VIOLENCE GIRL

VIOLENCE GIRL

EAST L.A. RAGE TO HOLLYWOOD STAGE
A CHICANA PUNK STORY

BY ALICE BAG

FERAL HOUSE

Feral House
1240 W. Sims Way
Suite 124
Port Townsend, WA 98368
feralhouse.com

Book design by Gregg Einhorn

ISBN 978-1936239122

Printed in the United States of America

10 9 8 7 6 5 4 3 2 1

For my husband and daughters.

VIOLENCE GIRL

One two three four! My band rips into our opening song. The music is loud, tight, fast and intense.

A wave of bodies surges at the front of the stage as the audience explodes into frenetic dancing. The music blaring at my back, I'm going to ride this wave. I grab the microphone from the stand and belt out the words.

She's taken too much of the domesticated world, she's tearing it to pieces she's a violence girl!

I'm bouncing on stilettos like a fighter in the ring, I charge out onto the edge of the stage, full of adrenaline and fire. I sing into the faces in the front rows. They are my current, my source of energy. I urge them to engage. I know there's something in them, some inner carbonation lying still, waiting to be shaken. It's fizzing in them as I shake them up. Shake, motherfucker, shake! I want you to explode with me.

I'm stomping, jogging and dancing all over the stage, teetering precariously on my high heels. I spot an area of spectators in front of Patricia, my bassist. Fuck that! No spectators, we're all participants here! I get up in their faces as I continue to spew out the words. Now they're dancing, that's right, keep it going.

She's a violence girl, she thrives on pain, she's a violence girl, you can't restrain!

I am in my element, *en mi mero mole*. There is so much energy coursing through my body that surely I am dangerous to touch.

Then I see him. A gnat on my windshield, a tiny insect in wire-rimmed glasses has moved toward the front of the stage. He stands facing Craig, my rhythm guitarist, flipping him off. I make my way over and the insect turns my way, sticking his insolent middle finger up in the air in defiance. Some people in the audience slam their bodies into him attempting to swat the bug, but he resists. I reach out toward him while still singing. I'll swat him myself. I reach to smack him but he backs away.

The gnat is emboldened now. I try to keep singing, the crowd is still with me but he is hovering in my peripheral vision. He has moved closer, middle finger still in the air. I dance over, lean over the front row and swing at his face. He is squished in and can't move more than a few inches back. I miss his face but as he's backing away I catch his glasses between my fingers. He looks at me, suddenly helpless. I smile at the gnat and hold his glasses up high as I bend and twist them into a wire sculpture. Gnat has been swallowed by the audience, his finger has submerged under the sea of punks. We are all dancing in unison. With great flourish I place the wire sculpture under my lovely high heels and smash the glasses to bits.

How did I come to unleash the wrath of Kali upon the world of punk? The answer to that question lies way back in my childhood and perhaps even before that, because the seeds of Violence Girl were sown way before I was even born.

THE PIT BULL TAKES A BRIDE

My father, Manuel Armendariz, was a self-employed carpenter, which meant that sometimes he worked a lot and other times he didn't work at all. He grew up in Mexico and always considered himself a Mexican; not a Mexican-American, not Chicano. Even on the rare occasions when he wore a suit, he looked like a laborer: bulky and strong, with a solid frame. His face was all up front, with a strong jawline that locked into place, like a pit bull. He had a disposition to match: alternately cuddly and ferocious. Manuel met my mother, Candelaria, on a bus in Mexico. She was shapely yet angular, like a cubist version of a woman with an hourglass figure.

My father as a young man.

My father was coming home from work, sweaty and covered with dust and dirt from a day of construction, when he sat down next to this very fashionably dressed lady. Instead of being put off, she started a conversation, and eventually my father said, "I'd ask you out to the movies, if I wasn't so dirty."

A smile would creep across my father's face as he recalled the memory, mimicking my mother's high pitched voice: "You don't look so dirty to me." My father always laughed when he told this story; since he actually was filthy, he immediately knew that my mother liked him. I imagine him dressed in his grimy khakis and T-shirt, bushy black hair turned prematurely gray by sawdust, holding hands with my stylish, soon-to-be mother in the dark *cine*, watching the screen as Pedro Infante woos his leading lady.

My mom, a cubist version
of a shapely woman.

Mom and Dad, early courtship.

Candelaria was also born in Mexico, the youngest of 15 children. Her family moved to the United States when she was still a small child. This was during the height of the Great Depression, and the experience marked her profoundly. She and her siblings grew up near a shoe factory in L.A. They would rummage through the nearby city dump, looking for a matching pair of castoff shoes they might wear but which they never found. If they were lucky enough to find a left and a right shoe of the same style, they were invariably different sizes. If one was only a bit larger, the problem could be solved by wadding up a piece of paper and stuffing it into the toe box. Candelaria was a dyed-in-the-wool pack rat who never threw away anything that could be repurposed or recycled. I like to think of her as being the original DIY-er.

Unlike my father, my mother considered herself American, or at least Mexican-American. Over time, she even came to prefer the "American" nickname of Candy over the nickname used by our Mexican relatives: Lala. This was a pattern of Anglo-remonikering that some of her children would repeat, including me: Alicia, who would become Alice. It might seem strange today, but the desire to assimilate was stronger in those days, when public swimming pools in East Los Angeles still had "white days" and "Mexican days." By the time Candy met Manuel, she was already a widow with five children from her first marriage, one of whom had died in infancy. She was married with her first kid before she turned 16 and thus spent practically her whole life being a mother. When I was older, I accidentally found my parents' marriage certificate, and, after doing the math, I realized that my mother had been eight months pregnant when they finally made it legal. It was obvious that my dad had waited until the very last minute to marry my mother. I confronted him with it, joking, "You didn't want me."

He replied, "I always wanted you. I just didn't want to get married."

My family's home on Ditman Avenue was tiny, even by the standards of a poor barrio in East L.A., and it was completely infested with brown German cockroaches. My mother waged a never-ending battle against these intruders, stockpiling every insecticide carried by the local five-and-dime, all to no avail. The cockroaches had long since won the war, and they humored my mother's futile attempts to eradicate them so long as she occasionally allowed some wayward *queso* or a bit of burnt tortilla to fall behind the stove.

My earliest memory is of being at Hollenbeck Park with my father. We are sitting under a tree. I am very young, but I'm not too young to pick up on the forced smile, the fake show of happiness that my dad tries to put on for my sake. There's a melancholy, pathetic cloud casting a shadow on our sunny day. Despite my child's understanding of the world, I can sense the emptiness that has wandered in to fill the vacancy left by my mother. She's missing from the scene because she's in the hospital and hasn't been home in days.

The memory fades there, but usually another image of the same park appears. I am older now, perhaps 6 years old. There is a bald spot on the hilly part of the park. A group of children have flattened large cardboard boxes and are riding them down the dirt slope like toboggans, kicking up clouds of dirt. I muster up my courage, grab a discarded box and join the strangers, who don't seem to notice me. I push off and feel the rush of excitement as I race down the hill. Some of the children get a much bigger box and climb onto it, one behind the other. The boy in front pulls his knees up to his chest, the others stretch their legs out in a V and pile on behind him in a choo-choo-train style. They have made a cardboard bobsled, but it's a bust—it crawls too slowly down the hill, looking like a big centipede as the kids try to propel the box with their legs akimbo. Unfazed by their failed experiments, the kids go back to single-person toboggans, or doubles on luges. The more adventurous kids go down head first, face up or face down. We take turns, speeding down, adding tricks as fast as we can make them up. I am a coward and I ride seated, holding onto the upturned sides of the cardboard. My tricks are simple: legs stretched out in front of me, then legs bent to my chest, but nobody cares. Nobody's looking at me. They're all planning their next trick, or enjoying their current one. The heat of the summer day and the activity has made

Posing behind a Chinatown cutout. That's my dad and a little monkey who looks a lot like me.

the kids sweaty, providing something for the flying dirt to adhere to. They all look like Pig-Pen from the Peanuts cartoons. Mothers start coming over to put an end to what will surely mean an extra load of laundry. My own mom waves me back; she's been sitting under a tree with my older sister, reading *Novelas de Amor* and *Confidencias*. The fun is over, but who would have thought that a few spontaneous moments of makeshift play with a castoff cardboard box, a dirt hill and a bunch of kids who were having too much fun to bother picking on me would be one of my happiest childhood memories?

PUT ON YOUR WHITE BONNETS, IT'S CINE TIME

I grew up watching Spanish-language movies. *Peliculas de La Epoca de Oro* (films from the golden age of Mexican cinema) were the ones my parents liked best. They'd seen them all before but would never tire of watching Pedro Infante, Jorge Negrete, Libertad Lamarque, Pedro Armendáriz and Silvia Pinal on the big screen.

There were plenty of movie theaters in the hood which showed these movies, and it was our one splurge as a family to go to the movies on *dos por uno* night, a buy-one/get-one-free special, usually offered on a different night at each of the theaters we frequented. My mom and I would split one admission, then my dad would wait outside for another solo male to come along and he'd split the admission with him. In order to cut costs even further, my mother would pack a half dozen bean burritos wrapped in foil along with some canned sodas and bags of chips or Fritos. Once inside the darkened theater, she would produce all of these from a seemingly bottomless bag of tricks, like the one Felix the Cat carried. If we were out of tortillas, my mother would make white bread, bean and cheese sandwiches. These were a tasty change of pace and probably a uniquely *pocho* cuisine.

As soon as the lights went down, we'd start passing our feast around, and before long we were transported to an impossibly glamorous black-and-white version of Mexico. It was escapism at its finest. In those days, you got to see two or three movies at a time when you went to the *cine* (cinema). Sometimes there were even live acts who performed in-between the films. The Million Dollar Theater in downtown L.A. was famous for its variedades. There, on weekend afternoons, we'd watch the first movie, then be treated to touring singers, actors, jugglers, comedians, dancers, ventriloquists, gymnasts, mariachis…you name it. The word variedades means "variety," and there was certainly plenty of that. Young men and women would walk up and down the aisles with large trays strapped around their necks, selling cigarettes and bonbons and candy. It was a total experience.

Back in the 1960s, Broadway was still the vibrant commercial center of downtown L.A. and an important part of Latino life in the city. The Million Dollar Theater was one of the few remaining grand movie palaces on Broadway, a baroque time capsule from a long-gone age of opulence and architectural craftsmanship. I especially recall the beautiful interior alcoves and balconies, where my family would sometimes sit to watch a movie. On one such afternoon, I was getting bored with the movie and asked my mom for some change to buy a toy from the vending machine in the ladies' bathroom. Those machines used to stock all kinds of goodies, from small plastic toys for fidgety kids to lipstick, combs and emery boards. To keep me out of her hair, my mom gave me some change and let me go back to the bathroom to get myself a little toy. When I got there, I discovered not one but two vending machines. The second vending machine didn't have a glass front showing all the different goodies that could be purchased. This puzzled me, and as I stood there wondering, a woman came up and put some coins in. She was rewarded with a little white paper bag.

Aha! I figured it must be a grab bag–type deal. I knew from shopping with my mother—who often bought grab bags of fruit and soon-to-expire bread at the market—that you could get more for your money if you were willing to take a chance. I was excited by the prospect of getting a really special surprise treat, so I put my money in the machine and turned the knob. Out slid my little white paper grab bag. I tore it open and pulled out a small, white pillowy-looking bonnet. It had two straps that didn't quite fit around my ears and I was disappointed that I couldn't get it to stay on my head straight away.

I ran back to the balcony, where my parents were seated about five rows up. I stood at the bottom of the stairs, and, proudly wearing the sanitary pad on my head, I called out to my mom, "I didn't get a toy but look what came out!" My mother, mortified, rushed down to me as some audience members suppressed snickers while others glared at me. My mom whisked me up and out of sight. I asked her why she was angry with me, and she couldn't quite say, except to tell me that "Those things are for ladies!" When I asked her how they were used, my mother couldn't tell me. The mystery of the little white bonnet would remain unsolved until sixth grade, when my teacher would show my class a film about the Miracle of Menstruation.

YOLANDA

I have very few memories of my toddler years, but one of them is of sitting at the kitchen table in a booster seat. My father, my sister Yolanda and I are eating while my mother putters around in the kitchen. I am watching my father intently, trying to emulate his moves. He takes a bite; I take a bite. He sips his drink, I sip mine. He takes a long, skinny bottle from the center of the table and liberally pours the red liquid contents onto his food, then takes a mouthful and savors it. I reach for the bottle but it's too far away, so I start fussing for it.

"No," warns my sister in a quiet voice. In toddler speak, the word "no" translates as "keep at it, they can hear you," so I insist until my dad takes the bottle from the table and holds it up right in front of me, just out of reach.

"Is this what you want? Is this what you want?" my dad asks, knowing full well that's exactly what I want. He laughs and unscrews the cap, handing me the bottle against my mother's protests. I pour the hot sauce all over my food just like my father and I take a big bite. A strange, stinging sensation starts to fill my mouth. Suddenly, I am howling in pain. "That's how she learns!" he says jovially. My sister shakes her head in a way that says we're all crazy.

My half sister Yolanda was 10 years old when I was born, so I literally and figuratively looked up to her. I remember her teaching me how to do the twist.

My sister Yolanda and me.

We had matching poodle skirts that my mother had sewn for us. In fact, we had numerous matching outfits. My sister had a little record player that folded away like a miniature suitcase and had tiny built-in speakers, so she could never play the music too loud, even if she wanted to.

When my mom wasn't home, I could always count on Yolanda to boss me around. I didn't mind. She didn't yell like my father was prone to do, and she didn't talk to me like I was simple, which my mother tended to do. My sister always took the time to explain things to me, at times seeming wiser than either of my parents.

But what I really liked about her was that she taught me about music. She was the first to play Enrique Guzmán, Los Teen Tops, the Beatles and soul music for me. She taught me to dance, and, in exchange, all I had to do was promise never to drink from her soda bottle (she said I left little fishies in it) and not to warm my feet under her legs in bed. I agreed long enough to learn the basics, then I reneged on both promises.

My sister and me in our winter finest.

In my eyes, Yolanda was the most beautiful girl in the world (not counting Sarita Montiel, who I considered the most beautiful *woman* in the world). When I was a little older and we moved to the Ditman house, my dad and I would watch beauty pageants together on TV. We'd take a pencil and paper and score the contestants. We'd see who could pick the most winners after each elimination round. Once, my sister walked into the living room while we were doing this, and I remember looking at her and thinking she could beat them all. After that, I hounded her for weeks, begging her to enter a beauty pageant. I could imagine my sister on TV, having a crown placed on her head and having a big bouquet of roses handed to her. She'd smile at us through the television screen and I would be jumping on the couch with joy! I was sure she'd be a winner, but my sister dismissed my pleas with a flattered giggle, and eventually I gave up.

Even though we grew up together, our age difference made our interests incompatible, so we didn't always spend as much time together as I would have liked, especially as she got older and discovered boys. I also had older half brothers who didn't live with us and a much older sister who was married and had a family of her own. I have a mental snapshot of being out driving with my brothers, Jaime and Ramon (later to become Jimmy and Raymond). I am riding in the front seat between them. As we pull up in the driveway of my home, I hear screaming and yelling coming from inside the house and suddenly my mother, father and Yolanda all tumble together through the screen door. One of my brothers picks me up and holds me protectively in his arms while the other rushes toward my parents. The whole family is in turmoil. I don't know what's happening, so I cry and cry and bury my head in my brother's neck. After that day, I don't remember seeing either of my brothers for a long time.

My sister was the only person other than my mom and me who ever had to experience my father's rage on an ongoing basis, and when I think of it now, it must have been harder for her to bear than it was for me, because he wasn't even her natural father. He was just some random ogre who beat up her mom. My sister and father rarely spoke to each other except in the most cursory manner. Yolanda had lost her real father to cancer at a young age. It would have been nice if my dad could have given her a father's love, but I don't think she wanted it from him. I suspect that Yolanda deliberately tried to make herself invisible when my dad was around. Whenever possible, my sister stayed out of the house.

When we moved to Ditman Avenue, Yolanda entered Stevenson Junior High School and met Angel Lujan, with whom she would eventually get married and spend the rest of her life. Yolanda spent most of her time after school at Angel's house. When she and Angel did come to our house, they could usually be found making out in the narrow space between the neighboring apartment buildings. Being a typical little sister, I'd sometimes spy on them and throw rocks at them, and Yolanda would toss back empty threats at me. It seemed like Yolanda had managed to find a little piece of happiness and a way to save herself from the ugliness that thrived in our home.

Yolanda died of cancer a few years ago. Being at my big sister's side during the last few weeks as she struggled to fight off the inevitable was heart-rending, because she was in excruciating pain. The type of cancer she had was incurable, and the doctors sent her home to live out her final days with her family. All we could do was try to dull her pain with morphine, but on the day she was sent home from the hospital, the nurse practitioner was delayed in getting to her house, and Yolanda began to moan for help as the drugs wore off. Panicked, Angel and I tried to figure out how to ease her suffering. I thought seriously of calling a friend who might have access to heroin. Finally, the drugs arrived and Angel, unable to see clearly through his grief, asked me to administer the painkiller into her mouth. "You can't give her too much," he said to me, but he needn't have, since we were both thinking the same thing. Yolanda was in so much pain by then that all I could think to do was to help her by ending it. Every time she awoke and cried out in pain, I gave her more morphine to ease her suffering. In the end, I honestly think I may have taken my sister's life by overdosing her on painkillers.

During Yolanda's final days I slept fitfully, dreaming of our good times and bad times together. After she died, she and my *mami* visited me together in my sleep, both of them smiling, happy, looking radiant as they had in the old days.

"Come with us, Alicia! There's a party that's just about to start, come with us!" they beckoned.

I was overjoyed at seeing them again, looking so wonderful, but then I remembered my own family and told them, "No, I have to stay."

DADDY DEAREST

My father was a monster.

By that, I mean that everything I know about the deep, dark, ugly side of mankind, I learned from my father. He was like a dark sensei, passing on his knowledge through transmission to an acolyte—me. It's not that he actually did every cruel and evil thing imaginable but that he tapped into the energy which makes humans capable of committing any atrocity. Some people believe that the archetype, idea or shared experience of divinity is contained within each of us. I believe that its polar opposite—the capacity for evil—is also carried within us all, like a latent gene.

My dad relaxing at home.

I used to think that the house we lived in on Ditman Avenue didn't have a dining room, which is perhaps not quite true. There was a small room between the laundry room and my father's bedroom (my mother slept on the couch) where my father kept his tools. It was full of saws, drills and other equipment, and my mom kept her sewing machine in there. Another family might have put a small dining table in there, but we had no garage and the sewing machine and tools were valuable, so it became the tool room.

One day I was playing outside when I heard yelling coming from the tool room. I ran into the house to find my mother trying to cover her bloodied face in shame.

"*Incate!*" (Kneel!) my father yelled. My mother obeyed my father, who then raised his hand to strike her but I rushed over and grabbed his arm.

"No, *Papi!* Please, *Papi,* no!" I tried to pull him back, but he pried my fingers from his arm, then he turned to spit on my kneeling mother. He spat on her over and over again as I desperately tried to push him back, using my whole body in a feeble attempt to block him from getting to her. He took a few steps back.

"You don't want me to hit her? Okay, let me go." I did, cautiously. "You spit on her!" he ordered.

"No," I replied, horrified that he would even suggest it.

"YOU SPIT ON HER OR I'LL KILL HER!" He raised his voice even louder and let go with a volley of curses directed at my mom, his face flushing a deep red. He was yelling so violently that his false teeth had loosened and suddenly the top half of his dentures flew out of his mouth and landed on the floor next to my mom. Now he really looked like a monster to me. The upper part of his mouth flopped loose and ragged, and spit sprayed out as he raged on, making unintelligible sounds. Losing his false teeth had made him even angrier. He yanked me in front of him and grabbed me by the shoulders, squeezing hard. "SPIT ON HER!"

The scene fades to blackness, like so many of my bad memories. It's a scary scene and I just can't bear to watch anymore, so little subconscious hands have been raised to cover my 7-year-old eyes. I don't know what happened that time; I don't remember how the scene ended. The police were frequent visitors at our house during my youth, because the neighbors often called them after a fight. My mom never pressed charges, she was afraid to. My older sister was rarely home. She was old enough to have a boyfriend and spent most of her time at his house. I don't blame her. As soon as she was able, she would marry her junior high school sweetheart and move out of the house.

Another day, I came home from school to find my mother with bruises on her body, face and neck. "Your father tried to kill me," she said. "He tried to strangle me." The neighbors had called the police and my father was being held temporarily. "He will be home tomorrow or later tonight," my mom informed me. "We've got to get out of here." We spent the night at my oldest sister's house. I remember lying awake in my sister's living room, wondering if my father would come looking for us in the middle of the night, wondering what he would do if he found us. My half brothers and sisters repeatedly tried to convince my mother to leave my father but she wouldn't. Years later, she would tell me that she had only stayed with him for my sake. She would not press charges because she was afraid of what he would do to her when he got out.

The next day I went to school and tried to pretend that everything was normal, but I couldn't think of anything except my mother's safety. Would she still be alive when I got home? Would my dad spend the rest of his life in prison for murdering her? I had often been told by my mother that I was the only one who could stop him. I felt impotent and guilty. My mother was only with him because of me, and I was the only one who could stop him but I wasn't doing it. I didn't know how.

My dad wasn't just a wife beater. He got in fights with men, too. I remember watching him punch a guy out at a movie theater, and, another time, he took on a group of cholos. These fights were always resolved by the police. Surprisingly, my father didn't do much jail time. I don't know how he got away with it.

SPOILED

"Quien te quiere mucho?" (Who loves you a lot?) he'd ask me every day.

"Tu!" (You!) I'd shout back. He spoiled me as much as he could, using whatever meager amount was left over after the bills were paid to do something nice for me or with me. We might have the smallest, most dilapidated house on the block, but, by God, we had to have a swing set. When it was back-to-school time, I'd be taken to K-mart to buy brand new clothes for the coming school year. They had to be on clearance or blue-light specials, because my mother didn't believe in paying full price for anything, but I usually came away with a couple of new dresses, shoes, plenty of socks and undies, plus my secret passion—stationery!

Despite the ferocity of my father's rage toward the world in general and my mother in particular, I had no doubt that I was the apple of his eye.

Dad used to tell me that I could be anything I wanted to be. He'd say, *"Mija,* you can be the first woman president, if you want to be." He was always telling anyone who would listen how smart and talented I was, and, after a while, I started to believe him. He made me feel special. Maybe that was a bad thing, because, as a result, I probably acted like I thought I was special, but it did give me a kind of confidence that has stayed with me throughout my life.

Because my father was self-employed and we lived in the barrio, his customers were sometimes other poor people who didn't have enough cash to pay for construction work. Others may have had money, but they enjoyed the art of bargaining, and my father was happy to find creative ways to get paid. He often traded his services for a wide variety of goods.

Once, my father worked for a man who owned a clothing manufacturing business. When the man seemed reluctant to pay the full amount of the bill, my father suggested that his daughter be allowed to pick out dresses from the factory's inventory to make up the difference. The man was happy to oblige. They took me downtown to the clothing factory, where I was shown a huge selection of stylish, form-fitting knit dresses hanging along the walls. I chose five or six of my favorites in their largest sizes and went into the bathroom to try them on, but only two of them fit; I was too fat for the largest size.

The owner of the dress factory was talking to my dad when I came out, but he stopped and looked over at me to ask, "Did you like them?" Without waiting for an answer he added, "You can have them all!" I was so embarrassed, I didn't want to tell him that I was too fat to get into most of them.

"I only want two," I answered politely. My father looked disappointed, and the man looked concerned.

"Look around, we have many," he insisted.

"No, I only want two."

I couldn't figure out how I was going to get out of this embarrassing predicament, when my father suddenly seemed to grasp the situation. He smiled knowingly at me, then turned to the factory owner. "You got off easy," he said as we walked away.

Another place my father had some sort of free-trade agreement with was a little place on First Street near Lorena in East L.A. called El Centavito (The Little Cent). We used to call it "El Sentadito" (the little seated one) because the shop attendant would frequently sit outside, keeping an eye on the goods he had for sale on the outdoor tables. El Centavito stocked all sorts of things. I guess it was a traditional five-and-dime, but with some exotic elements thrown in. You could get gift and stationery items along with stuff like Chinese paper parasols or Mexican pottery. I always felt like a queen, going to El Centavito with my dad, because the people there were really nice to me. I could pretty much have my pick of goodies, but my mom had taught me to only take one or two things, so I set my limit at three.

Me hugging my dad.

Sometimes, the neighborhood kids would be out on the street, playing, when we came back from one of our outings to El Centavito. If they asked to see what he'd bought me, they'd inevitably say I was spoiled. I detested that term because it was thrown at me so venomously, but now I can see that my dad had indeed spoiled me with little gifts and attention, and by instilling in me an unfailing sense of self-confidence.

Me on the carousel.

Wholesome fun at the park.

My father was not only indulgent, he was resourceful. He even figured out a way to turn a profit by taking me to the rides at Lincoln Park. I don't know what sort of deal he had with the carnival-ride operators there, but it was a good one. The scam went something like this: My father would buy a dollar's worth of tickets, then we'd head over to a ride. He'd hand the operator a ticket, and, at the same time, the operator would hand my dad back a bunch of used tickets. We'd go to the next ride, and my dad would hand me a used ticket and I'd get on the ride. Nobody blinked when I handed them a wrinkled-up, used ticket. This would go on until I'd had my fill of rides.

Not all the operators had this deal with my dad, but they all knew and were on friendly terms with him. As we were leaving the park, my father would spot a family heading toward the carnival rides. "Want to buy some tickets at a discount?" my dad would offer. "My daughter doesn't want to ride anymore." Nine times out of ten, they'd go for it. Then Dad and I would head home, holding hands as we walked through the park, happy to be together doing fun, wholesome stuff.

THE DONKEY BANK

There were times when I was growing up that my family had to be extremely frugal and do without, and there were times when I thought we were rich. Being self-employed, my dad rarely had steady work or a steady paycheck, but once in a while he'd find a large building project that would mean regular work for months. During those times of steady work, we'd live high on the hog, not bothering to save or put money away in the bank. My parents had both lived through the Great Depression and preferred to keep their money at home in different hiding places, like under a carpet or inside a prayer book; the very idea of saving money seemed to have no appeal to them. If we had money, we'd go to Tijuana and bet on the horses at Caliente Racetrack, or we'd take a trip to Mexico to visit relatives.

On one of our many trips to Tijuana, my father bought me a little white ceramic donkey bank. Every Friday, when he cashed his paycheck, he would hand me a crisp one-dollar bill to put into my donkey bank. "It's your college money," my dad would tell me. My father, who had been forced to work at an early age to help support his family and had only made it through the fifth grade, firmly believed that education could level the playing field. Not going to college was never an option for me, as far as he was concerned.

I treasured that little white donkey bank and soon moved it from its place atop the television to a table near my bed where I could look at it every night before closing my eyes and dream of going to college. I would become a brain surgeon or a pilot; not that I had any aptitude for those things, but my father liked to tell me I could be a brain surgeon. It was his way of telling me he thought I was smart, but I was too stupid to catch on. I thought he really wanted me to be a brain surgeon, so I promptly put it on my to-do list.

The donkey bank, proudly displayed atop our TV set.

In the mid-1960s, airline stewardesses were considered very chic and worldly, and I once mentioned to my father that I'd like to be an airline stewardess so that I could travel all over the world. "An airline stewardess?!" my father scoffed. "Why don't you become a pilot or own an airline instead?" Well, even though I was self-confident and very young, I could calculate that my chances of owning an airline were about the same as those of becoming the first woman president, so I set more attainable goals for myself. I would become either a brain surgeon or a pilot; and my little white donkey bank held the key that would open those doors.

The months passed, and my father's construction project was completed. He started to work as an independent contractor again, putting up business cards at markets or buying small ads in the local papers. The donkey bank was now nearly full, and each dollar bill had to be carefully folded nice and tight so that it would fit inside. Then the weather changed for the worse, and outdoor construction jobs became sporadic or nonexistent. My father scrambled for the less lucrative indoor jobs, like tile-setting or small repairs. The regular Friday night deposits to the donkey bank which had once been a ritual were disrupted; sometimes no money was deposited, sometimes we'd skip a week, and eventually the deposits stopped altogether. The donkey bank slowly migrated to the back of the dresser, where I didn't have to see it all the time. I did peek at it now and then, but it didn't make me as happy as it once had.

One fateful afternoon when I got home from school, I noticed the donkey bank was gone from its place atop the dresser. "Where's my donkey bank?" I asked my mom.

"I don't know," she answered. I began frantically searching for it all over the house until I finally discovered it, broken and half empty, laying on the floor of my mother's closet. I immediately ran over to my mother, planning to throw her lie back in her face.

"I'm sorry," she said. She was crying. "Your dad and I talked about it last night. We had to borrow the money to pay the rent. We'll pay you back." Of course, they never did pay me back. So much for my chances of becoming a pilot or a brain surgeon.

When my father got home, he knew immediately that something was wrong, because I used to run up to greet him as soon as I saw him. That day, I pretended not to hear him come in. I couldn't stay angry at my mother; after all, she hadn't promised me anything. She was practical, counted every penny and kept her dreams, if she had any, to herself. I felt most betrayed by my father. He was a modern day Daedalus, the craftsman in Greek mythology who constructs a set of wax wings for his son, Icarus. But unlike Daedalus, who had warned his son against flying too close to the sun, my father had pointed me straight at it and told me to go get it. My wax wings had melted, and I had fallen hard.

My mother told my father that I knew about the bank. He came over to apologize to me but I was angry and not in a forgiving mood. After several attempts to console me, my father eventually lost his patience with me and he left me with some harsh words of advice: "Never trust anyone but yourself. You're the only one you can count on."

DADDY'S KNOCKOUT PUNCH

My dad was a violent man. I don't know what happened to him to make him so angry at the world, but he went through life like a cocked and loaded gun. Even when we weren't the targets of his anger, the women in my family were often held hostage by his unpredictable rage.

**Believe it or not,
my dad is not angry here.**

In the summer of 1970, my mom, dad, sister and I were riding in the car, returning to East L.A. from a trip downtown. We were stopped at a traffic light when a car pulled up next to us. It was a warm day and both cars had all the windows open. My sister and I were in the back seat when the two men in the car next to us looked over and said something to us. My father immediately started yelling at them, but, just at that moment, the light changed and they sped away, laughing. My father yelled at my mother, "Follow them!" My mother was driving but my father stepped over and smashed her foot down on the gas pedal with his own foot, demanding that she catch up to them.

"What did they say?" I asked my sister.

"Something nasty."

The chase was on as we careened wildly through the streets of downtown L.A. My father yelled at my mother to speed up as the traffic lights changed from yellow to red and my sister and I were freaking out in the back seat, certain that we were about to be killed in a horrible accident. Both cars raced out of downtown L.A. and flew over the Fourth Street bridge, where the other men's car finally had to stop at a red light. The passenger got out of his car at the same time as my father leapt from ours. He looked just as angry as my dad and started yelling at him when my father suddenly unleashed a vicious punch to the man's jaw. The guy went down hard.

"*Levantate!*" My dad yelled at him to get up, but the guy seemed completely dazed and shook his head, motioning that he wouldn't or couldn't. His friend, the driver, got out of the car and put his hands up in the air, surrendering. "We're sorry, we're very sorry," he said as he cautiously approached his friend and helped him up. They backed into their car. My father never took his eyes off of them. He was still a cocked and loaded gun, and the two men were smart enough to recognize it. They got in their car and sped away, and just as quickly as it had begun, it was over.

It had all happened so fast. My father got back in our car. "What did they say?" I asked my dad.

"They insulted you and your sister," he replied.

"Yes, but what did they say?" No one would tell me. I never did find out what terrible words they had said.

I'M A BARBIE GIRL

Some of the greatest achievements in history have been the results of accidents: the development of penicillin, the discovery of the New World. Barbie accidentally helped me make my own great discovery when I was about 6 years old.

I had lots of Barbies when I was little. Okay, so maybe they weren't *real* Barbies — some were imitations, and they weren't all new. In fact, I don't know if I ever owned a *new, real* Barbie. I don't remember having Barbie shoes or real Barbie clothes; instead, my dolls wore scraps of cloth, tied with a piece of hair ribbon or a rubber band. A shimmery fabric scrap could become an evening gown, the cuff from a cutoff sock could be a strapless, casual day dress.

I had lots of naked, ratty-haired Barbies, and they all shared one boyfriend whose name was G.I. Joe. I didn't like G.I. Joe very much — he had too many ball-and-socket joints, and he looked short and stubby next to my trim, hourglass-shaped ladies — but as much as I wished and begged for a Ken doll, my parents never bought one for me. Despite the fact that they were a bad match and for lack of other eligible bachelors, my Barbies all dated G.I. Joe. Of course, the real fun was in getting dressed for those dates.

I was combing my Barbie's ratty hair for her big night out with G.I. Joe when I decided to steady the doll upright between my thighs to keep her from shifting while I worked on her up-do. I held the rubber band in one hand and a little brush in the other as I began my work, but I found that she still wiggled a little, so I pressed her tightly between my thighs and that seemed to help. After a few moments of combing her hair, I noticed a strange, tickling sensation in the place where my Barbie's legs were. It felt good and after a moment or two, I put the brush down and just focused on wiggling Barbie's long, firm, slender legs to continue to create the pleasant, tickling sensation.

Pretty soon, I was a devoted doll hairdresser. Under the pretext of styling all my dolls' hair, I enjoyed the sensation on a daily basis, until, one day, my older sister Yolanda caught on.

"I know what you're doing with those Barbies."

"What?" I asked, trying to look innocent.

"You know what," she continued. "I'm gonna tell Mom." I hadn't been aware that I was doing anything wrong, but I could tell by the tone in her voice that I would surely be going to the fiery place for tickling myself. I didn't understand why it was wrong. My dad used to tickle my neck and stomach, laughing and saying "Coochie, coochie," while I giggled until I thought I would pass out. Nobody ever acted like that was wrong.

"You shouldn't be doing that," my sister said sternly.

"I'm sorry," I said, and I truly was. "Please don't tell Mami, I promise I won't do it anymore." Miraculously, my sister agreed. I was so happy that my mom didn't have to find out about my wickedness that, the first chance I got, I went straight to confession.

I walked into the confessional at Our Lady of Victory Church, prepared to make a fresh start with Jesus. "Bless me Father, for I have sinned," I began with a few of the easy-to-confess sins: I didn't do my homework, I pretended not to hear when my mom said it was time for bed — sins that nice children commit and which one or two Our Fathers can easily erase. I was dancing all around the big one, trying to work up my nerve. I knew I'd have to say it or I'd go to hell, so I mustered up my courage and I finally spit it out.

"I did coochie-coochie to myself down there with the Barbie!"

Silence, pure, unadulterated silence is all that came back from the other side of the darkened screen separating me from my confessor. Had I shocked him? He was quiet for so long, I started to worry that there was nothing I could do to remove this sin. After a moment or two, the priest seemed to regain his composure and finally gave me my penance. I don't remember exactly what it was, a few Hail Marys and some Acts of Contritions. It was a breeze. I was a speed-prayer anyway — I could pray like an auctioneer.

On the way home from church, I felt like I was walking on clouds, as pure as an angel. I wished a car would run me down at that very instant, so I could die and go straight to heaven before I had a chance to sin again.

I was right to be afraid. Before too long, I would sin again.

CAVEMAN

I was playing outside when I heard the voices of my parents begin to rise. I stopped to listen, knowing that sometimes their arguments would only last a few minutes. Those were the good endings to their arguments, endings that meant we'd eat in total silence. By that, I mean my dad and I would eat on TV trays in front of the TV while my mom ate standing up in the kitchen. (Not once in my entire life did my mom eat dinner with us at home. She was there to make and serve dinner and warm up tortillas.) The happy endings to their arguments meant a cloister-like silence for the rest of the night. But this wasn't going to be one of those endings.

I saw my mom bolt out of the front door like a frightened cat. She was running in her flimsy *chanclas* (house slippers), and she nearly slipped and fell as she turned the corner around the pink apartment building in front of our house.

"Mami!" I yelled, but she didn't stop or answer. Seconds later, my father walked out onto the front porch. His face was still and focused, his eyes glazed over as if he were in a trance.

"Papi!" I cried out, but he couldn't hear me. He didn't react to me. He had checked out. He moved swiftly, not running, but with a long, steady, determined stride. He was an animal, hunting his prey. I ran after him, tugging at his arms but he swatted me away like an annoying fly. I fell on the steps of the apartment and rushed to get up. He walked on, unbuckling his belt. I tried again to hold him back but he pushed me away effortlessly, now gripping the folded belt with the metal buckle and prong dangling menacingly by his side.

In the distance, I saw my mother in a neighbor's yard, begging for asylum. For a second, I hoped she might escape but my father must have seen her at the same time and he took off straight after her. I tried to keep up, but I was no match for his speed. He reached her first and starting beating her with the belt in our neighbor's front yard. She fell to her knees after two or three blows. I couldn't see her anymore, but I saw my dad's arm swinging and I could hear the *whoo...whoo* of the leather belt lashing down over and over. By the time I reached them, my mother's face and arms were completely covered with blood and she had collapsed in the grass. My father reached down, grabbed a fistful of my mother's hair and began dragging her down the street in a public display of caveman might.

Blood streamed into mom's face as my father dragged her, head first, down the street and toward our house. The neighbors came out of their houses and stood on their porches, wanting to see what all the commotion was about as I ran alongside my parents, begging my dad to stop and let her go. But he wouldn't listen to me. I tried holding his legs, I cried and wailed and pulled at his arm, but he kept moving forward, relentlessly. I felt completely powerless to stop him from killing her, and I prayed to God that someone would help me. We had just reached the apartments and were about to turn the corner to our house when I heard the answer to my prayers in the distant scream of a police siren. My father stopped dead in his tracks and just stood there waiting for them, clutching his bloody prize by her mane.

The police immediately handcuffed my dad and put him in the squad car. My mother was helped inside by some of the neighbors, who cleaned up her cuts and tried to attend to her needs. After about 20 minutes, a policeman came in. He interviewed my mom, who once again refused to cooperate. The officer tried to convince my mother to press charges and even gave her information about a place where she and I could go to be safe from my father, but my mother said no.

My father came home later that evening. There was silence in the house that night, but tomorrow everything would be back to normal.

SUMMERS IN JUAREZ

I'm not sure how or when we started going to Juarez every summer. My mom must have been happy for the chance to get away from my abusive father. It seemed that as soon as summer started, my mom and sister would begin packing for our annual pilgrimage. My father never joined us—being summertime, it was prime work season for outdoor construction jobs, and my dad must have stayed behind to earn as much money as he could.

My mother had family in Juarez, so we'd take the train from Los Angeles to El Paso, and then a relative would pick us up at the border crossing and take us over to my aunt's house. We'd stay with my Tia Anita and my cousin Conchita. They lived in a small *vecindad* with a center patio and individual dwellings surrounding the little courtyard. Outside in the courtyard, the children would be given baths in large metal tubs. I remember the cold water being poured over my head as my mom bathed and shampooed me with the same bar of soap that would later be used for laundry. It was a shivery experience, but all the local kids endured it so I tried not to complain. I never wondered until now where the grown-ups took their baths. They must've been holding out on us.

In the center of the patio was a large stone sink with a built-in scrub board that would accommodate four laundresses at once. (I never saw a man do laundry there.) It seemed that every day was washday, a social event where the women joked and chatted as they worked their way through their baskets of clothes. There was always activity in that courtyard. We kids were asked to go outside and play almost as soon as we woke up. We had few toys, but we were creative. I remember a time when one of the older kids made a little race cart out of a wooden crate. We all took turns getting inside and pushing each other down the street. I pushed too hard and made one of the little girls crash and smash her lip. She cried and my aunt was furious with me. That quickly ended the speeding cart game. Even though I had caused the termination of our game, the other children did not blame or ostracize me. Being the wild, unsupervised kids that they were, they were used to accidents and being scolded or spanked by their caregivers. After a brief pause in the action, we ran off to make more mischief.

On days when we didn't get into trouble, we eagerly awaited the arrival of the *raspada* (snow cone) vendors who would come with their large blocks of ice and multicolored bottles of flavored syrups every afternoon. My mom, who had American currency — which used to be worth a lot, a long, long time ago — frequently treated the kids to raspadas because my mother was of the belief that you couldn't buy a treat for one child and let the others go without, so either we all got raspadas or none of us did.

One of the things I liked best about being at my Tia Anita's house was that there were always people selling things out on the street, not just raspadas and *elotes* (hot buttered corn on a stick), but lottery tickets, balloons, fortunes told by little birds in colorful cages who would pick a fortune for you with their beaks (for a small price). There were shoeshine boys and newspaper boys, fruit vendors who would slice up your choice of fruit — from coconuts to jicama, mangoes, cucumbers, cantaloupe and watermelon — and season it with lemon and salt and chili upon request. All these people were known as ambulant merchants, because they carried their goods, walking from street to street, calling out to people and announcing their wares, often with catchy rhymes or little songs to make you take notice. No one simply shouted out: "Pop-

Don't mess with the little girls of Juarez.

Look Ma, no hands!

sicles for sale!" Instead, it was "*Compre de pina para la nina!*" — a rhyme which translates into "buy a pineapple one for the little girl"; or "*Comprelo ahora, que aqui ahorra*" — a rhyme and a pun: "Buy it now because you'll save here." The streets of Juarez were alive with a symphony of traffic, songs, laughter, rhymes, colors and the sweet scent of fresh fruit and hot elotes.

I felt more than a little culture shock when we'd return to the United States at the end of summer. Summers in Juarez really cemented my pride in my Mexican heritage. It's true that East L.A. had a fair share of *paleteros* (ice cream men) and elote vendors, but I missed the raspada man and the bird fortunes, and the absence of fighting.

SE HABLA ESPAÑOL

"Se Habla Español." That's a sign you frequently see in the windows of businesses in East L.A. They know who their customers are, and they cater to their needs. It's too bad they didn't have that knowledge at Eastman Avenue School back in 1963.

I entered Mrs. Poundstone's kindergarten class as a Spanish-speaking student and I still remember my first impression of her. She was a thin white lady with horn-rimmed glasses and a short brown bubble-style bob, popular in the early '60s. She smiled a lot and spoke in soft, pleasant tones, like she was cooing to an infant. I was worried about leaving my mother, but Mrs. Poundstone's demeanor eased my fears, and I grudgingly agreed to stay while my mom left, "for just a little while."

No sooner had I taken a last glance at my mom as she walked out the kindergarten yard gate than Mrs. Poundstone began calling the children over to the carpet, where she was seated on a chair. We sat cross-legged around her, in what used to be called "Indian style." That's when the trouble started. Mrs. Poundstone held up a small carton of milk and another of juice and started talking.

"Blah, blah, blah, pica, blah, Uhleesha, blah, blah."

She stared at me, still smiling. I smiled back. She started talking again "Blah…blah…blah…pica… blah… Uh-lee-sha…blah…blah," she said again, at a much slower pace. She was still looking at me, but she was no longer smiling. I stared at her blankly. She pointed at me with her index finger and opened her eyes wider. I could sense that she wanted something from me but I didn't know what. I looked around for help but none was coming from the other children, who, for all I knew, were starting to get equally concerned about the direction this was heading. Mrs. Poundstone's voice got louder:

"BLAH…BLAH…BLAH…PICA…BLAH…UHLEESHA…BLAH… BLAH."

To punctuate each word she pointed that thin white finger at me menacingly and then she motioned with her hand for me to go up next to her. Suddenly, I got it. Pica means "poke" in Spanish. She wanted me to go up next to her so that she could poke me. I had done something wrong, which explained why she had lost her smile and was practically yelling at me. I burst out crying and ran to the window to see if my mom was still there, but she was gone. Thus began my first day of school as a Spanish speaker.

I later learned that Mrs. Poundstone had bestowed an honor on me by picking me to take in our milk and juice count. Uhleesha was my English name. It sounded ugly to me (no offense intended to any Uhleeshas out there). Ah-lees-ia sounded so much softer to me and was what my family called me, but if the teacher called me Uhleesha, it must be my new name.

I responded to Uhleesha in kindergarten and first grade, before my second-grade teacher, Miss Gibbons, completely changed my name to Alice. I actually liked Alice better than Uhleesha. It wasn't as pretty as Ah-lees-ia but it was difficult to mispronounce. So in second grade, I shed my hard-to-pronounce Mexican-sounding name and went with the foolproof, Anglo-approved Alice.

I have name issues. I go by Alicia Velasquez these days. You can't imagine how difficult that is for some people to pronounce. I am grateful for those who make the effort and don't insist on calling me Uleesha Valaskwez. I try to remind myself how, as a teen, I used to love Cher but always pronounced her name "Chair" until I took French in high school and figured out that Cher is a French word.

Miss Gibbons would go on to punish me for not learning English quickly enough. She constantly reminded me and any other kids who weren't fluent English speakers that we'd been in school for two years and shouldn't have any problem understanding things by now. Some of the children at our school were second-, third-, even fourth-generation Americans; they had learned English at home and were doing fine. Others had older siblings who spoke English to them, a benefit I lacked since my father prohibited the use of English in our house. "English is for school," he declared. "In this house, we speak Spanish."

So it was the first-generation Americans, like myself, or the recent immigrants — anyone struggling to understand the lessons — who bore the brunt of Miss Gibbons's ethnocentrism. She treated us like idiots, talked down to us and gave us easy work, as though our lack of English fluency implied we were mentally deficient. It simply made her job easier, because by giving us first-grade work, she saved herself the trouble of having to explain anything to us.

When we were done with an assignment, we were allowed to get a book to read from the bookshelf. Children at the bookshelf would sometimes whisper to each other in English without so much as a glance from Miss Gibbons, but woe unto those of us who spoke Spanish, because she would keep us in from recess if she caught us whispering to each other at the bookshelf. She seemed to have a built-in radar for any kind of Spanish speaking. I didn't know until then just how lucky I'd been to have Mrs. Poundstone as my kindergarten teacher and Miss Blye as my first-grade teacher. They had both been relatively kind and patient with the kids who were learning English.

My English language acquisition in elementary school was slow and painful. I know I didn't get all the information that a native speaker had access to in public elementary schools across the United States, because the lessons were given in a language which I barely understood. I had to devise my own ingenious method of learning English by reading comic books. My tutors were Archie, Reggie, Betty and the rest of the Riverdale High gang. *Memin Pinguin* taught me how to read and write Spanish. I got just enough information to move on to the next grade, and I began peppering my conversations with archaic expressions like "gosh" and "gee whiz," which only further sank my peers' low opinion of me.

THE QUEEN'S QUILT

Like so many kids who grew up poor, I didn't recognize it at the time. Everyone in my neighborhood was poor, so I had nothing to judge by. I remember one evening my father came home late from work. I was already in bed but he was happy and he came into my room with a wad of bills. For all I know, they could have been one-dollar bills, but I remember him sprinkling them all over my head, like raindrops falling from the sky. I fluffed them up, laughing happily along with my dad. It was then that he promised me I was going to go to college and that I could be the first woman president, if I wanted.

My mom and her beloved sewing machine.

Eventually, the rain stopped and we entered a prolonged dry spell. I remember my mother fretting over not being able to pay the rent, but my parents were both resourceful children of the Depression, and they devised a plan. One night after the sun had set, we got into our old car and drove downtown to the clothing manufacturing district, now known as L.A.'s garment district. My parents parked the car in the darkness across the street from a factory loading dock and told me to wait inside. I could see them clearly illuminated by the security floodlights as they approached a row of a half dozen steel dumpsters, lined up alongside the ledge of a loading dock. My father lowered himself into the first one, and his head disappeared below the edge for a few seconds while my mother looked around nervously. There weren't any chain-link fences guarding the dumpsters, but something about the way my parents were acting told me they were breaking the law. My father's head reappeared as he handed my mom several large bolts of fabric — remnants left over from the manufacturing processes of coats, pants and dresses. After they'd sorted through the first dumpster, they repeated the process until they had gathered a large assortment of scrap fabric, sample books and remnants from the ends of fabric bolts.

We hit several dumpsters over the next few weeks. I was never allowed to jump into a dumpster because my father said they were dirty and unsafe, but my parents had found a good source of heavy fabric that my mom could use to make quilts. These quilts would then be sold at the local swap meet along with any other salvaged items that had been rescued from the dumpsters. By night, my mom and dad climbed into bin after bin to collect the scraps that would enable our family to survive the financial drought. By day, my dad looked for work or scavenged for broken machines he could repair and sell, while my mom's sewing machine whirred nonstop.

My mother saved the softest, most luxurious scraps of velvet and velveteen that she came across and used them to sew a special quilt for me. It looked so plush and fancy that she called it my "Queen's Quilt." That name and the fact that my father called me *"La Reina"* (The Queen) made the quilt very dear to me. I still have it. Over the years, it's lost its plushness and looks a little mangy in spots, but it still brings me all kinds of warm, happy, hopeful feelings.

MUSICA, SWEET MUSICA

You could tell who was home at my house by what was playing on the radio. My mom loved listening to *radio novelas*, live studio performances of dramas, comedies or romances; my sister loved Motown and the Beatles; but for my Dad, *ranchera* music did the trick. Rancheras, often accompanied by mariachi, are usually performed in a hyper-emotional, melodramatic style befitting their subject matter, which is often the singer boasting about being on top of the world or bemoaning their latest betrayal or heartbreak. Seeing and hearing the performances of such greats as Lucha Villa, Pedro Infante and José Alfredo Jiménez almost certainly influenced my own peculiarly emotive style of singing, although I never consciously tried to emulate them when I sang in a punk band. Like latent hereditary traits, their stylistic influences just bobbed to the surface when my own moment onstage arrived. My older sister and mother preferred teen idol Enrique Guzmán singing "*Popotitos*," a Spanish version of "Boney Maroney." Many years later, I would sing my own version of "Popotitos" with Mexican Randy and the Metro Squad at a punk show.

I grew up believing that Mexican artists were getting their songs ripped off by American artists because I always heard the Spanish versions first at home and the English versions later on at school or on the car radio. My father, being a proud Mexicano, banned the speaking of English in our home, reasoning that we would learn it in school. This created some major challenges for me on the English-speaking front but ensured that I would always maintain a firm grasp on my mother tongue.

Concert for my dolly.

Early on, my father insisted that I learn to play the piano. I don't know what made him decide on the piano, but he had his mind set on it and I had to go along. At a very early age, I was taken to the Neighborhood Music Settlement in Boyle Heights. The school operated out of an old turn-of-the-century Victorian house where I met my piano teacher, Miss Dean. She was at least as old as the house and looked like she had powdered her face with the ashes from her cigarettes. Her teaching methods soon made the piano my least favorite instrument. She would sit next to me on the piano bench, gagging me with her stale breath and inspecting my fingernails before I was allowed to play. If they were dirty or if I'd put polish on them, she would give them a little slap with her hand and lecture me about her standards.

Miss Dean liked to remind me at each and every session to keep my fingernails clean and to keep my fingers curved. She would drawn in a deep breath before very slowly and meaningfully exhaling the word "cuuuurved," while at the same time demonstrating said curvature by putting her hands up in front of her face. "You must think of squeezing an orange," she would tell me as she opened and closed her crinkly, withered claws. This was before we'd even started the lesson.

When she finally got around to letting me play, she'd put on a metronome and wave a little wooden wand in time, as though she were conducting a full orchestra. In my mind, the wand confirmed my suspicion that she was really a witch. Miss Dean scolded me constantly because I was terrible at sight-reading. I would take the sheet music home, figure out how to play it, memorize it, then pretend to read while I played for her. "You've memorized the piece again!" she would shriek, before assigning me another piece and making me read it in front of her. I'd stumble through it during the lesson, then I'd take it home and memorize it. I hated my lessons with Miss Dean. I hated the prissy weekend recitals, I hated being indoors practicing the piano when other children were watching Saturday morning cartoons or making mischief outside.

After a couple of years, my dad figured out that he was wasting his money. He asked me what I wanted to play and my immediate answer was the accordion. I wish I could remember now why I was so smitten with the accordion. My father hated *nortena* music (rancheras were another story), and, on previous occasions, I had heard him badmouth the accordion. Perhaps just the thought of seeing his face when I said I wanted to give up on his beloved piano and take up the dreaded accordion gave me some sick satisfaction. I took accordion lessons for about a month, then I gave up. Nobody tried to stop me.

Back at Eastman Avenue School, my music teacher, Miss Yonkers, suggested that I learn to play the violin, but I heard myself making mistakes and I couldn't take it. I was bad and I knew it. I gave back the loaner violin as soon as I could. There was nothing else for it: I couldn't play anything, so I was going to have to become a singer. I knew that wasn't on my father's approved list of professions, but I tucked it away in the super-secret part of my mind.

A BITE OF THE HAM

Uncommon portrait setting.

My dad was a junker. He used to pick up stuff that was left out on the sidewalk on trash days and come home with rescued items he claimed would be as good as new, just as soon as he cleaned or fixed them. Often, these repaired items would go up for sale at the swap meet, where, for a while, my parents had a reserved spot where they sold salvaged and homemade goods. My mother preferred selling recycled clothes and homemade items, but my father was really into tools and hardware, and he had a special love for old cameras. He built up quite a collection by trading his junk for other people's junk, back when people actually bartered at swap meets.

My dad's favorite camera was an Argus C3 rangefinder, which he claimed was tough and sturdy and took the clearest pictures. He had so many old cameras around the house that I don't think I was more than 5 years old when I got my first Brownie. I didn't really like it. I didn't like having to look down into the box to compose the photograph, and I quickly lost interest in it. Only occasionally did I use the cameras he later gave me, with the exception of the Argus C3, which I eventually inherited and loved.

My dad would remain an avid photographer for many years. Unfortunately, he was more enthusiastic than talented. He didn't always choose the best subjects or settings, as evidenced above.

Besides, he had an ugly daughter as his favorite subject. Both my sister and my mother disliked posing for him, but I was a ham even then. I never suspected that years later the pictures would come back to bite me in the butt. So feel free to join in and take a bite of the ham!

In the following photos my father was experimenting with stop-action photography:

Laugh all you want, but I felt like a flying superhero when I saw these photos for the first time!

When I got older and became more self-conscious, I would no longer see the superhero in these photos. I only saw my body flaws and my ridiculous poses. I was mortified by these photos and tried to hide them anytime my mom brought family albums out to share with friends or relatives.

Now, I see myself differently again. I see a young girl who loved her father and was eager to have fun with him, who dreamed of becoming a superhero so she could defend her mother. I see a young girl who had little interest in or awareness of how others perceived her.

CALIENTE!

Caliente means "hot" in Spanish but it was also the name of a racetrack in Tijuana. Well, Agua Caliente was the complete name, but everyone just called it Caliente. I guess the abbreviated name better conveyed the postcard image of sunny Mexico, whereas Agua Caliente (hot water) only made you think of a bathroom faucet.

With my dad, it was always feast or famine. If he was working, we felt rich, and if he wasn't, we had to scramble for food and shelter. In times of plenty, we'd drive the two hours south from Los Angeles to the international border crossing and then on to Tijuana. My mom liked to visit the doctors in Tijuana; she claimed they were more attentive than American doctors and that the medicine was much less expensive. Despite being diabetic, my father rarely went to the doctor if he could help it. Instead, he liked to go bet the ponies.

Going to the horse races at Caliente was a real treat for me. As soon as we walked in, we were swept up in the excitement. There was an aura of old-time glamor and shadiness to it. It was the sort of place where one could find a wide variety of people from all walks of life, from the well-to-do who looked like Italian movie stars to American tourists in casual shorts, straw hats and newly purchased *huaraches* to regular working-class Mexican men in groups of two, three or four. The local women were never there, alone or in groups, unless they were accompanied by a man. They were usually well-dressed, within their means.

The first thing we'd do was get a program and a copy of the *Daily Racing Form*. I'd take the program, look at the upcoming races and circle the names of the horses with the most interesting-sounding names. If my mom and sister were with us, they'd go for the snacks. Food at racetracks is traditionally cheap, so we'd stuff ourselves, but sometimes, when we had leftover bean burritos from the drive down, my mother would make us eat them instead.

My dad liked to bet *quinellas*, so he'd pick two horses and I'd pick one and we'd box them. A quinella bet is one where you pick the horses that will come in first and second in any order. To box a quinella, you pay triple the amount for your bet, but your three favorite horses are covered if they should come in first and second in any combination. I knew way too much about horse racing for a little kid because my father was an avid gambler. He didn't make foolish bets, except where I was concerned. Oddly, my methods for choosing horses seemed to be just as effective as my dad's. We often won when we went to Caliente — not a lot, just enough to make it fun and keep us going back.

Sometimes we'd be so busy during the day in Tijuana visiting the doctor, taking pictures with goofy hats or sitting on donkeys painted to look like zebras that we wouldn't make it in time for the horse races, but that only made things even better because the one thing that I enjoyed more than an afternoon at the ponies was a night at the dog races.

Me astride the burro with my family in the cart.

The dog races seemed to move at a faster pace. They were easy to watch without binoculars, and being out at a race track late at night just felt a little bit naughty. It was very rare to see other children at the racetrack at night, except for the little kids who were forced to sell four-packs of Chiclets gum (three four-packs for a nickel). Most of the other tourist children were tucked safely in a hotel bed or back in San Diego by the time the dog races started.

Caliente all lit up at night was like an opulent pleasure palace. Surrounded by so much poverty, it was an oasis where locals and foreigners alike could escape to a place that was worlds away from everyday life. Over the years and to this day, one of my favorite pastimes is spending the day at the racetrack, making bets on horses with crazy names, eating racetrack junk food and drinking beer or a nice glass of scotch in the middle of the afternoon.

THE FUZZY QUESADILLA

Even though Dad seemed to enjoy beating up Mom on a regular basis, he never took his anger out on me. In fact, I was sort of a "daddy's girl." He doted on me. *La Reina del Mundo y de Otras Partes* ("Queen of the World and Other Places") is what he called me. I cherished the title and was very secure in the knowledge that my father loved me more than anything else. I was about 8 years old then, and over the years I had developed a bad habit of tasting my father's food whenever he was eating. If I liked what he was having, he'd usually let me have it or get me my own. This day was different.

In our tiny, cracker-box house on Ditman Avenue, we didn't have a dining room or a dinner table. Instead, we ate all our meals on TV trays in our small living room. One day, I passed by my dad as he sat on the sofa, reading a Spanish-language Western book and eating a quesadilla. I snagged a piece of it and smiled at him.

"Thank you," I said, but he didn't even look up. I figured he was absorbed in his book. I walked over to the TV, turned it on and sat on the floor in front of it, then I turned back to my dad.

"Can I have another piece?" I smiled. To my surprise, he threw the quesadilla at me. The two tortillas separated as they landed on the dirty hardwood floor. The exposed cheese worked like a magnet on the dirt and dust bunnies as the quesadilla slid under the TV.

"Pick it up!" he ordered. I did. The two tortillas were a mess; the piece that had landed face down was now peppered with debris. "Eat it all!" His voice boomed.

"No dad, I'm sorry," I said.

"Eat it all!" he repeated.

"No, *Papi*, please don't make me eat it!" My mother ran into the room and offered to make us both fresh quesadillas but my dad got up and stormed out the door.

For years, I had enjoyed some kind of diplomatic immunity from my father's wrath. On many occasions, I was able to step between him and my mother in the middle of a fight. Once, I even grabbed his leg and bit it, like an angry little dog. I guess I'd been easy enough to kick away as a little girl. I had never before been the target of his anger. Now that I was getting older, I was losing my immunity. I no longer felt safe.

THE WRESTLER

When I was about 8 years old, a new family moved into the apartment building next door. The father was a large, imposing Samoan man, and the mother looked like a lovely Tahitian beauty. The couple had four daughters, including a girl about my own age who told me that her father was a wrestler.

A wrestler! How glamorous and exciting a profession that must be! Thanks to my dad, I was an avid spectator of professional wrestling, or *lucha libre*, as it is known in Mexico. I had grown up watching Blue Demon, Mil Máscaras and the original wrestling movie star, El Santo, battle vampire women, zombies and Satanist cults. We watched wrestling on TV, broadcast live from the Olympic Auditorium in Los Angeles as well as lucha libre bouts from the Arena Coliseo in Mexico City. Some of the Mexican wrestlers worked the American circuit. In Los Angeles, some matches were designed to appeal more to lucha libre aficionados. I always found the Mexican bouts more colorful and eclectic than the American wrestling matchups. On lucha libre nights, it was not unusual to see women's wrestling or little people on the bill. Many of the costumes rated high on the tacky scale, but I always thought of that as a plus.

Matches were not just for a title; titles were for ordinary athletes. *Lucha-dores* were more than athletes — they were real-life superheroes with near mythic status. They didn't just stand for might and brawn, they often championed causes. Their matches were for higher stakes than a trophy or a belt; a masked wrestler might risk his anonymity by staking his mask against another man's prized Samson mane. But it was not just the hair or the mask that would be lost by the defeated wrestler, it was seen as a blow against whatever cause the wrestler stood for.

Heroes like Ray Mendoza stood for the indigenous underdogs, the Indians throughout Mexico who made up the poor and often marginalized lower classes. In Mexico, to say someone looks or behaves like an "Indio" was considered an insult, akin to being called a savage. It was widely rumored that Ray Mendoza was illiterate, but instead of that being a source of shame, it was seen by his fans as a sign of how far one could rise despite the lack of a formal education. El Indio, Ray Mendoza, was one of my childhood idols. Ray Mendoza had been a *rudo* who turned *technico* (aka *scientifico*) — a bad guy who turned good. He always kept the rough edges of a *rudo*, but being eight or nine years old, I didn't need to do a lot of analysis of what he stood for; El Indio was clearly for the common people. His brown skin and long black hair were a source of pride for him and for his fans who saw a bit of themselves reflected in this powerful wrestler.

I had the opportunity to see Ray Mendoza fight a bout in which he wagered his long, Indian locks. My parents and I went to the Olympic Auditorium that night to cheer on our hero. The place was loud, raucous, and the crowd was fired up. Ray's fight was the main event. I wish I could tell you who he was wrestling but I don't remember because it didn't matter. Ray fought valiantly in what turned out to be a very bloody brawl. We shouted and cheered him on until we were all hoarse, but in the end, he was defeated. As soon as the winner was announced, a chair was dragged into the middle of the ring and Ray's beautiful long black hair was cut off, right there in front of the packed audience at the Olympic and thousands of fans watching at home. I was nearly in tears. My hero had lost.

Through this seemingly vapid sport of *lucha libre*, I learned to understand the concept of duality at an early age. It was the same kind of duality that I experienced when I realized that I both loved and hated my father, that a rudo — a villain — could also be a good guy. It was as much a part of Mexican culture as eating a sweet apple with salt and chili or celebrating the bleak inevitability of death by making brightly colored sugar skulls with your name on them.

Our next-door neighbor turned out to be a completely different type of wrestler. He was an athlete, not a superhero. I, on the other hand, was a daughter of duality, caught up in a wrestling match between love and hate that was only in the first round.

THE DREAM

Children have all kinds of methods of avoiding going to bed. Mine was brushing my teeth. I'd brush my teeth so hard and so long that I'm certain that's why they wore out and got holes in them. I would have stayed in the bathroom all night if it meant not having to go to sleep.

Sleep was the land of bad things. Every night was a nightmare. I'd wake up crying or shaking, even cursing. Everyone was worried about my nightmares. I had heard my father's curses during my waking hours, and although I never used them in the daytime, I'd swear and punch and kick in my sleep. Sometimes my mom would have to wake me up, calm me down and then put me back to bed. Sometimes I'd sit up in bed, still asleep but arguing and trading foul insults with the people in my dreams. My sister, who used to sleep with me, hated when I did that; it used to frighten her.

I was about 8 or 9 years old when I started having a recurring dream. In this particular dream, I'd walk into my own bedroom (the one I shared with my sister) and it would be dimly lit by the filtered light coming through the closed, pull-down window shade. Above the window was a large, black taffeta bow, its long ends draped around the sides of the window. My eyes would move to my mother's 1940s-style vanity. Above the large circular mirror is another big black bow. Then I see my own reflection in the mirror.

I am grown up. I'm dressed all in black, wearing some kind of Catwoman-style leather jumpsuit. I have a whip in my hand. My eyes move to the bed where my father lies, sick and dying. He is feeble and looks at me, but he doesn't recognize me because I'm not a little kid.

"It's me," I say as I strike him with the whip, hard across his face. He lifts his skeletal hand to protect himself, just as I'd seen my mother do so many times in real life. In an instant, I see the recognition and horror in his eyes as he realizes who I am and what I'm about to do. He tries to cry out to me, but I beat him over and over with the whip, not ignoring his cries, but enjoying them. Our eyes meet, then lock: his frozen in horror, mine in delicious vengeance as I slowly whip my father to death.

MISS YONKERS AND THE ESCAPE PLAN

As I grew older, my home life became increasingly tainted by my father's violent outbursts and my school life was no better. Kids relentlessly picked on me, calling me all kinds of cruel names. One that sticks out was llantas (tires), a reference to the spare belts of fat I carried around my waist by this time. I guess you could say I was an early bloomer, except that the qualities which bloomed early were all the ones that would ensure I became a true misfit: I was snaggletoothed, overweight, unpopular and unwilling to follow the herd to fit in. Instead, I defiantly wore my women's-size clear plastic raincoat and go-go boots to grade school and cultivated my own isolation like a rare and beautiful flower. Although I was almost unbearably lonely, I felt unable to do anything other than cling fiercely to my individualism, which only aggravated my situation. The one ray of light in my dim schoolday existence was my music teacher at Eastman Elementary, Miss Yonkers.

Miss Yonkers and me.

Miss Yonkers was a tall, thin, pale woman with bright auburn hair that seemed sculpted atop her head. She dressed in bright swirls of color that completely covered her, from her dainty neck to her lovely, large feet. She projected an extraordinary air of confidence, which completely enthralled me. When she entered the room, there was no question that she was in charge and would tolerate no disruptions or challenges to her authority. She literally towered over all the other teachers at our school.

Miss Yonkers would achieve near heroic status in my life. Wielding her autoharp, bells, claves and maracas, she would come into our classrooms and try to teach us to sing. Often, she would single me out for special treatment. I would assist her when the group was to sing in rounds or if a harmony was required. For 30 minutes, once a week, when Miss Yonkers came into my world, I was happy — really happy. I felt important, valuable, good for something.

Miss Yonkers would later rec-ommend me to a company that was producing educational cartoons and needed children to sing some of the parts. She got me my first paying job. I made a whopping $100 the first time I recorded. At the time, the rent on my family's modest home

Me in the recording studio.

was only $60 a month, so the sum of a hundred dollars was a small fortune to us. I remember the producers taking us out for what we considered very fancy Mexican food. I think it was at an Acapulco restaurant. Up until then, the fan-ciest place I'd ever eaten was the top-floor red room at Clifton's Cafeteria in downtown L.A.

It was then I realized that music was to become my lifeline, my escape plan.

LOS GUERRA

When I look through the photo albums that I collected from my mom's house after she passed away, I see pictures of myself playing with other children and I wonder why my recollections of my childhood always leave me feeling sad and lonely. Although I was unpopular, I did have some opportunities to play with other kids, but the majority of the time, I felt like I was engaged in parallel play. For one reason or another, I was unable to connect with most kids, but I played with them anyway. It was either that or play alone — which I did the majority of the time. Maybe the things that were happening in my life were affecting me in a way I could not express or share with other children.

One person who I did eventually get close to was my friend Viola Guerra. I met Viola shortly after moving to our house on Ditman, and she would weave in and out of my life over the years. We didn't see each other much at school, but we did visit each other's homes. The Guerra family lived at the corner of our block, next to a bar called The Branding Iron. Sometimes, Viola, her two younger brothers and I would sit outside on The Branding Iron's rear-exit steps, under the colorful red and amber lights. It was a little safe cubby for us to gather in until a drunk would stumble out of the bar, trip over us and puke in the gutter.

The Guerras were a large family of eight or nine kids; Viola was the third youngest. Her household was run very differently from mine in that everyone had chores to do at all hours of the day. What good did it do me that my own mother never made me help her with chores when anytime I wanted to play with Viola, I had to help her finish her chores before her mother would give her a break? Viola made beds, hung, folded and put away laundry, washed dishes, made homemade flour tortillas, refried beans, swept, mopped and dusted. To me, it seemed like cruel and unusual punishment.

With everyone so busy at the Guerra household and the adults preoccupied with other matters, the kids often took unauthorized breaks and got into mischief. I remember Viola and her younger brothers climbing onto the roof of her house, then jumping onto the roof of the front patio, then leaping again to the roof of the front house. These buildings were not all connected, and a fall would have meant at least a broken leg. The Guerra kids were like circus performers working without a net.

I loved going to Viola's house because I got to experience a home full of brothers and sisters, and I think she enjoyed coming to my house because I had only one sister living with me and she was rarely home, so I grew up pretty much like an only child.

One time, the Guerras were having a big outdoor party and Viola was allowed to invite me. I was about 9 or 10 at the time. I had never been in the front house, which also belonged to the Guerra family, but this was a special occasion. I entered the front house through the back door and was immediately greeted by the sight of a long dining table draped with a crisp, white tablecloth. Matching dishes and glasses had been set out for the party guests. Everything looked really nice, and I stood there taking it all in. Then I saw it. On a platter in the middle of the dining table sat a severed, cooked goat's head with the eyeballs still in the sockets. I have no idea how they cooked the goat to keep the eyeballs intact, but there it was.

"I hope you like goat," Viola said, laughing at my obvious shock.

"Unh, Unh," I answered, queasily. We agreed to go outside and have chips and dip instead. We found most of the other kids outside munching on snacks, while I imagined the brave adults were inside, devouring the goat's head or perhaps some of its other body parts.

I had just stuffed a big potato chip loaded with onion dip into my mouth when Viola's older sister Margie came over to us. She had a tall glass of soda and was taking tiny sips.

"Want some?" she asked us with a mischievous smile. The fact that Margie was hanging out with us was a big deal, because not only was Margie older and prettier than either of us, she was also popular.

"What is it?" Viola asked.

"Seven and Seven," Margie whispered, looking around to make sure no one heard her. "Try it," she offered, holding out the glass to us. I took it and hesitantly wet my lips with the drink. It was sweet with a bitter aftertaste, but not scary at all. Viola took a real drink, then smiled, eyes opening wide as she swallowed. We all started laughing and took turns drinking from Margie's glass. Bottles of Seagram's Seven Crown had been placed on the outdoor tables as centerpieces, along with bowls of chips, dip and bottles of soda. All of this had been left unattended while the grown-ups were inside, dealing with the goat. We managed to polish off the first drink, mix and start on another before the adults finished eating. When the grown-ups did come outside, we fled into the back house. I sat down on the couch.

"I feel funny," I reported. "My ears are hot."

"Mine too," said Viola. Margie was now laughing at us.

"You're drunk!" she pronounced. We all burst out laughing for no reason at all.

"You can't go home like that," Margie asserted. As the oldest, she was definitely in charge.

"Call your parents and ask them to sleep over." I did, and to my surprise, my parents reluctantly agreed.

That night we danced and laughed and distracted the adults while Margie played bartender. Eventually Mr. and Mrs. Guerra must have caught on, because they told us it was late for us and made us go to bed. There was no hangover the next day, no reprimands from anyone. We had gotten away with it and it had been fun. I knew then that someday booze and I would be good friends.

THE FANCY LADY

My mother put on her best dress, went into the bathroom and left the door open as she burned the tip of a black eyebrow pencil to soften it. I watched her as she applied the smoky, sable line along the base of her eyelashes. Next, she took a bright crimson lipstick, applied it to her lips and then wiped it off. It was an unusual event. My mom rarely wore makeup unless we were going someplace special, but it was midweek, my dad was away and we weren't going anywhere. As she walked over to me, I could see that she hadn't wiped the lipstick off altogether; she had only wiped away the inner, center part and left the color lining the edges of her lips. I thought the effect was very glamorous.

My mom in front of our house.

"We are having company today," my mom told me. My mom didn't have any friends, so it was a bit of a shocker for me. Except for relatives, she had never had anyone come over to visit. A lady was coming for coffee, and I was to be on my best behavior, she said. My mom gently suggested that I might enjoy playing outside for a while until the guest arrived, a suggestion I took only too gladly, seeing how vigorously she was now cleaning and not wanting to be roped into helping.

When the fancy lady arrived, I could tell right off that my mom was out of her league. The woman was wearing a hat and high heels. She smiled and said hello as she passed me and then knocked on our door as I watched from a safe distance. My mom welcomed her in. I tried to stay outside as long as I could, but curiosity got the better of me, and about 10 minutes later I went inside. My mom had set out a little TV tray with our nicest cups and saucers that actually matched and were never used. True, they were from the thrift store, but they were *elegantes*, cream-colored "china" with metallic gold vines around the rims of the cups and the outer edges of the saucers. She had a little matching creamer, too, and had bought (!) sugar cubes. We never had sugar cubes at our house — NEVER. It was then I realized just how much my mom wanted to impress this fancy lady.

Mom brought out a platter of *pan dulce*, but her guest seemed more interested in the coffee and hadn't taken a piece. "Good," I thought to myself, "more left for me when she leaves." I pretended to go to the bathroom, all the while lingering and trying to eavesdrop, but I couldn't make out what they were saying. I was about to give up and go outside, but I had to pass through the living room to get out. That's when it happened. As the fancy lady sat on the edge of our old couch with her high heels crossed at the ankle, holding my mom's "elegante" cup and saucer, I saw a big old brown German *cucaracha* crawling up her leg. I stopped to think for a split second. Should I say something and ruin my mom's chances for making a friend or should I....

"LOOK OUT!" I cried, unable to contain myself any longer. The cockroach was heading toward her skirt. The woman looked down and saw the cockroach racing up her leg and abruptly stood up, losing her hat in the process. My mom's "elegantes" came crashing to the floor as the lady started shimmying all over our living room. My mother apologized profusely, but the damage had been done. The gracious lady said it was all right as she hurriedly gathered her belongings and left, never to be seen at our house again.

Because our house was infested with roaches, my sister and I learned at an early age to shake out our clothes before putting them on, to rinse and wipe down our plates before putting food on them and to keep all food that wasn't refrigerated enclosed in plastic or airtight containers. These skills would serve me well years later when I'd move into the Canterbury Apartments in Hollywood, a place that would prompt the Go-Go's to write these lyrics in one of their early songs: "Living at the Canterbury, fighting off the roaches!" One night at Ditman Avenue, my sleep was disturbed by an itching feeling that seemed to move about my face. Half asleep, I slapped my cheek then felt a wet, squishy substance ooze between my fingers. I ran into the bathroom, turned on the light and looked in the mirror. To my utter disgust, there was a smashed cockroach smeared across my cheek; part of a wing, little legs still discernible, the other part of the roach clinging to my fingers. I scrubbed my hands and face vigorously with soap and water, then went back to bed.

The visit of the fancy lady coincided with a new chapter in my mother's life. Because her first husband had died of cancer, she decided to volunteer for the American Cancer Society. Over the years, this would become an important, empowering activity for my mom. She started dressing better, she went out and talked to strangers about cancer and the need to find a cure. This woman, who I had once seen as servile and often helpless, was advocating for those less fortunate than herself, and she was doing it remarkably well. My mother, I was soon to discover, had a competitive streak. She tried very hard to be the top fundraiser in our community. Now, when we went to the swap meet, she'd always take an hour or two to walk around with her little manila envelope, hitting people up for spare change to fight cancer. She made everyone feel that their contributions counted. I remember walking with her once, when she was asking for donations, and a man told her, "I only have a few pennies in my pocket."

She replied, "Pennies count, too." She gathered the man's pennies and as much spare change as she could. She made calls, went to meetings, passed out information tirelessly. I began to see a change in her and a slight improvement in her relationship with my father.

My dad, who had belonged to the carpenters' union for as long as I can remember, had never really pursued any of the posted union jobs. He liked calling the shots and enjoyed the feeling that he could stay home when he felt like it or work incessantly if he preferred. My father enjoyed telling tales of his days hopping the rails, working here and there. I think getting married to my mom had ended all that wanderlust and carefree lifestyle for him, but in his heart he secretly longed to be a vagabond. With union jobs, there were rules to adhere to; with lucrative contracts on the line, strict timelines were in place. Around this same time, my father finally broke down and signed up for a long-term union job. I thought my father would be miserable, but it was quite the opposite. The regular schedule, steady paycheck and hard work seemed to agree with him.

Now, as I reached the end of grammar school, the violent fights and arguments that had occurred once or twice a week diminished to once or twice a month, and I enjoyed the relative tranquility.

SCHOOL DAZE

I used to have an odd idea of what friends should be like. I thought friends were people who played with you, liked you and stood by you faithfully through thick and thin, but that's a pretty tall order and maybe that's why I always felt like I didn't have any friends. Early on, I figured out that I could be a school safety during lunch and recess, which would allow me to escape the humiliating ritual of roaming the schoolyard alone and purposeless, looking pathetic. Instead, I could roam the schoolyard, still alone but with a supposed purpose: to catch other students breaking the rules. Things could be much worse; I could insist on playing a team sport, get chosen last and then immediately be made "out"; or I could have the tetherball, kickball, or volleyball "accidentally" hit me in the face. These accidents happened more frequently when I played team sports, so being a safety seemed well, safer. I could almost even boss people around.

One year I was a hall safety. I'd keep kids from running down the stairs or halls and make sure they didn't scream or graffiti the walls. Most kids liked to be on the playground during lunch and recess, so the hall gig was dull. The following year, I switched to where the real action happens in elementary school: the girl's bathroom. Bathroom safeties were like capos in training. You could get your peers in trouble if they refused to obey you, and — what the hell — they hated me anyway, so why not? The threat of snitching was a powerful weapon, but I don't think I ever did snitch on anyone. It's a cultural thing. Nothing is lower than a snitch. But I didn't need to snitch — I was tall, fat and ugly, which probably helped me enforce the rules and was usually enough to keep kids from throwing wads of wet hand towels on the ceiling or locking the toilet stalls and crawling underneath, making the stalls inaccessible to all but the most desperate. As I said before, I was real good at cultivating my own isolation.

When I entered sixth grade, two things happened. It was discovered that I needed glasses, and I was miraculously moved to a class where the teacher liked me and recognized my genius. She promptly had me tutoring students, and, before I knew it, I was classroom president. I quit the safety gig and stepped up the tutoring. I was far from a straight-A student, but others were doing much worse, and, as the Spanish saying goes, *En el pais de los ciegos, el tuerto es rey* (In the land of the blind, the one-eyed man is king). That was me, I was the *tuerto*, and I was starting to be liked. Well, the adults liked me, anyway. I got to deliver a speech at our sixth-grade culmination ceremony, which I filled with big words that I learned from the dictionary because nobody I knew ever used those words. The fact that I didn't know how to pronounce some of them didn't become apparent to me until I got to Stevenson Junior High.

FATSO AND BOZO

Maybe I wasn't quite this big, but I felt like I was.

I was getting slightly better at making friends by the time I was about 10 years old, but there was a girl living on my block who had taken an intense dislike to me for some reason. She was a couple of years older than me, but because I was tall for my age, we stood about the same height. I don't remember her name because I never had a chance to learn it. The first time I saw her, she was walking down our street and I was standing out front by myself. I looked at her as she walked toward me, thought nothing of it and looked away, but she must have misunderstood my lack of interest because as she approached me, she glanced up and muttered "Fatso." She hurled the insult at me as though I were her lifelong enemy. It surprised me and left me speechless, but I didn't think about it for long because I didn't see her very often and we went to different schools.

A few months later, I was outside again. The shaded carport in front of the apartments was an occasional playground for me when no cars were parked there. I was minding my own business when she again passed by and yelled out, "Fatso!" Her insult annoyed me, but this time it was tossed at me with little conviction, and, truth be told, I was a little afraid of her because she was older, so I once again ignored the insult.

This verbal abuse went on for the next several months. Finally, the summer before I entered seventh grade, I felt I had to stand up to her. The next time she crossed my path and called me Fatso, I was going to say something. No sooner had I made a commitment to talk back to her than she came walking down the street. A group of neighborhood kids were out in the street, playing baseball. They weren't playing with me, but they had seen me. My enemy walked on the opposite side of the street from where I stood and called out at the top of her lungs for all to hear.

"FATSO!"

This time, I was prepared. Because her reddish brown hair was very frizzy and poofed out on either side of her head like a certain famous red-haired clown, I decided that I'd found a weak point in her appearance and went for the jugular.

"BOZO!" I shouted back. The kids in the street heard me and thought the nickname was fitting. There was even louder laughter for my response than there had been for her initial insult, because, after all, people insulting me was old hat. Caught by surprise, it was her turn to be speechless. I had struck directly at her insecurity. Within a day, all the kids were calling her Bozo. It became her nickname, and she hated it. Most of all, she hated me for giving it to her. Now, when she walked down the street, she would keep to the side opposite from me. She would still call out "Fatso" as she passed, but I threw "Bozo" right back at her. We had our own little Cold War going.

After school one day, I went across the street to play with my friend Viola and some other kids in Griselda's front yard, which was directly across from our carport. Bozo was walking home from school, and as she passed by she saw me. I wasn't usually on this side of the street, so it must have caught her off guard.

"Fatso," she called to me as usual.

"Bozo," I replied, but this time she stopped in her tracks.

"What did you say?" she asked, staring at me.

I trembled inwardly, but I realized that I had to stand up for myself.

"I said…*BOZO!*" Bozo dropped her school books to the ground and charged at me, pushing me into a thorny rose bush in Griselda's front yard. I swung at her blindly, too surprised to realize that I was in the middle of my first real fight. It seemed like we were mostly just pushing each other around in a weird, frenzied dance. We took turns knocking or pushing each other into various bushes. Every now and then, a punch or slap would make contact but I couldn't really feel anything. Eventually, Viola pulled us apart. She was the only other kid around who was big enough and had enough experience fighting with her brothers that she wouldn't shy away from a fight. Bozo said nothing, she just picked up her books and walked away.

"Who won?" I asked.

"You did," my friends said, but I knew they were lying. I knew there was no way I'd done anything but dance around with that girl.

Viola walked me home, pointing out that I still had rose bush thorns stuck in my arm and fingernail holes where Bozo had clamped onto me. I felt no pain at all. The adrenalin rush was incredible.

"You stuck up for yourself," said Viola. I smiled, knowing that I had indeed finally stuck up for myself. More importantly, I had found a thrilling new sensation, the experience of losing oneself in the heat of battle and the giddy adrenalin rush of the fight.

STEVENSON JUNIOR HIGH

Stevenson Junior High is where I served a three-year sentence after leaving elementary school. I was in science class, learning about modern medicine, when the teacher asked which antibiotic would cure a certain infection. I was still riding high from my smarty-pants sixth-grade year, and I raised my hand high.

"Penny-celeene," I said, stressing the syllables as one would in Spanish.

"Which one?" my teacher asked again. He was either confused or just setting me up for the punch line.

"Penny-Celeene," I repeated innocently.

"*Penny-celeeeeene?*" he mimicked quizzically and then paused for effect. "Oh!!! You mean PENICILLIN?" The class burst out laughing. It was very funny. Asshole.

That experience marked the beginning of an exciting year. One guy thought it would be hilarious to throw dog biscuits at me in Algebra class. He didn't think it was so funny when I went over and dug my fingernails into his flesh, clawing bloody red gashes down his face. Because he was a gentleman and only threw dog biscuits at girls but drew the line at hitting them, he vented his anger by picking up his desk and hurling it out the window of our second-story classroom. The teacher sat at his desk and pretended nothing happened.

I made Lamplighters, which is what the Stevenson honor society was called. The Biscuit Thrower christened me "Hunch Butt," which was horrible because even I had to admit that it was funny and therefore had legs. A group of marauding boys threw an orange at my ass as I crossed the field. It exploded and left a big wet spot on my pants. The students in the yard fell over themselves laughing at me. My anger simmered as I plotted a million ways of exacting revenge, none of which would ever come to fruition. I saw a group of *cholas* jump a girl in the gym locker room. They mercilessly punched, kicked and dragged her around by her hair, literally mopping the floor with her before the coaches found out what was happening.

I'd had a growth spurt in sixth grade and was almost normal weight, but by seventh grade my weight caught up with my height and then some. I was 170 lbs. and wore a size 20 in women's dresses. I had buck teeth, frizzy hair and glasses, and I was completely lost in that savage, evil place named after the author who had written about bloodthirsty pirates and the hideous Mr. Hyde. None of the things he wrote about were as scary as this East L.A. middle school that was named in his honor.

Before the year was over, I had signed up for Service, also known in some circles as Lapdog. I worked in the student store for a semester, and then my past came back to haunt me and I was assigned to the girl's bathroom. I tried to enforce as much as possible, but I couldn't control the gang jump-ins that took place all the time in that bathroom. I would've felt bad if someone had been beaten during my watch, but these girls were willing participants. It meant so much to them to be accepted by these surrogate families that they were willing to have their asses kicked. It seemed to me that they were even sadder than I was. My parents might have been fucked-up, but I knew they loved me. I didn't want or need a surrogate family.

I was lost during my first year at Stevenson Junior High. I had no clue how to parlay the few social skills I had picked up during my last year at Eastman Avenue School and make them work for me in this new setting. The school was big and overwhelming. The kids from a nearby housing project called Estrada Courts had their own gang called *Varrio Nuevo Estrada*, or VNE. They were a huge gang at the time, and today they're one of the biggest and oldest gangs in L.A. One of their rivals was another large gang called White Fence, or WF.

Although I grew up in East L.A., I never felt the presence of gangs when I was in elementary school or at my home on Ditman Avenue. Oh, I'd see the graffiti on the walls, and there was a family on our block who was deeply immersed in gang culture. The parents were gang members and the grandparents were *veteranos* (respected gang elders), and the kids, although too young at the time to be actual gang members, were expected by their family to be gang members someday. But most of the families on our block were not in gangs; they were just poor, working-class people with a desire to get ahead.

I didn't really understand the gang mentality. What were they fighting for? An old, overcrowded apartment building, a liquor store, a bus stop — all of it was prized turf. I saw them as divided and conquered, fighting over scraps from the master's table instead of pulling up a chair to join the dinner party. I couldn't relate to their goals. They didn't seem interested in becoming brain surgeons, or pilots, or president of the United States, like I was. They didn't want to live in a house like the one the Brady Bunch had. They wanted to rule their turf, grow old and become veteranos.

Needless to say, I knew very little about gang culture but soon found myself in the middle of it. In East L.A. at that time, it was impossible to escape it. It was not unusual for rival gangs to drive slowly around the perimeter of our school football field, trying to find a particular target. Sometimes their bullets found their intended victim, but just as often, "civilians" (non–gang members) sitting in the bleachers studying their textbooks or watching a game got caught in the crossfire. Every so often, someone would post a bulletin about a memorial service for one of my classmates.

It was like trying to sit in a classroom in the middle of a combat zone. Just when you started thinking you were in a regular school, you'd walk into the bathroom or gym class and see someone getting jumped in, or you might see someone spray-painting a wall, or sniffing the paint from a plastic baggie. Stevenson had lots of other problems besides gangs. There were plenty of drug dealers on our campus. It was the easiest thing in the world to buy reds, whites, black beauties, yellowjackets, joints and nickel or dime bags. I avoided these during my first year, but would eventually sample a little of everything while I was there.

That first year was the hardest for me. I wanted so much to do well, but doing well only meant that someone would threaten to beat me up if I didn't let them copy my work. It seemed that the answer was to not do so well. Maybe I shouldn't strive to make Lamplighters — scholastic achievement only meant you'd be labeled a nerd and made you an easy target. Yet, if I didn't do well, I would have to contend with my father's wrath. My looks didn't help, either — being fat, wearing glasses and having crooked teeth

Me at Stevenson Jr. High.

didn't win me any friends. I looked the part of a stereotypical nerd, and even some of the least popular kids at school teased and bullied me. I was at the bottom of the food chain.

It was during this school year that I started to go home and go to bed while the sun was still up in the sky. My sister had already married her junior high school sweetheart. My mother had started working as a teacher's aide. I was all alone and my best friend was my pillow.

In eighth grade I wised up, totally by accident. I was still in Service but now I was working in the girls' vice principal's office. This was exciting, high-stakes stuff. I started making friends with the female thugs and ringleaders of the gangs at school. They were always being called down to the VP's office, and they always had to wait a long time with nothing to do. With no magazines or weapons to keep them entertained, these girls would eventually talk to me. They were nice, too.

"Do you know why they called me down? How much do they know?" they'd ask. Pretty soon, I was on friendly terms with *cholas* from rival gangs and, believe it or not, I even had one or two stick up for me. I started to appreciate them. They had so much style, they were so fierce-looking and they didn't take shit from anyone. There was a code of loyalty between them that I admired, but not enough to endure the jump-in ritual.

I don't know if being around all these cholas started to rub off on me, but one day, one of my usual tormentors pushed me as I was walking up the stairs, and, without thinking, I immediately turned around and pushed her back. She was a couple of steps below me on the stairs and had a Bic ballpoint pen clenched pointy-side-in between her teeth. My open hand shoved the point of the ballpoint pen into the back of the girl's throat, causing blood to come gushing from her mouth. The ambulance was called and I was suspended from school for two weeks, during which time I enjoyed watching TV and having no homework.

I might as well have brought some 8-by-10 glossies and a Sharpie to sign autographs when I finally returned to school. I was almost famous. People smiled at me and said hello to me in the halls. I found four friends to eat lunch with (one of them was Viola), and my days of dodging projectiles and taunts were over. I took shop as an elective the following semester and learned how to make a plastic shank.

CHICANO POWER!

Late in the summer of 1970, just as my summer vacation was coming to an end, the National Chicano Moratorium Committee organized a huge march through the streets of East L.A. to protest the war in Vietnam, the many Chicano soldiers who were being drafted and sent overseas to fight it and the higher-than-average mortality rate among Chicano soldiers.

My father never liked the term *Chicano* because he believed the word was derived from a derogatory term used when he was young and working as a bracero. He was fairly cynical about politics and didn't usually get involved in political demonstrations. This time, however, he surprised us by volunteering to take us to the march. We parked our car near the 7 (now the 710) Freeway, just a couple of blocks away from Whittier Boulevard, where the march was already underway. We walked up the street and were able to find a spot where my sister and I could see. I think we were expecting a parade, but there were just a lot of everyday-looking people: mothers, fathers, kids and students with signs, crosses (to symbolize the fallen soldiers) and fists pumping in the air, some chanting "Chicano!" while the onlookers would yell back "Power!" I remember being most impressed by the Brown Berets, and being totally dazzled by their coolness. They had a paramilitary look, with boots and uniforms, and even had some female members.

After a while, my sister and I begged to join the march, but my father was looking uneasy. The crowd was swelling and we found ourselves being pushed back. My father, sensing something was wrong, pulled us back even farther. To my surprise, we saw police cars parked along the side streets. Not 10 minutes had passed from when he'd forbidden our participation than we saw a young man throw a beer bottle toward the marchers, then quickly run and disappear into the crowd. There was no one following him, but we could see a wave of people push back as he shoved his way through the crowd. I couldn't see where the bottle landed, but I did see the results. Suddenly, people were shoving and yelling. More projectiles flew through the air; one hit the roof of one of the police cars. Pandemonium broke out as the crowd pushed in all directions, trying to get away from the volatile situation. And then, just as suddenly as it had started, it ended, as the attackers fled on foot through the crowded sidewalks. A few cool heads tried to calm people down and reorganize the marchers, but my father rushed us back to our car and drove away. As I watched out the car window, I could see the policemen on their radios calling for backup and getting out of their cars. I thought they might have been waiting until things stopped flying through the air before stepping in, but they didn't seem to be too concerned with catching the people who threw the bottles. I could see parents holding their children's hands and trying to stand their ground as we turned the corner and sped away from the danger.

At home, we watched the news on TV and heard that a riot had broken out when a bottle had been thrown at a police officer. From my perspective, it had been a minor altercation and the police had made no attempt to catch the individuals who had been throwing bottles in the first place. A reporter named Ruben Salazar, who was favorably disposed toward the Chicano movement and had been an outspoken critic of police brutality, had been shot and killed by a deputy sheriff. The riot squad had been called in to clear out the demonstrators, using tear gas and batons, resulting in dozens of injuries and three deaths. I remembered the worried faces of those parents clutching the hands of their small children as we drove away to safety. I couldn't believe that what had started as a peaceful march protesting a war halfway around the world had turned out to be so ugly.

I will never forget that day, August 29, 1970, for two reasons: One was that I had never before realized that I was part of a minority group, and I felt good about being part of something as powerful as the Chicano Movement; the other was the understanding that this group had enemies who weren't afraid to throw bottles at us or shoot us. Throughout my early childhood, policemen had been the knights in shining armor who had rescued my mother from my father's vicious attacks. In my eyes, they had always lived up to their motto, "To Protect and Serve." That day, I saw my knights like the other people in my life: Their capacity for good was matched by their capacity for evil. It almost seemed like diametrically opposed impulses had to exist for the world to make sense. My own world was coalescing into a ball of love and hate, trust and treachery.

A NEAR ESCAPE

I heard the rumble of the bulldozer coming to demolish my house. The metal arms slid under the creaking floorboards, lifting the cracker box off its foundation. "Oh no," I thought, "they must not know we're still in here.

"*MIJA!* WAKE UP!" It was my mom tugging hard at my arm. "It's an earthquake!" she said urgently, pulling me out of bed and under the doorway. Jolted awake but still half asleep, I watched our little house bouncing up and down, whining like a colicky baby on its mother's knee. Standing there between the bedroom and living room, I saw a huge crack spread diagonally across the wall. Photographs, knickknacks and dishes crashed to the floor. While my dream of the bulldozer had been scary, the reality of this strange phenomenon was just surreal. I felt as if I was looking out through someone else's eyes, shielded by a calm sense of disbelief at the destruction, unperturbed by my mother's distress as our home literally fell to pieces around us.

During the past few months of school I had been going to bed increasingly early, often while the sun was still up. I think I was hoping to sleep my life away. My father had started frequenting a local billiard hall after work, and my mother worried that he'd squander the little money they'd been saving to buy a house. My mother had accepted a job as a teacher's aide at my old elementary school, and my father was working steadily. For a while, the goal of buying a house had made it possible for them to keep an unspoken truce, but now that truce was on shaky ground.

As soon as it became apparent that my father was running late for dinner, my mother would usher me into the car, drive me to the pool hall and send me in to get him. I hated doing this, because kids and females were not usually welcome at pool halls. Everyone would turn to look at me as I walked in, then they'd turn to look at my father.

"Dad, *Mami* says to come home for dinner."

I could see the pained look of embarrassment on my dad's face. Not once did my father leave when I asked him to. Instead he would send me away, simmer for an hour or two, then come home angrier than ever. The fact that my mother would challenge my father's authority and cause him to lose face by sending his daughter to tell him it was time to come home infuriated him and inevitably led to a fight. Now that I was getting older, I started to see how my mom's actions played into the cycle of violence they were both trapped in. It was easy for me to predict the outcome of some of the things she did or said to him which would trigger a beating, and I wondered why she couldn't see them and avoid setting him off. I felt guilty for thinking these things because I knew my mom didn't want to be beaten, but I couldn't help but feel that she was somehow contributing to her own victimization by staying around and pushing my dad's buttons. Now I could feel my anger spread from my father to my mother, and I wondered what role I played in all of this.

I was 12 years old, and it was hard to think about all these things. I still felt powerless and trapped, and I was tired of being in the middle of my parents' fights as well as the fights and humiliation at school. I cherished the fact that I no longer suffered from nightmares, because now I could escape into a deep black sleep, and part of me wanted to stay there forever. I was trying to build a fortress to hide myself in. I didn't want to be caught up in my chaotic environment, to see any more fighting, endure anymore ridicule, so I tried to shut off my feelings and withdraw from life. Now, in the middle of this massive earthquake, I felt immune to my mother's panic.

The little house on Ditman took quite a beating from that 6.6-magnitude quake. No one came by to inspect the house, but my father declared that we had to move out. My parents redoubled their efforts to find a house we could afford to buy, eventually settling on a house just a few blocks away, on Bonnie Beach Place.

It had a huge yard, and even though the house was small, it seemed palatial compared to the house I had grown up in. The move was uneventful, and pretty soon we settled back into our old routines. I continued to keep my feelings bottled up, until one afternoon when I got home from school.

My mother was hysterical. She had cuts and bruises all over her body and claimed that my father had tried to kill her. I tried to calm her down and convinced her that we should go see a divorce attorney. She finally agreed, and we drove out to the neighboring town of Montebello that afternoon. Sitting in the female attorney's office, I felt hopeful that my mother was finally going to put an end to our troubles. She spoke with the lawyer for a long time and pictures were taken of her injuries, but when the attorney asked my mother to sign the paperwork that would allow her to file the suit and represent her, my mother refused. She had changed her mind again.

I saw the fortress that I had painstakingly built starting to crumble around me. My mother's inability to act — even to defend her own life — sent my anger rising to the surface. How stupid I was for allowing myself to hope that things could change for the better.

LA CAPIRUCHA

I had lost count of the days and nights we'd spent on the train. After the first day, the air conditioning had broken down and our mid-class air-conditioned cars became little rolling ovens. Most people made their way back toward the rear of the train, where the wooden benches didn't stick to the backs of our legs like they did on the Naugahyde seats and where the windows were not sealed shut to keep the failing air conditioning from escaping. These windows let in gusts of warm air that blew through the train car, invigorating the weary travelers as they watched the sometimes lush, sometimes barren landscape of Mexico spread out before them.

At each station along the way, the train would no sooner shudder to a halt than a swarm of vendors would engulf it from all sides. Men and women bearing large flat baskets on their heads sold sandwiches; little kids rushed up with plastic bags of sliced fruit, others sold candy or Chiclets, still others offered delicious-smelling steamed tamales on paper plates, or homemade *champurrado*. I felt sorry for the people in first class who couldn't open their windows and were stuck with the white bread sandwiches, potato chips and soda pop sold on the train.

Being a thrifty soul, my mother always insisted that we finish the food we'd brought with us before we got anything from the vendors. She purchased a package of Gansitos, a sort of Mexican Twinkie with jam and creme inside, and offered it to me if I ate something nutritious first. She handed me a hard-boiled egg that was packed in foil. I don't know if she'd packed it herself at the onset of our journey or if she'd purchased it when I wasn't looking. I'd like to think that she wasn't deliberately trying to poison me, but no sooner had I finished eating the egg than I began to feel sick. The remainder of that journey was spent curled up on the wooden bench, clutching my aching stomach, the taste of that rotten egg stuck in my throat.

When we finally arrived in Mexico City, D.F. (aka La Capirucha), I was blown away by its size and beauty. I had been there before, shortly after the city had hosted the 1968 Olympics, but the idea of putting on your best clothes for company must have endured long after the athletes and TV crews had gone home. Mexico City had continued to grow, modernize and dress up for company. There was a beautiful new Metro that made most points of interest in this sprawling city easily accessible. My father's sisters lived just a few blocks from a Metro stop.

My Tia Josefina had a small, two-bedroom house which shared an enclosed courtyard with a neighbor's house in back. It was a longstanding family tradition to stay with relatives when visiting from out of town. My aunts' two-bedroom house was already home to Tia Josefina's four daughters, one son, my Tia Agustina and Tia Josefina herself, so arrangements were made for the younger girls to stay in a rooftop room that was constructed above the rear house.

At the back door of my aunt's kitchen stood a large stone sink and clotheslines for doing laundry; beyond that, a switchback stone staircase led out to the temporary rooftop quarters I was to share with my cousins, while my parents were given my aunt's master bedroom. I was thrilled at the thought of not sleeping in the room next to my parents, and I loved the rooftop view.

Dad, mom and tia Agustina in Mexico City.

These trips to see his family always brought out the best in my father. We spent most of our time doing all the standard touristy things: trips to the pyramids, the zócalo, the basilica, Xochimilco…but this time my father wanted to go beyond our usual travels. He suggested we take a trip to Monte Alban, in Oaxaca, and he wanted to see Veracruz, too. These destinations were further away from Mexico City than we'd ventured before. My father suggested taking a flight. My mother was terrified of flying, but going everywhere on trains and buses was going to take a big chunk out of our vacation time. My father eventually convinced my mother to give air travel a chance, but my mother was trembling from the moment we booked the flight up until the pilot had completed the ascent. "*Siento que me muero*" (I feel like I'm going to die), she kept saying over and over again, and nothing we could say or do would ease her anxiety. As soon as the plane reached cruising altitude and the free soft drinks and peanuts were passed out, my mother calmed down and declared that flying was not so bad after all. We got to see a lot of different Mexican cities that way, using my aunt's house as home base and booking short flights on Mexicana.

We were all feeling really good about this trip until one morning. I was up on the rooftop with my cousin, and I heard a familiar commotion coming from my aunt's kitchen. I ran toward the edge of the roof where I could see right into my aunt's open kitchen window. My mother and father were fighting. It took only an instant to assess the situation. My mother was backed up against the sink, my elderly aunt Agustina was trying to put herself between my father and mother. Dad was enraged and ready to strike. I turned to run down the stairs when I heard my mother's bloodcurdling screams and the sound of my father hitting her. Without thinking, I leaped from the top step and vaulted perilously down about 15 feet through the open air, landing hard on the concrete stoop at my aunt's back door. My aunt Josefina ran toward me, certain that I had broken my ankle but I'd merely slipped a bit on landing. Quickly regaining my balance, I dashed into the kitchen where I started pulling my father away from my mom. I didn't feel like a helpless little kid anymore. I pushed hard and was able to wedge myself in front of my mother. I was angrier than I'd ever been in my life.

Now I was screaming in my father's face: "STOP IT! STOP IT!" For the first time in my life, I wasn't begging him to stop, I was demanding it. I got up close, staring him down, daring him to hit me. I couldn't stop to feel scared, I had to act. Instead of the confusion I'd felt in my little scuffle with Bozo, I felt hyperaware, like time had slowed, like I had superhuman powers to leap through the air, stop time and push this monster off my mother. Something inside me had snapped and there was a surge of wild, powerful energy racing through my entire body.

I forced my father to contend with me long enough to allow my mother to escape. Tia Agustina helped her outside while my father was focused on me. Tia Josefina held onto my dad warily, afraid he was going to strike me too, but he wasn't resisting. His eyes were locked on mine, and, for the first time, I think he saw that I wasn't a little girl anymore.

JUKE BOX

There are some kids at school who give off an air of maturity and coolness that demands attention and respect from both teachers and students. Diane Apodaca was one of those girls who seemed aberrantly self-possessed for an eighth grader. She was well liked and respected by her peers and teachers. We shared the last class of the afternoon during my eighth grade year at Stevenson Junior High. I don't recall the subject, but I do remember that we often had to plug away at our work quietly while the teacher worked at her desk. One afternoon we were at our desks, silently working on our independent assignments, when Diane interrupted the silence.

"What's on the jukebox today?" Diane asked me.

"What?" I replied, perplexed and surprised that she was addressing me.

"You were singing," she said. "You always sing or hum while you work. Didn't you know that?"

"No," I replied, embarrassed. Oh no, I thought to myself, she's going to make fun of me.

I was about to apologize when she said, "It's nice, you have a good voice."

I couldn't believe my ears. I was getting a compliment from Diane Apodaca and the other kids were agreeing with her. Students who had never shown any sign of knowing that I existed were now nodding their heads in agreement with her.

"So, what's on the jukebox?" she repeated with a big warm smile.

I was too embarrassed to sing anything for the rest of the day, but it wasn't long before I'd give in to my subconscious singing and humming while I worked. Pretty soon, the kids in that class started calling me "Jukebox." When I'd sing a song they liked, they'd sometimes call out, "Turn up the jukebox!" and if they didn't like it, they would call out, "Change the record!" I even started taking requests, and nobody ever told me to shut up, not after Diane said she liked my singing.

Now when I walked down the hall, I'd be greeted with shouts of "Jukebox!" It sounded odd to me at first, but I learned to like it. Diane had singlehandedly saved me by giving me a new nickname and validating my singing. Jukebox quickly replaced the calls of Hunch Butt that I'd had to endure in seventh grade. It seems like such a small thing when I write about it today, but, believe me, her kindness made a huge difference to me during my junior high school years.

TOUGH GIRL MAKEOVER

After my first year at Stevenson Junior High, I spent a good part of the summer dieting, trying desperately to lose weight and make myself look better for the upcoming school year. In eighth grade, the addition of false eyelashes to my everyday makeup ritual instantly hardened my appearance. The first time I glued on those eyelash strips I spent the whole day looking loaded, watching the world through half-closed lids. Eventually I would whip my weak, sissy eyelids into shape with enough strenuous workouts that by mid-year, I could double up on lash strips for special occasions.

Trying out a harder look.

My morning ritual went from rolling out of bed and brushing my teeth to a full 45 minutes of piling on layer after layer of makeup. Sometimes, I took a tip from the cholas and added dramatic liquid liner to accentuate my eyes, but I couldn't leave well enough alone and I sometimes painted on tiny lower lashes, like the Mod models I'd seen in magazines. The new look added several years to my appearance, and it wasn't long before Viola's older brothers allowed us to sit in the back seat and go cruising with them down Whittier Boulevard. I got bored with cruising after about 10 minutes. Listening to loud music on the radio was fun, but being stuck in traffic, trying to look into other people's cars from the back seat of ours was difficult and not worth the effort, as far as I could tell.

The Boulevard was much more exciting in the day, when my friends Rita, Viola and I would walk or take the bus there. We'd spend the day shopping for records, then finish off with a trip to the movies. My favorite theater in East L.A. was the Golden Gate Theater, on the corner of Whittier and Atlantic. The Golden Gate was practically a movie palace and always seemed out of place in its humble surroundings, but as you walked through the covered entryway to the ticket booth you had a chance to transition from the mundane to the glorious. The place felt like a castle. I saw *Billy Jack* and *The Sound of Music* there, though not as a double feature. Although the Golden Gate was beautiful, we frequented the Boulevard Theater more often, because it was less expensive and you could usually get two or three older movies and a cartoon for the price of admission. The Boulevard seemed to cater to horror fans. I saw lots of good cheesy and bad cheesy movies about vampires, demons and monsters, like *The House That Dripped Blood, The Fearless Vampire Killers, Mark of the Devil*, countless (no pun intended) Christopher Lee movies and *Andy Warhol's Frankenstein*. Sadly, they were checking IDs on the day they showed *Fritz the Cat*. I was so bummed!

Now that we were teenagers, another source of entertainment opened up for us. Viola's older sisters, Margie and Irene, invited us to dances at Kennedy Hall, where kids only slightly older than us would rub up against each other while slow dancing, then head over to the tables and benches on the sidelines and make out. I was not pretty and I'd usually only get asked to dance once or twice in the entire evening, but I did a lot of looking around. I saw a buxom girl from my school getting hickies all over her neck and chest from a guy who spent about two minutes looking at her face before heading south. It made me want to laugh, seeing her sitting demurely with her low-cut blouse while this guy plunged his face into her cleavage. I couldn't help but think that he was having more fun than she was. As I stood there pondering what it felt like to get a hickey, I could hear the soundtrack in the background. On any given night at Kennedy Hall you might hear Thee Midniters, Cannibal and the Headhunters or "oldies but goodies" being played by the legendary Huggy Boy. I was invisible here, watching the others dance and embrace. Nobody made me feel uncomfortable, but I knew that I was different somehow. I felt like I was wearing a costume that had allowed me to peek into someone else's life.

STEREOPHONIC

When we made the move to the house on Bonnie Beach Place, one of the first things we purchased (aside from the house itself, which was a whopping $8,000) was a stereo console. It was state-of-the-art, built into a very fancy dark-wood cabinet. It had am/fm radio and played records. I was now able to stack several records at one time on a spindle at the center of the turntable and a new record would automatically drop into place when the previous one finished playing. It was a decadent extravagance, and my dad and I played it all the time, much to my mother's dismay.

No sooner was the console in our house than I bought my first 45: "Band of Gold," by Freda Payne. I LOVED that record and played it over and over, until, out of sheer irritation with the endless repetition, my mother gave me money to buy some more records. I bought the Archies' "Sugar, Sugar," The Supremes doing "Stop in the Name of Love" and Aretha singing "Respect." It wasn't long before I monopolized the DJ duties. First thing in the morning, I'd stack my records or crank the radio; it drove my mother crazy, but it got me out of bed early, and God knows I had to be up early, what with my strenuous makeup routine.

At school, I became more outgoing. Hiding behind the tough-girl mask made it easier. Once the camouflage was in place, I added another defense mechanism to my arsenal: humor. After years of reading *Mad* magazine, I could trade witty quips with the best of 'em. Eighth and ninth grades were my funny years. I had logorrhea, projectile humor; funny things would come spurting out of my mouth without my having any control over them. The result was that I made more friends, but my grades went from A's and B's to C's and D's.

During my funny period, I made friends with a girl at school who was also a bit of a comedian. She would spark my voyage of musical discovery by introducing me to the music of David Bowie via the record *Hunky Dory*. She also introduced me to the man I would fall madly in love with for the next four years. That man was Elton John. The first time I heard the song "First Episode at Hienton," I was hopelessly smitten. Elton and especially Bowie were making music that sounded nothing like the oldies, ranchera and soul music I'd grown up with. It was a soundtrack that was totally different from the music played at the dances where I had felt like I was wearing a costume.

I quickly embarked upon a campaign to raise money to buy albums instead of the 45s that I'd been collecting. My mom kept us on a tight budget, and an occasional 45 wouldn't break the bank, but LP records were too expensive, she said. Pretty soon I was mowing the lawn, washing her car, taking out the trash; I did whatever she didn't like doing to support my growing music habit. I ventured to the FM rock stations like KMET and KLOS, where I discovered more music that was not popular with either my family or most of my friends. I found this new music becoming increasingly important to me, and I sought out others with a similar interest. As often happens, life provided the answer in the form of a friend, a new girl at Stevenson named Rita Barrett, who loved Led Zeppelin. Her family had just moved to East L.A. and she didn't know anyone. She wore vaguely hippie-ish clothing, like an army jacket with different patches sewn on and a pukka-shell necklace. We hit it off immediately.

I'd found myself. Listening to rock music and talking about it felt like I was discovering my way home. I made new friends who were all rock fans, but not just ordinary rock fans; they understood the appeal of rock artists who were pushing against convention. It was one thing to like Led Zeppelin and quite another to like David Bowie and Elton John, who were seen as total freaks by most of the kids at my school. There was a lot of homophobia in the early 1970s. Elton John was closeted at the time but he wore outrageous outfits that raised speculation about his sexuality. I was convinced that Elton was straight and that someday I'd meet and marry him. Bowie was openly bisexual, a relatively new concept to teenage kids in East L.A. and one that was very threatening to a culture which preferred clearly defined gender roles.

Around this same time, the movie *Lady Sings the Blues* came out. I was already a Supremes fan, so I enjoyed the movie without the burden of having to compare Diana Ross to Billie Holiday, since I had never heard of Billie Holiday before. I bought the soundtrack and through that I also became interested in finding original music by Billie and Bessie Smith. I fell in love with both of them and the way these two very different yet powerful women expressed themselves through their music.

I was in the process of redefining myself. The tough-girl look and attitude had helped me, but I didn't fit in with gang culture; my class-clown antics had negatively affected my grades, and my love of rock music had not won me general popularity but it had gained me a few quirky friends who appreciated my offbeat taste. There had always been a soundtrack to my life and I had always loved music, but up until this point, it had been selected for me by others — my father, sister, teachers, peers; my surroundings had dictated the soundtrack for my childhood. Now there was a new sound in my life, a self-guided audio adventure. My world was becoming stereophonic. I imagined myself in a musical where people sang to each other instead of speaking and spontaneously broke out into dance numbers. My heroes were artists who defied society with their music, their outrageous clothes and unconventional sexuality. Suddenly, everything was gloriously colorful and open to endless possibilities. Everything good in this new music, appropriately called *glitter*, spilled over into the way I looked at my life and myself.

BORRACHERAS

Homeroom is the class that counts. If you're on time to homeroom, you're good for the day, because it's the morning's official class count which is sent down to the office that establishes you as absent or present. Oh sure, they take attendance in each class, but that attendance doesn't get noticed until it's written in a tiny box on a report card at the end of the year. By then, most parents just look at the grades.

Viola, Rita, Olivia and I were discussing our strategy for taking the day off from school. The plan was to leave our books in our lockers, sit through homeroom so that our parents wouldn't be called, then sneak out the exit closest to our homerooms and meet down at the five-and-dime at the corner of Whittier and Indiana.

Everything went according to plan; in fact, it was easier than I'd imagined. As soon as all four of us were at the meeting place, we made our way to a less visible location. Once we were on a side street, Viola lit up a Kool and passed it around. I had never smoked before, but I really wanted to be as cool as my friends, so I took a drag. Smoke exploded from my throat and nose as I coughed uncontrollably. The girls laughed at me and continued passing the smoke around, mercifully skipping me when my turn came. I was grateful that they hadn't pressured me into smoking. As much as I wanted to be like them, my body's response was making me look like a sissy each time I took a drag.

We had no real plan aside from not going to school. It was early, and most of the shops and businesses on Whittier Boulevard were still closed. We walked toward Laguna Park, stopping to play on the swings for a little while until we noticed a car slowing down and the two young men inside looking at us. Just as I was starting to think that they thought we were cute, one of the girls commented that they might be truant officers, narcs or gang members. I had recently taken to studying the way characters talked on TV shows like *The Mod Squad* in another attempt to look cool, and I thought this might be the perfect opportunity to try out my new vernacular.

"Do you think it's the *fuzz*?" I asked.

"*Stoopid*!" Olivia laughed.

Olivia was somewhat new to our group, and hanging out with her brought with it a certain risk. She was widely suspected of belonging to White Fence, the gang, and although she had skillfully skirted the issue on the occasions we'd asked, she was far from safe in a school that was dominated by rival gang VNE. Just the fact that we were with her made all of us targets. Now we were in danger, vulnerable to attack in an empty public park. As soon as the car turned the corner and was out of view, we ducked behind the building that housed the public pool. We watched from our hiding spot as the car rolled slowly back into view. Now we could see the guys inside scouring the park for us, but we'd temporarily lost them and they sped away.

We weren't sure if the men in the car planned to return but staying at the park was clearly a bad idea. We left and continued our aimless meandering. We decided to pool our lunch money and try to score a bottle of Ripple, Thunderbird or Strawberry Hill. We knew there was always someone willing to trade a lunch ticket for a cigarette, so we wouldn't have to go hungry. We had done this before and already knew which booze was in our price range. Strawberry Hill was too sweet and Thunderbird too harsh; we opted for the Ripple.

We waited outside a liquor store on Whittier Boulevard until we saw a man walking toward the entrance. As he neared the door we called out to him, "Would you buy us a bottle of Ripple?" We were all talking at once, smiling and trying to be flirty without really knowing how, girls trying out the power of our gender, too naive to know where that power came from yet intuiting its strength. We didn't have to ask twice: The man went into the liquor store, bought something for himself, and on his way out, he handed us a brown paper bag with the bottle of Ripple inside. "Thanks, mister!" we giggled.

"You didn't get it from me," he replied, immediately regretting his decision to be our accomplice. He distanced himself from us as fast as he could.

"Let's go to Calvary!" I said. The girls looked at each other, a little surprised at my suggestion that we visit the local cemetery, but it was so close, so tranquil, so utterly devoid of narcs, cholos and truant officers that it made sense.

We carried our little brown bag and walked to a shady spot under a tree. We passed the bottle around and, after a few minutes, I got up to read the tombstones. They were fascinating to me. Here were a couple of sweethearts buried side by side. The dates told who died first and at what age. I imagined their short, bittersweet lives. There was so much history right there at my feet. I was lost for a while, making movies in my head about people I had never met, dynasties headed by a Beloved Father or Grandfather, a Beloved Wife and Mother. Sometimes whole families were buried together, side by side. I could imagine who'd cried at who's funeral, who'd lost a child, who'd died alone.

"It's time to go!" My friends interrupted my daydream. They looked a little funny to me, like they were sharing some private joke. I must have missed it while I was walking around, looking at the gravestones. We happily made our way back to Stevenson to grab some lunch and resume classes.

Back at school, we secured lunch tickets easily enough but had to eat quickly because we were late. We went to our next class and tried to pretend we'd been there all day, but halfway through the lesson, a monitor came to my classroom and asked to collect me. I was wanted in the nurse's office. I got a queasy feeling in my stomach that had nothing to do with food or booze.

Turning the corner at the bottom of the stairs, I saw someone being carried off on a stretcher by paramedics. "Alicia? Come in here," ordered the nurse. She shined a flashlight into my eyes and asked me to perform a few equilibrium tests, then authoritatively pronounced me high. "What have you taken?" she asked. It was clear there was no use in lying, so I told her I'd had a little bit of Ripple.

"Not that," she said impatiently. "What kinds of drugs have you taken? Your pupils are dilated." I hadn't taken any drugs so I was very surprised by her lack of medical knowledge.

"I haven't taken anything other than the Ripple!" I argued.

"Your friend's life is in danger if you don't tell us what she took," she warned me. "She is going to have her stomach pumped." The queasy feeling in my stomach had been justified; one of my friends was on that stretcher but I could see they were trying to frame her.

"We didn't take any drugs. She doesn't need her stomach pumped!" I insisted. I was told to wait in the nurse's office. I knew from my days as an office monitor how the administration operated. One of my friends would be waiting in the vice principal's office, another one in the principal's office, and I was being held here. We were being kept separate so that we couldn't corroborate our stories. I knew our parents had probably already been called.

I was right. When I saw my father's face as he found me sitting in the nurse's office, I felt truly ashamed. He had obviously left work early to come deal with my problem. He and my mother said nothing to me. They had just come from meeting with the principal, who had suspended me from school for a week. They waited until we got in the car. Then my father broke the silence.

"Are you all right?" he asked quietly.

"Yes," I said. Then he took my face firmly in his hand and turned it toward him. "I want you to tell me the truth. If you tell me the truth, everything will be okay. If you lie to me, you will be sorry." I knew what he had been told: that my friends and I had taken drugs and that the nurse had confirmed this upon examining us.

"I didn't take any drugs," I said, stubbornly looking him straight in the eye. I fully expected to be slapped but he released his hold on my face.

"I believe you." I never loved my father more than at that moment when he took my word against everyone else's.

HIGH INFIDELITY

I cheated on Elton all the time. I had a crush on a boy at school who didn't know I was alive. I'd never had a conversation with him but he'd smiled at me once as I passed him on my way to class, and that was about as much attention as any boy had ever paid me, so he seemed like a good candidate for my affections. He was a popular kid on the student council who went by the nickname Cowboy. We had absolutely nothing in common; nevertheless, I crushed on him in secret and he slowly took over the spot that David Cassidy of *The Partridge Family* had occupied in my heart for so long.

My other infidelity was daydreaming about Bruce Lee's body. I am a fan of a well-toned bicep, and Bruce Lee certainly trumped Elton in that department. *Fists of Fury* had sparked my interest in kung fu. Now the release of Bruce's new film, *The Chinese Connection*, added kindle to spark, and I couldn't get enough of Lee, or of kung fu in general. Apparently, I wasn't the only one. It seemed that the supply couldn't keep up with demand. People like me, infected with kung fu fever, were begging for scraps from Hong Kong cinema. The demand was temporarily met by horribly dubbed Chinese martial arts movies where actors talked through clenched teeth or closed mouths or would open and close their mouths with no words coming out. Exuberant foley artists provided thunderous sound effects at the hero's lightest slap. It was laugh-out-loud funny and gave me my earliest appreciation for films which fall into the bad-in-a-good-way genre. The stories were basic. The good guys and bad guys were clearly defined, with no ambiguity, which was exactly what was missing in my life, where, confusingly, people were both good and bad.

These movies were filled with underdogs, filial bonds, promises to never fight again, thwarted bullies. The plots were interchangeable, but the fighting was choreographed like Fred Astaire and Ginger Rogers in old black-and-white movies; they made it look easy. Well-staged fight scenes always excited me and made me smile. The more unbelievable and outrageous the circumstances, the better! One scene that stands out in my mind is a fight where the Shaolin master suddenly executes a handstand and literally starts kicking butt. As his opponents try to counter attack, the master switches from a handstand to supporting his entire upturned body on one index finger, doing all his fighting with his legs and free arm. It was absolutely hilarious and completely riveting.

I don't remember all the names of the movies I saw, but films like *Five Fingers of Death*, *Seven Blows of The Dragon* and *Fearless Fighters* seemed to be in every theater in East L.A. Many of these movies included female fighters alongside the men. These martial artists were given equal status with their male counterparts, and any thug who thought he was going to have an easy time with a female opponent had another thing coming.

I fantasized about being a kung fu master. I wanted to be like those beautiful female martial artists with their fabulously ornamented jet-black tresses, long sideburns and straight bangs. They were thin and agile, delicate but not fragile and sometimes they ended up kissing the likes of Bruce Lee. Who wouldn't want to trade places with them?

Comic book superheroes, masked wrestlers and Shaolin masters provided me with the role models that were lacking in my life. What was a girl to do? Elton just wasn't satisfying all my needs.

GOLDEN

The television ad promised golden, sun-kissed locks if I used their product. All I had to do was spray my hair with Sun-In and go outside. I followed the directions, saturating my coal-black hair with the spray and then letting it air-dry in the sun, but my hair was so dark that the sun had no power over it. This gentle method was not designed for people like me, with coarse, jet-black hair, but those ads had worked their influence on me, and now I had my heart set on those golden streaks. I'd have to call in the big artillery.

In the old days, hair color was mixed with heavy-duty peroxide, and you could buy a light blonde color at the drugstore that would lift your hair several shades. I know, because that's exactly what I did. Of course it was a gamble; you didn't get the color on the box right away. With black hair you'd get a brassy, deep red the first time, then a copper color, and, if you kept at it and didn't burn your hair off, after multiple treatments you could end up with a lovely rusty blonde, a color I tried to pass off as strawberry blonde.

I've always had a problem knowing my limitations. When I was very little, my father made me believe that I could be anything: president, brain surgeon. I just added blonde to the list. When I looked in the mirror, I didn't see what others saw — the cheap dye job, the broken, crooked teeth and braces, the bulging midsection. I saw myself through my father's eyes. I was a beautiful blonde, and if the world thought it could limit me or beat me down, then it had another thing coming. I would never be a beaten woman.

That summer of '72 I was golden, and I wasn't the only one. My world expanded beyond the everyday concerns of East L.A. when Munich, Germany hosted the Summer Olympics. Making history was an American swimmer named Mark Spitz, who captivated the attention of people all over the world by winning seven gold medals, a record which stood unbroken for over three decades. I became a fan of his and of the Soviet gold-medal gymnast Olga Korbut, but not for the same reasons. Spitz was ruggedly handsome. His nearly naked freestyle stroking was just about the sexiest thing I'd ever seen. Olga, on the other hand, was beautiful to watch. She made strength look graceful and flawless technique look effortless. A fierce competitor with a deceptively inno-cent face, she would later receive a *Star* magazine "groupie" makeover.

At that time in my life, I looked up to groupies. I thought they had style, sex appeal and chutzpah, and I imagined their lifestyles were quite glamorous. I wondered if Olga Korbut knew what she was in for when she agreed to let the makeover team at Star dress her up. I, for one, wholeheartedly approved of her new look, and my appreciation for her increased.

Tragedy struck at the Olympics that year when a group of Israeli athletes were murdered. Because he was Jewish, Mark Spitz was perceived as a potential target and left the games early. That fall, I started ninth grade and I drew a huge, poster-size charcoal portrait of Mark Spitz for art class. It won me a summer scholarship to the Otis College of Art and Design in Los Angeles. I was promptly kicked out for fighting with another student.

The following spring, a loudmouth, braggart tennis player started making news with his sexist statements about women in tennis. I had absolutely no interest in tennis, but I found myself getting angry. Later that year, the loudmouth, Bobby Riggs, would challenge Billie Jean King to a tennis match which would become known as the Battle of the Sexes. It was at that point that I realized for the first time in my life that there was a name for what I was and still am — a feminist.

The Battle of the Sexes was like no other tennis match I've ever seen. It was more like a lucha libre bout. The amount of theater that went into it and the things that the athletes stood for was every bit as important as (and perhaps even more important than) the athleticism. Billie Jean was carried in on a golden litter trimmed with bright pink feathers. She looked like an Egyptian queen. She handed Bobby a squealing baby pig for his male chauvinistic pig statements.

Billie Jean King didn't just defeat Bobby Riggs that September day in 1972, she triumphed over sexism and male chauvinism, and men and women who championed equality of the sexes all over the world celebrated with her. News of her victory reached all the way into East L.A., where a bottle-blonde teenage girl whose world had been rather small up until this point suddenly realized that a woman who refused to play by the rules could change everything.

LAST MANGO IN MEXICO

"It's the last time I'll be able to see Mexico," said my father dejectedly. He'd had to leave work the previous week after experiencing an insulin imbalance at a construction site where he was working on a narrow beam five stories above the ground. His vision blurred and he'd started feeling confused and disoriented. A co-worker helped him down, and my father was sent straight to the hospital, where the doctor reprimanded him for completely ignoring his diabetic condition, which he'd known about since childhood. Not only was dad overweight, he constantly binged on donuts, pan dulce and Mexican soda pop. Now it was too late; my father's kidneys had been permanently damaged.

His doctor informed him that they would begin preparing him for hemodialysis, a treatment by which a person's blood is cleaned and filtered by a machine when the kidneys can no longer do the job. Once the treatment was underway, my father would have to be hooked up to the machine four to five hours a day, three days a week. My father felt utterly defeated.

Even though we couldn't afford to go back to Mexico so soon after taking on a mortgage payment, my father insisted on taking one last trip to see his sisters, so we flew out. My Aunt Anastasia (Tasha) and her family met us at Aunt Agustina's and Aunt Josefina's house. My father had many brothers and sisters, but he was closest to these three sisters and especially to Josefina, who was closest to his own age. My cousin Agustin, Josefina's son, had recently passed away, so my father was the only man in a house full of women.

It was a wonderful trip. Because of my father's delicate condition, we enjoyed simple activities like picnicking in Chapultepec Park and lunch in Xochimilco. My cousins and I walked to the local *panaderia* for fresh pan dulce every day and took an empty basket and dishcloth to the *tortilleria* for fresh, hot tortillas sold by the kilo every afternoon. We bought sliced mangos, coconut and jicama from the fruit vendor and sat eating on my aunt's patio, enjoying each other's company.

One day, my family was sitting in my aunt's living room, telling stories about their youth. I walked away for a minute to take another piece of pan dulce from the table when I heard my father snap at something my aunt Tasha said. Suddenly, he was up on his feet.

"*Don't ever say that again!*" he shouted. "*None of you!*" He was standing in front of Tasha, looking down on her, trying to intimidate her. For a minute, I thought he was going to strike her, but Josefina was able to calm him down and get him out of the room. My mother moved closer to Tasha and apologized for my dad's outburst, but my aunt was a large, powerful-looking woman and my father had not frightened her. She simply stood up and helped herself to another cup of coffee. Her composure thrilled me. Later, I asked my aunts about the comment but nobody would share any details with me.

"Your father wants it forgotten," my Aunt Tasha said. "We'll leave it alone." Aunt Josefina later told me that my father had bad memories from his childhood and that he hated their grandmother, but that was as much as she'd share with me. I had never considered that my father was still powerfully affected by his own childhood memories.

That was the last time that my father ever had the strength to threaten anyone. When we got back home, he started his hemodialysis. Each visit left him weaker and more tired. Eventually, he was unable to do any heavy jobs. That's when my mother stepped up.

My mother was in her mid-50s when she started accompanying my father on construction jobs. Out of necessity, my father taught her how to do flooring, tile-setting, roofing, painting and minor repair work. To practice her tiling and building skills, my mother took all the leftover pieces of tile my father had accumulated over the years from different projects and tiled and expanded the laundry room in our house. It was perfect. She arranged the mismatched tiles artfully and I thought it looked better than if she'd used just one type of tile.

It was the first time in my life that I'd seen my parents treat each other like friends and partners. My father still held his contractor's license, but it was my mother who did most of the work while my father supervised and coached her. My mother's self-esteem rose exponentially, and on days when she wasn't working on a construction job she could be found repairing things at home. She had found a new lease on life.

It's strange to think that a fatal illness is what finally brought peace and harmony to our family.

THE PAN DULCE DIET

In one way or another, I have been battling with weight gain since elementary school. Before that, everyone said I was just hanging onto my baby fat a little longer than most. I had role models like Shirley Temple, whose chubby legs and cherubic smile were considered cute. It wasn't until some kid at Eastman Elementary threw my lunch bag in the trash, saying I was too fat, that it occurred to me I might not be so cute and chubby.

In those early days, my mother tried to help by denying me food, but that only made me feel like she was withholding her love. She made a spicy guacamole one day and wouldn't let me have any; ditto for the mango shakes that she knew I loved and would prepare for my father. Eventually, I'd make her feel guilty and she'd give me a little bit. I felt like I was winning, but I was only making things worse for myself. I wasn't thinking of the humiliating public weigh-ins we had at school, not while the creamy taste of a warm tortilla smothered with guacamole caressed my tongue.

I was terrible at dieting. I remember the doctor telling my mother that she could help me lose weight by making me eat salad more often. One afternoon after hearing this, my mom was out running errands and I got hungry. I boiled a couple of potatoes, chopped them up, scooped out about half a jar of mayonnaise, sliced up a hard boiled egg my mom had in the fridge and I made myself a big bowl of potato salad. By the time my mom got home, all she saw was me licking the spoon.

"What were you eating?" she asked.

"I made myself a salad, like the doctor said," I responded. I had no concept at all of how much fat or how many calories were in different foods.

"What kind of salad?" my mother asked suspiciously.

"Potato salad, that's my favorite!" I chirped, proud that I had made the salad all by myself.

"Oh no!" was all my mom could say, shaking her head from side to side. "It should be mostly lettuce, Alicia." She must have been exasperated, because she only called me Alicia when she was fed up with me.

I felt bad about my silly salad mistake and I made a point to start reading more about nutrition. Once I learned a little bit about how calories worked, I felt ready to try again. Although I was no longer as heavy as I had been in the seventh grade, I still had weight issues. After my dad's final trip to Mexico, which had centered around food and conversation, I felt like a boa constrictor was wrapped around my midsection whenever I buttoned up my pants. I was sick and tired of the diet plans we got at the doctor's office, plans with impossibly bland and boring food, but since I had a little bit of knowledge of how calories work, I decided to make up my own diet and include the things I liked:

Alicia's Pan Dulce Diet #1: Every morning upon waking up, have a tall glass of low-fat milk and one piece of pan dulce. Unlike donuts, pan dulce is baked, not fried, and therefore much better for you! In the middle of the afternoon, eat one piece of fruit with a cup of coffee, then go to kung fu class, where you will get good and sweaty. You want to get on the fast track to a black belt, so be sure to give it your all! After class, starve yourself until about 3 p.m., then open up a can of Campbell's Chicken Gumbo soup and eat the whole thing. It will leave you feeling nice and bloated for the rest of the day.

I followed this diet for about two months, and I had to re-think the way I thought of food during that time. Up until then, eating had been a sensuous experience. Before, each bite of a good meal was an exquisitely stimulating oral sensation that led to deep physical satisfaction; now, eating the same thing every day meant the thrill was gone. The experience was like putting gas in the car — tedious but necessary. I stayed on the pan dulce diet until I got down to about 118 pounds and had to buy myself new skinny jeans. Once I started at Garfield High, I continued to lose weight. I had a book from the library on yoga and started doing that, as well as trying to learn cheers and cartwheels so that I could try out for the cheerleading squad.

I liked my pan dulce diet so much and it had been so effective that I started inventing new diets based on my favorite foods:

Alicia's Awesome Chocolate Diet: In the morning, take a glass of low-fat milk and add powdered chocolate Quik. Enjoy with a chocolate *concha*, chocolate Donettes or Gems. For lunch, you may have a Big Cherry or a Cherry-O-Let, a cup of chocolate pudding and/or chocolate milk. Sit on the grass at school with your tasty lunch and eat while reading the school newspaper, the aptly named *Garfield Log*. Go very light on dinner; you may have a Fudgesicle or perhaps more chocolate Quik.

My mom had stopped telling me what to eat after the first few weeks of the pan dulce diet. I guess she figured it was a phase. My new chocolate diet was different. It was downright dangerous, and I was too stupid to know it. One warm day, as I was walking home from Garfield, I started to feel dizzy and faint. By the time I got home, I must've looked sick. My mother sat me down with a glass of ice water and called the doctor. He asked me to come in immediately. After poking my arm for a blood sample, he told my mother I was anemic, and then my mother told him about the chocolate and pan dulce diets.

I was severely reprimanded and told to stop dieting. It was strange to have a doctor tell me to stop dieting because usually they were telling me the opposite. I gladly followed the doctor's orders, took my vitamins and iron and went back to eating. Quesadillas, burritos, mole and enchiladas made a triumphant return to my dinner plate. From time to time, my mom would open up a box of frozen spinach, boil it and try to sneak it by me as a side dish, but it never worked.

FRIENDS AND BAPTISMS

I wonder if I can find a way to blame my parents for my lack of friends. After all, my mom never had any friends. She kept busy by meddling in her children's lives, not that anyone ever complained. My mom was a sweetheart who would give you the clothes off her back if she thought you needed them. She liked nothing better than checking in on her kids to make sure we were doing well. My father had business friends, but he only saw them when he was at work, and he certainly never brought anyone over to our house. We were an isolated family unit.

My mother's meddling took a bold turn when my brother Raymond married a Protestant woman named Mary. When my mother found out that their child was not going to be baptized, she concocted a successful plot to kidnap the baby and baptize him in secret. Actually, kidnap is too strong a word. She borrowed the baby under false pretenses, rushed him to a "real" church, then, by lying to a priest, secured the infant's salvation. Of course, the plot was later revealed, and my brother and his wife were very upset that my mother hadn't respected their wishes. My mother remained unrepentant, insisting that she had to baptize the baby so that he wouldn't end up in Limbo, which is a place between Heaven and Hell where infants are trapped if they die in a state of original sin. In my mother's Catholic world, we are all born in a state of original sin, passed down to us from Adam and Eve's transgression in the Garden of Eden. The Catholic sacrament of baptism basically gives a clean slate to children who are too young to atone for their sins. My mom's description of Limbo made me imagine a place in the sky with millions of babies and toddlers crawling around on the tops of clouds, never knowing true happiness. I could see them standing on fat, wobbly baby legs holding onto the locked Pearly Gates, never able to enter the kingdom of Heaven. The thought made me sick. I wasn't disgusted by the babies or the parents who didn't have them baptized; I was disgusted that God wouldn't allow them into the kingdom of Heaven.

My brother and sister-in-law eventually got over my mother's kidnapping and started coming around again. I loved my sister-in-law, Mary, because she would talk back to my dad and she could hold her own in an argument, never backing down. Their arguing made others uncomfortable, but they seemed to enjoy their heated discussions. I liked to listen to them, even though neither one ever changed their point of view. It was fun witnessing their verbal sparring, but I would later learn that engaging in passionate debates was not everyone's idea of fun.

My parents' friends were all family. My brothers and sisters were all grown up, and while my mother filled her days with housework, visits to the *sobadora* and finding ways to help her children, my father read incessantly and kept to himself.

My mom didn't have much faith in American doctors. Whenever she or any of her children got sick, she'd subject us to the ancient cures passed down by healers and *sobadores*. If I had a stomachache, out came the yerba buena or lemon grass tea. I didn't mind the minty taste of yerba buena or the subtle citrusy hint of flavor in lemon grass or the hot lemonade I had to drink if I was catching a cold; but she had a large variety of other, more bitter herbs to choose from. Sometimes she'd come home with little brown bags of dried leaves that I was told would cure my ailment. From them, she would concoct vile-tasting medicinal drinks whose chief benefit was that they would induce nausea and vomiting.

I used to make fun of my mother for favoring what I considered to be superstitious folk cures. It didn't boost my confidence when she'd pass an egg or a tomato over someone with a fever so that the foods would draw off some of the heat from the afflicted, or that she'd frequent a *sobador*, a sort of massage therapist who's brusque jerking and tugging could untangle your intestines or align your body for maximum health. Often, these cures were combined with prayer, incense, candles or oils. I called her methods *brujeria* (witchcraft), which made her pretty angry, but she suffered my ignorance. I thought myself so much smarter than her; it was only much later that I would come around to questioning the supremacy of Western medicine and admit that maybe my mom's herbal cures and aromatherapy were helpful.

Not all of her beliefs grew on me, though. I had been raised as a Catholic, but, as I said before, my mother's brand of Catholicism incorporated elements of Mexican folk beliefs and superstition. On previous trips to Mexico, I had seen people walking on bloody knees, making their way up to the Basilica de Guadalupe to pay off a debt to *La Virgen*. My aunt told me that she had promised La Virgen to make the journey from her house to the basilica on her knees when one of her kids was sick. Her faith impressed me, but the logic of it all eluded me. My mother told me stories of people she knew who had spent their childhoods dressed in a saint's vestments as a sort of payment for the saint's intervention. Still others were known to place a statue of *San Martin de Porres* in a headstand position until the saint would find them a suitor. The idea of bargaining with God or holding a saint hostage made no sense to me at all, and doubt chipped away at my religious beliefs.

I identified more with my father than with my mom. I, too, enjoyed reading incessantly, and I was comfortable being alone most of the time. At our Bonnie Beach house we had a proper dining table, and although we rarely ate meals together, when we did, my dad and I just ignored each other and read our books while eating. My father read his life away. He always had his paperback westerns with him in the car, the bathroom, at the dinner table; even while watching TV he'd shift back and forth between the screen and his book. My mother never ate with me and my dad; she was always busy warming up tortillas or doing something else in the kitchen.

I used to watch reruns of *Leave It to Beaver*, and there was a part of me that longed to be like the Cleaver family, who sat around eating meals together, discussing the day's events. June Cleaver would never kidnap a baby, put a tomato on Beaver's forehead if he had a fever or spend all her time in the kitchen warming tortillas. I bet Beaver would have turned out much differently if she had.

GARFIELD HIGH

When our sentence was finally up at Stevenson Junior High, half the kids went on to Theodore Roosevelt High School in Boyle Heights, and the other half went to James A. Garfield High School in East L.A. I went to Garfield, the school with the low academic standards immortalized in the movie *Stand and Deliver*. Garfield was much calmer than Stevenson had been. There was still the gang element to contend with, but most of the kids who belonged to VNE had gone on to Roosevelt. At Garfield there wasn't one strong, dominant gang. Instead, there were members from Varrio Nuevo Estrada, White Fence, Mariana Maravilla and Little Valley, to name just a few, but with no single gang able to assert control, the atmosphere seemed somewhat less confrontational.

Drugs were also less plentiful. Marijuana and alcohol provided the popular recreational highs. There was a new group of kids here that I hadn't seen at Stevenson called *stoners*; they were easygoing and non-threatening. In fact, Garfield as a whole was sort of easygoing and non-threatening. The problem with Garfield was that nothing was challenging. The expectations were so low that you could get a good grade just by showing up. I took classes like Communication, where we'd sit around and "rap" about our feelings; Poetry and Rock, where we analyzed the lyrics of Bob Dylan and Joni Mitchell. In French class, I was introduced to Sheila singing "Pendant Les Vacances," and I learned the lyrics as one of my assignments. The classes were fun, but I had a nagging feeling in the pit of my stomach that this was not the road to the White House or medical school.

Thanks to my ninth grade art teacher who put in a good word for me, I was able to take an advanced art class, where I caught the teacher's attention by drawing a forest. In the foreground, three trees had been cut down, the branches morphing into human limbs, knots on the trunk resembling rib cages and pelvic bones. My teacher liked it and my subsequent drawings, which were sort of surreal. What she called my "style" had developed over the years due to my habit of doodling in the margins of my notebooks. The abstract shapes of the doodles would often turn into something unexpected, subconsciously extracted from my daydreams or the teacher's lecture.

My art teacher conferred a special honor on me. She selected three students, each of whom would design a mural for a different building on campus. I had hoped to do one of the odd surrealist pieces that my teacher liked so much, but she surprised me by asking me to draw something cultural. She suggested a pyramid in the background and whatever I wanted in the fore-ground. This idea intrigued me since I was a big fan of the movie *The Ten Commandments*, which my family watched every Easter. So what if I couldn't do one of my wacky pieces, at least I could design something that would make Ramses proud. Without discussing it further, I immediately set to work on the sketch for the mural.

I went to the library and checked out several books on Egypt. I copied the pyramid from one book and put it in the background as my art teacher had suggested, then I copied the sphinx from another book and put it in the fore-ground. I was a good copier, and I composed my mural design almost entirely by rearranging the images from various books onto my page, but due to a lack of knowledge of Egyptian hieroglyphics, I allowed myself the freedom to styl-ize — or maybe I should say bastardize — the glyphs. I was pretty pleased with the end result. I thought I had captured the essence of Egyptian culture.

"The committee loved your design!" my teacher announced just one day after I'd turned in my drawing. She walked me out to the preselected wall so I could visualize my mural on it. Then she let the guillotine fall. "They just want you to change it to a Mexican pyramid."

"But a Mexican pyramid wouldn't make sense with the sphinx," I reasoned.

"Well, maybe you could change that to an eagle on a cactus, or put some-thing else that makes sense in the foreground." She smiled at me as though I should be grateful, but I couldn't hide my disappointment, and I asked her why. I wondered if there really was a mural committee, or if she was just mak-ing me jump through hoops for her own sadistic pleasure.

"Most of the students here are Hispanic," she said. "We want something that reflects their culture." I told her I'd have to think about what to draw and she seemed happy with that.

For the rest of that afternoon I found myself getting angry every time I thought about the mural. I didn't understand why they would give me a wall if they didn't like what I'd done. I didn't understand why Hispanics could only want to be around Mexican pyramid murals, I didn't understand why this white art teacher was telling me what Mexicans like. I love Mexico and Mexi-can culture, but I didn't want to do the same sort of murals that were every-where in East L.A.

I realized that I hadn't been chosen because they thought I was a good artist, I'd been chosen because they thought I was a good copier. I turned down the project the next day.

GO BULLDOGS!

We wait in line outside the gym. Some girls practice their routines, others stretch for splits, some just repeat the words to their cheer quietly to themselves, like a prayer they are cementing firmly in their memories. I don't do any of those things. I can't because my stomach is tied up in knots, and I'm so nervous that I have to go to the bathroom every 15 minutes.

My sister Yolanda, who graduated from Garfield several years before I went there, had once mentioned in passing that she thought I'd make a great Garfield cheerleader someday. Because that offhand comment came from my adored big sister, it became an instant goal of mine.

As soon as I began my sophomore year at Garfield, I started observing the cheerleaders. Garfield had an amazing cheerleading squad. I believe they were state champs the year I was there. These people were trailblazers. In a time before cheerleading was recognized as a sport, they performed incredibly precise and daring feats. I was thrilled that my sister thought I could be as good as them; it meant she really believed in me, and I wasn't about to let her down.

The first thing to do was figure out what they were cheering about. I only learned the little I know about football so that I would understand which cheers were appropriate during the course of a game. I didn't feel comfortable shouting "First and 10, let's do it again" without knowing what "first and 10" meant. I attended the cheerleading and football practices before and after school, and after a while the cheerleaders started to say hello to me when they'd see me in the bleachers. I would watch them carefully, then go home and practice in front of a full-length mirror. I went through each movement slowly and deliberately, making sure my body memorized the right angles, my hands were slightly cupped but never overly curved, my wrists never broke the smooth, straight line from shoulder to fingertip. My voice had to be loud, with each word clearly enunciated. My braces-accessorized smile should be wide enough to reflect sunlight and blind people in the top row of the bleachers. I trained like a real athlete.

By the time cheerleading tryouts came around, I had already been complimented by several of the varsity cheerleaders for my precise execution of their cheers. My roundoff, cartwheels and splits were just okay, but overall I felt like I had an excellent shot at making the squad.

The only thing I hadn't prepared for was nerves.

Now, here in this long line of girls all wearing white shirts and gym shorts, I fight to keep my breakfast down. The wait seems interminable. As I get closer to the gym door, I feel the urge to run away or to cry. Then the door opens and I'm on autopilot. I run in cheering and doing cartwheels. I introduce myself with a cheer. It's flawless and the judges clap for me. I start my second cheer. My arms and legs remember the perfect angles they've rehearsed, my smile takes up half my face and then all of a sudden my loud, clear voice runs out of things to say. I search my mind but draw a blank. The cheerleaders look at me. They're waiting, still smiling.

"That's okay, you can start again," says one of the girls who had complimented me just a few days ago, but I can't start again. I feel the urge to vomit, and I run out of the gym and straight to the girls' bathroom.

When the cheerleader list is posted the next day, my name isn't on it. Some of the varsity squad members come up to offer their sympathy. "We've seen you do that cheer perfectly, what happened?" one of them asked.

"I guess I just got nervous," I replied, grateful that they'd at least seen me do the cheer correctly.

I wanted so badly to make Yolanda proud of me. I wanted her to see me win a state championship cheerleading trophy. I wanted to lead the huge crowds that gathered every year for the Garfield vs. Roosevelt game, a long-standing rivalry that is now known as the East L.A. Classic, and pretty much everyone in East Los goes to at least once in their life.

Next year, I thought to myself. Next year.

GLAM, BAM, THANK YOU MA'AM

Me wearing my prized Elton pants with metallic silver letters,

What started as normal admiration turned into a full-blown obsession. I'm not sure how or why it happened, but I decided to buy everything that Elton John had ever recorded. I searched through the bins at new and used record stores, and pretty soon I had a complete collection of Elton's early work. My mom and dad had come to terms with the fact that the stereo, which was supposed to be for the whole family, was really mine, and they let me move it into my bedroom. I listened over and over to my records, and I memorized the lyrics. I read *Circus* and *Creem* magazines as well as *Star Groupie* magazine religiously. I bought every magazine or newspaper that mentioned Elton's name. I called him *Reg* (his real name is Reginald), knew where he bought his shirts and where he bought his eyeglasses. It became a sport to know as much as possible about Elton.

Pretty soon, even my rock-loving friends started to think I was a little crazy—looking through the dedications in my Garfield yearbook, the phrase "to a crazy girl" pops up over and over. I made new friends who were also rock fanatics. I found my musical taste was becoming more focused on glitter-rock artists who injected elements of theater, art and glamour into their performances. I went out with boys who liked to talk about Elton John, Freddie Mercury, David Bowie and Marc Bolan. Eventually, it occurred to me that many of my male friends were gay. It seemed like the most natural thing in the world. Like me, they had fantasy love affairs with these androgynous rock stars. My world started opening up again as it had when I first entered middle school. At that time, I had started to understand what it meant to be a Chicana; now I was looking beyond that.

One afternoon during lunchtime, the Garfield High MeCha organizers had set out a table to recruit new students for their organization. I remembered the cool Brown Berets I had seen at the Chicano Moratorium a few years back, and I was excited to think that I was finally old enough to be a Chicana activist and maybe even a Brown Beret, but the people I met that day snickered and whispered conspiratorially to each other as I walked toward their table. Instead of telling me about their organization, they asked me why I was wearing what I was wearing. They made me feel rejected even though they didn't outwardly insult me; their sideways glances and smirks let me know what they thought of me.

Instead of being open and welcoming, they seemed cliquey and judgmental to me. I was proudly cultivating what I thought was my new glam look. I wore sparkly platform shoes and tight jeans with the word *Elton* cut out of metallic silver fabric sewn down the side of my leg; and since I was going though a skinny phase, I wore my shirts open in the front with about 50 strings of beads to cover up my not-very-voluptuous chest. I guess I looked a little too freaky for them, and they thought I couldn't seriously care about Chicano politics, but they were wrong.

A long time would pass before I would call myself a Chicana again, but that was my own fault. I never should have let a snobby little clique keep me from doing anything I really wanted to do. Many years later, I found out that there were some very cool, creative individuals in this group, but I never made it past the welcoming committee to meet them.

I started asking my mother to drive me to Hollywood. Sometimes my mom would give me and a friend a ride, or my friends' parents would give us a ride. We'd dress up in something wild and go roller-skating on Hollywood Boulevard; sometimes we'd buy ice cream at Swenson's or take off our skates and go into a record store. I especially loved peeking at the sexy lacy undies at Frederick's of Hollywood.

I met lots of interesting people in Hollywood and learned about the latest clubs and discos. Like moths attracted to a flame, people flocked to the Boulevard from all over the country, individuals who were more open to new ideas, chasing different dreams. Pretty soon I had friends from all over Los Angeles. My school friends were still around, but in the evening I'd go home and talk on the phone for hours to friends from Hollywood, San Gabriel, Montebello and other suburbs.

I didn't feel like I had anything to keep me at Garfield, so I asked my parents if they could send me to a school where I could learn something, and, just like that, I was out of there.

AUDIOPHILIAC

My mom and dad had been shopping at thrift stores for years, and as soon as I started collecting records I noticed that there were always lots of records and books at thrift stores; in fact, they were so plentiful that you could often buy them for pennies. I got my first encyclopedia that way. Sure, it was a few years old, but in the days before the Internet, having a home encyclopedia was very handy. I hoped to someday have an entire private library.

Collecting the back catalogs of Elton John and David Bowie led to used record stores, where you could usually find something worthwhile in good condition, but in thrift stores you had to inspect the vinyl carefully to make sure you didn't throw away money on a scratched record. While looking through the stacks of used records for the stuff I liked, I often found things I'd never heard of but which intrigued me. Sometimes I'd take a chance on a wild cover. Not all my purchases paid off, but at thrift-store prices, I could afford to take a chance on lesser known artists, and I could get great deals on old standards. I loaded up on the Kinks, Dave Clark Five, Aretha Franklin and Koko Taylor, as well as a number of K-Tel compilation records, which featured popular songs by less prominent artists.

I no longer took my cues only from the radio; I ventured out and acted on my hunches. I chanced upon the New York Dolls and a band called Kiss that way. Although both bands were good musically, it wasn't just the music that appealed to me. It was the way they dressed and the messages they conveyed. The New York Dolls were challenging gender stereotypes, and Kiss just looked like comic-book superheroes. I loved them right away.

In the spring of 1974 I was only 15 years old, but I pulled up my shortest pair of cut-off jeans over a red lace garter belt so that the straps peeked out from beneath my shorts. I attached a pair of provocative black fishnet stockings to them and strapped on red-glitter platforms. I slipped into a red silk Chinese top, donned a sequined hat and applied as much makeup as I thought I could get away with. Only then was I ready to go. I was going to see Kiss in concert, and I wanted to look grown up. I'd bought a long, pearly-white cigarette holder in Chinatown, and, because I didn't smoke, I bought cigarette-shaped gum to stick in the end, to help create the illusion of sophistication. My father stopped me at the door.

"She can't go out like that," he told my mother.

"Oh, you're so old-fashioned, that's what they wear these days," my mother replied.

My father looked at me again. "Are you sure?" he asked my mom. I held my breath.

"Of course!" My mom reassured him. "She's young, she looks cute in that." I knew what my father was thinking, and I knew he was right, but, God bless my mommy's innocent heart, she condoned my outfit.

When I got to the Long Beach Arena, I was shocked to discover that Kiss was the opening act and I was just going to make it to my seat in time. Kiss was playing with two bands I had never heard of before: Wishbone Ash and Camel. I'd been to the local scalper and had great floor-level seats, so I made my way down to the floor in a hurry, but on the way down, I met a really cute, friendly girl who complimented me on my outfit. She was wearing an outfit with the same level of cuteness as mine (I believe it was a blue Chinese dress) so I returned the compliment.

"Are you here to see Kiss?" she asked.

"Yeah," I responded.

"Me too."

"I don't know who those other bands are!" We both started laughing. Her name was Trudie, and I only spoke to her briefly but I would remember her when she'd come back into my life, years later.

I spent that summer collecting used records and books, and lots of big concert experiences. I permed and bleached my hair the afternoon that Rod Stewart played the L.A. Forum. Not surprisingly, it burned and fell off in crunchy clumps, so I wrapped my head in a turban and unsuccessfully tried to mix glitter rock with old Hollywood glamour. I must have looked like a mixed-up groupie, like Lana Turner meets Sable Starr, a combination which could only have happened in my mind. I had great seats and tried to look mysterious and aloof.

The big concerts were fun, but it was at a small battle of the bands at Montebello High School that I would meet my future friend and bandmate, Marlene, and a fun-loving photographer named Gilbert who would encourage and support us.

GROUPIE TRAINING MISSION

Audiophilia in a teenage mind can take some odd turns. The more I listened to music and got to know musicians through their songs, interviews and articles in music magazines, the more I fell in love with them. And by love, I mean that crazy, obsessive infatuation that passes for love in young adulthood.

Groupies were an example of teenage audiophilia taken to one possible conclusion. Obsession can make you want to consume, caress, submerge in and make love to the object of your affection. I could relate to groupies, and even though I wasn't sexually active, I had a sexually active imagination. I thought I dressed like a groupie, but maybe I was just too awkward to get it right.

I heard of a local glam band called Batch, whose lead singer looked like David Bowie and wrote beautiful songs, so I went to see them play a show at Montebello High School. As I walked down the aisle of the auditorium, I

Makeup O.D. in the photobooth.
Me and Marlene.

spotted an empty seat next to an attractive, red-haired girl and sat down next to her. She was friendly, very sweet and talkative. Her name was Marlene. We made small talk while one band tore down and another set up their equipment. She jokingly referred to herself as a groupie (at least I thought she was joking) and asked me if I was one. I told her I was a groupie-in-training, and we both laughed. We found that we had a lot in common. She too read *Creem*, *Circus* and *Star Groupie* magazines, she liked the same bands I liked, we even knew some of the same people. She was two months younger than me. We clicked immediately.

I guess the only major difference between Marlene and I was that she was really serious about being a groupie. After Batch played, we went up to the front of the stage and loitered, trying to attract the band's attention. Instead, we attracted the attention of a young photographer named Gilbert, who was a friend of the band. Gilbert was a little older than us, and he'd taken pictures of all kinds of bands. We were impressed by him and nearly lost sight of our initial objective. The band was almost packed up and ready to go when Marlene made her move. She went over to the bass played and started talking to him. Gilbert and I watched her from a distance, laughing when we saw the bassist take out a pen and write down Marlene's number. Marlene got his number too, then smiled and walked away. She was so cool! I was so impressed that when she walked over to us, I practically grabbed her and started squealing, but she signaled with her eyes that that would not be cool.

Marlene, Gilbert and I all exchanged phone numbers. The band had been good, just as my friends had said, but Marlene was the real discovery. I called her just a few days later to see if she remembered me and she did. She confided in me that she had already talked to the bassist and that they had a date. We talked for hours, mostly about music but also about sex. She told me about her sexual escapades, and since I didn't have any to tell, I just listened and enjoyed her stories. Marlene answered any questions that hadn't been answered in the pages of *Cosmo*. She gave me a step-by-step tutorial on how to give a blow job and explained to me that it had nothing to do with blowing. Pretty soon, Marlene and I were talking on the phone every day after school. When we got a new rock magazine or the new *Cosmo*, we'd discuss the articles like two well-read scholars; we were nerdy about the amount of information we stored.

After her date with the bass player, Marlene told me all about it in detail. She was turning into a mentor for me.

"You should go out with the lead guitarist," she decided. I didn't particularly like the lead guitarist, but I thought of it as a sort of training mission. I don't remember if we got his number from Gilbert or from Marlene's bass player, but we got it and I called him.

It was difficult trying to make small talk with a guy I had never met in person. I had only seen his band once so I didn't even have that much to say about his playing. I tried to be glib and witty, and I guess I did all right because we talked for a while before making plans to meet in person. When we did meet, our conversation was awkward and strained. Guitar guys can talk for hours about their playing, their gadgets and instruments, but the more I sat there listening to him drone on about those things, the more I realized that I was bored. Why was I sitting here listening to a guy that I didn't find attractive talk incessantly about his technical prowess? He didn't ask anything about me, we only talked about him. I made up an excuse to leave after about 20 minutes.

I felt like a failure as I walked away. I hadn't completed my training mission and Marlene would feel sorry for me but I couldn't help myself. Something inside me told me that I should be aiming higher. I didn't want to play a supporting role in someone else's life. I wanted to be the star of my own life.

SACRED HEART OF MARY

"Are you a practicing Catholic?" the lady behind the desk inquired.

"No," I replied honestly. It had been a very long time since I'd stopped going to Mass on Sundays. With the exceptions of weddings and Midnight Mass on Christmas morning, I never went to church anymore. I questioned whether it had been a good idea to apply to this all-girl Catholic high school.

My niece, Virginia Jr., who was also entering 11th grade, had attended Sacred Heart of Mary High School immediately upon release from junior high. She and my oldest sister, Virginia Sr., had told my parents how much they liked the school. I had an odd relationship with my eldest sister. We didn't grow up together, and there was such a big age difference between us that I thought of her as an aunt and of her children — who were my nieces and nephews — as cousins. Even though my sister's kids had gone to the same schools and were close to my age, our experiences and interests were galaxies apart. That isn't to say we didn't talk to each other at family gatherings, but we were never close. Nevertheless, my sister assured my parents that her daughter Virginia would help me get acclimated if I was accepted at Sacred Heart.

I don't know why they let me into Catholic school, but they did. My family and I were thrilled. I was especially excited about wearing a uniform. I loved my pristine white shirt, the little plaid skirt, the black-and-white shoes worn with '50s-style bobby socks. Wearing that outfit transported me to a mythical time when things seemed simple and innocent — the era of *Leave It to Beaver*. I'd read the book *American Graffiti*, and it probably damaged me.

My niece kept her end of the bargain. She introduced me to all her friends and they let me hang out with them until I got to know people on my own. It was a tiny school, so I quickly learned people's names and interests. The school was so small that just being the new girl was newsworthy. I was interviewed for the school paper and exposed in all my quirky splendor. Strangely enough, the people here were not at all threatened or made uncomfortable by my quirkiness. The uniform helped; without my platform shoes or my glittery outfits I was just like everyone else. I told my new friends that my name was "Ziggy," after the Bowie record, *The Rise and Fall of Ziggy Stardust and the Spiders from Mars*. No one had ever called me Ziggy at Garfield except my friend Louie Mendoza (who changed his own name to Dory, as in *Hunky Dory*, another Bowie album). I had made it seem like everyone called me Ziggy at my old school, and everyone here followed suit.

At Sacred Heart, I was as much a roamer as a loner. I floated between the different cliques during lunch and recess, but I didn't really belong to a permanent pack of friends. These groupings were much more fluid and open than they had been at Garfield or Stevenson.

The girls at Sacred Heart were curious about me: "Why did your parents send you here?" "What did you do?" "What was it like to go to school with boys?" These and many more burning questions made me an interesting person to talk to at recess and lunch. I was a woman of mystery, a blank screen on which these nice Catholic schoolgirls could project their fantasies of what a bad girl from public school might have done to make her parents lock her up in an all-girl parochial school. I told them the truth, that I just wanted to go to a better school, but I'm not sure they believed me.

I was always made to feel welcome as I drifted through people's little groups, telling my dull tales of life at a coed high school. When I wasn't drifting, you could usually find me sitting on the ground reading a book. I remember reading *Helter Skelter: The True Story of the Manson Murders*, by Vincent Bugliosi and Curt Gentry, while at Sacred Heart. It creeped me out so badly that no one could talk to me or come up behind me without my screaming or freaking out. I moved my reading area to the center of the patio where no one could sneak up on me without my seeing them or their shadow first.

It was nice being at this school of friendly girls — about as far from the scariness of Stevenson, Garfield or the Tate home on Cielo Drive as could be — but something was wrong with me. Here were all these smiling faces, but I still had no idea how to turn a smiling face into a real friend.

THE MARBELLITE

I joined the staff of the school newspaper, *The Marbellite*, almost as soon as I got to Sacred Heart of Mary High School. Unsure of my writing skills, I opted for what I thought would be the easy way out: I volunteered to be the resident cartoonist. To my delight, the teacher agreed. It turned out that I sucked at drawing cartoons, which was much more difficult than I'd imagined. You couldn't just copy a picture the way I'd done in the past, you had to have something to say; you had to infuse personality into the characters. I had no idea how to do that, and after a few lame attempts I decided to try to write an article instead. But first I needed material.

A year before, a friend and I had passed ourselves off as journalists to gain admittance to the brand new American Music Awards, where Elton John's album *Goodbye Yellow Brick Road* had been nominated for Best Album. This award show was new and hungry to generate as much press as possible, so we took advantage of their weakness and got on the press list. No one questioned the two writers from *The Derrick Diary* or took the time to realize that ours was a high school newspaper. The actual taping had been a lengthy snoozefest. Our big star-sighting was Bernie Taupin, who had nodded a greeting our way as we walked by him in the hall. The celebrities that were there weren't the ones we were interested in. Elton lost to Charlie Rich.

Despite our less than thrilling experience, the show had thrilled the nation. It was moved to a larger venue and the organizers were being more selective about who got on the press list. In the weeks leading up to the show, I bombarded them with calls that they easily ignored. When I finally spoke to someone, she informed me that yes, she realized that we had been invited before, but now the show was more popular and we were off the list.

Never one to take no for an answer, I decided to show up anyway, to see if I could figure out a way to sneak in. By sheer coincidence, Elton was again nominated for an award. Hoping for better luck than the previous year, I decided that our odds would be better with greater numbers on our side. I got together a small gang of Elton fans, and our posse showed up early to wait outside the venue. With the precision of a military operation, we broke off into teams to ensure that Elton wouldn't slip past us, and to see if anyone could find an unguarded way in. True, this was supposed to be about reporting on the awards show, but stalking Elton was clearly more important than journalism.

We met a few people who worked behind the scenes as they went in early, one of whom was a man named Sherwood Schwartz, who stopped to talk to us and find out why we were there. We must have looked suspicious because he didn't help us get in, but I still thought he was a really sweet man. I was a bit star-struck because he had produced two of my favorite TV shows: *Gilligan's Island* and *The Brady Bunch*. While I was distracted with talking to Sherwood Schwartz, the lookouts had spotted Elton's gold limousine and ran over to inform me. EJ had quickly slipped into the building and his limousine was now pulling up to a parking space behind it. We rushed over en masse, but it was too late. The security guards were annoyed with us, and though we tried to evade them, they caught up with us and evicted us from the property.

We regrouped and got some snacks from a store across the street, then sat down on the sidewalk, watching as fancy cars, stars and paparazzi started to arrive. I ripped open a bag of Wampums and took a bite of my Chic-o-Stick, reflecting on the day's events. It could have been depressing to be literally on the outside looking in, but it was actually kind of fun sitting there on the ground, snacking, laughing at ourselves, loving Elton. We'd met a cool TV producer, spotted Elton's limo and had been chased away by security guards; nothing to write a newspaper article about, but it sure beat staying at home.

HEY BABY, WANNA RIDE?

A long, long time ago, Los Angeles was a city with a marvelous electric railway system linking all the local suburbs to what was then the pulsing heart of downtown L.A. This system was popularly known as the Red Cars. Somewhere along the line, the profits of running an effective, fuel-efficient system were calculated to be less than the profits that would be generated by building freeways, cars and gas stations, so the Red Cars were demolished and their tracks were ripped up.

As a student, I had a cheap bus pass, so I could go anywhere in town, but it could take several transfers and a very long time to get to my destination because L.A. is a sprawling city. I often got rides from my mom, who was a very good sport about schlepping me around. At 15, I wanted to go places without having to ask my mom for a ride. A driver's permit was what I needed.

Luckily, the good nuns at Sacred Heart of Mary had hired a new Driver's Ed teacher and had put me in his class. His name was Mr. Mmm Mmm — I mean Mimm — and he made the boy-deprived young ladies at Sacred Heart of Mary giddy with delight, especially me. I thought I didn't know how to flirt, but suddenly I learned. I found myself saying provocative things, smiling as I walked up close to his desk, making sustained direct eye contact until Mr. Mimm looked away. It was great, and it made Mr. Mimm nervous, which only made it more fun.

One day, I wrote down the lyrics to Elton John's song *Teacher I Need You*. I changed a few words so that it would fit my gender and put the note on his desk before class.

> *Oh teacher I need you, like a little child*
> *You've got something in you to drive a schoolgirl wild*
> *You give me education in the lovesick blues*
> *Help me get straight come out and say*
> *Teacher I, teacher I, teacher I need you*
> *I had to write a letter to tell about my feelings*
> *Just to let you know the scene*
> *Focus my attention on some further education*
> *In connection with the birdies and the bees.*

The whole school knew I had a crush on Mr. Mimm. Some of the girls in class saw me put the note on his desk and shot me conspiratorial glances as he walked in, picked it up absentmindedly and started to read. His face went red. Giggles bubbled up across the room as his blushing continued. He put the note down and tried to start the lesson, but he was flustered and tripped over his words, which only made the giggles impossible to contain. I put on my best poker face and listened attentively.

I had several older friends from other schools who did have permits and even driver's licenses. I went to rock concerts with them or dancing at The Other Side and Rodney's English Disco (at the tail end of its popularity), and later at the Sugar Shack and Gino's. Those discos played glitter rock and alternative music like the soundtrack from the stage play, *The Rocky Horror Show*, which had been a big hit at the Roxy Theater on the Sunset Strip. I hadn't seen the play, but my friend Paul had, and he knew all the dialogue by heart. He quickly cast me as Columbia and taught me my parts. He of course cast himself as Dr. Frank N. Furter. It wasn't unusual to see the dance floor jammed with people doing the Time Warp. Many of my friends were in various stages of gayness; some were openly gay, some were closeted, still others — like me — were aware of bisexual feelings but in the exploratory phase.

I had my first French kiss on the dance floor of the Sugar Shack. She was a nice girl who was trying to make another girl jealous, and I was very happy to help out and discover what a French kiss felt like. There were no fireworks with her, but it was fun.

My annual yearbook dedications from this time reveal what my peers and classmates thought of me:

> "To a freaky girl…"
> "The weirdest girl I know…"
> "A crazy girl I know…"
> "You are a freaky, weird and crazy girl."

I don't know what they were talking about, because I don't think I was that strange. The people who I hung out with after school and on weekends didn't think of me as a crazy girl, they didn't think I was strange; they also enjoyed dressing up, seeing bands, dancing, drinking, staying up late and feeling completely open to anything the world had to offer.

At the end of the summer of 1975, *The Rocky Horror Picture Show* premiered in West L.A. A bunch of my glittery friends and I dressed up in costume and carpooled to the United Artists Theater in Westwood for the opening. We waited outside the theater for hours, entertaining ourselves by reciting the play, singing the songs and making new friends. The movie was a smash hit. Half the audience had already seen the play or knew about it from someone who had. We sang along with the music, talked back to the screen and went back again and again.

L.A. had grown too small for us. We belonged in Transsexual, Transylvania.

CHEERLEADER, TAKE 2

Fresh from my extracurricular dance lessons in Hollywood and my mastery of the Time Warp, I decided to try out for cheerleading again. This time I didn't freeze up like I had when I tried out at Garfield the year before. Compared to Garfield, this school was really small, and the competition wasn't as stiff, so I easily earned a spot as a junior class cheerleader, and I spent many a recess and lunch break practicing

Me at cheerleading camp.

cheers and pyramids. I told my sister Yolanda about it, thinking she would be impressed and proud of me, but by then my sister had a little baby to look after and cheerleading was the furthest thing from her mind.

I soon learned that the role of a class cheerleader was to organize Spirit Week and foster a climate of unity within each class. We cheered our classes on in any interclass competition, including, but not limited to, academic, athletic and even fundraising events. Sometimes the class cheerleaders would join the SHM cheerleaders in loud and noisy support for our all-girl sports teams. We were known as…er…don't laugh, the *Scooters*.

GO MIGHTY SCOOTERS!

Our mascot was an elephant.

These all-girl sporting events were a far cry from events such as the ELA classic, a football game so popular that it is usually held at the East L.A. college sports stadium because neither Garfield nor Roosevelt high schools can hold the amount of spectators wanting to see the game. Needless to say, Garfield cheerleaders were highly visible, highly competitive and a source of pride for the entire student body and the community.

There was a different sort of pride at Sacred Heart. Girls' sporting events were not well attended nor were they held in large venues, but girls actually played here. As I attended more of the school's games both home and away, I started to take a different interest in sports. I remember watching my classmates playing basketball and thinking that I might be good at sports if I just put my mind to it, and it made me appreciate the game in a new way. In the past, I'd thought of basketball as a tall man's sport; not being a tall man meant I could never aspire to anything beyond the role of spectator. Not that I wanted to be anything other than a spectator; I'd been bad at P.E. ever since I could remember. Here at Sacred Heart of Mary, the girls encouraged each other to try, and their best was good enough. They didn't need to sublimate their desires, feel intimidated by hot jocks or compete with boys' teams for gym or court time. It seemed to me that an all-girl school was a pretty good place to be a girl.

Of course, I never fully abandoned my dream of being part of a championship-worthy cheerleading squad, so when tryouts for the boys' school across the street came around, I put aside all the good, sisterly feelings that went along with being a junior class cheerleader and decided to go for it. I talked to one of the Sacred Heart cheerleaders who I thought was especially good and asked her if she would be trying out for Cantwell.

"No," she said. "I like cheering for the girls."

"I like cheering for the girls, too, but hardly anyone comes to the games," I said.

"That's why they need us," she smiled, and that was the end of that. A part of me faltered for a minute as I watched her walk away. I had a feeling that she was right, but I didn't have time to listen to the little voice in my head that told me my old goal had an expiration date.

The open auditions were held on a Friday afternoon and were attended by girls from local parochial schools, but because we were just next door I think SHM girls had an advantage. I only had one coed class — French class was held at Sacred Heart, and the boys from Cantwell High School attended. The boys in my French class were the only people I knew at Cantwell. I hadn't done my homework or researched the politics of trying out for a place on the cheerleading squad, but apparently there were politics that I should have been aware of.

Once again, I waited outside the gym for my turn, but I maintained my composure. The stakes didn't seem so high this time around. I'd already figured out that my sister was not going to be as impressed as I'd imagined, so the pressure was off. I ran into the gym, cheering. I'd been working on a nice cartwheel and round off and now I had a chance to show them off. I made no mistakes this time; my face muscles cramped from the sustained, enormous smile, and I was relentlessly, obnoxiously peppy. When I finished my cheer, I felt supremely confident.

CHEERLEADER, TAKE 3

On Saturday morning, I got a call from Cantwell High School. I had made the varsity squad for the following school year. Finally! I'd worked so hard for this. I was jubilant. I imagined myself at the state competition, executing perfectly synchronized movements better than dancers in a Busby Berkeley movie.

The following Monday, one of the Cantwell varsity cheerleaders stopped me in the hall.

"Did you get a call from Cantwell this past weekend?" she queried.

"Yes!" I replied, unable to contain the huge grin that spread over my face.

"Did you make it?" she asked nervously.

"Yes!" I thought she was going to congratulate me, but instead she looked at me as though I'd kicked her in the stomach.

"You were the only one I didn't know about," she said cryptically as she walked away.

I didn't know what she meant until later, when I saw the other cheerleaders around her. The girl who had stopped me in the hallway appeared to be crying, and every now and then the people in her group would look over at me as though I was responsible for her tears, which, it turns out, I was. As a junior, she had expected to keep her place on the varsity squad for another year, but something had happened. I — the evil new girl who had never even been to a Cantwell football game — had taken her place on the varsity squad, while she — who had given the Cantwell Cardinals one of the best years of her life — was put in JV. I felt a little bit bad for her because she was a nice girl, but in the end it was her dreams or mine, so I ignored the guilt and started practicing with the squad.

Cantwell Cardinals

The girls on the varsity squad were cute and bouncy and loved to flirt with the boys. I'd show up ready for work and they'd be giggling, talking to a football player or some other passing boy. I had no interest in making small talk with jocks, so I found this routine a boring waste of time. I tried not to roll my eyeballs up to the top of my head, but if they accidentally went there, who could blame me? I reluctantly took on the role of task master.

"Maybe we should start? Can we start now? Come on everybody, let's practice!"

I knew I was cramping their style, but I couldn't help myself. One afternoon as we were going through a drill, I asked that we do it again because I thought it was sloppy. That was my final faux pas. One of the girls turned to me, obviously irritated.

"Alice, we don't want to win championships or be perfectly synchronized. We just want to make the guys feel good and appreciated so that they can do their best."

It was an epiphany for me. It never even occurred to me that they had no goals beyond making the guys feel good. I felt sick and angry, but I knew that I was the only person I could be angry with. I quit just before the Cardinals' first game. I would've felt bad, but I knew that the girl I had replaced would take her spot back in a heartbeat. I smiled a big, fake cheerleader-smile and tried to make a graceful exit. Just to prove that I wished them well, I baked up a batch of chocolate chip cookies with little bits of Ex-Lax for them to enjoy after practice.

DON'T DREAM IT, BE IT

Early in 1975, Cher got her own TV show, and I got the word that Elton John would be doing a guest performance. A group of us ditched school to wait outside the CBS studios and stalk Elton John. I met obsessed Elton fans from several other schools that day, including Patricia Rainone, a lovely, long-haired beauty from Saint Paul High School in Whittier, and Thelma Melendez, the cousin of a girl who went to my school. Thelma was as fixated on Elton as I was. Instead of feeling like rivals, Thelma and I supported and encouraged each other. We understood each other, we exchanged trivia and talked about Elton long after others had tuned us out. We were a couple of geeks.

Patricia liked Elton, too, but she was a more moderate fan where Elton was concerned. She only turned maniacal when the subjects of Freddie Mercury or Tim Curry came up. Like me, Patricia was also a *Rocky Horror* fan, but unlike me, she had actually seen the play at the Roxy. As we sat in the parking lot of the CBS building waiting for Elton to drive up, we had plenty of time to get to know each other. We discovered that we were both fans of Queen, Bowie, Kiss, the New York Dolls, T-Rex and many others. We became fast friends.

As the day wore on we began to think that we would never see Elton, but suddenly hope appeared. A limousine drove through the parking lot and then slowed down in front of us. The person in the back seat rolled his window down and that's when we saw him: Michael Jackson, not Elton. Michael smiled and said hello to us, and asked us what we were up to. We all chattered excitedly and he hung onto every word,

Me and Patricia at Knott's Berry Farm

seeming to enjoy our adventure vicariously. I got the feeling that, given the chance, he would have hung out with us that day, and it put us in good spirits. Surely if we had seen Michael Jackson and he had bothered to slow down to engage us in conversation, Elton would do the same.

I guarded the front entrance while Thelma was stationed at the back. Unfortunately, my stalking was in vain, and I didn't have the opportunity to make personal contact with the object of my affection, but Thelma did (which gave her bragging rights for the rest of the year). I was disappointed, but it just made me realize that meeting Elton as a crazed teenage stalker wasn't going to cut it. I had to figure out a way I could meet him when I was as famous as he was, so that he would pay attention to me, which goes to show you just how crazy I was.

Back at school, my enthusiastic idol worship brought out the inner groupie in other girls. Pretty soon, open displays of affection for the likes of John Denver and Keith Emerson started popping up all over Sacred Heart of Mary. I maintained an intense letter-writing friendship with a girl at SHM known as Poonie. She'd write long, detailed accounts of her secret fantasies involving the English progressive rock group Emerson, Lake and Palmer. I'd respond with my own fantasies about Elton John. The only problem was that we wrote the letters during class when we were supposed to be taking notes, not passing notes.

Eventually, Poonie's mom intervened, and Poonie suddenly stopped talking to me. She claimed that I had drawn her into my fantasy world and that she had since rediscovered her direction. It made me sad that she had ended our friendship without us ever having an argument or disagreement.

She later claimed a full page in my yearbook to write an open letter in which she explained that she had pushed through the glitter and craziness to find the real me. She believed the real me was in dire need of help and she offered to help me, which was nice of her. I suppose she thought I was delusional, and I guess in some ways I was, only it wasn't because I was an obsessed Elton John fan, or because I spent my time in class daydreaming, or because I was a full-fledged Hollywood fag hag. By then I already knew I wanted to be more than that. In fact, my goals and dreams were so large in relation to what society expected of me that, had I stopped to think rationally, I might have given them up.

YOU WISH!

After my relationship with Poonie fizzled, I started hanging out with another girl at Sacred Heart of Mary named Charlene. Most of the girls at SHM had come up through the Catholic school system together and knew each other from parochial elementary schools. They had friendships with roots reaching all the way back to kindergarten. Being the new girl made me an interesting novelty and people wanted to know me, but my friendships had tiny roots. Charlene had other friends whom she'd known much longer and much better than me. Sometimes I got the feeling that her old friends resented the fact that she was now exhibiting signs of liking David Bowie and had decided to go by the more androgynous name Charles instead of Charlene. She also had an increased appreciation for the glamorous, swishy fags that I hung out with. Although I can take no credit for the refinement of her taste, I suspect that her friends would happily blame me for the changes in her. Luckily, Charles didn't seem to mind annoying her friends.

Charles had an after-school job caring for a bedridden old lady. Charles cleaned her house, helped her dress, prepared food for her and kept her company. Sometimes Charles would invite me over to the old lady's house, and we'd chat while she went about her cleaning and cooking. One particular afternoon, Charles invited me to work, and we hopped on the public bus right after school. We made our way to the back of the bus and watched another girl from our school get on after us. We smiled at her, but apparently she didn't see us because she looked the other way. The bus was crowded and Charles and I rode standing, holding onto the rail, teetering at stops with our arms full of books. Each time the bus stopped, our bodies would swing and we'd start laughing as we struggled to keep our footing. We made jokes and giggled until we got to our stop. We got out the back door, and, coincidentally, the girl from our school got out at the same stop, only she exited through the front door. She walked ahead of us and didn't stop to say hello. Charles and I looked at each other, surprised. Sacred Heart of Mary was a tiny school, and nobody there had ever been snobby to me, so I was surprised that she would snub us. It must be a mistake we reasoned; maybe she didn't see us. Even though neither Charlene nor I knew her very well, we knew that she was a junior, like us, and we were all wearing the same uniform, so, out of courtesy, she should have at least waved at us if she had seen us. "Hello!" we called out, but she didn't turn around. It became obvious that she was deliberately ignoring us, so we decided to ignore her, too, and went on with our conversation. The girl was about 30 feet ahead of us when she suddenly turned around.

"Stop following me!" she yelled at us. This caught us off guard, because following her was the furthest thing from our minds. We were perplexed.

"We're not following you," I replied.

"It's a public sidewalk!" Charlene added. The girl turned away from us and continued walking. A few minutes later, she crossed the street. "Oh great," said Charlene. "We have to cross that way, too. Now she's *really* going to think we're following her."

At school the next day, this girl started telling people that Charles and I were following her. Charlene's friends gave us the scoop just before break time. The girl was convinced that Charles and I were lesbians, trying to accost her. I was certain that someone had leaked my kiss at the Sugar Shack to the general school population. Charles and I couldn't imagine why she'd think that we were after her, but as I was walking to my class the girl looked me in the eye, and I was not about to look away. I stared back at her.

"I know what you are," she said cryptically. The idea that she thought she knew what I was when *I* didn't even know what I was made me angry. After all, I'd never had a boyfriend or girlfriend, and I'd only kissed one girl. I was still in the exploratory phase.

"You don't know shit!" I replied in a tone that said *don't fuck with me.* "Even if I was a lesbian — which I may or may not be — what makes you think I'd be interested in you?" I was so disgusted that I was practically spitting the words at her. I couldn't believe this ugly, homophobic girl thought she was an irresistible lesbo magnet. She stared at me without saying another word. I thought we would come to blows because we were standing so close to each other, but she turned and walked away. "YOU WISH!" I shouted after her.

I never had any issues with exploring my own sexuality or with others exploring theirs, and while I had lots of gay friends, I'd never before been the target of homophobic accusations. I think that experience made me even more committed to the cause of gay rights and freedom of expression than I already was.

THE COSMO GIRL

"Are you a Good Lover?"
"Ten Raging Sexual Fantasies"
"What Real Orgasms Feel Like"
"Facts and Fallacies about Love-Making"

These are just a few of the articles that were featured in *Cosmopolitan* when I was growing up. It was a magazine that would shape my views on sexuality more than anything else.

Even though the Catholic church opposed any artificial method of birth control, thanks to the Pill, many Catholic women were enjoying sex without the worry of an undesired pregnancy. I hoped to one day be one of them; unfortunately, with my hormones raging and my thirst for sexual knowledge growing, I was living in an information desert. My mother couldn't even name any body part below the waist and above the thighs. She simply used the expression *down there*, as in, "Do you have cramps, *down there*?" The idea of my mom explaining anything about sex was unimaginable. At school, even the progressive nuns avoided the subject. All I had was my rock magazines, where rock stars sometimes mentioned a sexual escapade in passing, and Cosmo, where you could read a whole article written by what I imagined were sophisticated, sexually liberated women.

The more I read *Cosmo*, the more I understood that everything I knew was wrong. I had grown up with the message from my community, church, television and movies that nice girls waited to have sex until after marriage. Despite the fact that my mother was eight months pregnant with me when she married my father, she had told me that virginity was important. It was different for her because she had been married before and had children from a previous marriage. I'm not sure what she meant by that, but I gathered that sex was like smoking marijuana: Once you tried it, you became addicted.

My mother sent out some confusing messages. When I decided that I wanted to switch from sanitary pads to tampons, she became alarmed. "Tampons are only for married women," she warned, "you will damage yourself if you try to use them." That scared me for a long time. Virginity, as my mother defined it, had everything to do with having an immaculate hymen. A girl without a hymen was simply not marriage material unless she was a widow, like my mom had been when she met my dad, and then — *woo-hoo!* — everything was okay.

Cosmo filled in the gaps in my sexual education. Helen Gurley Brown, editor-in-chief of *Cosmopolitan*, had made her mark in a post-pill world as the author of the bestselling book, *Sex and the Single Girl*. Even the title was scandalous! The book's main character is a sexually liberated, single woman who many people believed was based on Helen herself. If you were to pick this book up today, some of the passages might seem dated, but to appreciate a cultural phenomenon, you have to try to understand it in the context in which it occurred. Helen was a maverick who ensured that her readers had up-to-date information about the little-discussed subject of female sexuality, and she provided women with the inspiration to advocate for themselves in the bedroom as well as in the workplace.

It was from *Cosmo* that I first learned what an orgasm was, what oral sex was, and much, much more. It was from reading *Cosmo* that I finally came to understand that touching myself *down there* had a name; it was *masturbation*, and no, I wouldn't go to hell for doing it; in fact it was common, normal and… hallelujah, I had permission to do it again!

I guess *Cosmopolitan* may have also been responsible for my increased interest in sex and in losing my virginity. It had taught me that sex and marriage didn't necessarily have to go together, and, if I understood correctly, that meant there was no reason to marry for a long, long time. It made me question the double standard which labels a sexually active man "a stud" and a sexually active woman "a whore." I remember, later in life, one guy telling me, "I won't think less of you if you sleep with me on the first date," to which I replied, "I won't think less of you, either." The nerve, assuming that I needed his approval to do what I wanted to do.

I thought my definition of promiscuity around that time was very progressive. It had less to do with the number of sexual partners you had and everything to do with your reasons for sleeping with people. I don't know if it had been influenced by a *Cosmopolitan* article, or if I finally just synthesized *Cosmo*'s values. In my book, a woman could have as many different sex partners as she wanted without necessarily being promiscuous, because women are different and have a wide range of sexual appetites; however, sleeping with someone as a means to get something other than sexual pleasure seemed like promiscuity to me, because it meant you were not motivated by an honest desire for sex but were having sex because you felt there was no better way to get what you were really after. This bothered me, mostly because I'd known so many girls who had been looking for a love relationship and thought they could get it by giving in to a sexual relationship that they didn't want. That, to me, seemed promiscuous. I wished they'd read *Cosmo*.

Over the years, my views have changed but I think Helen Gurley Brown would still approve. I don't label people "promiscuous" anymore, even if they want something other than sex from sexual encounters. I just think of the word as a term by which society tries to regulate and suppress human sexuality.

HAIR DO'S AND DON'TS

I looked around to see that nobody was coming, and when I was certain that I hadn't been followed, I took out the little silver primary scissors that I had tucked into my sweater pocket. I'd borrowed them from my classroom, and I was on an emergency makeover mission that had to be done quickly and stealthily.

The golden mane I'd been so proud of just a couple of years ago had gone through some experimental changes, but my hair had never gone back to a — heaven forbid! — natural color. Once my hair was light, it was easy to play with. I went for strawberry blonde, then copper penny, then the darker, deeper shade of auburn that I wore today. I was adventurous with my hair, bold and confident in the knowledge that if something went wrong, I could always cut it off…which was what I was just about to do, here in the girl's bathroom at school.

It wasn't my bright idea. I'd seen another girl do it in the bathroom the week before, at break time. She had a large pair of haircutting scissors which she'd opened up in order to use the open blade, as a barber would use a razor. She'd taken the blade to the hair framing the sides of her face, and, within five minutes, produced fluttery, feathered angel wings which swept stylishly away from her face. Just a few months later, a real TV angel would perfect and popularize the style. It was the Farrah Fawcett 'do, in its infancy.

I've always been a hair-hopper, and my personal appearance has been guided by a desire not so much to look pretty as to project certain qualities. I wanted to look creative, innovative and daring, and if pretty happened along the way, it was a bonus. I didn't want a feathery hairdo, but I did want to give myself a little bathroom makeover. With my dark auburn hair, I thought I could pull off a Bowie-esque look, like the one he'd sported on the cover of the album, *Aladdin Sane*. I grabbed my little silver school-scissors and started chopping away. My hair was getting shorter and shorter, but instead of standing up stylishly like David Bowie's, it did an annoying, wavy thing at the top of my head which made me look more like Lucy Ricardo than like a glitter rocker.

I'd been in the bathroom about five minutes and had managed to mess up my makeover. Now, I had to think fast, because the teacher would think I was either sick or up to no good. I panicked. "How can I fix this?" I thought to myself. While I was thinking, my hand kept chopping away at the sides of my head automatically until I noticed that I could see my scalp. I had cut out a bald spot about the size of a quarter on one side of my head, and as I looked around to inspect the rest of my hairdo, I saw another bald spot about the size of a nickel on the other side. I didn't even have time to cry, because just then the bell rang. I quickly turned on the faucet and let the water carry the evidence down the drain.

I tucked the scissors back in my pocket and ran back to Mr. Braimer's room. Most of my classmates had already left. I apologized for taking so long and Mr. Braimer gave me a curious look but said nothing. "Good," I thought to myself, "it must not be that obvious." I dropped the scissors on a random table when the teacher turned to greet the new group of girls that was walking in, and I ran to my next classroom. At the next class, everybody noticed.

"Ziggy, what did you do to your hair?!" my friend Susan asked.

"Me? Oh, nothing." I said. I started hanging out with Susan after one of her good friends got pregnant and moved away. Susan had started taking cosmetology classes in Long Beach while she was still in high school. Her mother and aunt owned a salon in Alhambra, and you could say peroxide ran through her veins. She was naturally talented in the hair-color department. Because Susan needed a guinea pig on which to practice her lessons and I needed to stop giving myself bald spots, we made a good pair. We'd go to her mom's shop after-hours and mix up fun colors to dye my hair.

Eventually, Susan also became infected with my offbeat aesthetic and learned to appreciate glam. At the cosmetology school, she found herself making friends with more gay men than she'd ever known in her life. Our friendship blossomed as she, too, became an accidental fag hag. She introduced me to some of her gay hairdresser friends, and before long I had gone from self-inflicted bald spots to modeling at hair shows.

I even dated some of her gay hairdresser friends. I guess it was strange, but we didn't know any better. We innocently held hands, cuddled, kissed and went on dates, but we never slept together. I loved my gay boyfriends, but after a while the Cosmo Girl in me wanted to find someone that wanted more than kisses and cuddles. My longtime crush was closeted, so although he wrote that he loved me in the yearbook, I didn't know what he meant by it. It was a confusing time to be me. I still loved Elton but my fantasies were becoming more and more unsatisfying.

LITURGICAL CLUB

If someone had told me I'd be joining Liturgical Club and Christian Action Club in high school, I would have laughed at them, and if you ask me now how it happened, I don't know that I can come up with a good reason; only that the girls in the club were friendly and invited me to join. Actually, it was oddly satisfying to participate in religious rituals, even as I was moving further and further away from considering myself a Christian.

Participating in the mass and organized prayer was a chance to commune with people who were focusing their intentions on accessing their spirituality. I don't think it mattered that we didn't all hold to the exact same beliefs; we could have been an interdenominational group, as far as I was concerned. What was important was that we all felt that the repetitive formal rites somehow aided us in our individual and joint quests for spiritual growth.

The Christian Action Club was a youth volunteer group that tried to help out in the community. It had little to do with Christianity and much to do with just being a responsible member of the community, but I guess when you're a Christian, this is called being a good Christian or a good Samaritan.

My two years at Sacred Heart of Mary provided me with the opportunity to explore my unanswered questions about God, Christianity and the nature of good and evil. My religion teacher, Sister Angela, was a sweet, petite, intelligent woman with a spunky Clara Bow haircut, who welcomed my questions and tried to answer honestly, without trying to persuade or convince me of anything. I appreciated her approach; I think I would have resented any other.

In her class, we were given journals and time to write every day. We could even take the journals home and fill them up with our thoughts or questions and turn them in the next day. Sister Angela would promptly read and respond to each person, every afternoon. Although she was Catholic and I no longer agreed with all Catholic teachings, I found that we both had a hunger to understand the nature of God. I was surprised at how much we had in common. I remember asking her about a bumper sticker I'd seen that read, "When God created man, She was only joking." Sister Angela explained to me that because God is made up of the Holy Trinity — the Father, the Son and the Holy Spirit — some people viewed the Holy Spirit as the feminine aspect of God. The concept of the Trinity was always difficult for me to understand, and assigning masculine or feminine attributes to God felt to me like a distortion of the original concept. Nonetheless, I liked Sister Angela's explanation and the fact that she was not dogmatic but open to considering that more than one interpretation of the Bible was possible. I'd have many more years to ponder the nature of God and to come up with a satisfactory answer for myself, but just being able to have a dialogue with Sister Angela meant the world to me.

She really threw lots of new concepts at me, and challenged me in ways that no one else had up until this point. She introduced me to the idea that time was not linear, that religious doctrine can be interpreted in much deeper ways than I had been taught; and she helped me to think of God as a concept rather than as an anthropomorphic entity.

Our textbook for that class was *Good News for Modern Man*, a contemporary translation of the New Testament. Each class meeting, we'd read selected excerpts and discuss them. It was really fun, because everyone was encouraged to speak and share their beliefs. No one was ever laughed at, and no idea was too outrageous or ridiculous. Sister Angela provided a safe environment in which all felt valued and respected, and she behaved as a mediator rather than a teacher, so that we felt like we were determining the course the class was taking.

Sister Angela took a group of us to see the stage play *Jesus Christ Superstar*. Afterward, we wrote in our journals about it. I wrote about Judas. I felt that Judas had been put into a position where he was predestined to be a villain. God seemed to me to be a big puppeteer in the sky, pulling all the strings in a production where he already knew and controlled what each character was going to do. "Hadn't Jesus known all along that Judas would betray him?" I asked in my journal. "How can Judas change his mind? How can Judas have free will if an infallible God is certain of his betrayal?" That's when Sister Angela introduced me to the concept that time is not linear.

"God is omniscient" she said, "and because time and space do not exist as you and I usually think of them, God knows what happened, what is happening and what will happen."

This idea blew my mind. I had a really difficult time understanding how God could know what I was going to do before I knew what I was going to do. It smelled of determinism to me, but, of course, I didn't know that word yet.

Later, I would take a Comparative Religions class at SHM in which I would have the opportunity to read about and discuss the beliefs of different people as well as visit various places of worship and interview their congregations. There was always a sense of respect and exploration in these classes. The study of religion and the hunger to know more about the nature of God — and to understand my own nature — were subjects that would continue to occupy much of my time and energy for the rest of my life.

MERCURY RISING

"Did you hear that Elton's going to be in a movie?" my friends at school asked me, but of course I already knew all about it. I'd been reading about Elton's upcoming cameo in Ken Russell's film version of the Who's rock musical, *Tommy*, for months. The movie had received lots of media attention, not only because the Who was a hugely popular rock group, but it also featured a star-studded cast, including Ann-Margret, Elton John, the Who, Tina Turner, Eric Clapton, Jack Nicholson and Oliver Reed. The story revolves around a little boy who becomes deaf, dumb and blind after a traumatic experience. This boy grows up to become a pinball champ by defeating the reigning Pinball Wizard, played by Elton John.

As soon as the premiere date, time and place were made public, I gathered up my stalker friends and we arrived early to wait outside the theater and perhaps catch a glimpse of Elton. As the day wore on, the crowds began to swell, but my friends and I kept our places at the front of the theater. The news media arrived and set up cameras and equipment everywhere; they didn't make us leave, but they did block our view, like a barricade between us and the celebrities. When the actors and musicians began arriving, the energy was tremendous. Fans and stalkers of all the other stars in the movie were there, but no one screamed louder than me when Elton John arrived. I must have caught his eye because the TV camera panned over to me screaming and holding my hands up to my head, looking like I was going to pull out my own hair. Little did I know that my parents were watching me act like a lunatic on our television back in East L.A. They must have been so proud. All my screaming was for nothing, though, because I didn't come any closer to meeting the man of my dreams; in fact, he probably would have run in the other direction if he'd seen me coming and there had been no TV cameras present.

Once the celebrities had entered the building, the crowd started thinning. My friends and I walked around the corner and there, shining like a golden nugget in a prospector's pan, was Elton John's gold limousine, parked on the street with no chauffeur in sight. We walked around the holy vessel, looking in the windows for a hint of some object belonging to Elton when a brilliant idea came to me. I *must* have a souvenir to show Thelma, the other crazed Elton John fan who had surpassed my number-one fan status by actually meeting Elton during our Cher-show campaign. But what could that souvenir possibly be? There was only one thing I could take without damaging Elton's beautiful limo, so I ducked down and started unscrewing a tire valve cap. I felt certain someone would come over and stop me, but nobody did. Once I'd loosened the cap, I clutched it tightly, as though it was a diamond ring and not just a piece of hard black rubber. I tucked the valve cap into my bra, next to my heart, and when I got home, I made a little hole in it and hung it on a chain, which I wore to school every day under my uniform shirt. While some girls wore holy medals next to their hearts, I had my own holy relic. I felt a bit like the guy in the movie, *The Adventures of Priscilla, Queen of the Desert,* who finds a bit of his favorite Abba member's poop and keeps it in a tiny bottle that he wears around his neck.

I didn't know then that my admiration had reached ridiculous levels. Every time I had a new close encounter with Elton John, it fed my obsession and kept me babbling about him for weeks.

My friend Patricia had been doing her share of babbling about Freddie Mercury of Queen for some time. Now she and I were driving out to the Santa Monica Civic Auditorium to see them. Patricia lived in Whittier with her mother, and the drive to my house alone took a good 30 minutes if you left before rush hour. The drive from my house to Santa Monica was at least another 40 minutes, sometimes even longer if traffic was bad, as was often the case in Los Angeles. Still, we always opted to drive ourselves rather than ask a parent for a ride because it made us feel grown up and independent.

We were lucky enough to have really great seats for Queen. The band was fantastic, and Freddie Mercury's vocals were breathtaking. Patricia couldn't get enough of him. She seemed to know the words to every song. Sometimes she would look at me and point out something he'd done or said that she thought I might not have caught. She was a Freddie expert, and now I knew what she felt like when she listened to me talk about Elton. I could tell that she was in another world — Freddie's World — and all I could do was smile at her. It felt good not to be the only madly obsessed fan.

THE SUPPORTING ROLE

Marlene started writing to Cherry Vanilla in New York City. Cherry was a Warhol actress, a DJ, a poet, but what was most important to us was that she was a super-groupie.

> *Fuck you, all you rock star guys*
> *Who come to me with cocks on rise...*
> *Fuck you and your groups select*
> *Who come to me with Cocks erect...*
> *Fuck you cuz you just don't know*
> *This lady's head beyond a blow...*

These are just a few of the lines I remember from one of Cherry's poems, called "To the Muddy Minded Members of the Music Media." She goes on to condemn the narrow vision of her celebrity lovers in the rest of the poem. It made me a little sad to read it because she wrote about the men she admired and would have gladly helped but who were too self absorbed to look for any depth in her. They saw only one aspect of her when she knew she had so much more to offer. Even though there's disappointment, in the poem, at not being appreciated, there's also a spirit of defiance in her writing and a desire to prove their assessment of her wrong. I liked her spunk and the fact that she had taken the bad taste of being undervalued and turned it into a poem that made two teenage girls on the other side of the continent question what they viewed as a glamorous lifestyle.

Marlene shared all of Cherry's mail with me, and we both treasured her letters. She seemed stronger and wiser for having been through so much. She did PR for David Bowie early in his career. He hired her after watching her performances in Andy Warhol's *Pork*. To us, she was a star and a super-groupie who had bothered to take the time to share her triumphs, setbacks and inner secrets with us, even though we were just a couple of schoolgirls she had never met.

Marlene and I read and re-read Cherry's poems. Eventually, Marlene started writing her own poems about her groupie experiences. My favorite was a poem she wrote about Batch, where she describes each member as a different type of cookie. The attributes of the Ginger Snaps or Coconut Macaroons cleverly reflected the attributes of each band member. On the same page, she drew a picture of herself holding up a cookie tray. She looked like a thin, glammed-out Ruby's Diner girl. In the speech bubble, she wrote, "I have made a fabulous Batch." I thought Marlene was quite good at poetry, and I enjoyed reading her poems, but I was never inclined to write any of my own.

Cherry's poems helped me realize that some groupies had the same mentality as the cheerleader who had told me she just wanted to make the guys feel good. There was an air of glamour and popularity that went along with both roles, but there was also a risk that the importance by proxy conferred upon those who supported the music or athletic stars could make a girl forget that she should also have goals of her own, even while playing a supporting role.

Once I understood this, the knowledge had a domino effect in my life. Over time, it also started to affect the way I saw my role as a fag hag. Even though I was around guys that I considered very good friends, I spent an inordinate amount of time in gay clubs as a sort of cheerleader for my friends. Of course, there is a certain amount of cheerleading and supporting that goes into being a good friend, a good fan, a good spouse or a good parent. Healthy relationships are reciprocal and thrive on mutual encouragement, but there is a point at which people sometimes get lost in the vicarious thrill that they get from other people's accomplishments and forget to chase their own dreams. I was at that point, and I had to find a balance.

I had seen my mother define herself completely as a wife and mother, only to blossom when she finally started to take a stronger and more active role in charting her own path. I had long ago dared to dream of becoming a singer; now that dream was calling me. I knew if I could take some of that cheerleading enthusiasm and dedication, that fag-hag loyalty, that groupie passion and channel it into achieving something that I truly wanted, I could not only chase that dream down, I could catch it.

I was now in my senior year of high school, and, aside from singing every day, I hadn't done anything to move closer to my goal of being a singer. I decided to try out for the school talent show, and I made it.

The previous summer I'd taken my eyeglass prescription to Optique Boutique, the place where I knew Elton had bought a pair of my favorite glasses. I scrimped and saved, doing odd jobs around the house and even working for a short time as a dreaded telephone solicitor for the *Los Angeles Times*, alongside Marlene. The job didn't last long, but it did put a few extra pennies in my pocket, and after begging my parents for the amount I didn't have, I bought myself some real Elton John glasses with my own prescription in them. I wore those glasses every day, and it was a senior privilege to wear your choice of shoes, so I teamed them up with platform tennis shoes. I was quite a sight in my huge Elton John rhinestone glasses, Catholic school uniform and platform tennies.

Me in my Elton phase.

It must have been those platform tennies and rhinestone glasses that made me feel like *Elton Jane* and inspired my performance in the talent show. I borrowed a feather boa, pulled on my favorite pair of jeans with *Elton* written in silver metallic letters, strapped on my highest platforms, and, of course, my rhinestone glasses, and I took to the stage as Elton Jane.

I was back posing for my father, hamming it up, flying high. I strutted across the stage singing *Saturday Night's Alright for Fighting* like I was really Elton John. My classmates got up on their feet and clapped along with the song, and with their help I felt like a rock star. I wanted that feeling to last forever.

OUT TO LUNCH

Twelfth grade meant you were entitled to two important perks: free choice of footwear, and off-campus lunch. I didn't have a car in high school, but many of my classmates did. Sometimes I was invited to tag along with the fast ("sports car") girls at school by virtue of having a dance class with one of them.

Stylish, sophisticated Doreen Mercado was pretty, lean and an impeccable dresser, but in Modern Dance class she was an unabashed ham, just like me. We swished around like two Isadora Duncans caught in a windstorm, or sometimes one of us was Isadora and the other was Martha Graham, squatting in front of Isadora like a Sumo wrestler as Isadora whirled and twirled around her, like a spider spinning a web around a fly. Our bodies made up all kinds of stories.

Doreen was a car-less fast girl, but she made up for her lack of wheels by being so undeniably cool. She had long, wrapped and manicured nails, frosted hair that looked like she went to the hair salon every day before coming to school, and an aloof air of worldliness. Doreen hung out in the world of MG Midgets and Datsun 240Zs and chivalrously held the door open for me when she walked in. Off-campus lunches with the fast girls usually meant a quick trip to a burger stand, but a whiff of locker room and secondhand pot smoke were sometimes part of the fun.

I remember my first freeway ride in Nana's MG Midget. Speeding along like a bat out of hell on the Hollywood Freeway, I was terrified that the tiny car would collide with a gnat and we would be sent spinning out control. I dug my hands into the seat cushion and smiled at Nana as I tried to make my fear look like excitement. I didn't want to be exposed as the total fraidy cat I was beside these ultra-cool super vixens. On this particular night, I had been invited to a party at one of their friends' houses. Their friends were lesbians, so I think the fast girls thought I would fit right in. I was greeted warmly and offered chi-chis, or maybe it was piña coladas, but they were coconutty, smooth and sweet, so I drank up. It was a nice evening, but I didn't really have that much in common with the lesbian girls. Because I was a total music freak/Elton stalker first and foremost, gender, sexual preference, ethnicity and class all faded to secondary attributes. This fact became important a short while later when I would meet up with a whole community of music freaks and artists.

I took off-campus lunch whenever someone with a ride invited me, but sometimes I'd just walk off campus by myself. There was a liquor store and a burrito place not too far from the school, but the burrito place was usually too slow for me to eat and walk back, so I'd just walk to the liquor store and grab a rock magazine and some chips or candy. On one of these solo walking lunches, I chanced upon a new publication on the stands. It was called *Punk* and looked like something between a comic book and a rock magazine. The articles were shorter and the writing less formal than *Creem* and *Circus*, and they wrote about less popular but more interesting groups that weren't like the mega rock stars profiled in the other mags. I walked back to school reading and stuffing chips into my mouth. I devoured the magazine just like the chips, and promptly called Marlene to tell her about it. The magazine featured new bands like the Ramones, Television and Patti Smith. I immediately subscribed and sought out the music they were writing about.

When Patti Smith played at the Roxy Theater in Los Angeles, in January of 1976, I was there, completely unprepared to have my mind blown, but Patti gave me an unforgettable blow job. She came onstage, a skinny, makeup-less wisp of a girl, and before my astonished eyes and ears she transformed herself into a superhuman androgynous, sensuous, venomous, writhing shaman, spewing words like poison darts that pierced and destroyed my stereotypes. She held me enthralled with the magical power of a rock deity.

Patti completely changed the way I thought about female performers. Most of what I'd seen before her were beautiful women with silky voices. Even those women, who were primarily known for their powerful voices, were often repackaged and made over by record companies so that they would approximate the accepted definition of "attractiveness." Patti was different; her sensuality came from within. Her power was in her words and her presence; it didn't come from the sweetness of her voice, because her voice wasn't sweet; her power came from the brutal conviction in it. It didn't come from makeup, high heels or typically feminine dress; it came from her raw sexual androgyny.

MOONAGE DAYDREAM

I floated on the effects of my Elton Jane performance, and for a good two weeks after the talent show my classmates addressed me as Elton Jane. After my brief moment in the spotlight, I tried to figure out how to make it last.

When I was just a little girl, I'd had a dream of being onstage with an all-girl band. It was such a happy dream that it stayed with me for a long time. In the dream, I wore white go-go boots and a mini-dress. I was the lead singer. It wasn't a rock lineup; my subconscious dream band looked more like Josie and the Pussycats teamed up with the Archies. Betty and Veronica were backing me up on tambourine and keyboards. We all wore outfits that might have been designed for the Jetsons. The dream was due for a makeover.

I called Marlene and told her I was going to form an all-girl band. She supported me wholeheartedly, and now I was the one talking her ear off with my plans, while she cheered me on. It didn't take long to drag her into my girl-band scheme, along with our Freddie Mercury–obsessed friend, Patricia.

At Sacred Heart, most of the girls were busy charting their futures. The campus buzzed with talk of aptitude tests and college applications. Instead of sharing in the excitement, I felt anxious about having to declare a special interest in one career path. I had never seriously considered being any of the things my father wanted me to be; I had simply been happy to imagine myself as the first woman president, or a daring Amelia Earhart, piloting a plane around the world, or a brain surgeon, saving lives while making buckets of money. But now that I really thought about the possibility of pursuing any of these careers, I realized that I had simply been allowing myself to fantasize. I was like Walter in *The Secret Life of Walter Mitty*, daydreaming myself into different roles without ever picturing myself doing any of the work to achieve them.

I had to think long and hard about a serious college action plan. Going to college was not something that was up for negotiation. My father and I had always spoken about my future plans, and no matter how they'd changed over the years they always included going to college. Now, although I wanted to form a band, I knew that I still had to go to college even if I didn't know what I'd study. I'd been told for years that the things I did and didn't do in school would affect my ability to get into the college I wanted, but since I didn't know what I wanted, I hadn't paid much attention. I made it through my entire high school career without ever doing a single scrap of homework, spending my

Glammed out graduation photo.

days listening to the teachers while simultaneously writing notes, daydreaming or doodling. Even though I'd somehow managed passing grades and good test scores, I knew I wouldn't be going to Harvard. There was a part of me that was conditioned to feel that I needed the safety of a good college education, and I stressed over making the right choices. But there was also a side of me that couldn't wait to ride life like a cowboy on a bucking bronco, just get on and hang tight. In the back of my mind, I heard my father's voice telling me *you can be anything you want*, and I believed him, but I didn't want what he wanted for me. I wanted fame, money, power and rock stardom.

Now that I was older, my parents went out together more often, which left me alone at home. I liked it. I could spend hours on the phone in those days. Sometimes, if there was no one to talk to, I'd play dress-up by myself. I'd paint my face and paste a gold or silver star on my forehead where a bindi might go, or I'd glue sequins on the outer edges of my eyes, or take my eyeliner and paint a tiny heart-shaped beauty mark on my cheek like I imagined Marie Antoinette might have done. I had a treasure trove of gaudy thrift-store clothes, sparkly and glittery platform shoes, hats and wigs and gloves to play with.

Alone in my bedroom I'd crank up the stereo volume and strike poses in front of the full-length mirror on my door as I sang along with David Bowie:

> *I'm an alligator, I'm a mama papa coming for you*
> *I'm a space invader, I'll be a rocking rolling bitch for you*
> *Keep your mouth shut, you're squawking like a pink monkey bird*
> *And I'm busting up my brains for the words.*

WHAT'S IN A NAME?

As soon as there were three of us girls in on it, and the dream of starting our own rock band seemed plausible, Patricia, Marlene and I spent hours on the phone coming up with ridiculous names for our band project. As has been the case with every band I've ever started, the name and concept came first. We narrowed it down to two finalists: Lipstick and Femme Fatale. Lipstick reminded me a little too much of Kiss. I couldn't picture anything more than a pair of glossy red lips, and both the *Rocky Horror Show* and the Rolling Stones had already

Marlene studying for the A.P. groupie exam.

milked the luscious-lips shtick. Femme Fatale sounded like a woman in a '40s film noir, wearing a dark trench coat and sunglasses, cautiously surveying the train station as she boards the Orient Express. The femme fatale I pictured might be running toward or away from trouble, but always in a pair of stylish stiletto heels. Despite this mental image, that's not where the name came from.

The word femme is French for "woman," and it had popped into my head not from my two years in French class with Miss Sarkisian but because it was the name of a line of cheap cosmetics I used. La Femme was one of the first companies I'd known to carry black nail polish and lipstick. Now that I think of it, it probably wasn't the first but it was definitely the first to make it to my neck of the woods. Aside from the black polish and lipstick which Marlene and I liked — and Patricia was especially attached to — La Femme offered all the fun, garish colors that my friends and I gravitated toward, and most of their cosmetics could be had for 99 cents or less at any beauty supply store. The femme fatale I imagined was a far cry from freaky, overly made-up teens like us, but the incongruity of it didn't faze us.

Even though the name and concept of the band were still in their infancy, Marlene took it upon herself to get things moving. She was the first one of us to start taking guitar lessons. Marlene's father had a guitar, so there would be minimal initial expense involved — just the price of the lessons themselves. I also think that, because Marlene's parents were divorced, asking her dad for something always got results because her daddy wanted to come through for her. My dad, by contrast, was hardly working anymore and had already been burned on all my prior flings with instruments, so I had to wait.

Marlene learned quickly and had a natural affinity for the guitar. By the time Patricia and I had our first guitar lessons, Marlene was already learning barre chords. Because I was just learning the names of strings while Marlene was practically a rock star in my eyes, she took pity on me and taught me how to play "Smoke on the Water." Listening to myself play that song stiffly, struggling with my inexperienced, clumsy fingers, rushing to stay in time with the beat while finding the right strings, I wondered how I'd ever get to the point where I wouldn't have to stare at my fingers while playing. Luckily, we were three experienced fans, so we became each other's earliest fans and cheered one another on. Now when we went to concerts, we looked at musicians in a new way. We noticed the amps they used, which foot pedals created which sounds. I remember the thrill I got the first time I saw a guitarist playing chords I recognized. It was exciting to imagine myself playing those same chords.

One afternoon, Marlene and I got bored and decided to paint ourselves up in geisha makeup. We wrapped ourselves in kimono tops that we wore over our jeans, then licked some big foil stars and stuck them to our foreheads — like no self-respecting geisha would ever do — and headed for the carnival that had set up in the J. C. Penny parking lot in Montebello. We walked around, and pretty soon we attracted the attention of a couple of carnies.

"Why are you dressed that way?" they asked us.

"We always dress this way," I replied, lying through my chipped teeth.

"We're in a band," Marlene explained. Before I knew what was happening, Marlene told the two guys all about our band and invited the carnies to her house, because her mom was working late and wouldn't know they'd been there. They showed up at her door right when they said they would. I have to admit they were kind of cute in a dirty, gross, never-takes-a-bath sort of way. Marlene brought out her guitar and handed it to one of the guys who said he played a little. Marlene and I asked him to play us a song, and he played one that he wrote himself. It was called "The Itchy Sitchiation." (Yes…*Sitchiation*.) It was a funny little song in that "Achy Breaky Heart" sort of way that makes you want to either laugh or vomit, depending on where you grew up. I grew up on the vomit side of the tracks, so I was just about ready to send the carnies packing when, after having softened us up with their foreplaying, they approached us about the possibility of swinging with them.

Now, I'd read every single *Cosmo* I could get my hands on in the past few years, but I had no idea what they were talking about until they finally explained it in nauseating detail. Not only did they want to have sex with us, they wanted to have sex and then trade partners. These boys were not Brad Pitt and George Clooney by a long shot. Yes, it seemed that we had gotten ourselves into a truly *itchy sitchiation*, but we opted to wound their achy breaky hearts and sent the carnies back to the funhouse and the Tilt-a-Whirl.

Some Femme Fatales we were!

FREE AT LAST, PART 1

In June of 1976, I graduated from Sacred Heart of Mary High School. I was 17 years old, and my only career goal was to become a rock star.

Of course, I couldn't tell my parents that, so I decided to sign up for classes at East Los Angeles College, a small community college where I could sample a few different classes, hopefully figure out what I was going to study and get in some general credits before declaring a major. I got a part-time job at J. C. Penney in Montebello, and I paid for my tuition with it. My parents had agreed to provide room and board and lend me their car me as long as I went to school.

I took a wide variety of subjects, including philosophy, history, theater arts, photography and astronomy. I had already taken a theater-arts class here at ELAC during my senior year of high school, having been encouraged by my friend Paul Marish after he had molded me into his very own *Rocky Horror Show* Columbia. He knew I could dance and sing, but acting was something I hadn't tried. My first time out, I was cast as a cancan girl in *Ten Nights in a Bar Room*; not very challenging, but for the following production I was promoted to a singing villager in *Fiddler on the Roof*. In *Fiddler*, I had a featured solo part as a Cossack dancer. Every night, I started as a sweet-singing village girl with a short verse to sing, then I strapped my boobs down, gave myself a scruffy beard and turned into a male dancer. It wasn't fun getting all butched up, but it was worth it because I had the spotlight to myself while I balanced a bottle on my head and did deep knee bends to a Russian folk song. That dance always got lots of applause, even the one time when the bottle fell off my head. After the dance I had to hurry and wash my face, unstrap my breasts and put on my girlie clothes so I could sing another two lines as a young girl. Talk about gender confusion!

Theater class was fun, but I have to admit that even though the thespians were a really nice, fun-loving bunch, they had a different sense of humor from mine, and very different interests, and I once again found myself feeling like a misfit.

Astronomy class was great. I loved learning about the stars, distant galaxies and time travel. The possibility of contacting alien civilizations appealed to the Trekkie in me, but there was only one astronomy class at ELAC when I was there, so I didn't have a chance to explore the subject in depth. I have to admit that I was also scared, because I'd been told that you had to be good at math to be an astronomer, and I sucked at math.

I was also very interested in history. I had a growing fascination with books about Nazi Germany, my interest having been piqued by a book about the White Rose, a German youth resistance group which inspired me tremendously. I wanted to understand what had made Hitler such a terrifyingly effective monster. I wanted to learn how Joseph Goebbels's propaganda had helped convince the German people that they were doing the right thing. I wanted to know what Dr. Mengele hoped to accomplish by torturing and sacrificing so many human beings. I wanted to so completely understand the Holocaust that I would be able to see it coming and try to prevent it from ever happening again.

Nazi Germany wasn't the only historical subject that interested me: Ancient Egypt, Greece and Rome were also intriguing subjects. The whole of Asia, Africa and the Americas had histories I knew practically nothing about, and all I knew about Australia was that they had kangaroos. I was poorly educated, and I knew that the solution to that was to read as much history as possible. My lifelong love affair with books may well have begun at this time. Unfortunately, I'd have to read on my own time, because I couldn't think of a job where I could use a degree in history, so I decided against it as a major but kept it as a possible minor.

The subject that eventually won my heart and my major emphasis was philosophy. The word *philosophy* means "lover of wisdom," and I loved nothing more than taking a subject and examining it from every angle, constructing and deconstructing arguments, spotting fallacies, arguing for and then against something just to make sure I understood it from different points of view. My high school friend Susan had also taken philosophy, and we would meet every day before class to discuss our reading. Then we'd go to philosophy class together, and after class we'd tear apart any unresolved arguments. Sometimes we'd spend all day on a single argument, and if one of us couldn't sleep, we'd meet later for a cup of tea or coffee at a 24-hour diner and continue our philosophical discussions long into the night. I became so obsessed with philosophy that it completely replaced my love of Elton John.

Only one thing came between me and my new obsession: my lifelong dream of becoming a singer. My Femme Fatale bandmates kept me focused on practicing. We looked for female musicians in the newspaper, and we weren't having much luck, when our search was interrupted by an unexpected graduation gift.

FREE AT LAST, PART 2

My parents didn't have a lot of money, but upon graduation I was given the choice of a used car or a trip to Europe. I quickly surmised that I could always borrow the car from my parents, so I opted for the trip. It was one of the best decisions I've ever made. The trip was sponsored by the school and involved a tiny bit of studying. We usually had one or two short classes on politics and culture in each place we visited, and had to keep a journal. The marginal academics made it possible for those of us attending to earn college credit and get a discounted travel rate while having the opportunity to see the world. In the space of a month, I got to see Spain, England, France, Austria — with a day trip to Germany — and Italy. It was an unforgettable trip that only made me want to see more.

In Spain we stayed in Barajas, Madrid. A girl in my study group who I had never met before sat at my table during our first combined student/teacher meal. We both eyed a couple of cute waiters at the hotel as they served us *paella valenciana* and smiled at each other, knowing we had the same idea. By breakfast the next day we had become friends and had secured dates with the waiters, but we had to figure out a way to sneak out. We had a 10 p.m. curfew, but my new friend and I decided to wait until the teachers did their final room-check before making our way outside to the parking lot where we would meet the waiters when they got off work. The plan worked beautifully, and that night we were taken to a Polynesian restaurant, where we drank a sweet, intoxicating concoction out of a volcano through extra-long straws and then did some drunken smooching in the car. Spain looked wonderfully lit up at night, and my trip was turning into the kind of learning experience I liked best!

In Italy, my new friend cried over her Spanish waiter, but I was too enamored of the pasta and gelato to give my guy another thought. I must have gained about 10 pounds in six days. We went to Rome, Pisa and Florence, where a famous statue of a young man named David will make you forget any schoolgirl crush. We also saw the pope wave from a window in Vatican City, but all I can remember is the cannelloni and the fact that the Italian kitchen staff at the hostel couldn't understand when I asked for some "agua" and mimicked drinking water. They had to call several people out to watch me pour imaginary water into an imaginary glass and then pretend to drink it all the while saying, "*Agua, agua.*" Finally an older woman looked at the others and smiled. "Aqua!" she said. Brilliant!

In France, we stayed in the red-light district just across the street from the Moulin Rouge. Luckily, I spoke a little French and I had studied the country's history for two years in Miss Sarkesian's French class, where she had regaled us with stories of French culture, Versailles and the French Revolution. I felt like I was walking through a history book, except when the French people were hating on us for being Americans. In one restaurant, we were waiting to be served for a very, very long time, so I asked a friend for some change for the jukebox. No sooner had I selected my songs than the owner began yelling at us, something about, "You Americans won the war!" I didn't really know which war he was talking about or what it had to do with us, and we tried to make peace with him but he wouldn't be swayed. He unplugged the jukebox and threw us out of the restaurant.

In Austria, I nearly caused an international incident when a drunk at a pub grabbed my ass and in response I immediately clocked him. He had obviously never tried this with a girl from East L.A. before. His friends rushed up, my friends rushed up, and again we had to leave. Salzburg, Austria was my least favorite place. I mean, I love *The Sound of Music* as much as anyone, and I tried to picture myself singing "Doe, a deer, a female deer" as I walked down the street, but the place left me cold…literally, it was the coldest place I'd ever been, and I was not prepared for it. We stayed in private homes, and, at night, under the down comforter, I started to miss East L.A., my mom and dad and my Femme Fatale bandmates.

London, England was our last stop before heading home, and I was glad to be in a place where Americans were not hated. England was fun, but because our English and American cultures are so similar, I started missing home again. My mind started drifting back to Femme Fatale. I wondered if my friends had been practicing and whether I'd be able to catch up to them on guitar.

When I got home, there they were, waiting for me. They had missed me as much as I'd missed them. I don't know if they thought I'd never catch up to them on guitar, but what they told me was that they had talked about it and they'd decided that I should concentrate on being the lead singer. They didn't want me to bother learning to play guitar because Margot would be doing the guitar playing and Patricia had decided to play bass. I was happy to be able to focus on what I really wanted to do, so we were on track again.

At the end of summer we got an album by an all-girl group called the Runaways. We liked their songs, and their music didn't sound so polished that we couldn't play it, so we started trying to learn their songs. We were wrong.

We weren't as good as we thought we were, and nowhere near as good as we wanted to be. The Runaways were not as technically proficient as some of the groups we liked, but they had made an album, they were all girls, and they were getting airplay. It inspired us, and pretty soon we were playing along with them, singing *"Dead end kids in the danger zone, all of you are drunk or stoned..."*

ROCKET FROM THE TOMB

With Femme Fatale again on the front burner, the girls and I were getting together more often. I was still working at J. C. Penney, which was getting more depressing as fall arrived and the days grew shorter. Some days, I'd go in when the sun was coming up and leave when it was dark. There were no windows in the lingerie department, where I worked, and I usually took my own lunch in a paper bag and ate in the back room in order to save money. The place was lifeless, and with no natural light it felt just like a tomb. I was buried alive, away from the sunlight I craved, and I felt like a vampire in reverse; I was withering without the sun's rays.

My work was tedious, and, by virtue of seniority, the old woman I worked with bossed me around and gave me the crappiest tasks to do. Sometimes people would come in with coats or umbrellas and I'd ask them what the weather was like outside. I was hermetically sealed away from the world, and I counted every agonizing tick of the clock. Each hour lasted a century. I started to doubt my sanity. *How could it still be the same time it was two hours ago?!* If this was what it meant to have a regular job, then I had no choice — I'd either have to make it in music or commit suicide. The only reason I stayed at J. C. Penney was because I needed the money, and they allowed me to have a flexible schedule that made it easy for me to continue to take classes.

I was still going to East Los Angeles College and was mostly focusing on philosophy and photography classes, as well as some general education. I also continued to try other things, like anthropology and chemistry, the latter being a subject I dreaded, and with good reason too. I sucked at it, but it was a requirement, so I bit the bullet. I was still seeing Susan and my gay disco friends, but Marlene, Patricia and I managed to play together regularly and to do research — going out to see more bands.

I hardly spent any time at home now, which was a good thing, because even though my parents didn't get into the bitter arguments that used to climax in my mother being beaten, our neighborhood was changing, and it wasn't always fun to be around. Our neighborhood in East L.A. had been pretty quiet and peaceful when we first moved in, but now there were drug deals taking place on the corner of our street, and if you followed the little trail of bread crumbs on the sidewalk, they led back to one of our neighbors' houses.

Early one evening, my dad had fallen asleep after an exhausting afternoon of dialysis, and my mother was puttering in the kitchen, making dinner. I was sitting on the porch, reading a book, when a flatbed pickup truck full of young men screeched to a halt in front of the house where the bread crumbs led. The young men jumped out of the cab and piled off the back of the truck and ran to the neighbor's house. When someone came to the door, the men pushed their way in and, after a few minutes of yelling, they dragged one of the inhabitants out into the street. I watched from my porch, partially obscured by plants and a safe distance away, as the people who tried to come out of the neighbor's house to aid the man being pulled away were hit over the head with lead pipes and beaten back into the house. The captured man was dragged around to the back of the pickup truck where a rope was quickly tied around his ankles and calves and the other end was fastened to a metal tow pin on the back of the truck. It was something you might see in a Western movie, only instead of being dragged by a horse, this guy was going to be dragged by a truck. The driver got in while the other men hooted and hollered, cheering him on. People inside the house screamed too, but not in the same way. I watched, transfixed in horror as the truck sped off down the street with our neighbor being dragged helplessly over the asphalt. I presume they went around the block because it came back from the other direction just a few minutes later. The truck stopped and one of the men got out. I couldn't tell if they were planning to back up over what now looked more like a pile of torn, bloody rags than a man, untie him or simply check on him and drag him some more.

During the brief pause, another car screeched onto our block. There were four guys in this car, and they were yelling. The noise was escalating as the people inside the house, emboldened by seeing their own reinforcements show up, forced their way out the door. My mother, hearing the commotion, came out to the porch and made me go inside. I did, but I peered out my window, still unable to tear myself away from the chaos that was happening just a few yards away. My view was now partially obscured but I could hear the screaming and yelling, and I realized that at least one of these men had a gun because I could hear it being fired. One of the men ran into our yard and vaulted over the fence, trying to avoid being captured or killed by his enemies. The sirens of approaching police cars sent everyone running back to their vehicles.

My mother turned to me hastily and said, "You didn't see anything." I knew I would never forget the man who was dragged by the truck. I don't know whether he survived the attack. The police went door to door asking if anyone had seen anything. We all said no.

RODNEY B AND
THE FOWLEY CONNECTION

A few nights later, my bandmates and I went to see a band at the Starwood. We were milling around when we spotted Rodney Bingenheimer in a corner, quietly eating a basket of French fries by himself. His slight build and big round eyes gave him a boyish appearance. He sported a cockscomb reminiscent of the Bay City Rollers or Bowie circa Ziggy Stardust. Rodney was a sort of celebrity to us, his English Disco had been at the heart of the glitter scene in Los Angeles and he was known to be very well connected in the music business

"Go talk to him," Marlene suggested.

"You talk to him," I snapped back. The girls ganged up on me, and I was elected to go tell Rodney about our new band. I knew I wasn't voluptuous like Marlene or striking like Patricia, but I was young and naive and they told me Rodney would like that, so I walked over.

"Hi, Rodney," I said stiffly.

"Hi," he replied shyly, smiling at me. "Want some French fries?" he offered the basket up to me.

"No, thank you." His kind offer instantly put me at ease and I began talking to him about the band that was playing, and then about the band I was forming.

"Give me your phone number," he said. "I'll help if I can."

When I walked back to my friends, they made fun of me. "*Ohhhh, Rodney,*" they teased as though I'd just been making out with him instead of talking to him at their request. "You gave him your phone number?" I don't know why they asked, because they'd been watching us the whole time, giggling and making faces at me behind Rodney's back.

"Yes, I gave him my phone number and told him about the band. He promised to help us if he can."

We went back to watching the band and thought nothing more of Rodney, until a few days later when I was awakened by my phone. My mother was holding it in one hand, having brought it into my bedroom after I tried to ignore it. "It's a man," she whispered to me, holding her hand over the mouthpiece.

"Hello?" I mumbled into the receiver, half asleep after staying up until the early-morning hours at a 24-hour coffee shop with Susan the night before.

"Alice?" a strange voice asked.

"Yes, who is this?" I asked curtly.

"I got your number from Rodney Bingenheimer," the man began, my ears perking up immediately upon hearing Rodney's name. "We are holding auditions for an all-girl group, and Rodney told me about your group." Yes! Oh Rodney, you wonderful man, you remembered me!

The man was still talking. There was something irritating about his voice; he was not as pleasant or warm as Rodney. I met his gruffness with my own. "Excuse me," I interrupted. "Who are you?"

"My name is Kim Fowley, I'm a record producer." I knew who he was. We hadn't been listening to that Runaways record without doing a little research on them. Fowley was credited with not only helping to assemble the band and co-write the songs but with being a strong force in shaping and promoting them. He started listing his accomplishments, and I assured him I knew who he was.

"So are you looking for an all-girl band?" I asked, getting a little nervous now that I knew who was on the other side of the phone.

"Not exactly, I'm looking to *assemble* an all-girl band, similar to the Runaways, and I want to invite you and your band members to the audition." That didn't sound as good as I'd hoped, because all of us would have to audition separately.

"Rodney tells me you're a singer," he continued.

"Yes."

"Can you sing something for me now?"

Now? Damn it, I had just woken up and I was caught off guard. "What do you want me to sing?" I couldn't believe I'd just said that.

"Sing whatever you want," Kim told me. I drew a blank. Which songs did I know the words to?

"*I'm an alligator...*" the song came out of my mouth before I had a chance to weigh my options. I sang halfway through David Bowie's "Moonage Daydream" before Kim stopped me.

"That's fine," he said. "Come on down to the auditions so that I can see what you look like, and bring the other girls."

I don't remember if I gave Kim the girls' phone numbers or if I called them and told them. It doesn't really matter, because we were all very excited and swore our allegiance to each other. No matter what happened, we agreed it would be all of us or none of us. Femme Fatale would stick together, with or without Kim Fowley.

When we got to the audition there were more female musicians than I had ever seen in one place. Most of them were friendly and outgoing. The process took a long time, but it wasn't bad. I'd hoped that Femme Fatale would be allowed to audition all together, but we had to audition separately. As Kim narrowed his search, he put different people together in different combinations. After hearing some of the other girls sing and play, we were pretty certain that we hadn't made the cut, which, surprisingly, didn't disappoint us all that much; after all, we were true beginners.

Outside the audition room, we struck up a conversation with a cute guy who was there with his sweet but very shy baby sister. The sister played drums, but she didn't tell us this herself, she only nodded when her brother, Michael, told us about her. She seemed to be a little younger than us, maybe 15 years old, tops. She had very little experience, which was okay with us, because that was what we had, too. Michael encouraged us to form our own band.

"You don't need Kim Fowley," he told us, and there was a certain quality about him that made you want to believe him. Before the day was over, we'd found our fourth member and a self-appointed band manager.

THE MANAGER

Michael immediately invited us to his house to jam with his sister, so Marlene, Patricia and I made the trek out to the South Bay after work one evening. The drive was long and the traffic infernal, especially during rush hour, when crossing downtown L.A. ranks right up there with having a root canal. It was especially grueling for Patricia, who lived in Whittier, which added at least an extra half hour to her journey.

When we arrived at Michael's house we expected to get right to work, but there was a drawn-out ritual of hanging out and talking that had to happen first. We waited for over an hour before asking about Michael's sister, who was conspicuously absent. I don't remember if Michael made an excuse for her that first day or if he gave us the bad news right away, but I do know that he was really angry about his sister's lack of interest in joining the band, and, although it should have sent some red flags up for us right away, we were just too young and naive to follow our intuition.

"She doesn't want to do it," he told us flatly.

"She doesn't want to play drums?" we asked. "Or she doesn't want to be in a band with us?"

Michael, Masque Era manager on stage at the Smokestack

"She's lazy," Michael said, neatly avoiding the question.

That left us all a bit confused, because we didn't know whether she was insecure about her playing, in which case we could encourage her, or if she just didn't want to be in a band with us. Sensing our disappointment, Michael jumped in again.

"Forget about her. You girls don't need her. I'll manage you anyway," he said, smiling at us as though it was no big deal to have lost our drummer. We had assumed that Michael wanted to manage us because he wanted to help out his sister, but since she wasn't going to be in the band after all, we wondered why he wanted to work with us.

That first night, we just talked. Well, Michael did most of the talking, and we listened. He told us we were going to be great. He said we were lucky Kim Fowley hadn't chosen us, because we were destined for better things. He told us about his own musical experiences. He was a working guitarist, and he promised us we would one day be at his level if we just followed his simple instructions. We were children, and he was dangling lollipops in front of us. We were hooked.

We started making the trip out to the South Bay several times a week. Every time it was the same ritual: hurry up and wait. Sometimes we had to wait while Michael took a shower, blow-dried his hair or talked on the phone. Then, we'd make long-term plans for the band. Sometimes he'd give us a music history lesson. There was a lot of talking and very little work. Eventually, we got down to songwriting. After a few weeks, we succeeded in completing the one song Michael assigned us. It was called "We Love the Show," and the idea for the song originated with him. It took us a really long time to figure out lyrics, because it wasn't anything that any of us felt like we wanted to write about.

Marlene could come up with great, funny, clever lyrics on the spot and had written several songs before we formed the band, but even she was stuck on "We Love the Show." The truth is, it sucked. Even worse, we sucked. Femme Fatale was heavily influenced by our musical heroes, and "We Love the Show" was probably a bit more ambitious than we had any right to attempt. During this period, we were still listening to our old favorites like Queen and Roxy Music while at the same time absorbing the new sounds coming out of the New York punk scene, like the Ramones. Playing covers of the Runaways and the Ramones was just about our speed, but that didn't keep us from trying the more complex, glitter-influenced music that also appealed to us. We were practicing less — now that we were driving two hours to our manager's house — than we were when we practiced in Marlene's living room, but we were under Michael's spell.

Michael had a girlfriend when we first met him, but after a while he broke up with her and starting putting the make on Patricia. That's when things got really crazy. Suddenly, Michael started trying to play weird power games with us. There was always the waiting game. No matter what time we showed up, Michael was never ready to do anything, but now he also started talking to us about spiritual enlightenment. The subject fascinated me, because I missed discussing religion with Sister Angela, and there were philosophical elements to spiritual enlightenment which were right up my alley, but Marlene and Patricia were disturbed by it, and by the fact that these lengthy discussions often happened when we were supposed to be rehearsing. They also didn't think that Michael was simply interested in discussing spiritual enlightenment, religion and philosophy; they thought he was trying to convince us that he was a kind of guru who we were supposed to follow blindly.

I didn't realize until Patricia confided in me that much of the enlightenment discussion was really aimed at convincing Patricia to give in to his advances. After a while, the girls started getting fed up with Michael, but I was still enjoying my visits out to the South Bay, where we went to various rock shows and parties. I remember crashing one party at a very nice house in Palos Verdes, where I chanced upon the girl I had met at a Kiss concert a couple of years before: Trudie. We reintroduced ourselves, and I, feeling somewhat embarrassed and definitely out of place in these upscale surroundings, confessed that we had crashed the party. I expected her to say that she had crashed, too.

"Do you happen to know who lives here?" I asked Trudie.

"Yes!" she answered, and then she introduced me to her friend Helen, who would later become known to me as Hellin Killer. Around this same time, I also met a tall, Peter Frampton–haired drummer who had a great sense of humor and who always looked at me as if he could see through my clothes. His name was Jeffrey Ivisovich, and he was a friend of Michael's who often stopped by the house when our band was practicing.

Michael soon insisted that we change the name of the band from Femme Fatale to Masque Era. He also said that we should spell it M-A-S-Q-U-E. "You will be entering an era when it will be difficult to tell who is a friend and who is an enemy. It's as if people are wearing masks," he told me. "It also refers to your show. A masque is a form of entertainment involving theater and music — it's a double entrendre," he tried to explain, but I was stuck with the image of a masked ball and Venice canals. Nonetheless, it occurred to me a year or two later that Michael might have been a prophet.

A LONG-HAIRED BOY WITH X-RAY VISION

One Saturday afternoon, Patricia and I were at Michael's house when Jeffrey, the long-haired boy with X-ray vision, showed up. Michael asked Patricia to run an errand with him, leaving me and Jeffrey alone in his house. Jeff and I were attracted to each other, we'd flirted with each other whenever he was at Michael's, and no sooner had they walked out the door than we got to the business of getting to know each other much better. I had never taken my clothes off in front of a man and was very shy at first, but Jeff was older and his kisses and gentle reassurance made me feel beautiful and desirable. Within minutes we were rumpling the covers on Michael's bed.

Jeffrey with Rocky and Bullwinkle

I liked Jeffrey but I was a true, dyed-in-the-wool *Cosmo* Girl. I did not expect or want Jeff to be my boyfriend just because we'd done "it," as my friends and I used to call sex — "The Big It," to be precise. There had been no romance between us, only sexual attraction. Jeffrey made the bed, and when Michael and Patricia got back, he and I were sitting in the living room talking. I thought we both looked innocent enough, but on our way home, Patricia turned around in the car and stared at me.

"Well?" she said, her eyes inspecting me mercilessly.

"Well, what?" I replied.

"WELL, what happened?" she demanded. I laughed and we exchanged secrets.

Patricia was smitten with Michael, so it was still fun for us to go out to the South Bay, but we were frustrated that the band was not making progress. "Michael and I were thinking that it might be a good idea to put an ad in the *Recycler* looking for female musicians," Patricia told me.

"Yeah, it sounds like a good idea. Let's talk to Marlene and see what she thinks."

Marlene was all for it, and later that week we called in our ad, listing our musical tastes and limited playing experience. As soon as the ad came out we got some calls, but not all of them were from girls. We often got calls from guys wanting to be the stud in the all-girl band, but we ignored them. We met a hippie drummer who lived out in the wilderness and tried to convince us to change the name of the band to Squat and Gobble. She played fairly well, but she liked hippie rock, wore sandals and no makeup, and just didn't have the same aesthetic as us, so we decided not to work with her.

A lead guitarist named Reena auditioned for us. She was good, and her boyfriend roadied for Zolar X, an L.A. band that dressed like extraterrestrials and were favorites on the glitter scene, so we knew she was on the same wavelength. She wore satin and glitter and just as much makeup as we did. We snagged her. Finally, we got a call from a cute, blonde college girl; I think her name was Cindy. She was pretty, smart and well-adjusted, but we decided to overlook those unusual qualities because she really wanted to learn and was willing to let us dress her up. She was also open to taking drum lessons from Jeffrey, who had agreed to help us in any way he could.

Masque Era was ready to start rehearsing. We agreed to make the first rehearsal at my house in East L.A., because it was the most centrally located. Michael, our manager, didn't show up, but Jeffrey was there. He helped set up the drums and provided us with feedback and encouragement. We rehearsed

Marlene and Patricia focus on getting it right.

our one original song, "We Love the Show" over and over again, and followed with a few lame covers, just to get loosened up. My mother and father retreated to their bedroom, and my mom only came out to offer us food. She always had something cooking, and nobody was allowed to get away from our house without having something to eat or drink; it was unthinkable. Rehearsal was followed by feasting, and there was a sense of celebration in the air. Finally, we were on our way.

Jeffrey and I were seeing more of each other. We still didn't think of ourselves as boyfriend and girlfriend, but it seemed to be working out that way. Other changes were afoot. Kim Fowley, dissatisfied with the selection of female musicians he had auditioned for Venus and the Razorblades, had given up on the concept of an all-girl band or an all-girl band with a male singer. He was now holding auditions for guys, specifically drummers. The next time I saw Jeffrey, he had big news for me. He had auditioned for Venus and The Razorblades and was their new drummer. Kim was good at generating press, and pictures of the newly formed band were immediately distributed to the press, along with interviews — mostly of Kim — in which he hyped his new venture.

Jeff was on his way, too...or so we thought.

FLASHBULB, PHALLUS AND SHADES

In the pre-punk days, we all had nicknames like Alice Phallus, Marlene Mattress and Patricia Delicia. At concerts, we were often escorted by Flashbulb Gilly, a photographer Marlene and I had met at a band concert at Montebello High School. Flashbulb, who's real name was Gilbert Leos, was a little older than us, but when you're a teen, age differences are measured in months, and the older you were usually corresponded with the amount of respect you got.

Flashbulb was a bit of a star to us. He had been going to concerts longer, and he photographed bands. He was friendly with many of the club owners, managers and local groups. Going to a show with Gilly always meant getting backstage. Gilbert was daring and fun. He would hide us in the trunk of his car and drive to the Fiesta Drive-In, in Whittier, where he would open the trunk and release us after we'd made it past the ticket window. Once in the car, we would all get drunk while watching a movie, and if we didn't feel like getting in the trunk he would turn off the headlights, put photo albums over the tire spikes and we'd drive into the drive-in through the exit. He would turn off the speaker box and encourage us to make up our own dialogue to go with the action on the screen, often to hilarious effect. At concerts, he was often on the guest list of bands that wanted live pictures of themselves, but sometimes, if he was taking all of us out and he couldn't get us all on the guest list, he'd open the back door at the Whisky and sneak us in; or we'd go in during sound check and hide backstage or in the bathroom.

Gilly took us to rock shows hosted by the local indie rock station, known as the KROQ Cabaret shows. A few of those shows were held in the basement of the Columbia Pictures Studios on Gower Street. I met future Plunger Trixie Treat at one of those shows. She was very pretty and sweet, and we became fast friends. She walked around like she owned the place. She seemed to know everyone, and I was impressed by her lack of pretentiousness. Unlike many people who tried to seem more important than they were, Trixie was happy to be a music fan.

I also met another interesting character who would be a fixture in Hollywood for years. He was a Marc Bolan–looking guy who always wore sunglasses. I'd seen him before at shows; he was always alone, and even inside a dark bar or nightclub he kept his shades on. One night at Columbia Studios I went up to talk to him, but the East L.A. part of me surfaced subconsciously, and instead of asking him a more relevant question, I asked him, "Hey man — where are you from?"

He looked at me, surprised. "I'm from Greenland," he replied, smiling. "My name is Danny." I said hello, but I immediately realized that I'd sounded like an idiot, and I made a hasty retreat. For years after that, I would see him alone with his ever present sunglasses at shows around L.A., and I'd address him as Danny From Greenland. Later, I learned he also went by another name: Danny Shades.

After Masque Era's rehearsal in my mother's living room, Marlene commented on my energetic singing style. "You should have a stage name that conveys that," she said. My boyfriend, Jeffrey, the drummer, had recently changed his name to Nickey Beat, and I thought it suited him very well and had really helped him define his stage persona. I thought about it for a few days and finally came up with a name I liked. I called Marlene.

"I thought of a name for myself," I told her excitedly.

"What is it?"

"Adrina," I said.

"Adrina?" Marlene sounded confused.

"Adrina Lynne, get it? Like adrenaline?" I enthused.

There was silence on the phone that seemed to last for centuries, and then, finally, laughter. "Adrina Lynne is perfect!" Marlene said, cracking up, but that long pause had made me unsure of my choice.

THE HIT LIST

If you turned on the radio in early 1977, Leo Sayer might make you "Feel Like Dancing," or you could be "Torn Between Two Lovers," by Mary MacGregor. You'd risk either being "Blinded by the Light," by Manfred Mann's Earth Band, or being called a "Rich Girl," by Hall & Oates.

Punk had begun making waves in this sappy cesspool of sameness as early as 1976, and there were a few bands playing L.A. at the time who were listening to the jungle drums beating in New York and absorbing elements of the new style. These bands bridged the gap between glitter and punk, providing a transitional sound that was later dubbed "power pop" or "new wave," and they played shows at places like the Whisky a Go-Go, Columbia Studios and the Starwood. Songs and guitar leads got shorter, tempos got faster, clothing got tighter and darker, but there were still no local bands playing what I would describe as punk. Masque Era was certainly not punk, although we were all listening to the Ramones by 1976. Because mainstream radio wouldn't dare play records by Television or the Ramones, there were only a handful of people I knew who had heard of these bands, and fewer still who actually liked them.

Some of the real heroes of punk come in unlikely packages. In 1977, Rodney Bingenheimer was a quiet little man with a soft voice. He sported a haircut that belonged on a Bay City Roller: choppy on the top, with spiky bangs and longish sides. He went out to see local music often, and could just as easily be seen alone as flanked by touring rock stars. Rodney really deserves a starring role in any punk history book, because, despite his timid exterior, he was passionate about music. As a DJ at KROQ starting in 1976, he had the courage to play music that nobody else in Los Angeles and very few across the country would.

Some punks thought that because Rodney had been at the forefront of glitter rock, his switch over to punk was somehow disingenuous, but I don't believe that. Many of us who were part of the early L.A. punk scene transitioned into the new music. We didn't materialize out of a vacuum without any musical roots; we weren't born clad in leather jackets or ripped fishnet stockings.

It was Rodney's radio show on KROQ where most of us were first introduced to the sound of punk rock, giving us our first taste of new records that were often difficult to find. Rodney was an enthusiastic supporter of new bands, and, later, when we started putting out our own records, Rodney was usually the first, if not the only, DJ in town to play our small, independent releases.

When the local punk scene eventually got underway, radio became completely meaningless to us, because no one listened to the radio…except for Rodney's show. We quickly became each other's fan base and supportive audiences, but in those last few months, when we were waiting for the end of the world, *Rodney on the ROQ* provided the audio sparks for our own creative fuses.

1977

As we turned the corner into 1977, everything we'd previously only read about in *Punk* magazine, *Creem*, *Circus* and *New York Rocker* was about to come busting down our doors. Marlene, Patricia and I had been listening to the Ramones' first album for nearly half a year, enough time to learn their songs, which were right at our playing level.

When we first heard the Ramones, we weren't sure what to make of them. Imagine listening to Queen's *Bohemian Rhapsody* and then hearing *Beat on the Brat* for the first time. No other band on the planet was doing what the Ramones were doing: It was simple, exciting, and it completely fucked up the way I thought of rock music — in a good way. When the Ramones' first record came out, a lot of people thought they were just one big joke. Their two-minute songs with no guitar solos and sparse, repetitive lyrics made some critics dismissive toward them.

More palatable to the mainstream was Blondie, another of the New York underground bands that made an impression on us. Even though Blondie's sound was more pop and accessible than the Ramones, it was still very different from what was being played on the radio in those days, and what ordinary people were accustomed to hearing. Blondie got lumped into the punk category mainly because of the venues they played and the bands they were associated with. There was a broader label that was being used at the time for bands like Blondie that were innovative but a bit on the pop side: new wave. I would always consider Blondie new wave rather than punk.

Rodney Bingenheimer had been playing Blondie's single because he was the only radio DJ in town with any real vision. The band's single, "X-Offender" (changed from "Sex Offender"), was considered provocative for the time because the lyrics made reference to handcuffs and sex with a police officer. Blondie was different enough and fun enough to appeal to the growing numbers of ex-glitterati who were now trading in their satin for black leather, in homage to the Ramones, and their platforms for Debbie Harry–style stilettos.

Up until now, the music scene in Hollywood had been going through a transitional phase. 1976 had seen the sparkle of glitter fade like a Christmas tree left up for too many weeks after New Year's Day. Some of us, myself included, still hung on to our tinsel and just added layers of ripped-up hose, spiky heels, leather and industrial-strength eyeliner over our recycled glitter outfits. But the young music audience in Hollywood was going through a metamorphosis and was about to burst forth as an entirely brand new creature.

Rodney Bingenheimer was still at the forefront of championing new bands on his weekend show on KROQ. His was the only station in town that was playing punk, new wave and power pop. KROQ supported local band concerts at a venue called the KROQ Cabaret, where groups like the Berlin Brats, the Dogs and the Nerves bridged the huge gap between glitter and punk. But in a world that was about to radically change, some of these bands would wear the scarlet letter of power pop, radio free or post-glam in a town that was ready for PUNK. Others, like the Berlin Brats (who became the Mau-Maus) changed with the times.

Early in '77, the Ramones and Blondie played a series of shows in L.A. and Orange County. They were but the first swell of a tidal wave that was about to engulf me and my world.

THE MIDAS TOUCH IN REVERSE

"Kim Fowley has the Midas touch," Jeff told me one afternoon following a Venus and The Razorblades rehearsal. "Only it's the Midas touch in reverse. Instead of everything he touches turning into gold, everything he touches turns to shit."

Jeffrey photobooth promo shot.

Fowley had assembled a good band, but with his abrasive, domineering personality and his attitude toward the band members — which was by many accounts disrespectful — the band was struggling. Jeff, who was now going by the name Nickey Beat, had always been outspoken. He had a flair for making colorful statements that sometimes took people by surprise. I'm sure Fowley found Nickey's irreverent sense of humor and unwillingness to hold his tongue annoying. Fowley fancied himself a Svengali, but he wasn't that clever. He tried to intimidate and shock people with offensive language, but most of the younger musicians in Hollywood thought of him as an old fool who used the little power he had to try to find someone to stroke his needy ego. I don't remember if Nickey quit Venus and The Razorblades or if Fowley fired him. In any case, it was a blessing for Nickey.

Meanwhile, Masque Era was also severing ties with its manager. Michael's religious and philosophical interests had Marlene and Patricia fed up. To tell the truth, that was one aspect of Michael's personality that never bothered me, but my allegiance was to my girlfriends, so we all agreed to part ways with him. Masque Era only rehearsed one or two more times before things started falling apart. Our drummer was busy in school and couldn't find time for the drum lessons Nickey had offered her, so she decided to quit. Our wounded little band was hobbling around, unable to get on its feet, but Patricia and Margo were still practicing and getting better and better. As for me, I always practiced using my own methods. I cranked up the stereo in my room and sang into the full-length mirror that was built into my bedroom door. I danced and posed and made faces at myself. In this respect, I was much more in keeping with my older influences like Rafael or Pedro Infante than my American and British rock idols.

Rafael was a Spanish movie and pop star. He had made a lasting impression on me with his dramatic, passionate singing style, while Pedro Infante… well, Pedro could wrap me around his finger with his romantic songs, bring out the feisty side of me when he was telling someone off or yank a tear from my eye if he was doing a sad song. Rafael and Pedro didn't just sing a song: they delivered it, they exuded it; they lived it. Every word was audible, every syllable and inflection in their voices meant something. Imagine comparing a silent-era movie star to a modern actor; Pedro and Rafael did with their voices what silent actors did with their gestures. They were outsized and playing to the last row of the theater. At the time, I didn't realize that Pedro and Rafael had more to do with how I felt about music and performance than did David Bowie, Elton John or Freddie Mercury. My earliest musical heroes, Aretha Franklin, Bessie Smith and Freda Payne, had also left an indelible mark on me that I wasn't even aware of.

Aside from practicing, we worked on songwriting, read about bands from the New York punk scene in *Punk* magazine, and went to as many shows as possible, all the while going to school and working full time. Even though we kept running up against road blocks, we never stopped working toward our goal of having an all-girl band. We nurtured our dream, we talked about it like it was going to come true, we made plans for when we would become famous. I don't know about the other girls, but I even practiced my autograph.

Instead of feeling sad or hopeless because we'd lost our manager, my bandmates and I felt like we had lightened our load. We were re-energized. The long drives, long waits and lack of results had chipped away at our enthusiasm, but now we were ready to take matters into our own hands. Nickey, too, was relieved to be free of Kim Fowley's tyrannical ravings. We'd all thought that we could trust a manager, give him power over our careers, and that the manager would turn us into rock stars, but we couldn't have been more naive. Not that you can't trust people, but you do have to be the captain of your own ship. It was time to reverse our misdirected courses.

"FIND MY FINGER!!"

Patricia and I camped outside the ticket-seller's shop. Patricia had called in advance, and they had assured her they had excellent seats for the Queen concert at the L.A. Forum, so we parked outside and prepared for a long night. We'd packed some snacks, blankets and music, and were the first to line up the night before the tickets were to go on sale. It was a cold night, but as more and more people started to arrive, the atmosphere changed into a Queen-fan slumber party. A patrol car eventually came by, but after talking to us and seeing that we were all well behaved, they allowed us to keep our places in line.

After a long, sleepless night, the ticket-seller finally showed up and opened the door for us. Patricia and I were the first ones in. As soon as the man behind the counter handed us our tickets, he smiled at us.

"You are going to be very happy with these," he said.

Patricia took the tickets. "We're in the first row!" she screamed.

"Front row, center," the ticket-seller clarified. "Let me show you your seats." He pulled out a seating chart and pointed our two seats, dead center in front of the stage. "That's you two," he laughed. Patricia and I started screaming and jumping up and down like we'd just won the lottery.

The people outside pressed their faces against the window and as we walked out they asked, "What happened?"

"We've got front row, center!" we said to our slumber party friends. Now everyone was electrified. Patricia and I got in her car and drove away to have breakfast, but we were so giddy that we couldn't even eat. We went back to her house and blasted Queen in her bedroom as we started counting down the days until the concert.

When the night of the Queen concert finally arrived, Patricia and I put on our best black-and-white outfits and belted out our favorite Queen songs in our loudest voices as we drove out to the L.A. Forum. Other drivers on the freeway looked our way as the music, singing and excitement spilled out of our open windows.

When we got to the Forum, Patricia literally had to stop me from skipping. She was always the level-headed one, and I, being a few months younger, looked up to her and followed her example. I could tell she wanted to skip, too, but instead she walked regally to the usher and handed him our tickets. We felt important as the usher walked us to the front of the stage and showed us our seats. I'd always thought you had to know somebody to have those kinds of seats, but it turned out that all it took was a good ticket broker and a willingness to camp outside with the masses in an urban parking lot.

When the band came onstage, we realized that even though we had excellent seats, the stage at the Forum was huge and the only person that we were really close to was Freddie Mercury. The rest of the band might as well have been a block away. It didn't matter. We loved all of Queen, but if we could only be close to one member, we were glad and thoroughly satisfied that it was Freddie. He was five feet away from us, and we could see every gesture, the sheen of perspiration on his skin, his Adam's apple move as he sang, "*Somebody to love...*"

Me and Patricia on the way to see Queen.

"Did you see that?" Patricia asked.

"What?"

"He looked straight at me!" she exclaimed.

"He did?" I replied, a little confused.

"Yes, didn't you see him?" she asked, annoyed.

"Oh, yeah, yeah he did." I hadn't noticed Freddie looking at her, but she looked beautiful that night, and I believed her and smiled inwardly at her excitement.

It was wonderful seeing Freddie up close, feeling like he was singing every song to you personally. I was so happy for Patricia, imagining how I would've felt if I'd been that close to Elton John and he'd looked at me while he was singing. Surely I would have fainted or rushed the stage and tried to rip his clothes off. But this was Patricia's night, and I was glad to be along for the ride.

About halfway through the set, the lights dimmed. It was time for a quiet love song. Freddie was talking and pouring wine into a crystal wine goblet. He looked out into the front row and handed the glass to the audience. He seemed to be handing it directly to Patricia, who got up to take it. She was on her feet with the goblet in her hand but suddenly another girl in the front row, thinking that the wine glass was for her, lunged for it just seconds after Patricia had accepted the offering. Now, she also had the glass in her hand. Patricia had her eyes on Freddie and Freddie's were locked on her but the other girl had her eyes on the glass and she yanked it hard. Suddenly, the spell was shattered as Patricia let go of the broken glass and jagged shards of crystal and wine flew everywhere. Freddie looked concerned but continued to sing. I rushed up to help Patricia, who seemed to be hurt.

Now she was screaming something at me but I couldn't hear her. The concert music swelled and drowned out her voice, but I could see a look of panic in her eyes. She showed me her hand and all I could see was what looked like the stump of a finger that had been chopped off and was bleeding profusely. I called the security guard over.

"She's hurt!" I yelled at him as he rushed over with his flashlight. He put his arm around her and started to lead her away as I rushed back to our seats to grab our bags and jackets.

"Find my finger!" Patricia yelled to me. I ran to the front of the stage and looked on the floor but it was pitch black and I couldn't see a thing. The security guard was now also yelling at me, telling me to go with them.

"I need you to come with us," he said. He was afraid Patricia was going to pass out.

We were taken to a first-aid location where they tended to Patricia while waiting to transport her to the emergency room. "Find my finger, Alice!" she kept yelling at me.

"I tried, it's dark down there...I can't see anything!" I tried to explain. "Can you go with me?" I asked the security guard.

"Go quickly," the paramedic barked at us. "We're getting an ambulance for her."

"They can sew it back on if you find it!" Patricia's voice echoed down the hall after us as the security guard and I flew back down to the auditorium floor.

There was another security guard already posted at the front of the stage. The two guards and I went down to the front row and they shined their flashlights while I bent over and searched all over the ground near our seats but we couldn't find the severed piece of Patricia's finger. People were looking at us, including band members. We were disrupting the concert and the head of security came and told the guards they couldn't shine the flashlights anymore. The ambulance was there and they needed me to go with my friend.

I was ashamed to face Patricia without having found the rest of her finger but there was nothing else to do. I rode with her in the ambulance while she cursed and grimaced in pain. I was sick with shame that I hadn't punched the girl who'd grabbed the glass, and worse, that I hadn't found the piece of missing finger. Once at the hospital, they stitched her wound closed and wrapped her finger in white gauze.

"I don't know if I'll ever play bass again," she said sadly to me. We held each other, crying in silence, not knowing what the future held for us.

BIG FAT LIAR

After Patricia's finger-chopping accident, Masque Era was in a holding pattern. Patricia had lost about half an inch off her index finger. It doesn't sound like much but it looked pretty bad.

We had to allow time for her wound to heal before the doctor would even consider giving her any hope of plucking the bass strings with her fingers again. Even using a pick so soon after her accident was painful. Everyone tried to support her. We met musicians who had similarly lost a part of a finger or fingers and still played quite well. Marlene and I called her every day and never let her stop believing that we'd one day have a band together.

It was a time of transition for all of us. Marlene — who had always lived with her mom in a one-bedroom duplex in Montebello — had decided to move with her father and brother into a larger house near East L.A. College. Marlene's father and brother led very different lives from Marlene's and her mom's. Her brother was soon to become a Jesuit priest, and her father was a kind, quiet but somber man. Marlene's mother had always been gregarious and fun-loving, but in this new household our late nights, concerts and teenage escapades in Hollywood were severely curtailed under the watchful eye of Marlene's father.

My own father was also keeping an eye on my behavior. With Patricia in recovery mode and Marlene adjusting to her new surroundings, I was spending a lot of time with Nickey Beat, who was now officially my boyfriend. He'd introduced me to his father as his girlfriend, and I guess things between us had just taken their natural course. We both enjoyed each others' company,

Patricia displays her wounded finger.

and despite the fact that Nickey was not romantic in the typical sense, he had a creative, sweet and original way of expressing his feelings. He never bought me flowers, but he bought me a can of spray paint so I could paint my clothes; instead of rings or jewelry, I got a rubber drain plug fashioned into a pendant on a ball chain; instead of love letters, I got little rhymes mailed to me on the back of humorous postcards.

Romance came after sex in our relationship, but it was what we both wanted, so
it was a good fit for us.

I helped Nickey move into a tiny
bachelor apartment in Hollywood, on
the corner of Santa Monica and Vine.
The place was disgusting, and the yel-
low-and-brown-stained toilet and sink
took several energetic scrubbings and
bleachings before they came clean. We
disinfected all the surfaces with Ajax,
409 and Lysol, and decorated the place
with Nickey's odd collection of colorful
toys, gadgets and found objects. There
was even a lovely used catheter hanging
on one wall. Nickey was a true magpie;

Me and Jeffrey/Nickey

anything shiny found its way into his collection, as did any unusual tool that
inspired curiosity. I didn't know it then, but I should have realized that this
strangely decorated place would turn into our little circus-themed love nest.

My father didn't like me hanging out with Nickey. "He's a little old for
you," he told me. But instead of getting me to listen to him, his criticism only
prompted me to lie to him when I was going to spend time with Nickey. It
makes me sad, now, to think about lying to the only person who had believed
me when I told him that I hadn't taken drugs, and who had taken my word
over that of the authorities at my junior high school. But sex messes with your
mind. After a while, I thought I was in love, and I couldn't imagine giving up
Nickey just because my dad thought he was too old for me. I don't really think
it was Nickey's age that worried my dad; more likely it was the palpable sexual
tension between us that could never be fully suppressed when we were in a
room together. I have no doubt that my father had picked up on this and was
trying to save me from making a big mistake.

One evening, I lied to my parents and told them that I was going to the
movies with Nickey. When I came back late that night, my father asked me
what I'd seen. The movie *Rocky* was still out in theaters around this time and
it had caused quite a buzz, so it instantly popped into my head, and before I
knew it, I blurted out, "We went to see *Rocky*."

"Tell me about it," my father said. Of course, I didn't know very much
about it except that it was about a boxer. I felt like a fool then, Nickey had told

me to tell my father we had seen a French movie called *Children of Paradise*, probably because he figured my dad would be unfamiliar with it.

"I don't want to ruin the plot for you," I tried to evade the question.

"Oh, that's okay. I'm not going to see it," my dad insisted. "Just tell me one thing," he said. "Does he win or lose in the end?" I figured it was a Hollywood movie and the odds were in favor of him winning, so I placed my bet on that.

"He won," I lied, smiling at my dad as he turned to walk away.

"Oh," he said quietly, not looking at me and dropping the subject for good.

I couldn't stomach lying to my parents, and when I talked to Nickey about it, he suggested we move in together. I was 18, only months out of high school, with no real skills and a head full of rock 'n' roll dreams, so I decided to put him off, but only for a little while.

THE PARENT TRAP

"You will always be our daughter, and we will always love you," my parents had told me my whole life. Whenever I did something wrong, instead of simply punishing me they would attach the *we will always love you* sentence to whatever reprimand or consequence they administered. As a result, I think I'd been relatively unrebellious. I realized at an early age that any child-rearing mistakes they may have made with me were a result of their own private demons and had nothing to do with their love for me; so for someone with a fucked-up childhood, I thought I was remarkably well-adjusted, but that doesn't mean I considered myself a "good girl," or that I always listened to my parents.

Spring of '77 brought spring fever along with it. I'd spend long afternoons with Nickey up in his apartment, visiting him every chance I got. One afternoon, I arrived at his apartment to find him looking distraught, his eyes red and his clothing disheveled. "We're going to be sad today," he told me as soon as I walked in. "My brother drowned."

Nickey's brother liked to surf but he'd been pulled by a rip tide into a cave which is where his body had been found. As he told me about the accident, this older guy who had seemed to me so carefree, strong and independent melted into my arms like a little boy. I think our relationship changed that day, as I drove him to his father's house. We talked and listened to each other and allowed the sadness to wash over us.

We didn't know then that the cycle of life and death was playing itself out inside my body. I thought I'd come down with a bad flu when I started waking up with nausea. When it got really bad, I asked my mother if she'd drive me to the doctor. The idea that I might be pregnant hadn't even crossed my mind. Nickey and I had used condoms and I thought I had nothing to worry about, but I was wrong.

"You're pregnant," the doctor told me in front of my mother. I was shocked, completely taken off guard. I looked to my mother. Her face betrayed no emotion. She looked at the doctor instead of me.

"She is too young," my mother said to the doctor. "She's not ready to be a mother." The doctor looked first at me and then at my mother.

"I am going to leave you two alone for a few minutes," the doctor told us, sensing that we had matters to discuss.

I fully expected my mother to yell at me as soon as the doctor left us, but she didn't. She just looked at me and waited. "I'm sorry, mom" I said, tears welling up in my eyes. Now I was a little girl, breaking down, unable to deal with the consequences of my own actions. I was ashamed. I didn't feel like a Cosmo Girl anymore. I felt like a kid trying on her big sister's high heels and falling flat on my ass. A million thoughts raced through my mind, the first being that my mother was absolutely right: I was too young to be a mother.

"Do you think you're ready to be a mother?" my mom asked me.

"No," I answered. I was openly sobbing now.

"Stop crying," my mother scolded. "We can solve this, but your father can never know about this. Do you understand?"

"Yes." I knew my father would find a way to blame my pregnancy on my mother. "Dad won't ever find out," I promised.

My mom, the doctor and I scheduled the abortion for the following week. There had been no discussion beyond the brief exchange my mom and I had in the doctor's office. On the drive home, my mother and I hardly spoke. I don't think either of us really knew what to say. At home in my room, I didn't call my friends. I lay in bed, thinking about having an abortion. The nameless, faceless cluster of cells inside me, a potential life…some might say already a life, but not me. I didn't believe it. I had a friend who'd had a baby and I used to joke with her, saying that it wasn't fully human because it seemed oblivious to its surroundings. I'd tell her, "One of these days, God's going to give that baby a soul." I meant it as a joke, but it was a cruel thing to say, especially in light of the fact that my friend's baby later died before turning a year old. After the funeral, she pulled me aside and told me that my comments had actually made her feel better when the baby died, because she hadn't been able to bond with it and my words had made her feel that it wasn't her fault. Now, my stupid remarks came back to me. When does this cluster of cells get a soul? I remembered what my friend had said to me and thought about how convenient it is to be able to rationalize that which makes our choices easier.

After my friend had her baby, she could never go out with us anymore. She rarely had time to just chat or hang out. I could see on her face that the baby was like a tiny vampire, sucking the life out of her. It wasn't even cute. All it did was drink, cry, poop and pee, and you had to hold its neck up very gingerly or you could break it. As far as I could see, it had pretty much ruined my friend's life. She'd had to quit school, and her once lively, playful eyes were now dull and tired.

Back in Hollywood, Nickey had somehow managed to get arrested for jaywalking on his way back from the laundromat. Because he didn't have any identification in his pockets at the time and he looked unkempt, the police had hauled him in for vagrancy and forced him to spend the night in jail for the minor infraction. I felt bad about having to give him more bad news after his night in jail, but I had to. Although I was confident that Nickey would agree with my decision to have an abortion, I didn't want him to know I had made the decision without him. So I simply told him I was pregnant and waited to hear his reaction.

"I can't marry you," he said, to my complete surprise. I had no intention of marrying anyone. The fact that Nickey thought I was telling him of my pregnancy because I wanted him to marry me caused my anger to flare and instead of telling him he didn't have to worry about marrying me, I picked a fight with him.

"Oh, am I not good enough for you?" I asked bitterly.

"It's not that…" he tried to say something, but I don't think he could have said anything that would have made things better. I had shed my skin, every nerve was exposed and every attempt to touch me hurt. The discussion deteriorated and pretty soon we were pointing out each other's flaws and talking about how incompatible we were, both of us saying mean, hurtful things in a futile attempt to protect ourselves. We were a couple of angry children, calling each other names. We broke up that night. It would be the first of many breakups. It was just too much for us — the idea of being pregnant and having an abortion, the feeling of being trapped, it was all creeping up around us.

I was irrational and angry, angry at myself for not being more careful, angry at nature for not making Nickey get pregnant instead of me, angry at *Cosmo* for making me think I was sexually liberated before I was sexually responsible. Beyond that, I was just plain scared. I knew it would be painful. I could imagine sharp objects being inserted into my vagina and it made my eyes water just to think of it, but I wouldn't let myself cry anymore because I was even angry at myself for being scared.

Only my mom kept me grounded.

THE ABORTION

Dark eyes loomed over me, holding my gaze as I lay helpless on the operating table. "Count backwards from 10, slowly," a voice instructed. I did as I was told.

"10, 9, 8…" The world and all its troubles vanished.

I awoke to an intense yet dull throbbing pain and the sight of my mother, sitting on a chair beside me. "You're fine," she told me softly, holding my hand. "You're just going to be sore for a little while." She pulled out a can of Seven-Up that she'd stowed in her purse, her bag of tricks. "Are you thirsty?" she asked, holding the can up to me.

"No," I replied. She put the can away. I brought my knees up to my chest and started to ball up like a fetus, trying to find a position that would relieve the pain, but the pain followed me.

It wasn't the worst pain I'd known.

I'd had my appendix out the year before, and that time I'd awakened in the operating room. A bright overhead light was being pulled away by a latex gloved hand while simultaneously, a sword was thrust into my abdomen. I screamed until the pain killers were injected into my body and my breathing began to grow steady. Two men came in and lifted me from the operating table onto a gurney, except they didn't lift me — they placed the gurney next to the table and tried to slide me across, pulling my stitches as they did so. I screamed again, involuntarily spitting out a stream of curses. The men showed no mercy now; I'd angered them and they continued to move me around, each minor shift pulling the fresh wound. I felt the blade thrust into my abdomen again and again. I spat invectives and curses all the way to my recovery room. Every metal door divider on the ground caused pain as the gurney jumped over it; crossing the bumpy terrain between the smooth hospital floor and the inside of the elevator was torture and once on the elevator I knew I'd have to get off, so I could expect more. I screamed and cursed until another blissful needle came to my rescue. Later, when I spoke to some of my friends and family who were waiting to see me, they laughingly told me that they could hear me cursing all the way in the waiting room.

By comparison, today's hospital visit was just uncomfortable. "I'm just having very bad cramps," I told myself. My mother was there, holding my hand. She was all comfort and love, no reprimands, no guilt.

A nurse walked in. "How are you feeling?" she smiled at me. It was strange, she was happy. This was not a life and death situation, this was commonplace for her and she could smile about it.

"I'm in pain," I replied, sitting up, all tucked in like a ball.

"The doctor has prescribed some pain medicine for you," she told me, then she looked at my mother. "You should fill those right away because as the anesthetic wears off, her soreness will get worse." The nurse looked at me again. "You still look a little groggy to me."

I nodded.

"Why don't you go drop off the prescription and I'll have her ready to go when you come back."

I dozed off and on for a little longer as the nurse puttered in and out of the room and eventually woke me. "Can you stand?" She helped me out of the bed and handed me my clothes. "Do you need help getting dressed?"

"No," I replied, so she pulled the curtain and let me dress. Before long my mom was back, ready to drive me home. It was only three blocks from my house to the hospital. The whole day had gone by so quickly. I'd gone into the hospital early in the morning, shortly after my father had left for work. I had been a scared little animal then, following my mother, letting her do all the talking. Now it was evening and my father would be back home soon. My mom put me in bed and covered me up, gave me my medicine and cup of hot *yerba buena* tea.

"I'm going to tell your father you have bad cramps."

I nodded. It was true, I did have bad cramps, but I felt happy and relieved that my mother loved me so well and that I was no longer pregnant.

WHAT A WEIRDO!

Once the baby crisis was over, Nickey and I apologized to each other, made up, and life went on as usual, until one afternoon when the phone rang at my mother's house. It was Nickey on the other end, telling me he had just passed an audition for a new band. He'd been looking around for something new ever since parting ways with Kim Fowley and his latest creation, Venus and The Razorblades.

The move to Hollywood from San Pedro was designed to facilitate that search. Musicians all over L.A.'s far-flung suburbs knew that Hollywood was the place where both touring bands and cutting-edge local acts could be seen and possibly discovered. I could hear Nickey's smile over the phone. He was in a great mood and said he had a surprise for me.

"What is it?" I asked.

"You'll see," he replied cryptically.

I drove out to Hollywood later that afternoon and as he walked up to meet me, I had to do a double take. I found myself staring incredulously at the guy whose long, beautiful locks had once reminded me of Peter Frampton's. His hair was chopped off in a haircut that reminded me of the self-styled creations I used to give myself in the girl's bathroom at Sacred Heart of Mary. I thought it looked awful, but he was so happy and excited that I didn't want to spoil his mood. I decided to keep my harsh hair critique to myself as he babbled about his new music project.

The band was the reason he'd cut his hair, he told me. They had made it a condition of playing with them. That made me a little angry, because Nickey was a talented drummer and I didn't see why he had to put up with this. I was surprised he'd acquiesced. Nickey didn't like preconditions either, but it seemed that Nickey wanted to be in this band badly enough to let these fashion bullies dictate what kind of hairstyle he could have. In fact, Nickey, who had once been quite meticulous about grooming his golden ringlets, had already stopped at the drugstore to buy some hair gel to help him put the right touches on his punky cut.

He was completely energized and seemed positively giddy when he talked about his new band. "We're called the Weirdos. You're going to like this band. They have a look that doesn't go with long hair," he added, justifying their ultimatum. "But that's not all, we have to dress in these wild outfits," he explained. He excitedly tried to paint a picture of the band for me with his words, but I was having trouble imagining it. All I heard was "art school." The other members of the band went to some art school that I'd never heard of called CalArts. I pictured a bunch of guys with paint-stained smocks, berets, paintbrushes and goatees.

A few days later, Nickey and I paid a visit to the thrift store to buy Weirdo clothes. Nickey's selections were brightly colored pants and shirts with stark, bold prints. He was great at picking clothes and wasn't above pairing little boys' shirts or women's blouses with his trademark crotch-embracing pants. I wanted to show my support by wearing my

Nickey Beat with punk cut

own Weirdo-inspired outfit to his upcoming show, but without having seen the band before, I had no idea what to expect or what to pick for myself. I decided to stick to a cautious black plastic jacket (a poor girl's patent leather), fishnet stockings, a miniskirt and some gray suede fur-lined ankle boots.

Back at the tiny apartment on Santa Monica Boulevard, I watched nervously as Nickey put together different outfits. A picture was slowly starting to materialize in my mind. I was certain that the Weirdos were going to be a circus- or carnival-inspired band. It was a scary thought. I hoped Nickey knew what he was doing and that he wouldn't be sporting a red rubber nose onstage.

THE ORPHEUM SHOW

April 16, 1977, is the day that forever changed the way I thought of music. Nickey had been practicing with the Weirdos and Patricia Rainone, and I had driven out early because we'd never been to the Orpheum Theater and didn't want to get lost. As we waited outside, we noticed a small, giddy group with two brown shopping bags full of groceries. They were talking loudly and smiled at us, so we said hello. They introduced themselves as the Germs and said they were the opening band for tonight's show. As they talked, they pulled out snack boxes from the paper bags. Some of the crackers and squirt-cheese went into mouths, but some was just being crushed and played with.

"These are our props," their lead singer, Bobby Pyn, explained. I didn't think too much about it. They were all laughing and goofing around, so I thought he might be joking and that they were in fact just snacks to keep the band going. The guitarist kept telling us his name was Guy Tar. He pronounced the name with a French accent, so it sounded like *Gee-tahr*, and Bobby Pyn was constantly spouting off jokes. Here are a couple of his best ones — which I remember well because I repeated them for weeks after I heard them:

> *Question: Did you hear about the guy who got his left side cut off?*
> *Answer: He's all right now.*
> *Question: Did you hear about the guy that got his right side cut off?*
> *Answer: He's lucky to have what's left!*

Clearly, Bobby Pyn had a silly side.

Patricia and I hung out outside with the Germs for a few minutes before going in to get our seats. People filed into the small theater quickly, and the show promptly got underway.

The Germs went on first. I was excited for them because I knew it was their first show, and I didn't believe what they'd said about not knowing how to play; well…I didn't believe them until they started playing. Suddenly, the drummer, Donna Rhia, started banging on the drums with all the skill and enthusiasm of a toddler behind a drum set. Lorna Doom couldn't stop giggling but gamely tried to play along, alternately looking at Donna and Guy Tar for cues. Guy Tar, who later told me his "real" name was Pat Smear, played a noisy guitar with plenty of feedback. He swung his guitar around as he played. He looked at the other members, making eye contact and nodding his head to signal changes; he seemed to be the musical director. At the front of the stage, Bobby Pyn uttered cacophonous sounds and began emptying the market bags of their contents. The most memorable use of these props was when Bobby smeared peanut butter and mayonnaise on himself. I'd noticed earlier that there had been a loaf of bread in the bag and wondered if we'd all be treated to a Bobby sandwich, but I never had a chance to find out, because, just a few minutes into their set, the Germs literally had the plug pulled on them. They had put on a horribly wonderful show. The audience booed, cheered, whistled and clapped.

Next up was a group called the Zeros. These guys looked like a combination between the Ramones and the Sharks from *West Side Story*. They looked cool and sounded pretty much like they looked. Their music was fast, edgy and pop at the same time. The fact that they were Latinos also made an impression on me. It wasn't unusual to see one or two minorities represented in an integrated band, but aside from my trips to Mexico (where all-Latino bands were, of course, the norm) I hadn't seen anything like it on the new music scene. I immediately liked the Zeros and hoped to see them again.

After much anticipation, it was time for the Weirdos to play. Even before they played a single note, the band's appearance as they walked onto the stage put a smile on people's faces. The group was decked out in what looked like an explosion at a paint factory. Wild splashes of colors burst from their clothes. Some of the clothing was just loud, thrift-store reject stuff that no person in their right mind would want, a mishmash of '60s neon brights, but much of it was designed especially for the show by the band members themselves. The lead singer, John Denney, was covered from head to toe in spray-painted pants and shirt, with black and colored electrical tape forming criss-crossing designs in random patterns. His straight brown hair seemed to have been cut by placing a shallow bowl over his head; he wore very short bangs reminiscent of Napoleon or a Roman emperor. The rest of the band wore equally stunning outfits, and the audience grew expectant.

As the band tore into their first song, the audience was collectively swept off their feet in a wave of euphoric sound. The music was loud and aggressive but melodic at the same time. Like the Ramones, the songs were simple and fast but the Weirdos also had an amazingly sick and twisted lead guitarist who took the simple tunes and pinched them until they screeched and made your body want to move in rhythmic spasms. The lead singer was a demented escapee from a lunatic asylum who ambled around the stage, twitching out his repetitive, monosyllabic lyrics. His gaze was utterly detached, he seemed to be singing to hallucinations on the walls. The rhythm section was the heart of this strange organism, pounding and throbbing and pumping adrenaline into the veins of everyone in the building. Now the audience was infected with the madness, too. We screamed in delight after every song, clapping hard until our hands hurt. The energy built with every song until we thought we couldn't possible take anymore. We were smiling and grinning like crazy people: Could this really be happening? Could this band possibly be this amazing?

At the end of the set, the audience was in love. We stood with our hands held up in the air, three fingers forming a W as we chanted in unison: "Weirdos! Weirdos!"

COALESCENCE

It was the best of times, it was the worst of times — in music, that is. It was the age of excessively opulent guitar solos; it was the age of stripped-down, three-chord songs. It was the epoch of record company megastar-making machines; it was the epoch of do-it-yourself recordings and promotion. It was a winter of despair and a spring of hope.

It seemed that after the April Orpheum show there was a sudden change in focus. We had been observing the revolution in progress on the East Coast, enjoying the way in which our punk rock founding fathers and mothers challenged the stale old, self-indulgent rock establishment. Now we could see our own roles in that revolution. The night that Mexicans, Weirdos and teenagers with more courage than musical skill could take the stage and bring the house down was the night we all knew without a doubt that the old, tired, long-haired rock 'n' rollers were about to be ousted, kicked off their gilded thrones; and, incredible as it seemed, it was us — the rabble — who were going to do the kicking.

Patricia and I couldn't stop talking about the show for days after. We were eager to play. We were inspired, not only by the originality of the Weirdos or the musicality of the Zeros but by the sheer spunk of the Germs.

"We can do *that*," I told Patricia, laughing but very serious about actually doing it.

"We can do better than that," Patricia replied. Considering the fact that the Germs had nearly been pulled off the stage with a hook, I hoped we could do better. In spite of the fact that we had been trying unsuccessfully to get a band together for months, her words never sounded truer. If Patricia, with her bandaged, nearly severed finger, believed in us, then so did I. If Bobby Pyn and his band of pranksters could get onstage, so could I. I think many people were inspired that night. It was as if someone had taken a torch to all of our ridiculous fears and self-imposed limitations. Suddenly, we could see that the rules meant nothing, that there were no insurmountable barriers, that everything and anything was possible, that we didn't need managers, and we didn't need to wait to be discovered. All we needed was the guts to try.

By the spring of 1977, a global revolution was underway. The wind had carried it to our western shores, where it allowed us to see that what passed for gold in Los Angeles was often just a shiny surface. Hollywood — the entertainment capital of the world — was Versailles, where a select few could enjoy the bounty and privilege, and those of us with our noses pressed against the windows had been too blind or too stupid to challenge their right to keep us out in the cold. I confess there was a side to each of us that might still secretly (or not so secretly) covet the riches of those privileged artists whose billboards littered Sunset Boulevard, whose inescapable music was pumped out of every elevator and every dentist office in town; but we realized that the new music was powerful, unstoppable and, best of all, ours for the taking.

Although the term *punk rock* had originated in New York City, the revolutionary spirit had reached England, where the term was taking on its own uniquely British definition. One of those British punk bands was the Damned, who had come to Los Angeles to play on a bill with New York's Television at the Whisky. The Damned's appearance was supposed to coincide with that of the Weirdos, Zeros and Germs show at the Orpheum Theater, but, unexpectedly, the Damned had been kicked off the bill and had ended up spectators at the Orpheum. Two days after the Orpheum show, the Damned were added to a Monday night bill at the Starwood, and pretty much everyone who had been at the Orpheum show was at the Damned's Starwood show. There was an electric current in the air, an unseen communication system that alerted everyone who cared about punk that something was happening that should not be missed. A scene was starting to coalesce.

The lead singer of the Damned, Dave Vanian, was a dark, handsome vampire who mesmerized the audience, though occasionally the spell would break and we'd be drawn into the insane world of the bassist, Captain Sensible, whose wild antics seemed slightly incongruous with those of the brooding Vanian. Somehow, the band managed to balance these two larger-than-life personalities. At the end of the night, Captain Sensible was naked, the audience was throwing change up on the stage and the age of L.A. punk was well underway.

GIRLFRIENDS

New faces and names quickly became familiar to me as the Spring of 1977 progressed. It seemed like the same 40 or 50 people in the Hollywood/Los Angeles area who were deeply into the burgeoning punk scene kept running into each other at parties and shows, and we became an extended family of sorts. Around this time, I met Belinda Carlisle, aka Dottie Danger. She told me she was the Germs' original drummer, which struck me as funny because I knew I'd seen the Germs' first show and a girl named Becky, aka Donna Rhia, had played drums.

Belinda wore short, sassy hair that looked more ice-skater than rocker-girl. She favored leggings that showed off her shapely, well-toned legs, and an over-sized, off-the-shoulder, ripped T-shirt, which was perhaps a modest attempt to disguise her sexy curves. The look was completed with dangerously high heels that made my 5-inch stilettos feel dowdy by comparison.

Belinda explained that she had been part of the band during the conceptual stage, and that illness had kept her from actually playing with them at the Orpheum show. I had the same feeling upon meeting Belinda that I'd had when I met Trudie Arguelles; these two girls were so warm, open and friendly that

Belinda Carlisle and me.
Photo by Jenny Lens

they drew people to them, seemingly without effort.

One afternoon, Belinda and I were hanging out on Sunset. We'd been to Licorice Pizza and Tower Records, and then we'd gone back to a nearby apartment. I don't remember who the apartment belonged to, but it wasn't too far from Tower Records. I remember thinking the apartment was really nice because it was so well situated to the Sunset Strip and had a lovely swimming pool surrounded by palm trees that reminded me of every cliché Hollywood postcard image I'd ever seen. Coming from a poor section of East L.A., I have to admit I might as well have been one of the Clampetts on *The Beverly*

Hillbillies. I'd never known anyone who had a cement pond in their own yard, even if it was a shared one.

Belinda asked me to help her pick an outfit for her date that night, and I did. We were both in high spirits when the phone rang. I could see from Belinda's expression that it was unpleasant news. She stood up and walked into another room. After a few minutes, she was back. Her date was going to be late. I was about to leave, but she asked me to stay and hang out until her date arrived, so I did. Belinda got dressed while we chatted, laughed and played records. After some time had passed, Belinda began touching up her makeup; an expectant feeling hung in the air, but we tried to ignore it and distract ourselves until it became clear that her date was running later than either of us expected.

"Let's go," Belinda finally said. "Let's get out of here. I'm not going to wait anymore." Her tone was angry, but there was also a note of sadness in her voice.

"Don't worry, he'll show up," I said reassuringly, but I could see that it was late.

"We don't need him. Let's go to the Rainbow. Do you want to go with me? You can be my date," she said. I liked the idea of being Belinda's date, so I agreed to go, even though I hadn't planned on staying out that late.

"Sure, I'll be your date. I already have a boyfriend, but you can be my girlfriend."

I think the thing that saved the evening was that we really did behave like girlfriends. Our mood changed as we wobbled up Sunset Boulevard in high heels, leaning on each other for support, our arms linked. We opened doors for each other, held hands, pecked each other on the lips, put our arms around each other and made each other feel special and beautiful. There was nothing more to it than that. It helped Belinda get her mind off her aborted date, and since I already thought of myself as bisexual, having Belinda be my girlfriend for the night was sort of like acting out a fantasy. My bisexual experiences would go beyond this innocent escapade, but not with Belinda.

After that night, we playfully referred to each other as "my girlfriend," but we never told people the details, and we always let them draw their own conclusions.

THE REVOLUTION WILL NOT BE TELEVISED

Even though the punk revolution was underway, I was still enrolled in classes and working a day job. I was already spending all my weekends in Hollywood, but now I often went to weekday shows and parties and then dragged myself to school or work first thing the next morning. I had never been part of any in-group, but with Nickey in the band of the moment, there was always somewhere exciting to go, people to see and things to do.

The L.A. punk scene was in its infancy, but already we all knew each other. It was a small group of people, about the same size as my graduating class in high school, and we were around one another constantly. We went to each other's shows, worked on each other's projects and inspired and supported each other. Sometimes we fought, too, but not that often.

I was going out all the time, but I couldn't help feeling that I was missing out on some of the fun because I lived so far away and frequently had to leave while the parties were still in full swing. I became fast phone-friends with Belinda, Bobby, Pearl Harbor, Jade and Zandra, DW and Natasha. These people, along with Nickey, were my lifeline to what was going on while I was at work. I couldn't go to every party or even every show — although I tried! — but whenever anything happened, it was immediately on the wire.

Patricia was also working a regular day job, behind the Revlon beauty counter at The Broadway, a department store in the Whittier Quad, a large mall at the time. She worked all week and did Irish dancing on the weekends. She was quite good at it, too. She had medals and ribbons to show for it. I loved when she'd show me one of her dances. She'd stand up super-straight — from the waist up, you could have balanced a book on her head; everything was going on below the waist. She kicked up her heels like nobody's business. It almost made me wish I'd learned *folklórico*, just so I'd have something to show her, too.

Because Patricia lived in Whittier and we spent a lot of time there, she and I also became good friends with Al, X-8, Steve Schumacher and Pooch from a new punk zine called *Flipside*, whose headquarters were in Whittier. We used to frequent a record store called Lovell's, in uptown Whittier, that had a pretty good record selection and friendly prices. We were all fairly young, and many of us still lived at home with our parents. One person who lived with his mother and was a regular chatterbox on the phone was Bobby Pyn. I remember having many conversations with him in the very early Germs days, before he changed his stage name to Darby Crash.

I was still enjoying my love affair with philosophy. I had taken an introductory class the previous fall at East L.A. College and had followed it up with more classes with the same teacher — Mr. Sims, whom I secretly had a crush on. As it turned out, both Bobby Pyn and I loved the subject. I had picked up my first philosophy books at a used bookstore in Whittier which had a cozy little section called Plato's Cave. Bobby was very focused on existentialist philosophy, and I strongly disagreed with certain schools of existentialism, so it was an endless source of fodder for arguments between us, the sort of intellectually stimulating arguments that young philosophers and budding rhetoricians live for.

It seemed to me that the kind of existentialism that Bobby championed sort of let people off the hook as far as moral responsibilities were concerned, since, according to Bobby, morality was entirely subjective. It appeared that what Bobby was saying was that if you could rationalize it, you could do it. We'd throw the most ridiculous examples imaginable at each other, such as, "What if a deaf, dumb and blind person was raised by wolves in the wilderness? Would they understand morality?" We were infants, batting at big concepts that hung like mobiles over our cribs without having the experience or wisdom to know any better. Conversations about morality versus rationality, determinism versus free will and the like often went on for days and even weeks, with the two of us acting like a couple of stubborn dogs, pulling at the same bone and whirling around in circles, kicking up clouds of dust. Neither Bobby nor I took ourselves too seriously, and we could laugh and make fun of each other when we didn't come to the same conclusion; in fact, I think we often took up the opposing argument for sport. Later on, that would change.

It was an exciting and hopeful time, when our ethical and aesthetic values were being demolished and rebuilt, where each one of us in the scene could challenge one another in an attempt to tear down the old icons and virtues. At the beginning, most of us were optimistic and wanted to build something new and better, but the nihilistic impulse to destroy was like a dark undercurrent that would eventually rise to the surface.

ISLAND OF MISFIT TOYS

Being part of a rapidly expanding but very tightly knit family, I sometimes imagined that we were alone in the universe. I suppose some people feel that way in high school or in college, when they first meet a group of friends with whom they feel they can really be themselves, a group who understands them and whom they in turn understand. This was a type of kinship that had been missing for most of my life, a sense of community that I had never known, feeling as I always had (and still often do) like a misfit, a weirdo, an outcast. As I write this today, it is easier to see that at some point in my life between being the fat loser in grade school and the Elton John–obsessed, glitter-damaged freakazoid in high school, I bought into this assessment of myself as *different*. I know that people might not always hold this view of me, but to this day I still go into situations where I'm meeting new people feeling fully prepared, guarded and expectant of the eventual moment when they figure out that I AM NOT NORMAL.

Handmade flyer for a Weirdos concert

That summer of 1977, we misfits, weirdos and outcasts established ourselves as a force to be reckoned with. The Whisky a Go Go, the Starwood, the Orpheum Theater, Larchmont Hall and Myron's Ballroom all opened their doors wide to welcome punk. The clubs made money because we all went to everybody's shows and promoted them as only young kids with boundless energy can do. We helped post flyers in record stores, or we'd go up and down Sunset, sticking flyers on windshields. Our very presence on the street brought attention to the music because we looked so different that tourists would often stop to take our pictures and end up talking to us about why we dressed as we did and what our music was about. Our home-sewn skinny-legged jeans, self-bleached hair stained with food coloring or drugstore dye, thrift-store finds combined with decoratively torn, slashed or painted clothing, made us a visual feast for out-of-towners and jaded locals alike, especially when you contrasted our look with the wide-legged polyester jumpsuits that were all the rage, the Farrah Fawcett haircuts and neatly blow-dried hairdos. We stood out, and the growing interest and attention we got helped our numbers swell.

In addition to our own growing scene, there was a punk community forming in San Francisco. The Nuns were one of S.F.'s first exports. They played the Whisky and the Starwood in early '77. The Nuns were more new wave than punk. Their sound was eclectic: they had elements of pop, punk and dark, almost goth-infused cabaret, done with a sense of humor. The only thing I loved more than watching a young, lean Alejandro Escovedo play guitar onstage was watching and listening to Jennifer Miro.

Jennifer Miro was the epitome of cool. She was positively regal. She looked like an Icelandic princess decked out in Jackie O hand-me-downs. I remember her singing in a slow, deep, rich, velvety voice: "*I'm lazy, so lazy, I'm too lazy to fall in love. It's such a bother, I'd much rather stay home and watch TV. It doesn't matter anyway, in San Francisco all the boys are gay...*" Those are the words I remember singing along with her anyway; I may have some lyrics wrong, but that's never stopped me from singing along. Another thing that I remember about Jennifer Miro is that she was big onstage. I don't mean fat, I mean tall and a magnet for the spotlight. The other Nuns often wore black, and Jennifer, with her long, platinum-blonde hair and porcelain skin, just reflected the light. Jeff and Detrick were good singers, too, and each had his own style. I guess that's precisely why their sound was so eclectic.

Some of the L.A. bands also began playing in San Francisco. The Dils, a band originally formed in Carlsbad, California, about an hour and a half south of L.A. proper, were one of the first of the L.A. punk bands to play the Mabuhay that summer. Like the Zeros, who were from Chula Vista, these bands played so often in Los Angeles that they were widely considered L.A. bands, despite the distance between L.A. and their true home bases. The Mabuhay Gardens was a Filipino restaurant located in San Francisco's North Beach district which also featured live music. The promoter was a man named Dirk Dirksen, who loved to heckle the bands as part of his shtick each time he introduced an act. Despite Dirk's obnoxious attitude, he championed punk bands, and it was because of him that so many L.A. bands were able to play San Francisco almost as often as they played at home.

The island of misfit toys that had been the very early L.A. punk scene could now be seen for what it truly was: a group of islands dotting the western coastline.

TUPPERWARES AND SCREAMERS

The Screamers played their first show at the end of May that year, but they had been building a buzz well before that. Tomata Du Plenty and Tommy Gear were transplants from Seattle, where they'd been co-conspirators in a popular avant-garde band called the Tupperwares. Tomata was an interesting-looking guy. His slight build combined with a sharp, angular face managed to make him look hard and frail at the same time. There was also a strange quality to his voice; the pitch was slightly high and the tone was like sandpaper. He talked in a fast, staccato manner that reminded me of the East Side Kids movies I used to watch on TV. Like the fictional East Side Kids (New York street-gang boys whose tough exteriors protected sweet inner cores), Tomata was one of the sweetest men you'd ever want to meet, and the hard, abrasive voice was usually uttering kind, funny, tender words.

Tomata was the first Screamer I met. I ran into him at a party, but like so many of the parties that I attended during that time, I have little idea who the host or hostess was. The same night I met Tomata, I also met the flashy, tough-looking Cherie the Penguin and her tan, buffed-out faithful companion, Tony the Tiger. I don't know if the three of them were there together, but they were standing together when I walked up. Tomata was the first of the group to greet me. He was a little older than some of the other punks. Perhaps noticing that I was still sort of fresh-faced, he asked me where I'd gone to school. When I told him I'd gone to a small Catholic school called Sacred Heart Of Mary in Montebello, he surprised me by having heard of it, telling me that he used to live in Montebello. His accent was East Side Manhattan, not L.A. Eastside. We struck up a conversation about — of all things — roller-skating. Tomata told me that he had also lived in Pico Rivera and used to go skating at the Rollerdrome. I had only known Tomata for a few minutes when we were both reminiscing like old friends about the pro-style inclined roller rink at the Rollerdrome, watching the T-Birds on television, the Garmar Theater and our favorite hangouts in Pico Rivera and Montebello. I couldn't believe that this odd duck could have survived on the Eastside but indeed he had.

I soon met the rest of the Screamers. Tommy Gear was a handsome, quiet, almost stern-looking man with what I thought were movie-star good looks. He seemed aloof and only nodded when he greeted me instead of actually using words. Despite his cool demeanor, I found Tommy Gear the most attractive member of the Screamers, which should have tipped me off right away, but I didn't figure out that he was gay for a good six months. The remaining members — KK Barrett and David Brown — I gradually got to know over time. I don't remember ever being introduced to them, I just remember that at some point we all knew each other.

The Screamers not only had the Tupperwares' history to recommend them, they were four attractive and stylish men who were at the center of everything. They had hosted the Damned when they had been in town the previous spring and were well connected up and down the coast. Their first show was widely anticipated and lived up to everyone's expectations. Tomata danced across the stage like a rooster, his spiky hair standing up like a cock's comb. His mannerisms were jerky, his neck bobbing back and forth, making his head move in a clucking motion. His vocals were gruff and syncopated; in some cases, true to the band's name, actual screaming provided the best mode of delivery. It wasn't the type of singing where delivering a melody mattered, yet there was melody to Tomata's style; it just wasn't sustained, but rather composed of short, dynamic acoustic bursts.

The group broke with rock-band tradition in its instrumentation, too. There were no guitarists in the Screamers: synthesizers, electric piano and drums provided the stark backdrop for Tomata and Tommy's commanding vocals. A forbidding mood was created, accented by the band's dress and demeanor, which could be imagined as a scene from a marriage of *Metropolis* and *Brave New World*, a futuristic experiment gone terribly wrong yet somehow beautiful to contemplate.

A WAR ON MANY FRONTS

The fumes were suffocating us inside Nickey's tiny apartment on Santa Monica Boulevard. We crawled out of the window onto a neighboring rooftop to continue our spray-painting, but the wind blew the toxic mist back in our faces. We coughed away, undeterred as we continued to work feverishly on our art projects, periodically climbing out of the tiny apartment's kitchen through the open window to gulp lungfuls of smoggy L.A. air. The projects were outfits for an upcoming Weirdos concert. Layers of spray paint and household paint formed abstract patterns on pants, shirts, skirts, even shoes.

By early summer of 1977, the Weirdos, the Dils, Zeros, Germs, Mumps, Backstage Pass and many others were playing frequently all over town. The

Me, modeling a freshly spraypainted miniskirt I made for a Weirdos show.

Weirdos had immediately built a following, and each show felt like an event. Nickey and I treated them as such and invested as much time in creating outfits and accessories as practicing music. Each show brought with it an opportunity to reinvent ourselves, to push our creativity a little further, until slowly the outfits, the music, the aesthetic was so much a part of who we were that we weren't just dressing up for shows. The clothes had turned into a second skin, and the music had become a heartbeat. Punk was changing us from the outside in.

What had started as a music scene was turning into a cultural revolution, a revolution that I regarded as deeply personal. Wanting to tear down the music of the bloated past had led us to a point where we had to challenge not only our musical choices but choices about everyday activities, from what we consumed to what we produced, from what we believed to what we found improbable, each reassessment promising to bring with it new insight, begging for change...Or maybe I'd just inhaled too much spray-paint making those Weirdos clothes, because, at the time, it felt like punk was the catalyst for something big.

Aside from preparing for shows by creating outfits, whole afternoons could be squandered making fliers for shows. Scraps of paper, old magazines (I especially loved using *National Geographic*), ransom-note-style letters cut out from newspapers, crayons, markers and glue were usually all we needed to entertain ourselves. It wasn't unusual for each band on the bill to make their own fliers for the same show. Often, the artist made his or her band appear to be the headliner, so if you just picked up a flier and didn't know what was going on, you might think the band you wanted to see was going on last, only to find when you got to the venue that they'd already played. Some early flier creators found making punk fliers an entertaining way to unwind from a day job; others who started as flier-makers found their calling and went on to become full-time artists, like Gary Panter and Mark Vallen.

Although some of the music press had noticed what was going on in L.A., most eyes were still on New York, and, around this same time, some of the British bands were starting to attract US media attention and release records. Los Angeles needed to produce and consume its own press. A phenomenon that supported the scene was the seemingly overnight emergence of fanzines. Of these, the granddaddy was *Bomp*—a fanzine started by Greg

A proof sheet from an early Weirdos photo shoot. The band's do-it-yourself aesthetic was a perfect match for us.

Shaw in 1970, when *Generation X, Lobotomy* and *Flipside* were all still in their respective incubators. Although *Bomp* added punk to their regular offerings, they seemed to favor pop and new wave music over some of the more raw or abrasive punk music. The newer zines focused on a smaller, newer cluster of bands, and not just on the bands but on all the people who were part of this tiny community. In this early stage, everyone felt like a rock star, and everyone could feel secure that his/her contribution was fairly received. It seemed to me that the early L.A. scene was unconsciously egalitarian. The bands, musicians, artists, press and everyone involved in the punk scene provided an accurate sampling of L.A.'s misfit population. We may have looked weird and even hard on the outside, but most of the people involved in the early scene were open to new ideas, friendly and cooperative.

SAN FRANCISCO

The cold night breeze nipped at my bare legs as we hurriedly tried to jump on a passing trolley. The conductor shook his head to indicate his disapproval of our suitcases. "You're not supposed to bring those up," he admonished. Belinda and I gave him our best pleading looks, and he reluctantly waved us on. The high-heeled slip-on sandals I was wearing were not built for this kind of speed, and the overstuffed suitcase I was carrying made my gait awkward and clumsy. I had never been to San Francisco and, thanks to the many a Rice-A-Roni commercials I'd seen over the years, I imagined that the old trolley cars were the principal method of transportation. Now here I was, hanging off the side of a trolley, trying not to lose my suitcase or my balance, enduring the dirty looks from the rest of the passengers, thinking that the people in the Rice-A-Roni commercials looked much happier than I felt.

Earlier that afternoon, Belinda and I had been talking on the telephone, bemoaning the fact that we had missed a chance to ride with the Weirdos up to San Francisco. They were playing two nights at the Mabuhay Gardens, which had become a regular home away from home for L.A. punk bands. "Let's go anyway!" I offered on a whim. I was laughing but only half joking.

"We could fly out," Belinda countered. Neither of us had much money, but in those days a ticket from L.A. to S.F. was not that expensive, and we were both working, so we could splurge. "How long will it take you to pack?"

We made a few phone calls to check on airfare and flights, and we agreed to meet at the airport a few hours later. I don't know what we were thinking. We both packed like we were going on a cruise around the world instead of the two-day mini field trip that it was. I used the same full-size suitcase I'd taken with me to Europe the previous summer, and it was just as stuffed. Belinda was on the same wavelength. We both arrived at the airport in high heels and skimpy L.A. summer clothes, carrying bulky luggage.

We bought our tickets and then sat down to wait for our flight, chattering incessantly about all the things we wanted to do in San Francisco. There were just a couple of little problems that never occurred to us: The airfare had eaten up most of our money, and we didn't know how to get to where we wanted to go. It had been such an impetuous decision that we'd had no time to get a tour book or ask friends for tips on getting around. We just got on the plane and expected things to work out.

Once we got to San Francisco and collected our luggage, we decided to take a bus into the city, because we didn't want to squander the little money we had left on a taxi. We looked out the windows, still happy and clueless about the fact that we were lost the moment we stepped off the plane. We got off at a busy intersection that seemed to be in the center of town. We had been told before that San Francisco was much easier to get around than Los Angeles, and we had faith that if we just asked around, someone would be able to point us in the direction of the Mabuhay.

The Mabuhay was on Broadway, and though the club was not popular enough to be readily known by hotel concierges or friendly folks at tourist kiosks, Broadway was a big street. A helpful citizen told us we could take a trolley through Chinatown and we'd be near it. That was exactly what we were doing, but now the passengers and the conductor were becoming irritated with our cumbersome bags, and we were feeling the urge to get off the trolley soon.

We got off in Chinatown and started walking. Soon we were looking in the windows of the inviting shops, but we were both cold and miserable by now and only stopped to ask for directions. At least we were on the right track. The merchant we spoke to pointed us in the direction of Broadway and told us to keep walking. Our feet ached, and somehow we had passed from Chinatown into Little Italy without realizing that we had missed Broadway. It was getting quite late now; we were certain the show must have already started.

We walked a long, long way before a kind stranger told us we'd passed Broadway, and we figured out that we had to turn around and go back. Remembering that we'd only had a complimentary bag of airplane peanuts for dinner, I suggested that we stop at a small bistro that sold pizza by the slice. We stopped and kicked our shoes off under the table, resting our tired feet while we waited for our slices. After dinner we felt ready to look for Broadway again.

Walking up to Broadway, we wondered how we'd ever missed it. There were lights everywhere and men standing outside the strip joints that dotted the street, barkers calling out to passing men, inviting them to come in and see a topless show or strip show. We were still looking for a punk club when, to our great relief, we saw a guy with a short-cropped haircut wearing a black leather jacket. It was Brittley Black of the band Crime.

In those days, if you were a punk and you saw another punk it was as though you were part of a secret brotherhood. I had never met Brittley before, but I walked right up to him and told him we were looking for the Mabuhay Gardens. "We're trying to make it to the Weirdos show," I explained. He looked at us with pity in his eyes.

"The show's over, the club's closed," he informed us. With no way of reaching friends and very little money in our pockets we were truly stranded.

LET THE GAMES BEGIN

I couldn't believe what I was hearing. After everything we'd been through to get to the show, we'd managed to miss it. Worse, we were stranded. Belinda and I had been counting on staying with Nickey or some of our other L.A. friends who had driven out for the show, but everyone had gone elsewhere. Brittley walked with us to a hotel a few blocks away in Chinatown called the Sam Wong, where visiting punk bands often stayed while playing the Mabuhay. I walked up to the desk and asked if Nickey or Jeffrey was registered, but he wasn't. I tried the other band members' names with no luck. Belinda and I didn't have a credit card or enough money to get our own room.

Brittley suggested we go back to the Mabuhay to see if we could find out where the band was staying. The club was locked up, but someone came to the door. He appeared to be Brittley's friend, and upon seeing Brittley he allowed us to come inside. Brittley chivalrously explained our circumstances to his friend at the club, but the friend didn't have a phone number for the Weirdos or any other info about where the band was staying.

"Why don't you leave your suitcases here? We'll go get a drink and some food and figure out what to do," said the friend. Belinda and I had just had a slice of pizza, but the offer of food and drink seemed attractive when compared to the alternative, which was sitting outside the Mabuhay in the cold, trying to figure out what to do, so we accepted. We walked to a parked car. Brittley opened the front door for me and the back door for Belinda. Up until this point, I had thought nothing of accepting help from our two new friends, but a little red flag went up in my mind when the simple act of opening a car door appeared to imply a pairing. I chose to ignore those feelings.

We stopped at a liquor store and the guys got out and bought chips, cupcakes, beer and a bottle of whiskey. Belinda was getting a little nervous. "I hope they don't think we're going to sleep with them," she told me.

"I don't think they think that," I tried to reassure her. Still, Brittley was pouring on the charm and I had to confess that I found him attractive. Privately, I began to wonder how the evening would turn out.

We drove to Brittley's house. A man was seated in the living room when we walked in; Brittley introduced us to his father. His dad didn't look very happy to see us, but he was cordial enough, welcomed us and asked Brittley to keep it down. Brittley ushered us to his room where he turned on the stereo and then left the room, telling us that he was going to get glasses and ice. We opened up the beer while we waited for him, but he was gone a long time and Belinda fell asleep on the carpet. Brittley came in with some ice and glasses.

"Good news," he said smiling at me. "My dad says you can spend the night, he just wants us to be quiet." He had been pleading our case all this time. He turned the music down again until it was just a soft soundtrack in the background, then he opened the whiskey and we drank it as we talked and joked. At first it was a small party atmosphere, but before long we were just talking to each other and eventually his friend probably started feeling like a third wheel and fell asleep. It was just me and Brittley now. I could see where all this was going. He came closer to me and kissed me.

Me and Nickey Beat.

"I have a boyfriend," I said. It was too little too late, but I was trying to show some restraint. Ignoring my words, he kissed me again and I kissed him back. I cheated on Nickey that night. I think I felt entitled to cheat because he had cheated on me on a previous trip to San Francisco with a girl named Jean Caffeine. He had come out with the band, and I'd later found out that he had slept with her. I'd been upset, of course, but I thought I had gotten over it after he apologized to me and promised to be faithful. I didn't hold it against the girl; I'd never met her and didn't expect any fidelity from her; for all I knew she might not even know about me. I held Nickey accountable, but even when I claimed to have forgiven him, I made a little mental scorecard, and from that day on I pulled it out whenever I was tempted to cheat. Now we're even, I thought to myself, laying in Brittley's arms that night…Now we're even.

We were so stupid then. Neither of us knew enough about relationships to understand that beyond a certain point, apologies and working things out are no longer an option. We would both continue to cheat, break up and make up, a cycle which would erode our romance but which really sparked our sex life.

We were bad to each other not because we didn't care about each other but because we were young and made our mistakes on each other. The next night after the Weirdos played, I confessed my infidelity. I had selfish motives for confessing. I just couldn't stand the burden of lying to Nickey. I didn't regret anything, because I felt I could justify my actions. Nickey blew a gasket when I told him. I offered to get another ride home, assuming that he would break up with me, but I think Nickey was keeping his own scorecard, and, after a few tense hours, we sat down and talked things over, and he forgave me. He held me tight, and I promised to be true, just as he had done. Our game playing had begun.

FRUITS OF THE RECYCLER

"It says it right there in the ad: FEMALE musicians wanted. What's wrong with these guys?!" I was exasperated. For weeks we'd been trying to find a drummer and rhythm guitarist for our band by putting ads in the *Recycler*, a free ad weekly publication widely used by Angelenos before the birth of Craigslist. We'd had success early on, finding a few female musicians in our incarnation as Masque Era, but now that Patricia and I really wanted a punk band, our search was coming up empty. For some strange reason, men kept responding to our ads. The latest guy, named Geza X, seemed to have all the same musical interests as us. He was sweet on the phone and really wanted to be in a band with girls, but Patricia and I were having trouble letting go of the original plan. Geza X was persistent and talked us into jamming with him and a drummer he knew named Joe Nanini.

Patricia's finger was still not fully healed, but she could play with a pick, and we had abandoned all hope of resurrecting Masque Era, instead focusing on Patricia's brilliant new plan. She had told me a story about going out joyriding with some of our friends. They were all bored and decided to put paper bags on their heads. They'd torn out eyes, nose and mouth holes, effectively constructing makeshift masks out of the bags. As they drove along the streets wearing these paper-bag masks, they'd slow down for approaching pedestrians and shout out to them. Patricia laughed as she retold the story of people's extreme reactions to them. She said people either burst out laughing or ran away in fear. As she was telling me this, she suddenly tossed an outrageous proposal at me: What if we wore bags on our heads when our band played? It sounded like a great idea, and we were excited and focused again.

Marlene's new home life was cutting into our original plan, and though we remained friends, she apologetically bowed out of the band. It happened that Patricia's school friend, Janet Koontz, played guitar. Patricia immediately drafted her for the Bags, and pretty soon the three of us were practicing in Patricia's garage. We started writing songs together. It's hard to say whose songs were worse. Janet wrote a song called "Fantasexing," Patricia and I collaborated on "Bag Bondage" and "Survive," humming parts to Janet when our limited musical knowledge got in the way of communicating an idea. We didn't know what we were doing, but we weren't about to let that stop us.

It was the idea of playing with bags on our heads that really appealed to Geza X. Geza was quite a salesman. He talked us into the audition. Patricia,

Janet and I went to his house in Hollywood and played in the living room. We knew after the first attempt at "Bag Bondage" that Geza and Joe made us sound good, so we would probably have to allow them to force their way into the band.

Joe was quiet and gentlemanly and immediately likeable. I didn't know what to make of Geza. Near the end of the audition, I asked him if I could use the bathroom. He offered to show me where it was, speaking to me in the same sweet, soft-spoken voice he had used on the telephone. Along the way he joked that he might not be able to find it because he hardly ever used the bathroom. He confided in me that he didn't poop anymore. I immediately scoffed at this but he insisted. "I don't eat regular food," he told me. "I only drink herbal teas and juices, so I don't ever poop anymore."

He was fucking with me...or was he? For the rest of the night, the thought of Geza never having another bowel movement kept creeping back into my head; no matter how I tried to suppress it and assure myself that it was bullshit, there was a nagging doubt. My mind wouldn't let it go. Could you get all your nutrients through juices? And, if so, would you really not have another bowel movement? I was still thinking about it on the drive home, when Patricia interrupted me.

"So what do you think, Alice?" Patricia asked.

"About what?" I replied.

"About what? About Geza and Joe!" Patricia and Janet had already said they liked them, and I thought it wasn't even worth discussing. It seemed obvious to me that they should be in the band, but I was still nervous about Geza. The guy was funny and nice, but even by my standards he was a little quirky. He was a weirdo to a weirdo, and he didn't eat food and didn't poop. Could I trust someone who didn't poop? What if all the shit was building up inside of him, ready to explode?

"Yes, I think they sounded good," I replied, somewhat distractedly.

"What are you thinking about?" Patricia asked me later that night. When I told her, she laughed at me. "You're too gullible! He was just messing with you." I felt stupid and decided on the spot I couldn't trust that Geza X, no matter how sweet he sounded.

THE CART BEFORE THE HORSE

In the spirit of the times, we hadn't been practicing for more than a couple of weeks when we put the cart before the horse. Our few rehearsals had taken place in the living rooms of Geza and Joe, and it was at one of these rehearsals that we met Joe's roommate or perhaps, girlfriend. I don't quite remember the details of their relationship, other than the fact that they lived in the same place. Her name was Charlotte Caffey, and she was a fellow musician who played bass in a band called the Eyes.

Charlotte was a shy girl with straight, long blonde hair, who smiled a lot but always seemed to be holding something back, like she was humoring Joe and Geza. I remember seeing her in a nursing-style uniform and assumed she was a nurse, but she never stuck around long enough for me to ask her. I don't know if it was the sound of our practicing that drove her out in such a hurry, or if she really was late for work every time the band was rehearsing, but our meetings were always warm, friendly and brief. During one of the short conversations we had as the Bags' members set up our equipment and Charlotte gathered up her keys and purse, she casually mentioned something about a rehearsal place opening up off of Hollywood Boulevard and Cherokee. The remark went unnoticed by me and Patricia; we were quite content to continue practicing in living rooms for free, but Geza seemed especially interested and suggested that our band check out this new place at the first opportunity.

It was near the end of August 1977, and a few days later — following the Screamers' example — we decided it was time to start promoting our band, even if we were nowhere near ready to play. We decided to do a combined photo session and bag parade to spark curiosity about the band. The first time we decorated our bags was so exciting. Each person infused their personality onto the brown paper using markers, crayons and assorted trinkets. I was so involved with my own cat-eyed bag mask that I didn't notice what Geza was up to. After 20 years of working as a schoolteacher, I can see now that Geza was like a little kid, deliberately trying to push Mommy's buttons. Geza had created the most offensive mask I could imagine. It had one long, horizontal slit opened up for the eyes to peek through, with no mouth or nose apertures. Bloody tampons dangled from the corners of the bag like graduation tassels. The effect was utterly disturbing. Patricia and Janet didn't like it either, but I think I was the most bothered by it. I tried to protest, but my objections went unheard, and, in the name of tolerance, I decided to let it go.

The rest of Geza's outfit was equally disgusting. He decided to accessorize his foil-covered legs with a pair of urine-stained white men's briefs. Joe Nanini wasn't much more tasteful. He went the minimalist route, wearing only a jockstrap stuffed with a brown-skinned, black-haired doll whose head peeked out from the top like a long-haired erection. By comparison, Janet in a purple miniskirt and Patricia in a black vinyl dress were dressed much more tastefully.

Having suffered some permanent damage in the aesthetic department after fashioning many a Weirdos show outfit, I sported a red T-shirt with buttons and toys pinned on it, black dance pants, bright green textured stockings with the reinforced crotch seams showing at my inner thighs, and my trusty Frederick's of Hollywood slip-on heels. Decked out in our gloriously tacky band ensembles, we gleefully placed the bags over our heads and marched out into the street. We turned the neighbors' heads from the moment we walked out the door, but the evening was just getting started.

The Bags' first public appearance: Joe Nanini in his doll-head jockstrap, Patricia in black miniskirt, Geza X in urine-stained men's briefs, aluminum foil and bloody-tampon mask, Alice in green tights and Janet in purple with shades.

BAG PARADE

Six of us piled into my parents' old Ford Falcon: the Bags, which consisted of Geza X, Joe Nanini, me, Patricia Rainone and Janet Koontz, plus Nickey Beat, who was coming along to drive and document the event with my tiny 110 Instamatic camera. Having Nickey drive was my idea; I didn't dare drive the car with a bag on my head for fear of being pulled over, and I didn't want to step out of character once I'd turned into a Bag. We were packed tightly into the car with our windows rolled down and our limbs sticking out. We drove down the street, calling out to people, waving, singing and generally trying in any and all ways possible to call attention to ourselves. Even if we had never formed a band and just dressed up and drove around all evening, flaunting our bag masks, the night would still have been a memorable, fun-filled event for me.

We drove out to Sunset Boulevard, and, because we were all penniless, we parked high up on a hill then had to hang onto trees and fences on our way down to keep from tumbling over on our stiletto heels. The bags over our heads afforded us a partially obscured view that didn't make balancing on the steep incline any easier, but we made it down relatively unscathed. We walked to Tower Records, where we split up and walked up and down the aisles. At first, pretending that this was the most normal thing in the world, I browsed the record selection. I always wear a bag on my head to go shopping, don't you? Picking up an album, I pretended to read the back, all the while scanning the periphery from the eye holes in my bag, watching people as they stared and pointed in shock and amusement.

A young Asian couple at the magazine stand boldly asked to take their picture with me. It was a wordless exchange: They held up the camera and smiled, and I found myself posing with my arms around strangers. I felt like a movie star. *Autograph, anyone?* Buoyed by our success at Tower Records, we walked up to Licorice Pizza for more of the same, and then onto the Whisky, where people were lined up from the ticket booth to the corner of the street, waiting for a show. Here, the crowd tried in vain to be cool and not react to us. We posed for pictures outside the club and ignored them, until curiosity got the better of the jaded rockers and they sent scouts to come over and ask what we were doing.

"We're in a band!" we replied, urging them to keep an eye out for us. "You can say you heard of the Bags first!" Geza shouted. As the scouts reported back to their groups, even those rockers who considered themselves too cool to care leaned over to find out who we were and what we were up to. Some smirked or shook their heads.

"Hey Bags, I'll keep an eye out for you!" one of the guys in the crowd shouted as we walked away. Maybe they were making fun of us, I really couldn't tell and I really didn't care. This party was just getting started, and I was having more fun than any of those people in line.

We got back in the car and headed back toward Hollywood Boulevard, a seedier part of town in those years. As we were driving, Geza suddenly had a brilliant idea, or so he said. "Stop here!" he told Nickey. "Let's take pictures at the police station!"

Patricia thought it was a bad idea. "You can't walk into a police station looking like that," she warned him. Then Joe and Nickey chimed in with their support.

"Yeah, let's do it!" Nickey parked the car. "We'll just ask them if we can take a couple of pictures. We'll tell them about the band." The boys were all in agreement now. I don't know if Janet went into the station with them, but I stayed in the car with Patricia. We watched them cross the street and wondered how far they'd get. Less than two minutes later they came sprinting back across

Bags hitchhiking in Hollywood, 1977

the boulevard, out of breath and laughing. The police officers had taken one look at Joe Nanini in his baby-doll jockstrap outfit and were outraged.

"Get out of here before I arrest you!" cried the officer at the front desk. Geza's attempts to explain the band's concept had fallen on deaf ears. "I said get out of here — RIGHT NOW!" the outraged police officer repeated as other cops started to assemble. Taking to their heels, the boys wisely decided to beat a hasty retreat and raced each other back to the Falcon. Nickey sped us away.

We had one more location to hit before calling it a night. The Hollywood Walk of Fame was such an iconic symbol of old-school Hollywood glamour that we wanted the Bags to have a chance to strut their stuff on it. We walked up and down the Boulevard, talking to strangers and posing for pictures. We walked in a line one behind the other, skipped, played follow-the-leader, and generally just acted like little kids. Our fabulous night of playing dress-up behind a mask was drawing to a close. We got back in the Falcon and started to drive away when chance made us take a turn from Hollywood Boulevard onto Cherokee.

WELCOME TO THE MASQUE

"I heard there's a rehearsal place around here," said Geza, looking around the street as we turned the corner.

"Yeah," Nickey replied, "they had a show at a place down in the alley. I think the guy runs it as a rehearsal studio, too." Before the rest of us knew what was happening, we had pulled over and Geza and Nickey were getting out of the car. After parading all over town in our bag masks and high heels, all Patricia and I wanted to do was to sit in the car and kick off our shoes, but there was no stopping Nickey and Geza. It seemed that once they settled on an idea, they had to see it through, so the rest of us waited in the car while the two boys went down the alley to investigate the new venue. After waiting for half an hour, we were starting to get annoyed; they had been gone a long time, and we were all tired and ready to start the long journey back to East L.A. and Whittier when Geza returned, whooping like a little kid with a brand-new skateboard.

"I got us a gig! We got our first gig!" I was momentarily swept up in the excitement.

"We do? Really?" I asked, offering a wide-eyed smile.

"When is it? Who are we playing with?" asked the levelheaded Patricia, refusing to be carried away before she knew the details.

"It's OUR gig, we're headlining!" We couldn't believe our ears. Geza had got us our first show, and the best spot on the bill. Now we were all cheering, until Patricia repeated her question.

"When is it?"

"We have just over a week. We're playing September 10th." That's when the cheering stopped.

"TEN DAYS?!" Doubt chilled our enthusiasm like a bucket of cold water thrown on a hopeful suitor. "Do you think we're ready?" "I don't know if we're ready…" "We only know five songs!" Everyone was talking at once, expressing our worries, but Geza remained convinced that we'd be ready and valiantly tried to talk us into it. Once again, Joe and Nickey sided with him.

"Come ooonnn," Geza whined in his sweetest, most boyish voice. It didn't occur to me until now that it was the women who were most concerned about being ready to play. I don't know if we were being cautious or if we were insecure, but in the end, the memory of the Germs playing at the Orpheum came back to me.

"We can do it!" I exclaimed. I wasn't really sure we could, but saying it aloud made it feel a little bit truer.

After trying to squeeze as much into the next few rehearsals as possible, I think we were able to come up with an eight-song set list. The day of the show, I spent all afternoon linking tiny gold safety pins together to make a sort of chain-mail vest. The task was excruciatingly slow and laborious, and I quit before completing it, so I had a partial safety-pin chain-mail vest. After the vest, I worked on my bag for a while before Patricia and Janet arrived and we made our way out to Hollywood.

We already knew the entrance to the Masque was in the alley, but we had no idea what to expect once we crossed the threshold. As you walked in from the alley, there was a long concrete stairway on the right leading down to the basement. The basement had a cavernous feel. The so-called club was nothing more than a bomb shelter, only it appeared not to have withstood the force of the explosion. Things seemed to be falling apart. There was a small room in the middle of this concrete labyrinth; it couldn't have been more than 10 feet square. That was the office, as well as the owner's bedroom. It held a twin bed, a lamp, a small desk-table and not much else.

The owner was a young Scottish guy named Brendan Mullen, whose thick accent and rapid speech made me ask him to repeat himself more than once. He was sweet and smiled timidly as he welcomed us into the office. Putting an arm out as though he was ushering us into a palace, he said "Welcome to the Masque!" His hospitality was charming, but we were eager to get out of the cramped little office.

The night of the show, we readied for our sound check. At the far end of the largest room was a small stage, not more than a foot off the ground. We set up and started testing the amps and microphones. It was all echoes and feedback, but having never performed with a real band before, I had no idea what to expect. I didn't think it sounded that bad, but Geza was an audiophile; he tried his best to adjust everything to make us sound better, and we didn't stop checking until he was satisfied. My vocals were quiet and I was having trouble hearing myself over the booming bass and shrieking guitars. Geza reassured me: "It'll sound a little different when people come in." I was happy about that, because I wanted to wow them with my vocal skills. Maybe it didn't sound good now, but Geza said it would change, and it would: It was about to get much worse.

INTRODUCING THE BAGS

I have said before that I don't remember much of the Bags' first show, and that is true in some respects. Some details of the show are fuzzy in my memory. I may not remember the songs in our set list, but I do recall in vivid detail the emotional roller coaster that was the Bags' first show.

Back at Garfield High School, I had waited in line for my turn at cheerleading tryouts. That time, the overwhelming sense of anxious excitement had been my downfall. Now the feelings are back. Once again, there is the familiar nervousness that manifests itself as nausea and an urge to urinate. Visiting the filthy bathroom at the Masque requires a hover-and-balance maneuver designed to keep my body from making any contact with the toilet or walls. Any woman who frequents dives in high heels and practices this particular exercise can boast some nice, firm quads and glutes from it, though failing to master the technique can mean toppling over face-first onto the wet, debris-covered floor. Luckily, I was good at it and didn't fall over.

Between trips to the bathroom, people come up to talk to me. They are friends, people I've met at parties or at other shows. I say hello and answer questions when asked, but I can't remember who I've talked to or what I've said. I feel like I'm on autopilot, a regular robot. It seems to me that the people standing in front of me are just pictures on a TV screen; I can see the show playing and can even interact with them, but I'm a long way off. The words to our songs fill my head, the incessant inner monologue voicing all my concerns.

"What's the next line? Oh, yeah, I know it…"

I can hear the band on before us. The songs are pop-y. Charlotte's onstage, the band is good, but the sound is muddy. My stomach turns again, but I walk it off.

As Charlotte's band packs up their gear, I see Bobby Pyn. He has a bottle in a small brown paper bag and offers me some. I take a large gulp. The alcohol burns all the way down to my chest, and the jolt makes me snap back into the present. For a few minutes, the drinking fuels me and I feel energetic. I start bouncing in place like a boxer about to step into the ring.

"Have some more," Bobby says, holding the paper bag up to my lips. I'm happy to oblige. "You're NOT going to wear that bag on your head," he tells me.

"Oh yes I am," I reply.

"No!" he says stubbornly. He's a bit on the intoxicated side.

"That's the plan," I tell him, laughing at him now that I realize he's really drunk. He puts his arm around my neck and holds the bottle up to my lips again, and I take another swig before walking toward the stage.

Standing behind the amps, we take off our coats and jackets specifically worn to cover up our stage clothes before the performance. We don't want anyone to associate our clothing with us. The members of the Bags are meant to remain anonymous, our identities hidden by our paper-bag masks with the only clues to who we are coming from the decorations on our masks and the clothes we're wearing. There isn't very much privacy near the stage and no designated backstage area, so our anonymity is compromised. But for the band members, putting on the bags and shedding our street clothes is almost more of a ritual which takes us from our ordinary state of being into an extraordinary one.

I don't know who introduced us. I don't know what they said, but suddenly I'm onstage and the minute I have the mic in my hand, I become the boxer again, jogging and jumping in place. There's too much energy in my body; I can't control it. The songs start. They're fast. I can't hear myself except for a ghost of a voice that seems to come from the back of the room; only it's not a ghost, it's me: That's my voice shrieking, screaming, singing. The bag on my head makes me feel like I am protected, incognito, free to act without restraint. The amps on the stage are too loud, they seem to be shooting out little pitchforks aimed at my feet. I can't keep my feet on the stage, they need to move. I feel like the person in an old Western movie where the gunslinger says menacingly, "I'll teach you to dance," and shoots bullets at his victim's feet. My feet are moving like that now; the amps are the gunslingers. There's no time to think. The lyrics to the songs come automatically, which is good because I can't be expected to focus and concentrate in the middle of this religious experience. The herky-jerky dancing is automatic, too. There is so much electricity coursing through my body that I am truly out of control, but I don't care. I couldn't stop myself now if I wanted and the release is like an exorcism — it feels so good.

Bobby's at the front of the stage. He's not really dancing; it looks more like he's swaying. He comes toward me. He loves me, he wants to hug me, but I'm trying to sing. He comes up to me again and puts his arm around my neck, successfully pulling me off the stage and into the audience, but what I mistake for affection is just an excuse to try to rip the bag off my head. I can feel him trying to rip it. He had threatened to do this when I first told him about the plan to wear bags on our heads. "Not you, you're not wearing a bag on your head," he had told me sternly. "I'll rip it off if you do." Now he is trying to make good on that promise.

I easily break away from his intoxicated hug and jump back on the stage, continuing to screech and writhe, but Bobby is not to be deterred. He's right up front now. With one bold tug he rips the bag open and I explode like a broken pinata. The torn bag is still clinging to my head. My view of the audience now comes from a gash at the side of the bag rather than the eye holes. As I move, the audience comes in and out of my sight line. Mercifully, Bobby grabs at the bag again and tears the rest of it off. I am exposed but not defeated. Our set is coming to an end. The audience is clapping loudly, cheering for us as we finish the last of our eight songs and walk off the stage.

The cheering continues in what appears to be a request for an encore. We don't know anymore songs and decide to play our first song again, figuring that no one will remember it. The band is elated; we play the song twice as fast as the first time. More cheers. The band walks off, but people are still demanding an encore. That is when I utter the sentence that I would never live down. I don't remember saying it, but Geza and Patricia told me I said it, so it must be true.

A member of the audience shouts, "Play another song!" I grab the mic stand and shout back into the microphone: "*Play my body, it's a musical instrument!*" Geza and Patricia would tease me for weeks afterwards. My face still turns red when I remember it.

PUNK IN THE AFTERNOON

In the aftermath of our appearance at the Masque, the club was unexpectedly shut down. Rumors flew that people had been causing problems in the street, that the cops had busted Brendan for not having a proper license, that someone had passed out in the alley…Whatever the real reason, the wonderful new venue was not available to us for the rest of the month.

We had hoped to rehearse at the Masque, but instead we started rehearsing at Wilshire Fine Arts Studios. The name is so deceptive. Not only was it not on Wilshire Boulevard, there was no fine art anywhere on the premises. The place was a large, three-story house located near Western Avenue and Beverly Boulevard, behind a Taco Bell. The house must have been gorgeous in its day, but it had been many, many years since then, and one had to look hard to imagine its former beauty. Now there was torn, dirty carpeting on the floors and chipped paint on the walls. The rooms were large, and there was a single bathroom on each floor. It also had long, narrow staircases that always tortured Patricia and me as we struggled to carry her heavy bass amp up the steep flights.

The studios rented cheaply, and, depending on the size of room, the type of equipment you needed and the time of day you wanted to rehearse (afternoons were the least expensive hours), you could usually get a room for two to three dollars an hour. The owner was a kind, patient man who seemed to have an open mind about all types of music. His name was Winston, but I remember him as Paul, because his appearance reminded me a little of Paul Winfield, in the movie, *Sounder*.

We would become regulars at Wilshire Fine Arts Studios, along with X, the Plimsouls, the Motels, the Alleycats, many other bands and one mysterious individual who played the same guitar riff endlessly for three hours every day. When we inquired about him, we were told that the guitarist was practicing Transcendental Meditation.

Thanks to Michelle Myers (who championed the new music), the Whisky a Go Go started having Sunday afternoon punk shows. Our band's connections with the Weirdos and the Germs paid off, and we were offered the opening spot on a gig toward the end of September. It's a good thing we went on before the Germs, because their shows could get a little messy. Once again, I had to fight off the nerves and excitement. Luckily, the Whisky had a backstage area where you could isolate yourself and mentally prepare for your show. It also helped in protecting the anonymity of the rest of the band members who were still trying to go with our original plan of wearing bags on our heads.

The band was much tighter this time, and the sound was much better, but I still wasn't used to singing over loud amplifiers and wasn't even aware that there were speakers on the stage called monitors that sent the sound back to the musicians so that they could hear what the audience is hearing. Unfortunately, monitors aren't effective if the amps on the stage are too loud or are aimed at you. When the band started playing, I realized that I was losing myself in the performance again. I hadn't noticed the first time we played, but there was an intense anger inside of me that turned even the most trite lyrics into a verbal assault. I felt like a woman possessed, and the ritual of being onstage was my exorcism.

Bobby Pyn was there at the front of the stage, cheering me on and trying to rip the bag off of my head as he had during our first show. This time, the height of the stage made it more difficult for him to get a firm grasp on my bag, but eventually he managed it and ripped it off. I lost a shoe trying to pull myself away from the crowd. I would pay Bobby back by grabbing at his clothes when it was the Germs' turn to play, but I don't think he minded that at all. The Germs were already starting to build a following. Bobby seemed to have people around him all the time. It's not unusual for bands to have fans, but it struck me as something a little different in Bobby's case; he seemed to be collecting people.

After they'd played, we all went back into the audience to watch the Weirdos. They played regularly and had been getting better and better since their first show at the Orpheum. They were constantly writing new songs and adding new creative touches to their stage show. Their fan base was expanding, and their concerts always ended with people screaming for encores. The Sunday Punk in the Afternoon show had been a success, and more would follow.

PEARL BEFORE SWINE

"Alice, I was really scared. They were saying really mean things to me. I thought they were going to hurt me!"

My friend Pearl Harbor was telling me about being picked up by the cops after a concert the night before. The two men in a car had spotted her as she walked out of the Whisky. She had noticed them following her in their car but hadn't turned to look at them head-on, wishing that ignoring them would make them go away. But the two men had not gone away. They continued to follow her at a distance until she was in a less crowded part of the street, then they pulled over. The passenger got out of the car. Pearl was relieved to see that the man was wearing a policeman's uniform. She assumed that he had mistaken her for a streetwalker because of her provocative, skimpy clothes, and although she found the mistake annoying, she knew she had done nothing wrong and figured they had nothing to arrest her for. The policeman frisked her and asked her to get in the back seat of the unmarked squad car. At that point Pearl became alarmed, but she was comforted by the knowledge that the worst thing the two cops would do to her was question and release her. Instead they drove around with her for hours, threatening and terrorizing her.

"They called me a slut. They told me I was ugly and cheap and that they should teach me a lesson," Pearl sobbed. "They wouldn't let me go. I pleaded with them but they wouldn't let me go!" I pictured Pearl in the backseat of the car in her miniskirt and fishnet stockings, scared. I tried to calm her down, but her story worried me. It frightened me to think that a couple of rogue cops were driving around Hollywood, terrorizing punk girls. I dressed every bit as provocatively as Pearl, as did many of my friends. The men had let her go eventually, but Pearl was shaken. She was absolutely certain that they intended to kill her and she didn't know why they had let her go, or, for that matter, why they had picked her up in the first place.

It was the beginning of October 1977, just a few weeks before Pearl's story would take on an even more chilling tone. On October 18th, the nude body of a woman described as a Hollywood prostitute was found raped, strangled to death and dumped near Forest Lawn Cemetery. It was to be the first in a series of abductions, tortures and murders committed by a serial killer who dumped the bodies of his victims in hilly areas of Los Angeles, a habit that would gain him the moniker the Hillside Strangler.

The news broke around Halloween, when a second murder victim was found in Eagle Rock, just northeast of downtown Los Angeles; a week later, another woman was found in nearby Glendale, and pretty soon the evening news was reporting a new victim of the Hillside Strangler on a weekly basis. Women all over Los Angeles were on alert. We made sure to have someone walk us to our cars at night, we locked our car doors and tried to travel in groups whenever possible, but despite our best efforts we were still at risk.

On November 23rd, Jane King was abducted off of Hollywood Boulevard, yet another victim of the Hillside Strangler. Jane's murder struck closer to home. She was a close friend of the Berlin Brats' Rick Wilder and an occasional guest at the Masque. Her murder sent shock waves through the punk community. Brendan hired a security guard to watch the door and help protect the safety of the female patrons. Little did any of us know at the time that one of the killers was a security guard.

Eventually, the police figured out that there was more than one killer. They'd also suspected that the killers were luring women into their cars by posing as police officers. When I heard this on the news, Pearl's story came racing back to me. Had she been in the car with the killers? Over the past few months since her encounter with the cops, Pearl had been going out less and less, until I had stopped seeing her altogether. I had fallen out of touch with her, or perhaps she had decided to stay away for a while. Knowing how hard it had been for her to tell me the story in the first place, I didn't want to call her or bring it up.

The killing spree eventually ended with the arrest of Kenneth Bianchi and Angelo Buono, two cousins who dressed as policemen, abducted, tortured and strangled their victims.

A SOBERING SLAP

Some memories come back like movies, others come back like a punch in the gut.

The sun is going down over the Pacific Ocean, deep blue and purple bruises spreading across the cold evening sky. The sea is restless, waves hurling themselves against the deck's support beams. We're on that deck, me and Nickey.

I've been drinking, perhaps too much, and my tone is loud and accusatory. I will not be mollified by Nickey's words. I wish I could remember the cause of this argument, but all I remember is the storm, a destructive storm washing over me; or maybe I am the storm. I want to tear everything down, drown it in my deluge, wash it clean and wait for the sun to dry up whatever remains. I am submerged in this feeling. Seeing Nickey through my watery eyes, I want him to feel what I feel, but he cannot match my emotion. On the contrary, he is trying his best to sail around the storm rather than face it head on. "You're a coward!" I cry, and even my words come out sounding wet, like I'm drowning in my own anger. I'm flushed with emotion and move within inches of his face, unleashing the storm, wanting him to drown with me. Suddenly, Nickey slaps me.

It's a sobering slap, so effective that I am frozen in place. In a moment of absolute clarity, the storm stops and I fall like Alice — deep, deeper into the rabbit hole. I fall into an abyss so black, so dark that I see myself for the first time. Everything falls away, Nickey falls away into the background. He is not important, the argument is not important. There is nothing, nothing at all except for me and the blackness.

I start to walk away. In the distance I can hear words carried on the wind. Nickey is apologizing, trying to explain, wanting forgiveness, but I can't be around him. It's not about him, it's about me. My stride lengthens as I cross the parking lot while Nickey tries to hold onto me. His fingers don't burn me with their touch, they annoy me, they break my concentration. I turn to face him.

"Don't ever touch me," I hiss in a voice that could turn him to stone. I don't feel sad anymore, I don't feel distraught. I'm not being tossed by a storm, and there is no storm within me; instead there is an icy, steely blackness that is clear and strong and leads to a place I never knew existed. I feel powerful and somehow detached from my body. I feel indestructible. Nickey's voice fades as I get into my car, lock him out and drive away.

I am driving but I feel transformed. I have tapped into something that exists within me but also outside of me. It is a universal dark force or energy, at least that's how it feels at this very moment. I replay the slap in my mind, but now I am seeing through my mother's eyes and, like a good director who doesn't like what she sees, I cut the scene and try the shot again; this time I see myself doing the slapping. Neither Nickey nor I are in this take, instead it is my mother and father. I am my father as I launch the blow, I am my mother as I receive it.

Many years before, I had vowed to myself that I would never be like my mother. I would never allow myself to be victimized. My 6-year-old self is taking control, and she only sees one way to go.

"*You are either a tyrant or a victim...*" little Alicia whispers to me in the darkness. "*...and you will never be a victim.*"

This black hole is oddly comforting. In it, I am capable of anything. I feel sorry for anyone who crosses me when I'm in the abyss, because I don't feel attached to anything except the darkness. I don't care if I get hurt, I don't care if I die, if I lose everything, because I can see that I don't have anything to lose. It's all an illusion, there is only this dark energy, and it will never die. The black hole exists only to consume.

I don't speak to Nickey for a couple of weeks, but I can't stop thinking about the feeling I had that night. It's gone now, and the memory of it drains me like a hangover.

THE AGE OF EXPLORATION

Nickey and I had established a pattern of breaking up and making up that was hard to keep track of. After the sobering slap, we had been apart for a couple of weeks before I decided to forgive him, with the stipulation that if he ever hit me again, I would leave him no matter what, even if he apologized. I'd end up keeping that promise.

"Make sure Nickey walks you to the car," mom told me. I was irritated at being treated like a little kid, but I knew she meant well. This was while the Hillside Strangler was still at the top of every news report. As if we weren't all painfully aware that a serial killer was on the loose in Hollywood, both the Skulls and F-Word had written songs about the Strangler, and Brendan had been told by the cops that they believed the killer frequented punk clubs.

My father tried in vain to keep me home, but his strong-arm tactics never worked; the more he tried to keep me in the house, the faster I ran out the side door, sometimes literally. The day he forbade my going out prompted me to pack some clothes and inform my parents that I was moving in with Nickey. I was gone for a few days before I called home and we came to a peaceful compromise: I would continue to go to school and live at my parents' house, and in return I would be allowed to spend the night at Nickey's on occasion. Protecting my virginity was a lost cause; my dad was just hoping I'd manage to stay in school.

It was odd spending so much time at Nickey's. Sometimes I felt like I was his special guest, other times I felt like we were playing house, except that he never once let me cook a meal for him. I just figured he wanted to treat me like a princess, but he always insisted that I sit and talk to him while he cooked and served the food. All I was allowed to do was eat, which I can't complain about, except for the fact that his favorite thing to cook was beef hearts, and as much as he tried to get me to like them, I never enjoyed them as much as he did.

Spending nights at Nickey's also opened up the door for us to explore other freedoms. After our mutual double-crossings, where we had each cheated on each other, we promised to be true to each other, but our fidelity had its limits. We decided that we were too young to be sexually exclusive, and since we both wanted to try new things, we came up with a solution to please us both: We could include others in our sexual exploits but we had to agree on the who, what, when and where of each situation, an ambitious goal that yielded mixed results. We ended up with friends in our bed, which sometimes worked out well and other times caused awkwardness and mistrust.

Compared to some of our friends, Nickey and I were somewhat less than conventional when it came to sexuality, and we made a lot of mistakes with each other because we were trying to be as sexually free as possible within the framework of a boyfriend-girlfriend relationship. Nickey wanted to live the sexually adventurous lifestyle of a musician, and I had been taught by Helen Gurley Brown to expect that sex could be enjoyed freely whenever and with whomever I chose; to borrow a phrase from the film *Down with Love*, I wanted to be able to enjoy sex *à la carte* — just like a male.

We were pushing the boundaries and limits in every other aspect of our lives, and sex was a big part of who we were as young adults, so it was a valid area for experimentation and exploration, just like philosophy, aesthetics, music and art. Of course, music and paint are much less complicated mediums for expression than the range of human emotions involved in sexual relations, so we ended up with some hurt feelings and messy scenes, but it was all part of the spirit of the time, and part of Nickey's and my development; in particular, I began to adopt a more sexually aggressive persona onstage with the Bags, one that was not traditionally female sex-kittenish or vampish but more like a sexual outlaw.

Imagine spending your entire youth and adolescence being told you're a fat, ugly loser, and one day you wake up to find yourself being courted and treated like a sexually attractive person by members of both sexes. I was like a hungry *huerfanita* turned loose in a panaderia; with so many flavors, varieties and choices available to me, I indulged my healthy appetite for sex free of any moral constraints. Being the lead singer of the Bags also allowed me to express myself onstage in a more forward, untamed way than most female performers up until that time. I was often accused of being too masculine in my performances. It wasn't that I was too sexual; rather it was that I was too aggressive, too violent, too *in your face* for a girl.

It didn't matter, because there was no way I was gonna stand in one place and sing into the microphone, and there was no way in hell I was going to allow the audience to just stand there passively either. You had to move — dance, jump up and down, spazz out, do *something*, or get the fuck out of Dodge. Once the Bags hit the stage and the music started, ego checked out and id took over, channeling my libido, my inner rage, whatever…I was free to be myself with no holds barred. It was the ultimate freedom.

THE MORE, THE MERRIER

By the autumn of 1977, new bands were popping up all the time. Seemingly every week, someone who had been in the audience the week before was now onstage in their own band. The Masque reopened in mid-October with a gig featuring a band called the Controllers. The Controllers weren't really a new band, in fact they had been one of the first bands to rehearse and play at the Masque from its inception, but they had never had a proper coming-out show, so I think of their October 15th show as their debut. Their music was tight, fast and melodic, and some of their songs were almost pop-y which was nicely balanced by the imposing figures of Johnny Stingray and Kidd Spike, who sang up front and played with a ferocity curiously incongruous with their lighthearted lyrics. The band would evolve and get even better over the next several months, with the addition of an old friend of mine named Karla Maddog on drums.

When punk came along, it was just the perfect vehicle to express who I was as an individual. It was something completely new and wide open. Just a couple of years later, that would change, and people would have to fit into preconceived notions of what punk rock was or wasn't; but the early scene had no such limitations, because we were the ones creating and defining it. If you had been at the Masque in 1977, you would have seen very eclectic shows, ranging from the Screamers to Arthur J. and the Goldcups, from Backstage Pass to the Controllers. There was no clearly defined punk sound, no dress code; all you had to do was show up and make your presence known. The movement was one of individuals and individual expression, each of us bringing our heritage and formative experiences with us in an organic and, in my case, unplanned way.

In late October, *Slash* magazine held a benefit concert at Larchmont Hall. A band called X opened that show. I had met John Doe and Billy Zoom before, and I liked them both. I had only one memory of Exene, and it was a bad one. Exene had an obnoxious little friend known as Farrah Fawcett Minor, a nickname she shared with Cheryl Ladd, who had been given the moniker after being selected as Farrah Fawcett Majors's replacement on the hit TV series *Charlie's Angels*. Exene's friend bore no resemblance to Cheryl Ladd; she was a short, dishwater blonde who dressed with no originality and showed up at parties to whisper about others. F. F. Minor was one those women who try to make themselves feel superior by claiming they aren't like ordinary girls, as though all women share an inherent weakness which she had managed to rise above. She was a racist, misogynist anti-Semite, and a wimp. If she had ever had the gumption to look me in the eye while spewing her malice, I would have happily punched her in the face, but she spread her poison in backhanded, cowardly ways that allowed her to avoid standing up for what she said.

I remember one time I was standing in the kitchen at a party when Farrah leaned over and whispered something to Exene about Mexicans. I heard the word *Mexican*, but I didn't hear anything else. She was looking in my direction, so I looked at her and said "What?" She looked away. "Did you say something to me?" I added.

"No, I was talking about something else," she replied. I stared hard at her until I made her uncomfortable enough that she left the kitchen. Years later, when I heard the X song *Los Angeles* (which is written about her) I remember thinking that the line "every Mexican who gave her a lot of shit" was about me.

Unfortunately, my extreme dislike of F. F. Minor had tainted my view of Exene. There's a saying in Spanish: *Dime con quien andas y te dire quien eres*, which means "Tell me who you hang out with and I'll tell you who you are." I realize now that it's not a very good way to judge people, but at the time, I was prejudiced against Exene because of her association with Farrah. My first impression of the band reflected that prejudice; I liked everyone but Exene. That early impression of her would change as I got to know Exene better, and my appreciation of her band would also increase.

There was another band on the bill that night that I hadn't seen before. The Avengers were a San Francisco band featuring a strong lead singer with a powerful stage presence and a unique sense of style. Singer Penelope Houston led the band to instant success. The audience loved them, and it wasn't long before we were all walking around singing their songs. L.A. quickly adopted the Avengers, who I think always felt as much at home in L.A. as in San Francisco.

The Dickies, who also played the Masque that month, were another band that scored an immediate home run with an approach to punk that was completely different from what we'd seen up until then. Some members of the Dickies were friends of the power pop band the Quick, who had in turn been influenced by Sparks, and the Dickies' vocals showed that influence. Their lead singer, Leonard, sang like a bratty little boy, taunting and teasing and inviting the audience to play along. The Dickies were really fun to watch, their songs had lighthearted lyrics, and they weren't afraid to use props onstage.

A couple of weeks after their Masque gig, Nickey and I went to see the Dickies at the Starwood. It was my birthday, and Leonard climbed the top of the stairs leading to the backstage door as he dedicated a song to me called "You Drive Me Ape (You Big Gorilla)." In a Tarzan-inspired move, Leonard tried to jump from the PA scaffolding, in the process breaking one of his ankles and spraining the other. I was watching him attentively since the song was dedicated to me, and I could see that he was really hurt, but the band didn't stop playing. After the show, Leonard was rushed to Cedars-Sinai, and I made Nickey drive us there. I felt somehow responsible and wanted to at least check on his condition, but we never got to see him because we weren't immediate family, and I suppose he was in no mood for visitors anyway. That little happy-birthday dedication would put the Dickies out of circulation for a month, and Leonard would do his next show in a wheelchair.

BOOT AND REBOOT

Before too long, Patricia and I were done with Joe Nanini and Geza X. We didn't seem to be on the same page. Geza in particular had a very different aesthetic, and some of the things he thought funny and clever we found infantile and obnoxious. The final straw came during a fight between Joe and Geza in the back seat of my car, which featured the boys spitting beer on each other and all over the windshield. Since I was driving, Patricia leaned over the seat to break the two apart just as they launched fists at each other, and she ended up getting simultaneously punched by both of them.

"YOU'RE FIRED!" she yelled at them, and that was that. Janet also got the boot — or she may have quit of her own volition; I think she may have had an offer from Kim Fowley to work on another one of his projects, but I can't say for certain. Whatever the exact reasons, the band went through a quick overhaul, but we never stopped booking shows.

Patricia and I put another ad in the *Recycler* seeking female musicians. This time we could boast of having upcoming gigs and we even had a little bit of press in fanzines and in *Slash*. Once again, most of the respondents were male. We auditioned people at Wilshire Fine Arts, booking rehearsal space for one night and allowing each person an hour. At the end of the night, Patricia liked a redheaded, curly-haired rhythm guitarist who looked a whole lot older than us and seemed nervous and itchy during the audition. I didn't like him. Truthfully, he just seemed kind of nerdy to me, and although I had been an uber-nerd growing up, I no longer thought of myself that way, and the last thing I wanted to do was go back to being lumped into the nerd category. Patricia spent the next hour talking me into it, and I finally, grudgingly, agreed to let Craig Lee in the band.

Patricia had swayed me with the argument that Craig had lots of good songs. Where we had struggled to write our eight-song repertoire, Craig seemed to have an endless supply of songs. He'd hand me four or five sheets of lyrics at each rehearsal and ask me, "Do you like any of these?" From there, we'd usually try them out, dump a few and keep only what we liked best. Craig always encouraged me to make any changes I liked and often allowed me to write my own vocal melody, which was a perfect situation for me, because I was all about melody.

I was the product of a school system that had stunted my language development through Structured English Immersion. Whenever I got stumped looking for a word, I tried to express myself using English cognates of Spanish words that I knew, but cognates can be tricky, and my strained translations often led to meaningless or awkward sentences. It eventually dawned on me that my lyrics sucked. Craig, on the other hand was a writer. He had written scripts for TV and had even sold some porn. The more I learned about him, the better I liked him.

We were still drummerless, but my boyfriend Nickey was kind enough to sub for us until we could find a permanent replacement. He was quite good, so we were only too happy to have him on loan from the Weirdos. To celebrate our new configuration, Dawn Wirth offered to take some photos of us at Hollywood Memorial Park (now called Hollywood Forever Cemetery). Nickey wore a mask, so that when we got our new drummer, he or she could claim to have been behind the mask. It was a silly idea, but aside from the fact that my *nalgas* are showing, the pictures were great.

The Bags at Hollywood Forever Cemetery, photo by Dawn Wirth.

The only problem with Craig Lee playing guitar was that he was primarily a rhythm guitarist, which meant we still needed to find a lead guitarist before our upcoming gigs. The *Recycler* once again brought another duo to our doorstep. A guy named Johnny Nation called us. He and his friend Ricky Stix wanted to audition for the band. The two seemed perfect. They were fun, friendly and could play well. We thanked Nickey for filling in and immediately started rehearsing with the new lineup.

It wasn't all that unusual for bands to change members frequently in the early days. As new people entered the scene, they'd often be recruited into existing bands or form new ones of their own. I recall Geza X forming a band called the Jerrys (named for his love of a certain comedian who was adored by the French people). I can't recall seeing them play, but Geza soon popularized the use of the term *Jerry* as a name for anyone who was being annoying or obnoxious while thinking they were funny, as in, "Stop being such a Jerry!"

READY FOR TAKEOFF

My parents seemed to have settled into a comfortable holding pattern, and, for the first time in my life, I witnessed a sort of friendship develop between them. Ever since my father's illness progressed to the point where he could no longer work without my mother's assistance, he seemed to have a newfound respect for her. She, too, seemed more sure of herself, picking up the slack by taking on small construction jobs under my father's tutelage. My dad, who still had his contractor's license, would go out, meet potential employers and bid the job, only accepting jobs that did not entail heavy lifting or that were too physically demanding. Ideally, he would accept small painting or tile-setting jobs that my mother could do with a minimum of assistance. My father would go with my mother to the job site and direct her through the things she didn't know how to do, which worked out well, because my mother was used to my dad's foul temper and was willing to work in a subservient role. In exchange, my father was grateful for my mother's help, which allowed him to feel like he was still the family provider even though it was mom doing the grunt work. He was happy in the role of instructor and foreman, but after a while my mom learned enough from him to be able to complete many jobs without needing him for anything but his contractor's license. When he realized this, he eased up on her, maybe even learned to treat her as an equal... Well, almost as an equal. He never hit her anymore. He wasn't strong enough, and even though he could still spew out cuss words like Linda Blair in *The Exorcist*, the fury in him seemed to have been tempered by age and the realization that he was dependent on my mother for everything.

I suppose for some men this arrangement would be emasculating, but my father was remarkably comfortable with allowing my mom to work and find her self-confidence through her new abilities. It's strange to think that a man who had a history of wife-beating had such a positive reaction to the new, self-sufficient woman my mother had become. He began asking her opinion about work and household finances, and even went to the market with her just as a social outing. Necessity and the demands of survival required him to swallow his pride.

With my parents doing well, I no longer felt like I had to stay around to protect my mother. I knew from an early age that I was the only thing standing between my father and homicide. Even as a little kid, my crying and holding onto my father's leg while he tried to beat my mom seemed to have some emotional if not physical pull on him. I had been in the role of defender for so long that whenever I contemplated leaving home, I always felt guilty about abandoning my mother and perhaps jeopardizing her safety, but the time had come for me to move out and move on with my own life. I had no idea I would be taking my parents' emotional baggage along for the ride as if it were a suitcase packed with my favorite dresses.

Nickey had regular paying gigs with the Weirdos and he was giving drum lessons to earn extra money, but my paltry savings had dwindled and I needed cash, so I decided to apply for a job at a Jack LaLanne Gym in Montebello. I don't know what prompted me to think I would be a good fitness instructor. I wasn't athletic, and although I was relatively thin at the time, I was out of shape; but I wasn't going to be deterred by feeling that I was unqualified. I wore high heels and a tight, slimming dress to the interview and was hired on the spot, not for my figure but for my bilingual skills. Nobody asked me how many sit ups I could do or how much I could bench press. They'd train me, the interviewer said while handing me a little bright orange smock that would be my uniform. All I had to supply was the black leotard and tights that would go underneath.

Training included learning the proper use of the equipment and a brief lesson on the major muscle groups, their functions and how to best stretch and develop each of them with or without weights. We were taught about nutrition and healthy diets. We were given guidelines for developing our own class routines. Each instructor would be responsible for at least one floor class and one in-pool class each day, in addition to training individuals and giving tours to new members.

In those days, you typically had men's gyms and women's gyms, sort of the way PE is segregated by gender in schools. At Jack LaLanne's, the week was split so that there were three men's days and three women's days. Sunday was split into a.m./p.m., so that men and women had equal opportunity to workout. We worked 10-hour shifts on the full days — 12 hours total, with an hour for lunch and an hour for dinner — and a five-hour shift on Sundays. I liked it, because although the gym closed at 10 p.m., there was still time to change and go out afterward, and I wouldn't have to work the next day.

Training was fun, but I especially liked teaching. I found leading the exercise classes invigorating because I could motivate people and get them to push themselves a little further each time. Women looked to me for answers, they confided in me, they trusted me. I felt proud of them when they achieved the results they wanted and commiserated with them when they slipped into old habits. In many ways, the gym classes were like being onstage. I was the focal point, but each person was there because they wanted to be, they brought their own expectations and energy into the mix, and we fueled each other. I was a good instructor, just the right blend of dominatrix and kindergarten teacher. It was my first experience with leading a class, something I really enjoyed and would return to later in life.

Meanwhile, Nickey had heard of an apartment building just a block away from the Masque, on Cherokee Avenue, where the rent was cheap, the apartments were large and the property manager welcomed punks. We made plans to investigate this place called the Canterbury as soon as possible.

MOVING INTO A NEW PLACE

Walking up the path through the slightly overgrown gardens leading to the main entrance of the Canterbury Apartments, I immediately noticed that this apartment building was much nicer than the place where Nickey was currently living. There was a dusty old fountain on the path which hadn't seen water in many years, save for the few dirty puddles of rain that gathered around its uneven base, but one could see it was a lovely touch that had once welcomed a more refined breed of tenant.

Beyond the fountain, the path opened to a circular courtyard, and beyond that to the main foyer. The stone floor clicked under the stiletto heels I wore in an effort to look my best, which meant I looked like a 1950s call girl with a too-tight thrift-store dress, pointy, red patent-leather spike-heel shoes and a matching red patent-leather purse. Nickey had also tried to present himself in the best possible light by not wearing out-and-out Weirdos clothes.

Nickey hadn't had a regular job the entire time I'd known him. He made his money from gigs, and since the Weirdos had become increasingly popular, he'd also started giving drum lessons. He did well in both jobs, but I was the one with the regular paycheck. My gig at Jack LaLanne's afforded me the hours I liked, a small amount of cash, and I was in better shape just for doing my job.

We knocked on the manager's door and were greeted warmly by a slightly heavyset black man who asked us to call him Reverend. "That's what everyone calls me — The Reverend." I felt more comfortable knowing that I was dealing with a religious leader, which was the only context in which I'd ever heard the term *Reverend* used — this being before the notoriety of the Reverend Jim Jones. I figured the guy would, at the very least, be responsible and trustworthy.

The Reverend was a good-natured, amicable man. As soon as he saw my meager but regular paycheck stubs, he offered to show us a nice "roomy apartment with a great view." He closed the office and escorted us to a small elevator with an old-fashioned expandable gate. The three of us got inside and the little box began moaning and groaning like a constipated old man trying to pass a large bowel movement. We barely made it to the top level, the fourth floor. (Several months later, the ancient elevator cable actually snapped, and the elevator remained inoperative, with the cable hanging outside of the cage.) Our apartment was right by the fire escape, and if you went out and stood on it you did have a lovely view of Hollywood Boulevard on one side and the Hollywood

Hills on the other. My faith in the Reverend was confirmed. The apartment felt spacious: The living room alone was about twice the size of Nickey's bachelor pad on Santa Monica Boulevard. The kitchen had room for a breakfast table, and it was equipped with a large refrigerator, a stove and lots of freshly painted white cupboards. The bathroom wasn't exceptional, just a pedestal sink, tub and shower, but it didn't have any of the rust and urine stains we'd had to deal with before, and the tiny white hexagonal tiles on the floor shined as though freshly scrubbed. A double-size Murphy bed was hidden discreetly on a side wall. It was a dream come true!

Punks who grew up in different areas of L.A. might have seen the Canterbury as a dangerous, run-down, vermin-infested flophouse, but you have to remember that I had grown up in a dangerous, run-down, vermin-infested neighborhood, so it's all a matter of perspective. For some, this was truly slumming, but it wasn't too far from where I'd grown up. Nickey and I couldn't wait to move in, and the Reverend was as accommodating and hospitable as a southern belle. We quickly signed on the dotted line and started packing.

My parents weren't thrilled about the move, trying every argument and trick to get me to stay at home, but my mind was made up. Once they figured out that they weren't going to win this particular argument, they reluctantly gave me their blessing.

"Take the Falcon," my dad insisted. "It's yours." I knew my parents considered the old Ford Falcon my car, even though it had been my mother's car. My father never drove anymore, so they kept the Dodge Dart that had belonged to my dad and gave me the Falcon as a parting gift.

My mother gave me an additional gift — a Sears credit card. "For emergencies only." My parents had no other credit cards. My mother was a devoted Sears customer, because, she said, they always stood by what they sold. All of our large purchases except for the family cars came from Sears. I think more than anything, the credit card symbolized my mother's trust in me. I only used it on a couple of occasions: once, to buy nuts to eat because I ran out of money and had a few days until payday, and another time to buy an umbrella because I was caught in the rain. Other than that, I kept the card safely tucked away. I wanted my parents to see me as independent, successful and responsible.

PROTECTING HOME TURF

In short order, the Canterbury became L.A. punks' messy little crib. I don't remember the order in which people moved in, but there were at least two or three punk-inhabited apartments on every floor, which made us feel like we owned the place. It also solidified our sense of community, because now we were seeing one another every day. The Masque regulars moved in: Lorna, Belinda, Chloe, Margo, Rod Donahue, Maicol Sinatra, Chase Holiday, Terry Graham and Jane Drano, Connie Clarksville, KK and Trudie, Sheila, Nickey and me...you could walk across the hall in the middle of the night and borrow a cup of rum from a neighbor, and nary a night went by without some kind of impromptu party breaking out in someone's apartment or at the Masque, which was only a block away. Brendan, knowing all of us, never charged any of us to get in — band or no band.

The guys at the friendly nearby liquor store came to know us personally and took us at our word when we claimed to be 21. The Two Guys from Italy charged a dollar for a huge slice of pizza and often gave us extras just for being regulars. Rum and pizza became my favorite breakfast combo. As a friend wrote on an old picture of us at the Canterbury: "...And life once again became a veritable Eden."

The punk scene was now growing exponentially. There were the creative refugees from other scenes, like the van packed full of Phoenix "Cactus Heads" that arrived one night at the Canterbury, disgorging its contents of

Kira Roessler at the Canterbury Apartments, 1978. Photo by Alice Bag..

Consumers, Feederz, future Germs and Bags after a hot, uncomfortable drive across the desert. Nickey's popular drum lessons brought new friends into our lives: The beautiful, petite and wickedly funny Shannon Wilhelm, the proto–Johnny Depp cool/bad boy Terry Graham and Masque tomboy/heartthrob/future Black Flag bassist Kira Roessler all signed up for lessons with him and were soon regulars at our fourth-floor apartment, as was Larry "Wild Man"

Fischer, who did not sign up for lessons but liked to come by and serenade us all the time.

Not everyone was welcomed. There were outsiders who were destined to remain outsiders, people who just didn't get it. These people were shunned by the early punks because they held onto values from another time or because they tried to destroy what we saw as ours. Musically, the outsiders were slick musicians with new, "punk style" haircuts, who wanted to take the music back to the studio heads (they were too school for cool); and anyone connected to the old music establishment, even marginally connected people like Kim Fowley, who was widely regarded as delusional and self-absorbed by most of us. He may have claimed to be a punk insider, but we considered him a joke. Another type of outsiders were people who thought that a leather jacket meant you could push a woman in high heels off the dance floor, steal someone's guitar or in any way try to destroy what we considered ours. All it took was a look at each other and that person would be literally body-slammed on all sides until they left the dance floor, if not the premises.

I didn't see the early scene as cliquey, but we did recognize that we had something special, and we wanted to protect it. I found myself getting in fights at concerts around this time. Holding my ground near the front of the stage had never been a problem for me. I loved the intense pogoing and euphoria that came from dancing with a sweaty crowd of people caught up in the excitement of the music. Almost always people looked out for each other, helping a fallen comrade get up if they slipped and being careful not to bump each other too hard. Now we were watching for those who were intentionally bumping or kicking maliciously. Sometimes people would try to bully their way to the front of the stage by hitting or pushing; girls were especially vulnerable, because many of us wore high heels, and a hard shove could knock a girl over. When a bully targeted any of my girlfriends, I stepped in. My protective instincts went into high gear and my fists were swinging before I could think about it. The experience was exhilarating and timeless, not unlike sex or any activity in which you are so immersed that time stands still. I always felt satisfied after a fight, like an ancient thirst had been quenched. Protecting home turf may have been the catalyst for a confrontation, but the thrill of a brawl was intrinsically pleasurable for me, and, eventually, I would learn to provide the catalyst if one wasn't readily available.

I guess I was protecting what I saw as my new home and my new family. I don't know if I picked up traditional gang values somewhere along the way or if these were values everyone shared. Maybe I was merely working through some latent childhood issues. I never stopped to think it through, but I do know that I started to get a reputation as a violent girl, as much for my stage antics as for my behavior in the audience.

The rage and aggression that were released onstage were like a leaky faucet that I couldn't completely turn off when the performance was over. Without my being aware of it, the pent-up feelings of anger were constantly dripping and starting to overflow into other areas of my life.

WINTERLAND

Los Angeles held its collective breath for the date of the upcoming Sex Pistols concert, in vain. When it became apparent that the Pistols would not be playing L.A., some of us were a little insulted, but the band had decided not to play any of the large American cities. For some unknown reason, they decided to play smaller cities in the Deep South. I'm not sure what the intention was, unless it was to push themselves closer toward self-destruction, which is exactly what they did.

San Francisco's punk scene was smaller than L.A.'s but it was still larger and more progressive than some of the other cities the Pistols played. Some newspapers later claimed that San Francisco had been chosen because it had the largest and strongest punk scene on the West Coast, and that would be incorrect. San Francisco had a thriving scene and it was and still is one of the coolest cities in the US, but, as Malcolm McLaren later stated, the Pistols avoided the major entertainment capitals of New York and L.A. because he didn't want to risk the band not living up to their hype.

I have to take a minute here to defend L.A. against the prejudice that plagues it. Unfortunately, we have always had to put up with people's assumptions that Los Angeles is entirely populated by superficial, rich beach bums and starving actors. That assumption is incorrect. Los Angeles is one of the most diverse cities in the world, and I am proud to say that our punk scene reflected that diversity. The early accusations and assumptions that people made about the L.A. punks being somehow lightweight or derivative when compared to San Francisco, New York or London would be proven wrong by history, evidenced by the numerous groundbreaking bands and styles that blossomed from our scene.

But I digress. Despite the slight to Los Angeles, we all felt compelled to see the Sex Pistols. Carpools were arranged, those who could afford it booked hotel rooms, those who couldn't afford a room made arrangements to sleep on friends' floors, and pretty much everyone who was part of the L.A. scene packed up to make the eight-hour drive up to San Francisco. Craig Lee wisely arranged a weekend showcase for us and the Germs at the Mabuhay Gardens, so we could at least catch some of the Pistols' overflow and make a bit of money to recover expenses for the trip.

Winterland was packed that night, leading more than one newspaper to marvel at the huge punk scene in San Francisco. In truth, probably half the crowd was from L.A., as well as other smaller cities in California, Oregon and Washington. Somehow, I missed the Nuns, who were on the bill that night, but I managed to see the Avengers, who played a great set. I think the band was well aware that they would be playing for one of the largest audiences of their career. They were well rehearsed and did one of the best shows I'd ever seen them do. The Pistols did not. That's not to say that their show wasn't exciting to watch, I had looked forward to the show and enjoyed the band's set, but the individual members seemed to be struggling. It was almost like watching a couple of friends bicker over dinner. The band's inner turmoil was palpable onstage, and it made me feel like an intruder eavesdropping on a private dispute. After listening to a few songs near the front of the stage, I allowed myself to drift back and ended up walking around the back of the auditorium, talking to friends before the show was over, which was very unlike me. I usually preferred to be up front, wrapped up in the excitement of the crowd and the music, but this show was different. The energy wasn't coming from the stage or the music. I watched Sid Vicious, who seemed to be the most connected to the audience, baiting and engaging them. He was charismatic, but there was a self-destructive air about him that made me uneasy.

Bags and Germs in San Francisco, 1978

The Bags at the Mabuhay with Sid Vicious rolling on the stage. Photo by Ruby Ray

A more private encounter with Sid would happen that weekend, when my friend Hellin showed up at the Bags' Mabuhay show with Sid Vicious in tow. We had already started playing when they walked right up to the front of the stage. It was very exciting for me, because I thought Sid, despite his masochistic streak and in all his wild, out-of-control glory, was coolness personified. Now he was standing in front of the stage watching me. He smiled, the sweet, crooked smirk of an adolescent, bobbing his head in time with the music and draping his wobbly self over Hellin's shoulder. They seemed very snuggly and smitten with each other. I could see them from the corner of my eye now and then, and I was trying to stay focused on my own performance, but the next thing I knew Sid was up on the stage.

He rolled around on the floor in front of the amps like a kitten playing with a ball of yarn, then he got up and came over to me and put his arm around me. I got the distinct feeling he wanted to share the microphone with me and join in the chorus of the song but I knew there was no way Sid could possibly know any of our songs so he just hung onto my neck, still smiling and swaying around the stage with me. He reached for the mic a couple times, but I hung onto it, because as much as I liked Sid, it was a Bags show, not karaoke night. It was very much like having Bobby Pyn onstage with me, except Sid was really having trouble staying vertical. After a few minutes he went down and started rolling around the stage again, in time to the music. I looked at Hellin who looked at me, and an unspoken understanding transpired between us. She helped Sid up and walked him toward the skinny wooden staircase leading up to our dressing room while we finished our set.

After the show, we were greeted by Hellin and Sid, who was barely conscious when we walked in. The playful, adolescent smile had faded and all that was left was the babble of incoherent speech. Hellin stroked his hair tenderly as Sid passed out on a bench in our dressing room. She was his angel of mercy, and she asked if they might stay up there until someone came to pick them up. We were only too happy to try to help, although I think Craig was truly worried that Sid would OD long before anyone could get there. It was kind of sad, seeing my idol all fucked-up, wondering if he was going to be all right. I remembered my old school friend who'd had her stomach pumped after having ingested too much booze and an unknown quantity of pills. I recalled the many times I'd seen kids OD in the nurse's office at Stevenson Junior High. I also recognized a little of myself in Sid. I could certainly get out of control, mostly when I was onstage, but also if I'd been drinking. A little bit of the coolness seemed to fade away, but not much. After all, except for our brief onstage encounter, I didn't know Sid at all.

There was a part of me that chose to ignore the side of Sid that was flawed. I wanted the Sid that I'd created in my imagination, a tough, troublemaking bad boy who challenged the audience with his defiant, unpredictable behavior, not the stumbling, incoherent Sid who had to be helped up the stairs. I chose to focus on my hero's admirable attributes even when I'd seen another side of him. I will always hold a special place in my heart for Sid. I can still see him with his bleeding, scratched-up chest and low-slung bass strap, better suited for knuckle-walkers. A few months later, when Hector from the Zeros would teach me to play bass, I would set my strap so that the bass hung as close to my knees as possible, in tribute to bad-boy bassist Sid Vicious.

TRASH THE TROUB, SAVE THE MASQUE

Upon our return from San Francisco, we discovered that while almost all the Hollywood punks were out of town watching the Sex Pistols implode, the local fire marshal had quietly slipped into the Masque to do a little demolition of his own. The results were disastrous for us. The Masque was cited for violations of several fire safety codes, the most significant one being insufficient exits. Brendan was required to immediately shut the club down until he could correct the violations and pass inspection. I'm not sure how Brendan intended to create more exits, but he was determined to keep the Masque open, whatever it took. Most club owners would have tucked tail and run for the hills, but, to Brendan's everlasting credit, he was a punk fan first and a club owner second, so he chose to stand and fight. Local bands, fans, sympathetic press and small independent record companies all came together to volunteer their services.

A huge two-day Save the Masque benefit concert was organized at a rented auditorium in the Elks Lodge (now the Park Plaza Hotel, near MacArthur Park). The Bags were slated to play, but just days after returning from San Francisco we'd fired our two latest members, one of whom we'd diagnosed as having kleptomaniacal tendencies. The pair came as a package deal, so we opted to dismiss them both. I think they were actually happy to go, as Ricky and Johnny hadn't particularly enjoyed the trip to S.F. with us, and the feeling was mutual. With shows booked for the next two months, we had to move quickly to fill their spots. The ads went up in the *Recycler*, but we couldn't find satisfactory replacements for our two expelled members. My boyfriend, Nickey — who was becoming the go-to guy for bands needing a drummer — once again came to our rescue. Even before the Elks Lodge Benefit we had a show booked at the Troubadour, a venue that didn't usually book punk bands, and Nickey already knew our songs from having filled in before.

The Troubadour show would come to be remembered as the first clash between the old-guard established clubs and a new breed of clubgoers. The "Troub," famous for launching the careers of such soft rockers as the Byrds, Jackson Browne and the Eagles, had hitherto resisted the impulse to book punk bands, but someone in the box office was watching their competitor, the Whisky a Go Go, filling the house with bands like the Weirdos and the Germs and decided to take a chance on the Bags. It was a decision they'd live to regret.

Just a few days before our show, a chance encounter at a deli with one of the Troubadour's favorite sons, Tom Waits, ensured that the night would live in infamy. But for this story to make sense, I have to take you back a few days.

There's a popular all-night Jewish deli in L.A. called Canter's. One night, the deli was crowded and a group of us were standing around waiting for a table. Canter's had an amazing bakery with well-stocked display cases that always captured my attention. On this particular evening, we stood around gawking at the goodies when my friend Lauren saw someone she knew. She introduced us and we made polite conversation, then we left her talking to him because our table was ready. I thought nothing of the incident, because I didn't know her friend was a celebrity. When Lauren rejoined us, she told us her friend, Tom Waits, had asked about my band and was interested in seeing us, so she had invited him to our upcoming show at the Troubadour.

We left the restaurant, but the topic of Tom Waits came up again later, and some of our group knew who he was. "He really liked you," laughed Lauren, "but he didn't like Nickey. He wanted to know why you were hanging out with 'that dipshit.'" When Nickey heard this, he was furious, but it seemed that by the date of our gig at the Troubadour, it had pretty much been forgotten.

The Troubadour had long rows of tables and chairs lined up to the front of the stage, for audiences to sit and listen to music as they sipped their drinks. There was a two-drink minimum strictly enforced to sit at these tables, but the punks who showed up to watch the Bags that night had a solution to that problem: They just dispatched with the furniture by chucking it into a big pile in the middle of the room.

Just before our set began, someone came backstage to tell us that Tom Waits was in the audience and sitting right up front. Nickey's temper flared as he recalled the insult from the other night, and he walked out onstage ahead of the band to call out Waits in public for "talking shit" about him behind his back.

"Tom Waits is a famous asshole. And he called me a dipshit. He called me a dipshit behind my back. Well, I'm standing right in front of you. You're a fucking bloody cunt!" Nickey taunted him as the audience roared its approval. Tom just sat at a small table near the front of the stage with his entourage and didn't immediately respond, but the gauntlet had been thrown.

The Bags launched into our chaotic set, which saw the club get ripped apart by our fans, like the scene in *Night of The Living Dead* when the zombies storm the farmhouse. I saw Dim Wanker, the bassist from F-Word, hanging from one of the club's rafters. Shit was flying everywhere, all hell broke loose;

I saw a chair sail through the air, missing Tom Waits's head by mere inches. He didn't flinch and stayed cool while bedlam erupted all around him, but his posse was taking notes.

Following our set, the audience was hustled out of the club. Normally, bands are encouraged to break down and load out their gear immediately after the set, but something was different this time. The Troubadour's staff was telling us to wait until the audience had left, and they wouldn't let us remove any of our equipment from the club. That's when we knew something was wrong, and we started looking for a way out. All the exits were blocked by burly bouncers and the doors were barred. We weren't going anywhere until the damage to the club and Tom Waits's reputation had been resolved.

Patricia and I were pushed out of the way while the bouncers and Tom's entourage made a circle around Nickey in the entryway to the club. Remembering the gang jump-ins I'd witnessed in school, I immediately thought they were all going to gang up on him and kick the shit out of him. I started to panic. Patricia and I began pushing frantically at the doors, trying to let some of the punks back in. Through a crack in one of the doors, I caught a glimpse of Hellin's face, and I yelled to her, "*Help us! They won't let us out!*" She and several others put their hands in and tried to pry open the doors before the bouncers pushed them shut again and locked them securely. We could hear our friends outside the club, yelling and pounding on the doors now that they knew we were in trouble.

It turned out that the circle was just to keep others from interfering while Tom and Nickey fought it out. It wasn't very long before they were both rolling around on the ground and the fight was declared a draw. The circle broke up and Tom's entourage whisked him away, at which point Patricia and I were allowed to scoop up Nickey, who couldn't stop talking about the fight.

"I had both of my hands in his mouth and I was going to rip it apart!" He raised his hands to demonstrate pulling apart Waits's mouth. We were just glad to have Nickey back in one piece. The Bags were allowed to escape with our hides intact, but the Troubadour was declared off limits for punks from then on.

After the Troubadour show, we were pretty confident that we could do the upcoming Masque benefit without a lead guitarist, but Craig was insecure about his ability to handle lead guitar, especially for our most popular song, "Survive," which began and ended with a jazzy guitar riff and begged for a scorching solo in the middle. A few days before the show, Craig suggested that we get a sub from another band, but his asking for permission turned out to be

Bags at the Troubadour flyer. Collection of Alice Bag.

a mere formality, because Craig and Nickey had already asked Marc Moreland about filling in. Marc was a fantastic guitarist, but he was already playing the benefit with his band, the Skulls, and he was worried that they would be upset if he played with another band. Nickey countered that he was playing drums in practically half of the bands at the benefit, which was sort of true. Could he play with a bag on his head to disguise himself? Marc asked.

"Yeah!" said Craig, "Let's all wear bags!" Nickey joined in the campaign. "It's not fair we get to be in the Bags but we never get to wear bags on our heads," he argued, but by this time, Patricia and I were done with the gimmick. They were hot, mine always got ripped off my head because of my proximity to the audience, and we hadn't worn them in months, so we saw no reason to go back to them. Patricia had begun to develop her distinctive proto-Goth punk look, and her pale beauty, set off by her unusually long black hair, was already garnering new fans for the band. "No!" we said decisively. "But Marc can wear one if he thinks his band will be mad at him," we offered as a compromise.

The night of the show, Marc happily sported a bag on his head (no tampons!), but with his distinctive Gibson Flying V and aggressive, squalling playing style, no one was fooled. Everyone knew that Marc Moreland was playing with the Bags, including his bandmates in the Skulls, and nobody showed the slightest concern or resentment. The spirit of the two evenings was one of cooperation, coming together for a common cause. At the end of the night, Craig came up to me and Patricia and said he'd had a great time, with one caveat: "I'm going to surprise you one day and wear a bag onstage," he threatened. But he never did.

This show was perhaps the first time the local mainstream media (in the form of the *Los Angeles Times*) officially took note of the burgeoning scene, estimating that approximately 500 punks had attended the two-day event. The Sex Pistols may have imploded upon reaching the shores of the Pacific, but our little homegrown movement of disaffected weirdos and outcasts was exploding.

WILD MAN'S SERENADE

I was awakened from a sound sleep by an urgent thumping at the door. Nickey and I looked at each other. Who could be calling at this ungodly hour? It wasn't even noon yet. Was something wrong? My mind started racing. Nickey quickly walked over to the door, but before opening it he called out, "Who is it?"

A sweet little voice began to sing: "*My name is Larry, my name is Larry...*"

Over the past few weeks, Nickey and I had befriended Larry "Wild Man" Fischer. He started coming over to our apartment at the Canterbury almost every day. Larry was like a little kid trapped in a full-grown man's body. He had wild, frizzy hair that stuck out from both sides of his head. He nearly always came into a room with a big smile on his face, often singing one of his old songs or an improvised new one. Nickey had his own knack for making up fun, silly songs, and I joined in once in a while, too, but mostly it was Nickey and Wild Man taking turns with songs like "No, No, No — Don't Want No Jello," or "Merry-Go-Round."

He didn't usually come over this early. Nickey cracked open the door with a slightly irritated, "It's still early, Larry." But Wild Man was excited, and he ignored Nickey's comment. He burst into the room, talking about how he'd met some people on Hollywood Boulevard who recognized him and had paid him to serenade them. Larry couldn't hold down a regular job, so singing on the street was his sole means of earning a living. Strangers would toss spare change his way in exchange for a song or two, but the people he'd met this morning had known who he was. They had heard the album that he'd recorded with Frank Zappa, and now he was giddy with the rush of his newfound celebrity status. They had given him a few dollars instead of the spare change he was used to getting, and suddenly Larry was feeling flush with cash and he wanted to share his good luck with us.

Larry had a long list of songs into which he would insert people's names. He might ask you your name and what you did and then he'd take his songs and add details about you to the lyrics, so a song like "My Name Is Larry" could turn into "*My name is Larry, My name is Larry, I have a friend, Her name is Alice...*" It didn't take Larry long to figure out that the more details about his listeners he put into his songs, the more they liked the song. The practice became a social passport for him and pretty soon he was singing the details of any given activity, narrating it as he performed the activity and including as many details about the people around him as possible.

Larry held out a crumpled brown paper bag; there were some pieces of bread and crumbs in the bag. "I bought this for us!" he chirped, offering me the bag.

"I'm not hungry, but thank you," I replied after looking in the rumpled bag. I excused myself, then grabbed some clothes and locked myself in the bathroom while Nickey fixed breakfast and chatted with Wild Man. Even though we were now living together, Nickey still wouldn't let me cook, clean or do any of the laundry. He was a bit of a control freak in that sense, but I didn't have any problem with allowing him the privilege of performing the domestic chores.

When I was sufficiently dolled up, I joined them in the kitchen, where Nickey had our breakfast ready. We hung out for a while, just talking, but the newly earned money must have been burning a hole in Wild Man's pocket, and he wanted to go somewhere. "Let's go to a movie!" he suggested. Nickey and Wild Man went out for a newspaper, and when they came back we chose a movie called THX 1138, an early George Lucas science-fiction film. As we were leaving the Canterbury, we picked up a few other neighbors who were hanging out the window of Shannon Wilhelm's first-floor apartment, which faced the center courtyard. Shannon often kept the window open, so when punks came and went, they often checked in with her along the way, kind of like a reception desk. Connie Clarksville, Shannon, Nickey, me, Larry and someone else I've sadly forgotten all squeezed into my old Ford Falcon.

In the car, Larry sang incessantly, making up songs about people we passed on the street and about each of us. We laughed the whole way to the theater. When we got out of the car, my girlfriends and I walked in front while Wild Man and Nickey followed behind, singing about us.

Once inside, we found seats near the front and side of the theater; not my favorite places to sit, but it was a special day for Larry, so we let him pick. Instead of sitting way off to one side, Shannon and I sat up front and the others sat behind us. During the previews, Wild Man kept talking, but we figured he'd pipe down once the movie started. We figured wrong. He kept trying to engage Nickey in conversation during the credits and Nickey finally turned to him and said "Larry, I'm not going to talk to you anymore now that the movie's started."

"I'm sorry Nickey, I'll be good," Wild Man promised. And he was good, for about 10 minutes. Then, during a quiet scene in the movie, we heard a teeny-tiny mouse voice begin to squeak in the dark: "*My name is Laaa-rry, my name is Laa-rry...*" We couldn't contain ourselves. We all burst out laughing, provoking shushes and dirty looks from the rest of the audience.

"Larry, be quiet!" I scolded, but I could see his face beaming and smiling at me, even in the darkness of the theater. A couple of minutes later, the little voice started up again, this time even quieter: "*My name is Laa-rry, my name is Laa-rry...*" Again, we burst out laughing and the more we tried to control ourselves, the harder it was to stop. This went on for perhaps another 15 minutes, until we decided we'd have to leave out of courtesy to the other people in the theater.

Nobody was mad at Larry — how could we be? Larry's childlike qualities were endearing. His unbridled enthusiasm, innocent desire to please and outspoken honesty made him lovable.

One day Larry came over while Nickey was out. He looked thrown off by the fact that Nickey wasn't there, so I let him come in to wait. The whole time, Wild Man looked concerned, but he wouldn't talk to me about it. After some time had passed, Nickey walked in and he and Wild Man went for a walk. When he got back, Larry wasn't with him.

"Is everything okay with Wild Man?" I asked Nickey.

"You know, Alice — you probably shouldn't let him in when I'm not here," Nickey replied. He didn't tell me what he and Larry had talked about, but I could see that he was trying to protect me. "Larry is a mental patient, Alice."

I didn't know the half of it, but I promised Nickey I'd tell Wild Man to come back if he ever came by while I was alone. Our friendship with the Wild Man needed to have limits, but he was now dropping by unexpectedly at all hours, and Nickey stepped into an almost fatherly role. He told Larry when he could and couldn't come over. At first, Larry looked a little hurt that he couldn't stop by anytime he wished, but after a few days he seemed all right.

Larry seemed to be going through a change. His youthful exuberance was gone and he seemed sullen and pensive now. Eventually his visits became less and less frequent and we fell out of touch, but I still remember Larry "Wild Man" Fischer as one of the sweetest, most creative and unique people I met at the Canterbury.

BUILDING UP STEAM

Shortly after the Elks Lodge show, I spotted Terry Graham at a party at the Canterbury. I had met him before when Nickey was still living on Santa Monica Boulevard, when a homeless Terry had spent a few nights at Nickey's apartment. Terry seemed like an ordinary guy then, wearing plain jeans and a nondescript shirt, but tonight he was wearing a bright red pair of bondage pants that caught my attention. Messy black hair, pale skin and dark circles under his eyes made him look like he'd been partying like a rock star and hadn't slept in days. I immediately liked his look, which I hadn't noticed before. The bondage pants made me see him in a new light. He just looked like he ought to be in a punk band, and I immediately set out to recruit him for the Bags.

I asked him if he was a musician and told him I was specifically interested in a drummer. When I asked him if he knew how to play drums, his answer was ambiguous: "Not really," he replied, but then he followed up with, "Well…I played a little in high school." To me, that was as good as a yes, so I asked him if he'd be interested in working with Nickey to learn some Bags songs and audition for the Bags, and he agreed. Thus was Terry Graham's fate sealed.

Photobooth shot of Rob Ritter, 1978. Photo by Alice Bag.

Around the same time, a caravan bearing a cargo of refugee Phoenician punks arrived at the gates of the Canterbury. They were a bunch of loud, crazy, fun-loving guys who were immediately nicknamed the "Cactus Heads," because they'd driven in from the Arizona desert. Packed into the van alongside members of the Consumers and the Feederz was thin, talkative Don Bolles, future drummer for the Germs, and thin, quiet, bespectacled Rob Ritter. Unlike Terry Graham, whose bright clothes and outgoing personality got him noticed immediately, Rob Ritter seemed to blend into the background for several weeks without anyone even knowing his name. Eventually, someone let it slip that Rob was a guitarist. I immediately pounced and talked him into letting us audition him.

Terry started studying with Nickey, and before long he became our neighbor, moving into the Canterbury with his girlfriend, a cute young blue-haired girl named Jane "Drano" Wiedlin. They had an apartment on the second floor. Jane and I quickly became friends. She, Belinda Carlisle (a fourth-floor neighbor) and I shared a passion for the '60s girl-group sound. We got together on a couple of occasions at Jane's apartment to sing along with the Supremes, and joked that one day we'd have a singing girl group.

Rob's audition went extremely well, as did Terry's, and by spring of 1978 the band was sounding stronger than ever. Our popularity continued to grow along with the scene, and we were now able to headline and fill clubs on our own. In April, the Bags

Jane Drano Wiedlin and Terry Graham, the Canterbury, 1978. Photo by Alice Bag.

headlined a show at Lazaro's Latin Lounge with X and the Dils opening. I was fixing my makeup in the club's bathroom when Jane Wiedlin and Margo Olaverria walked in.

"Guess what, Alice?" said Jane in her distinctively perky, high-pitched voice.

"We're going to form a band!" shouted Margo, without waiting for me to guess.

"You are?" I smiled, surprised but returning to my lipstick.

"Yes!" Margo started.

"It's going to be an all-girl band," said Jane.

"We're going to call it the Go-Go's!" Margo chimed in.

I put my lipstick down and turned to face them. "Who's in it?" They started rattling off ideas they had about who they were going to ask.

"We're asking Belinda to sing. What do you think?" Jane asked.

"I've always wanted to be in an all-girl band," I replied, surprising myself at the sudden surge of jealousy that starting welling up inside of me.

I could see the two girls briefly exchange looks, then Margo turned to me somewhat seriously and said "Well, we would have asked you, but you're already in the Bags. You wouldn't consider joining us and giving up the Bags… or would you?"

"No, no, of course not," I quickly returned to my senses. "Belinda will be great. She's a good singer," I replied, growing embarrassed that I'd practically jumped at the chance to be considered for their new project when I knew from firsthand experience that there weren't that many girl musicians around. Hadn't Patricia and I already tried to find them? The Go-Go's would probably end up a mixed-gender group like us, and while they were just starting, we already had a following and headliner status. Nevertheless, a part of me still longed to be part of an all-girl band, and over the years I would ponder that brief conversation with Margo and Jane, imagining the horrible band the Go-Go's would have been with a screeching maniac like me as their lead singer.

The Bags were in full swing now, having finally found a mix of personalities and musical tastes that meshed well. As we got to know each other better, we learned to complement each other's strengths, and the band grew tighter and better with each passing week.

BREAK IT UP!

Over the next few months, my life turned into an incessant blur of concerts, parties, alcohol, sex and occasional drug use. Nickey and I were each busy with our bands, and though we often went out together, we also went out alone or with friends. Temptation was at every turn, and our relationship was on shaky ground. We still cared for each other, but we rarely talked about things that mattered to us. Our relationship was based on mutual attraction and friendship, which seemed like it should be enough, but it wasn't and we started bickering about little things.

One day, Nickey asked to borrow the Falcon to run errands while I was at work. Since my shift at Jack LaLanne's kept me busy from 10 a.m. to 10 p.m., I saw no reason that he couldn't use the car while I was at work. I had long since transferred from the Montebello gym where I'd started to a facility that was much closer to Hollywood. Nickey woke up early and drove me to the Miracle Mile, a stretch of Wilshire Boulevard near the La Brea Tar Pits, and dropped me off.

"I'll see you at ten o'clock," he said as he drove away. But when 10 p.m. came around and the last person walked out of the gym and locked the door, I was still out there waiting. I was sure he'd come by at any minute, but standing alone outside in high heels, black tights and a bright orange smock that stopped at the top of my thighs, I was feeling cold and vulnerable. I started walking in the direction toward home. Wilshire Boulevard was desolate by this time of night. I had some spare change in my pocket and thought I might grab a bus, but as the Miracle Mile was largely a business district with offices that were open between 8 a.m. and 6 p.m., no buses came by at that time of night. What did come by was a lowrider with three menacing-looking men inside. They slowed and tried to talk to me but I did my best to ignore them. Up ahead, I saw a little liquor store, so I quickened my pace and I ducked into the store, hoping the car would drive off. I poured myself a tall styrofoam cup of piping hot self-serve coffee, gave the man behind the counter most of my change and walked back out into the night.

In a minute or two, the car appeared at my side again. The cholos inside were trying to play cat and mouse with me, but they picked the wrong little mousey to fuck with.

"How much?" One of the guys asked me, turning back to his friends for approval. They all snickered. Growing weary of their game, I stopped and turned to face them straight on. Holding the tall cup of scalding coffee to my lips, I blew a steady cloud of steam toward them.

"Look, asshole — this coffee is really hot," I said, continuing to blow the steam toward them. "And if you don't fuck off, at least one of you is getting burned." I made a point of looking in each of their faces so they could see I wasn't scared of them, and then it occurred to me that I really wasn't scared anymore. "You can do whatever you want to me, but I'm gonna make sure that one of your faces melts away." I stood firmly rooted to my spot on the sidewalk, tough as shit, challenging them like I'd seen the cholas do back at Stevenson Junior High.

"*Fuck you, bitch!*" they yelled as they drove away.

At La Brea, I turned up toward Hollywood Boulevard. My feet hurt like hell from 12 hours at work and then a long walk home in high heels. I thought to take them off, but the ground was cold and I was still trying to warm up with the coffee. Nickey was dead meat now, I just needed to get home so I could stick a fork in him. I passed Pink's, where the sight of lights and people made me feel like I had reached civilization again. I finally made it home, only to find that Nickey had completely forgotten about me. If words were weapons, Nickey would have died that night. He apologized profusely but I was not to be appeased. His thoughtlessness stuck in my craw, and my anger simmered.

A few days later, there was another party at the Canterbury, and a cute British boy showed up sporting a pair of black, zippered pants and a charming accent. Shannon immediately christened him "Zippers." We laughed at his InstaPunk look. I knew he was one of Belinda's discards, and I immediately wanted to dislike him, but my snubbing only drew him closer. Flirtation mounted over a week or two, and I invited him to attend a recording session the Bags were doing for Dangerhouse Records.

On the way to the Dangerhouse recording session, another one of Nickey's antics made me remember how mad I was at him. We were all crammed into the Ford Falcon when I suddenly felt something crawl over my foot. I screamed and swerved, taking my foot off the accelerator for fear of crushing whatever was down there. I quickly pulled off to the side of the road.

"There's a mouse in here!" yelled Patricia, who had caught a glimpse of the creature. I freaked out, screamed and jumped out of the car. Craig Lee was laughing and trying to calm me down, but I was beside myself and refused to get back into the car until the mouse was outside. The frightened mouse eventually ran out of his own accord, and we were only slightly late to our recording. It turned out that Nickey had borrowed the Falcon to take KK Barrett to get food for his pet snake and some of the food had escaped. Knowing that I .was afraid of mice, Nickey had thought it best not to tell me. Now I was furious at him.

Zippers and I went out for drinks after the recording, and the night ended with my cheating on Nickey again. Instead of confessing, I tried to break up with him, hoping to save myself the confession, but Nickey made the breakup difficult, and, in the end, I confessed my infidelity to force him to let me go. His response was to slap me. I walked away from him, remembering my promise to leave him if he ever hit me again. He'd made it easy for me. It was over.

SHANNON AND THE MOVING OUT SURPRISE

I made plans to move out of the apartment Nickey and I had been sharing on the fourth floor of the Canterbury. Shannon invited me to be her new roommate, and I immediately took her up on her offer.

Shannon Wilhelm at Calvary Cemetery, 1978.
Photo by Alice Bag.

I'd met Shannon Wilhelm shortly after moving into the Canterbury. She was one of Nickey's drumming students, but she'd long since given up on playing drums. She and I had become good friends, especially after Nickey invited her up to our place early one morning. We were coming home from an all-night party that had turned into a wild orgy. On our way through the courtyard we'd checked in at Shannon's first-floor window and she'd greeted us by saying she'd heard about the party and was sorry she'd missed it.

"Come on up and we'll catch you up," offered Nickey. To my great surprise, Shannon showed up just as I was getting into the shower. "Go on in," Nickey told her.

"Can I come in?" Shannon asked through the bathroom door.

"Sure, come in," I called out as I stepped into the shower. We chatted through the shower curtain for a few minutes until a naked Shannon suddenly stepped into the shower with me. We both burst out laughing.

"Listen, if you don't want to do this, we don't have to," she offered.

I gave her a quick kiss. "It's not that I don't want to, I'm just exhausted."

"I can imagine," she replied, and we burst out laughing again.

"You and Nickey can do whatever you like. I'm going to sleep," I said decisively, and with that, I dried myself off and put myself to bed, falling asleep within seconds. I don't know if Shannon and Nickey had sex that morning but it was her friendship and the honest way she dealt with the situation that made me feel like I could trust her.

As soon as she found out that Nickey and I were on the skids, Shannon showed her allegiance to me. "Let's go get your stuff," she offered. I went up ahead of time to tell Nickey I was taking my things and moving downstairs with Shannon. He blew a gasket, and we both started yelling at each other. In a moment of fury I took a beautiful metallic gold-flake guitar, a vintage Mosrite that Nickey owned but couldn't play, and swung it like a baseball bat chasing a home run, intending to smash it to pieces against the wall. To our surprise, the guitar survived the impact but the wall of the apartment caved in. Despite my foul mood, I started laughing, as did Nickey before walking out. "I'll leave you alone to pack," he said.

Shannon came up to help me and we started off gathering my clothes and makeup. When we were done with that, I surveyed the room, making sure I hadn't forgotten anything.

"Let's look in the kitchen. Do you have any pots and pans?" Shannon asked.

"No, Nickey never let me go in the kitchen."

"Why not?" Shannon's brow furrowed.

"Oh, he has his special way of organizing things," I replied, as if this was a common living arrangement. Shannon looked quizzically at me and without another word, she walked into the kitchen and began opening the cabinets.

"Oh…My…God!" she said, bending over and covering her mouth.

"What is it?!"

Lined up in a kitchen cupboard were dozens and dozens of water-filled glass jars, each with its original lid and label intact. Spaghetti sauce jars, peanut butter jars, all sizes and varieties were represented, all spotless, sorted and arranged with their labels facing forward. Shannon was doubled over, laughing hysterically. We opened another cupboard. Carefully flattened cereal boxes were on a shelf, arranged like books in a library. Every meal that Nickey and I had ever consumed from a package was represented in that kitchen. Boxes, cartons, jars were all still there like silent witnesses to what our life had been. There certainly was a system at work here, but I didn't want to know what it was, and I didn't want to see any more of it. Nickey had never intended for me to see it; that's why he'd kept me out of our kitchen except to sit down and eat.

The freakish quality of the kitchen was funny to Shannon and a little funny to me, but it also made me sad because I'd never taken the time to claim part of it or to know why Nickey had organized it the way he had. It was a side of him that I'd never gotten to know and would never have the chance to understand. Shannon and I picked up my few remaining personal items and I closed the door on my life with Nickey Beat.

WORKING THE FRONT DESK

Around the same time that I broke up with Nickey, I quit my job at Jack LaLanne's. I had enjoyed my stint there until a couple of the sales managers started pulling me out to do Spanish-language sales. I was happy to do the tours in Spanish, but now I was being pulled away from classes and training to sit in an office and explain the different gym packages. I hated being asked to pressure people into buying a membership; besides, I didn't make any commission on sales, so I was clearly doing work I wasn't being paid for. What I did instead was that once I was alone with the client, presenting the packages, I'd tell the women to take their time making a decision. I assured them that they could come back tomorrow and still get a good deal. Since nobody else who worked there spoke Spanish they never knew what I'd said. I still closed a few sales, but only when people were happy and comfortable with what they were buying.

Shannon Wilhelm, photo by Alice Bag.

The deal breaker for me at Jack La Lanne's was the dress code. We were expected to wear high heels all day except when teaching classes on the premise that it made us look more attractive and the members would want to look like us. The reality was that it was a sexist practice which no one had challenged. Many of us at the club would try to extend our time in the workout shoes we were allowed to wear when teaching a class by not changing immediately after the class. Being a troublemaker, I started wearing my workout shoes almost exclusively. I was constantly getting counseled for this infraction, and no matter how much I protested that it was an unfair practice, I would eventually give in and switch back to the high heels. I played the game of leaving the workout shoes on for a half hour after leading a class, then an hour, then two hours, until one day I got fed up with it. When the manager called me on it, I refused to put on the high heels. "Fire me if you want to, but I'm not switching back." I won out that time, but

I knew my days were numbered. My relationship with Jack LaLanne's, like my relationship with Nickey, was past its expiration date, so I quit.

Moving in with Shannon was good for me. We shared clothes, makeup, records and, most importantly, an overactive sense of humor. It seemed as if we were always laughing. It was like having a sister my own age. She was a strong, assertive woman, intelligent and vivacious. She could have been a silent movie star, because she could convey every emotion through gestures. All it took was a raised eyebrow or a puckered lip to know what she was trying to say.

Alone in our apartment we'd take turns picking records, and Shannon would dance around *en pointe* to Teenage Jesus and the Jerks or X-Ray Spex. Her small, lithe dancer's body alternated between smooth and jerky movements, interpreting each song like a punk rock prima ballerina. She introduced me to pancake makeup. She accented her huge eyes with heavy stage makeup, telling me, "It's meant to be seen from the back row," in a low voice that sounded like Greta Garbo's.

I sometimes felt like a receptionist in that first-floor Canterbury apartment. When we opened our windows, which faced the main courtyard, everyone that came in could look inside, and we could see anyone coming or going. After a while, people started checking in and out with us.

Punk rock parlor games at the Canterbury, 1978..

"Is Rod home?" a head might ask, poking through our window. "Would you tell Belinda I've gone out?" People would check in with us like it was the front desk of the Punk Plaza. Other times people would just climb in through the open window to save themselves the trip through the lobby. Suddenly, we were running Hangout Central. Got nothing to do? Look in on Alice and Shannon. We always had something to do, we'd play dress-up, try on wigs, paint our faces, take pictures, make collages or fliers.

We even made up an all-girl gang. It wasn't a gang in a negative sense—we didn't have fights with

Shannon Wilhelm wearing her Pyranas shirt in our Canterbury Apartment. Photo by Alice Bag.

rivals or any underworld connections. We were just a group of punk girls with edgy dispositions. The Pyranas, as our group was called, came out of a night of heavy drinking at Margo Olaverria's apartment. Shannon, Margo, Sheila, Jane and I were all sitting around boozing when someone started complaining about men. That's when we decided that the idea of a man-eating fish, like a piranha, was a good name for a girl gang, so we created it.

Our friend Sheila started talking about her ability to suck blood right through a person's pores. Jane didn't believe it, so we asked her to try it. Over Jane's strenuous objections, Sheila tried sucking on Jane's arm, leaving a nice little hickey, which Jane immediately started to complain about. The rest of us found this terribly funny and prissy, so Jane became the first Pyrana to be initiated by being subjected to a multiple hickey attack. She was drunk and not so mad while we were doing it, because it was all in fun, but the next day, when her boyfriend, Terry, saw the hickeys all over her body, he was furious. Jane promptly quit the Pyranas, but not before giving us immediate street cred by claiming we had gang-raped her.

COMMUNICATION BREAKDOWN

"Are you ever coming back to school?" asked my friend Susan, indignantly. Sue had gone to Sacred Heart with me and we'd taken general ed and philosophy classes together at East L.A. College, but what had really brought us close was our mutual interest in religion and philosophy. Sue and I could spend all day at Googie's Restaurant in Atlantic Square, drinking coffee and discussing philosophy. Now I only saw her when I went to visit my mom in East L.A.

"Not for a while...but I will finish school. I promised my dad." I could see she wasn't satisfied.

"Montebello is only a half-hour drive from Hollywood. You could come visit me, too." I tried again to coax a smile from her, in vain. We both knew that our afternoons at Googie's and our leisurely discussions were coming to an end, especially since my visits to see my parents had grown less and less frequent.

Sue and I played backgammon and sipped countless cups of coffee while she told me about the classes she was taking. I loved talking with her because we could discuss anything. We knew that no matter what the other person said, our role was to challenge it. We made each other work to justify our beliefs. It was about strengthening our rhetorical skills and clarifying our ideas. Our arguments were a friendly joust, never a personal attack. We made up hypothetical situations to examine the ideas that needed challenging. When a belief fell under the weight of scrutiny, it wasn't all wrapped up in emotional baggage. This approach gave us time to digest our changing values and let our emotions catch up to our minds.

The backgammon game was over. Sue brought out a deck of cards and dealt a hand of gin. The waitresses knew us and let us stay as long as we wanted, refilling our coffee cups so that they never seemed to have time to cool off. Susan's mother used to sing in the piano bar in the back of the restaurant, so Googie's always felt like home base when Sue and I wanted to stay up late talking. After the last hand was played, we reluctantly got up to leave. We promised to stay in touch, but as we left the coffee shop, each of us driving in opposite directions, I immediately started to miss her.

Life at the Canterbury was nonstop excitement. There was always a party, a concert or some other communal activity to keep us from ever singing songs like "Boredom" with any real conviction. But with all that activity came a lack of solitude and meditative time that I'd taken for granted at my parents' house. I guess the upside of not having many friends is that you have lots of time to think. Now I was surrounded by friends and didn't even need a phone to talk to them because all I had to do was walk to their apartment. I didn't have my long phone conversations with Darby anymore, although we'd still sometimes get drunk together and have discussions, but more and more often these discussions would deteriorate into quarrels. The recipe for a sure-fire Combustible Canterbury Cocktail was simple: take one part Darby Crash, one part Alice Bag, one part philosophy and three parts of any kind of alcohol. Mix well and serve straight up.

Although I had already stopped calling myself a Catholic by the time I entered Catholic school, I was still having trouble adjusting to the fact that the concept of God I'd come to trust and believe in was no longer serving me very well. I had outgrown it intellectually, but not emotionally. It was a topic that was especially painful for me to discuss with Darby, because he seemed so cynical about the belief in God.

"Alice, I don't know why you work so hard to prove the existence of something that doesn't exist." Darby would inevitably grow frustrated with my theistic tendencies.

"I'm not trying to prove anything to you. I'm just telling you what I think. I don't care if you believe it," I countered, somewhat defensively.

Darby laughed sarcastically. "Oh, wait — God *does* exist, he's a human construct, you made him up!" There was something to what he was saying; in some ways, I felt like I was creating the concept, and at other times I felt like I was discovering it.

"Everything you've told me about your God just tells me you're an atheist who's afraid to let go of her security blanket," he continued in a lecturing tone. A condescending half smirk, half grimace spread across his face. He was pissing me off.

"Don't try to tell me what I believe!" I was neither an atheist nor an agnostic. I believed in God, I was just giving the concept a much needed makeover and I wanted someone to discuss it with, not someone to force their own ideas on me. I hungered for knowledge, not lectures. I'd never been one to assimilate other people's views without thoroughly examining them. I was convinced that real knowledge was earned by thinking about something and figuring it out. It hadn't even occurred to me, in those days, that there might be other ways of knowing God. The attributes of God for me were just a hunch, a gnawing suspicion begging to be explored.

I longed for the days when I could write a journal entry in Sister Angela's religion class, and she would write back thought-provoking, insightful observations. Now, there was rarely even time to sit down and read a book. Everyone was so busy having fun that the big, important questions I once spent so much time contemplating were just an irritating buzz in my head. Even if there were people who shared my interests, I had presented myself as a party girl, so that's how most people viewed me. Darby was the exception, eager to talk big ideas, but he tended to proselytize. He was a born-again atheist, spreading the new gospel. With no Susan, no Sister Angela and no regular phone calls to Darby, I felt like I had no one to talk with, and my sense of isolation started to bloom anew in the hothouse warmth of sexual partners, friends, neighbors and fans.

One evening after an afternoon of drinking, Darby, one of his fans and I sat on the carpeted steps between floors at the Canterbury. Darby and I were having a discussion while his fan nursed a beer, looking bored. It began as a discussion of the nature of God, and, as it turned out, our understanding of the universe was very similar, but the discussion turned ugly when Darby again tried to push me into admitting that I was secretly an atheist. I'd had a hard time giving up my concept of an anthropomorphic God, and sometimes, quite involuntarily, I regressed to visualizing a picture of a white-bearded old man I'd seen on my mother's free calendar from the panaderia when I was 4 or 5 years old. Of course, I didn't tell Darby that, because I knew he'd make fun of me, but it was the truth. My mind was ready to toss out the imperfect shell that had contained and constrained a concept it could no longer house, but the picture-maker in my head tried to tie the old image to the new concept. My new concept of God was still developing and incomplete, so I wanted a discussion, hoping I could add to it. My discussions with Susan or Sister Angela were always voyages of mutual discovery, but I felt like Darby was pushing me in another direction. Our conversation became increasingly heated, and his friend, perhaps sensing the coming storm, came over and said she'd be back in a few minutes.

"Bring me a beer on the way back!" Darby called to her. As soon as she walked away, I took the offensive and steered the discussion away from God and toward Darby's friend.

"Why do you always have girls doing stuff for you?" I asked him.

"They like to do it," he laughed.

"They want to be your *friends*," I countered.

Darby defended himself by expounding on one of his core beliefs. "People need leaders, they want someone to tell them what to do, how to dress, how to think," he argued. Pretty soon, we were back to a discussion we'd had once before. Darby didn't feel that a leader had any moral responsibility to his followers. From Darby's perspective, a leader who achieved his or her own personal agenda was a good leader. From mine, a good leader helped his or her followers develop the ability to form and achieve their own goals. I'd seen some of Darby's fans fawning over him, and it made me disgusted at him more than at them, because he allowed them to fawn, he encouraged it. Before I knew it, I found myself getting mad, and I unleashed a mouthful of venom.

"You're pathetic, you need them just as much as they need you! If you don't see that, you're lying to yourself." I got up from my place on the steps, but the alcohol had made Darby bold, and he started spitting out accusations about my beliefs.

"Talk about lying to yourself! You're an atheist who's afraid to let go of God because you're a fucking coward!"

We each knew where the other's weaknesses lay, and we'd gone for it. Just at that moment, Darby's friend appeared at the bottom of the stairs. Darby and I were walking down now, yelling at each other, fueled by passion and alcohol; we'd lost our ability to have a rational argument, we were caught in a whirlpool. Perhaps sensing that her hero was out of control, Darby's friend was pulling on his arm, coaxing him down the stairs, but Darby decided to get in my face. It was like striking a match to dry tinder.

Instinct triggered my internal fight mechanism and I felt heat racing through my veins. I took a step backwards up the stairs to increase my forward momentum. The vantage point was much better from here and Darby looked small. I threw my weight down and, aided by the force of gravity, I landed a solid punch to his jaw. He grabbed my arm and tried to punch back but I don't remember sustaining any blows. We were tangled for a few minutes when his friend finally managed to pull Darby away. I stayed on the steps, yelling, and that was the end of my friendship with Darby.

MY VAMPIRE ROOMMATE

"It's just you and another girl?!" A look of concern began to spread over my mother's face. "At least a man can protect you, but two girls alone…" her voice trailed off into worried silence.

"It's very safe Mom. We have a bunch of friends who live in the same building. We look after each other." I managed to calm her before she worked herself into a panic.

"Ayyy, m'ija," she said, shaking her head, exhaling in defeat as she made her way to the kitchen. "Come on then, come get something to eat." This was my mom's way of saying she was dropping the subject. At my mom's house, gorging on her cooking was a way to solve all problems. There were always multiple pots of delicious Mexican food simmering on the stove. I made a point of visiting my parents once or twice a month; more often than that would have meant certain weight gain. Now that Nickey wasn't doing the laundry, I'd take a couple of loads to my parents' house and wash clothes while feasting on my favorite enchiladas, chiles rellenos, dulce de leche and capirotada.

Shannon's mom lived much closer to her, just a couple of blocks away, on the other side of the Masque, near the Egyptian Theater. We'd visit her, too, sometimes. She didn't have pots of food on the stove, but she was a natural storyteller and always entertained us with her yarns and dreams of snipers in the middle of the night.

Shannon and I were blissfully settled into our wake-up-and-party routine, but when we got tired of parties we could retreat for the day to visit our parents. Our idyllic trance was rudely shattered by the realization that we were running low on money. I was still coasting on band money and the little cash I'd managed to sock away when I had a regular paying gig at Jack LaLanne's. I'd hoped to use that money for a road trip. Shannon got stock dividends in the mail, but they were infrequent and barely enough to live on. Our mothers would have liked nothing better than to have us move back home, but neither of us considered that an option. Instead, we decided that a roommate who could split the rent with us three ways was the answer. We immediately had a volunteer. Our friend Sheila was spending lots of time at our apartment. She often slept on our couch while Shannon and I shared the Murphy bed; why not get her to pay rent? Shannon and I had been toying with the idea of taking a road trip for a few weeks, and if we had a roommate, she could look after the apartment and our belongings while we were gone.

Sheila Edwards was a walking vampire who believed that she was the reincarnation of Drusilla, the Roman Emperor Caligula's favorite sister. She had a strong, striking face, with features chiseled from cold funerary stone. She wore purple shadow beneath her eyes to create a deathly, hollowed-out effect. Dark, angry streaks of powder made her face look harder. On top of this, Sheila had a reputation for being crazy and belligerent; she'd once kicked her foot through a window at the Canterbury in a fit of anger, tearing up her leg pretty badly; but none of this deterred us from asking her to become our third roommate. She fit right in.

Sheila moved in with very few belongings. Unlike Shannon and I, who had records, books, clothes and makeup, Sheila carried all her worldly possessions in a compact duffel bag, which made the move quick and easy. That's not to say that any of us had many personal belongings. We certainly didn't have anything of value, but we did have a lot of attitude packed into that little studio apartment — too much attitude. Sheila and I were both used to being the Toughest Girl in the Room, and it was inevitable that we'd have to settle the matter of who was Queen

My vampire roommate, Sheila.
Photo by Alice Bag.

Bitch, so one day Sheila and I had a face-off. We started arguing about some inconsequential thing, and, of course, neither of us would back down. I began the primal, visceral dance common to all predators: circling, summoning my power, sinking into the depths of the black hole where there is no fear, not even the instinct for self-preservation, only the ability to destroy, to annihilate.

Finally, I reached the abyss and was ready to take on this opponent. Sheila and I came closer to each other until we were almost face to face, both of us baring our fangs. In the final instant before the attack, we looked into each other's eyes and something swept through me; it was the sting of self-recognition, like seeing my doppelgänger. Staring deeply into each other's eyes, Sheila and I saw only twin pools of abysmal rage, and it shocked us both. There was immediate danger — the threat of violence in our eyes, which were now laser focused on each other — but beyond the danger there was unspeakable pain and horror, a wildly beating heart of darkness. Sheila and I both realized it at the same time; it was like being stripped naked in front of each other, only much more personal.

Acting quickly, Shannon fearlessly stepped between us and broke the connection. "Are you going to fight or make out?" We both turned to look at her, and in that second the spell was broken. Shannon talked us down, until Sheila finally turned away and went out for a walk. When she returned a few minutes later, Shannon joked about our insanity until we couldn't help but laugh at ourselves. The thing that made Shannon so funny was that there was always an element of truth to what she said. She said the stuff no one else dared to say, she joked about our rage, our lunacy, our hang-ups and insecurities. It was impossible to take yourself too seriously around her, and in her mastery of the moment when Sheila and I almost came to blows over nothing, Shannon proved herself to be the real alpha bitch of our little pack.

Because Sheila and I got our confrontation out of the way early on, we never got that angry at each other again. From that split second of recognition, we learned to relate to each other better, and there was also an increased sense of respect that grew from that day. But the two of us would be like dark twins of violence and destruction who would have further misadventures over time.

THE BIG ROAD APPLE, PART 1

How delightful are the pleasures of the imagination! In those delectable moments, the whole world is ours; not a single creature resists us, we devastate the world, we repopulate it with new objects which, in turn, we immolate. The means to every crime is ours, and we employ them all, we multiply the horror a hundredfold.
  —*Juliette*, Marquis de Sade

For $75, we could get an unlimited 30-day bus pass that would take us anywhere we wanted to go in the continental United States. Shannon and I emptied our piggy banks and bought a couple of passes. We'd been wanting to take a road trip, but the old Falcon just didn't have the strength, so we decided to make the 72-hour bus trip to New York City instead.

We boarded the bus full of enthusiasm, but by the time we reached Barstow we were already getting bored. The bus stopped at Barstow for lunch, and we picked up some talkers who, to our dismay, decided to sit right behind us. One young man was particularly chipper and gabby, and within a couple of hours he was the single rooster clucking it up with the surrounding hens. He tried to engage us in conversation by asking about our hair and clothing. I had plum and black hair, Shannon's was purple and blue, but our clothing was only slightly unconventional — straight-legged pants and Converse tennis shoes. Shannon wore a home-stenciled white shirt that said Sex Pistols on the front. I was wearing an old, ripped Ramones T-shirt. We looked at each other when the rooster asked us why we were dressed this way.

"We're in a band," I said, which was true.

"Oh yeah? What band are you in?" asked the rooster.

"Not one you've ever heard of," I replied, hoping to shut him up.

Shannon and I looked at each other. She motioned first to my shirt and then to hers with her eyes, then she smiled her closed mouth, holding-in-a-secret smiled and turned to face the rooster.

"We're in the Sex Pistols," she announced. I wanted to laugh, but I stopped myself.

"I'm Susie Vicious," I added playing along.

"And I'm Jenny Rotten!" Shannon smiled triumphantly at the rooster and hens.

One of the women exclaimed, "I've heard of you! You all play that punk rock!" She was beside herself with excitement. We had turned the tables on the rooster, and he was losing his audience. It seemed that Shannon had inherited her mother's ability to spin a yarn. She invented tasty little kernels about our supposed past and upcoming tours, managers, bandmates and fans, and the hens pecked them up hungrily, but after a while we ran out of steam and let the rooster rule the roost again.

I was taking prescribed bronchitis medication which felt like speed to me and made me jumpy, prompting me to refill the flask of rum we'd brought along whenever we pulled into a bus depot that had a liquor store nearby. Shannon was also medicated — self-medicated. She'd brought a bottle of thorazine with her. I don't know how she got it, but she popped them constantly to keep herself relaxed or asleep during the long haul. Luckily, I'd brought some books with me, *The 120 Days of Sodom*, by the Marquis de Sade, and *Franny and Zooey*. I started off with J. D. Salinger the first day, and then started in on de Sade. All the while, the rooster clucked away in the background.

It was too much for me. I was drugged, sleep-deprived and had plenty of inspiration. My sick, sick mind got very creative, and I daydreamed scenarios every bit as twisted as those devised by the clever Marquis. I'd fall into a dazed half-sleep and dream about the tortures described in the book, while, behind me, the incessant babbling and cackling of the rooster was like sitting in a movie theater in front of a little kid who's kicking your chair for three days straight. At first, I wanted to turn around and strangle him in order to shut him up, but, by the third day, a quick death was too good for him.

De Sade's creative methods for prolonging agony had gone from repulsive to appetizing. Mutilation of the offending mouth and tongue would not only stop his talking, the activity would keep me entertained on the dreary, tedious journey. What started with my pinching his lips together and stapling his mouth shut with a staple gun flowed easily into grasping his tongue in fist and cutting it off at the base with a pair of scissors, not in one quick stroke but allowing the scissors to open and close several times in a biting motion that resembled the beak of a fierce, predatory bird, filling his throat with blood… but even these little fantasies seemed too tame, and my mind wandered to sicker pastures. Soon, I was sleeping happily in earmuffs fashioned from the rooster's own ears. I wished Shannon would wake up so I could spill my fevered dreams and forget them, but she slept on, and the sick little fantasies rotted and festered in my mind.

On the last leg of our journey, Shannon handed me her dog-eared copy of *The World of Suzie Wong*. "I'm not going to roll into New York City with you looking like you're about to bite somebody's head off," she joked. It was just what I needed — a syrupy, juicy love story where the protagonists are an artist and a prostitute. Dr. Wilhelm was right — it did wonders for my mood.

By the time we pulled into the bus depot in Times Square, Shannon was relieved that we had made it without my having inflicted bodily harm on anyone, and I was in pretty good spirits, too. It had been one hell of a road trip, but we were finally in the Big Apple.

THE BIG ROAD APPLE, PART 2

We arrived in Times Square later than expected; it was well past midnight instead of the early afternoon we'd been counting on. Shannon had arranged for us to stay with one of her old friends, but she didn't want to call this late because her friend had a stressful job and went to bed early. "She probably won't even answer the phone this late," Shannon told me. Instead, she called another old acquaintance who was kind enough to let us crash on her floor. After some 80-plus hours on a bus, stretching out our stiff joints was heavenly, and we fell asleep instantly.

When we awoke, we thanked our gracious hostess, who was leaving for work and told us to let ourselves out. Shannon called her friend, Liliana, who was concerned because we hadn't checked in as expected. She was working, but we were to meet her at her apartment later that afternoon. Liliana's apartment was on 23rd Street, just a couple blocks away from the Chelsea Hotel. We spent the morning taking showers, trying to get the smell of the road off our bodies, followed by a little walk before catching a cab to Liliana's apartment.

It was a typical New York summer, hot and sticky, but the tall apartment building had air conditioning that welcomed us the minute we stepped inside. I'd never lived in a place with air conditioning, so it seemed luxurious to me. The place was secure; a man had buzzed us in and then checked off our names on a clipboard before showing us to the elevators. They were well maintained and didn't groan on the way up like the Canterbury's. Liliana must have a good job, I thought to myself.

We knocked on Liliana's door and it was opened by a slightly pudgy young woman with dark, curly locks and big brown eyes set in a doughy complexion. As soon as she saw Shannon, she gave her a big hug, while at the same time a sweet little creature appeared at Liliana's side. She was smiling shyly at me. "Come in," Liliana beckoned, then, glancing at her daughter, she introduced us. "This is my daughter, Angela."

"Hi Angela," I said, crouching down to shake her hand. "My name is Alice." I was rewarded with a beautiful smile that melted my heart.

"I'm sorry," Shannon interjected, "Liliana, this is my friend, Alice." Social skills had always been a challenge for me, and I'd neglected to introduce myself first to our hostess. I stood up again to shake Liliana's hand, and she ushered us into the kitchen, where she'd prepared a meal for us — some kind of delicious, baked pasta casserole, which Shannon and I tried not to scarf down too quickly.

"That's real Italian cooking," said Liliana. "Not like the stuff you have in L.A., is it?" I thought of my mom's soupy, tomato-sauce-soaked spaghetti noodles and shook my head while gulping down the delicious pasta. As we chatted over dinner, we figured out a way to repay Liliana for letting us stay with her. Once we found out how much she had to pay for babysitting, we offered to watch her 5-year-old daughter while she was at work, and, after polite bargaining back and forth over the details, it was decided that two or three afternoons a week of babysitting was a good compromise.

That night, Shannon and I were eager to go out to see a show, but there was nobody we were interested in seeing. "Can we go to Max's Kansas City?" I begged Shannon. "I've heard so much about it."

We walked up the stairs of the legendary venue, where a local band was playing.

"Would you please hold these?" I handed Shannon my lipstick, money and ID.

She gave me a dirty look.

"I don't have a purse," I shrugged.

The band sounded pretty good, but there was nothing new about them and there was no wild dancing up front. We made small talk with other loners in the club; Shannon was great at talking to strangers, but after a few minutes we got bored and decided to try our luck at the restaurant downstairs. We couldn't afford any food, but we ordered a drink and drank slowly, looking at the menu while we pretended that we were having a hard time figuring out what to eat. Some of our new friends came downstairs with some of their friends and squeezed into our little booth.

After talking to our new pals for a while, Shannon leaned over and whispered in my ear, "I've got to go get something with these two." She pointed with her eyes. "I'll be back in five minutes." I had a sinking feeling that the something was drugs. Shannon had recently developed a taste for pills.

Shannon Wilhelm and me in New York, 1978.

When she and her new pals had been gone for about 45 minutes, I started to get really worried. The waitress came and asked us to leave, since nobody was ordering food. I checked the bathroom and then went back upstairs to see if she was there, but Shannon was not at Max's and I had no idea how to find her.

I was alone in New York City. I had no cash, no ID and, worst of all... no lipstick.

THE BIG ROAD APPLE, PART 3

What if someone had kidnapped Shannon and was planning to sell her into white slavery? What if she'd been drugged and raped or worse. What if she'd been killed? I said goodbye to our new friends and continued to hunt for Shannon outside of the club, looking for her in all of the parked cars. I searched for blocks around Max's Kansas City, wandering aimlessly, hoping to come across Shannon chatting in a dark corner or to hear her laugh, but it was no use. With a start, I realized I was lost. I'd been so upset and worried that I hadn't noticed where I'd turned or which direction I'd come from.

I found myself alone in an alley in the middle of the night with no money and no idea what to do. I heard a sound behind me: the lonely sound of a can being kicked. I turned around to see a shape emerging from behind a dumpster. It was a man, looking straight at me.

"YOU'RE LOST!" he yelled at me. It wasn't a question. I quickly turned away from him and my mind went into overdrive. I knew that in this situation Violence Girl would need to take over, so I summoned her. The frightened Alice faded as my shadow self began to grow immense, casting a looming, terrifying figure against the brick wall in the dim light of the alley. I felt a black wave come over me. I saw the faceless man running up behind me and I turned on him, a lioness ready to rip him to pieces. I saw myself tearing his flesh off with my claws, biting off hunks of flesh, spitting out his blood, gouging into his gelatinous eye sockets. He was beyond the point of fighting back, but I continued my assault.

It was a vivid fantasy. I turned to look at the man in the alley. He was in the same place, still kicking the can. "Good. Now I won't have to kill him," I thought to myself, feeling dangerous, feeling sorry for anyone who might cross my path at that moment. I knew that someone could hurt me, but I didn't care because I would hurt them worse and I would hurt them first.

I had walked in a big circle, and I got back to Max's just as the club was closing, the last few diehard customers walking to their cars or hailing cabs. Shannon was still missing, and I was still friendless and penniless. I called out to a guy and two girls, some strangers I'd questioned earlier.

"Which way are you going?!" They didn't know me at all, but I hoped I could make them feel sorry for me.

"Didn't you find your friend?" one of the girls asked me, showing some concern.

"No…and I don't have money for a cab. Do you go anywhere near the Chelsea Hotel?"

"No!" said the guy who was getting behind the wheel.

"But we'll drop her off anyway," said the girl.

"Thank you so much," I said, getting into the car quickly, before the driver had time to object. As we drove back to the Chelsea, I kept looking out the windows. I couldn't stop worrying about Shannon, but if I found her alive, I planned to kill her. The car stopped in front of the Chelsea. I didn't know our address, but I knew we were close by. We'd passed the historic hotel earlier that day, and Shannon had regaled me with stories about the many artists, writers and musicians who had made the Chelsea their home over the years. The apartment was just a couple of blocks away…but in which direction? Even if I'd known which way to walk, only Shannon had an apartment key. It was our first night staying with Lillian, and I didn't want to ruin things by waking her at 4 a.m.

I walked into the Chelsea, acting like I belonged there. No sooner had I walked in than I heard a voice call out "Alice!" It was Shannon. "I've been looking for you!" she added, but I didn't feel like listening.

"Where the FUCK did you go?!" I was raising my voice, and the two or three people in the lobby looked at me. Shannon pulled her shirt collar down and rested her head on a counter top.

"I'm sorry, I'm sorry! Here, chop my head off!" she said, doing a wide-eyed Lillian Gish impersonation.

"Arggggh" I growled, disarmed by Shannon's nervy playfulness. I was too relieved to see her to get really worked up. She led with a wide grin that dissolved into a hug.

"Did you worry about me, honey? I'm really sorry. It just took longer than I thought."

"I don't want to know," I groaned. "Can we go home now?"

After that night, things got easier. I learned the names of the two main cross streets, the nearest subway station and Liliana's phone number, and I never again gave anyone else my money or ID to hold. I also learned that our hostess was a prostitute who supported herself and her angelic daughter with her earnings. In the evenings, after dinner, Liliana would describe some of her transactions, detailing her contempt and disgust for men in general and her customers in particular. It was a stark, black-and-white contrast to the watercolor world of Suzie Wong I'd just read about. Liliana seemed to regard men as something lower than swine; the only sweetness in her life came from her daughter, Angela.

We spent our afternoons being tourists and playing with the beloved little Angela. We took her everywhere, and she was never bratty or whiny. She reminded me of the child I never was: Her childhood was innocent, blissfully unaware of her mother's struggles. She was a cherub who woke us up in the morning by singing along with the *Grease* soundtrack until Shannon and I knew all the words to every single song. I couldn't help myself—I fell in love with that little girl, and I dreamed of saving her from what I saw as a situation that would end badly, but I knew that I would soon have to leave her. Besides, I was a mess myself, in no position to save anyone, barely able to save myself.

A few nights later we found out that our friends from San Francisco would be playing in town. We went to see the Nuns at CBGB and later hung out with them, posing for pictures on the roof of the Chelsea Hotel. I met a young, flirty guy named Johnny Angola who wanted to show me the Empire State Building. "Meet me there tomorrow morning," he said and then stood me up. We saw former Plunger Trixie Treat who was working at a punk store called Revenge. We fell into the brisk New York pace and squeezed as much fun as possible into every moment, until one day we woke up and knew it was time to go home. Back at the Canterbury, the rent was due, the band was waiting for me and, to tell the truth, we missed our L.A. family. We said goodbye to Liliana, hugged and kissed Angela for as long as we could, then we headed west.

Me, Angela and Shannon in New York City, 1978.

275

HOME AGAIN, HOME AGAIN, JIGGITY JIG

Hoping to avoid the bus trip experience on the way home, Shannon and I pooled our resources and bought plane tickets back from NYC. Our roommate, Sheila, came to meet us at the airport, but since she had forgotten which flight we were on, she decided to use the LAX public address system to page arriving passenger "Alice Douche Bag." (Alice Douche Bag was my full stage name in the Bags.) She somehow convinced the suspicious airport personnel that the name was German. Shannon and I were wandering through the airport terminal when, to our surprise, a voice came over the LAX loudspeaker paging "Alice Deutsche Bag."

It felt really good to be back in our own apartment, to see our old friends, to play our own records and see our favorite bands. Not that we hadn't enjoyed the vacation — it was grand, and we met some fun people — but, as Dorothy was fond of saying, "There's no place like home." My bandmates put me to work as soon as I got back, quickly organizing a rehearsal schedule, and Craig set about booking our shows. Sheila and I decided to go out looking for part-time jobs together, because Shannon and I had come home just in time to pay the rent and I couldn't afford to wait around for the next gig. I had spent all the money I had in New York and on the plane ticket back, so we looked through the want ads.

One job that caught my eye was a help-wanted listing for a front desk clerk at the Roosevelt Hotel, a fancy old place on Hollywood Boulevard known for hosting many of the Hollywood movie legends. In the late '70s, it had lost a little of its sparkle, and we thought we might be able to sneak one by them and get jobs there. Sheila and I put on full costumes just to go pick up applications. I put on a short wig which I borrowed from Shannon and did my best to ease up on the eyeliner. Sheila, too, tried her best to look normal, but as soon as we walked into the lobby, the raised eyebrows and worried stares told us that everyone could see through our disguises. The front desk clerk reluctantly gave us each an application to fill out, then told us that the manager had just left unexpectedly and that we should leave the applications with him. We could tell we were being given the brush-off, but we didn't understand why.

"We look okay, don't we?" I asked Sheila, discreetly sniffing myself to see if I was emitting any foul odors.

"I think you look good. How do I look?" Sheila responded, looking in a mirror to check her makeup.

"You look good too," I replied, confused. We were so far out of the mainstream by this time that we had no idea how to even fake it.

After filling out the paperwork, we waited for a long time before the front desk clerk deigned to speak to us again, and when he did, it was in a curt manner with a fake smile. Sheila and I walked out of the Roosevelt's fancy lobby feeling defeated. Just as we were approaching the corner, a big white Cadillac that was leaving the hotel rolled up to the stop sign. The conservatively dressed, middle-aged woman driving the car looked at us briefly, then continued to roll forward, nearly hitting us as if we were no more consequential than two random tumbleweeds blowing down Hollywood Boulevard. Sheila swung her purse over her head and slammed it down hard on the hood of the car, prompting the woman to open her door and start to get out. Sheila immediately went ballistic and rushed over to her. Following Sheila's lead, I started to bang up the car with my own bag. The male passenger began yelling at the woman to get in as he locked all the doors. Sheila was screaming at the driver: "*Were you going to run us over?!*"

"*Learn how to drive, asshole!*" I shouted, still pummeling the car. We were like wild apes, leaping around the vehicle, yelping and screeching, banging the hood and doors with our purses. The couple looked terrified as we unleashed all our frustration on that Cadillac. They drove away in a squeal of rubber. As soon as they were gone, Sheila and I broke out in spontaneous, irrepressible laughter. We didn't feel defeated anymore.

"Who cares if they don't hire us, someone will," I told Sheila.

Sheila just smiled and said, "Your wig is falling off."

Eventually, we were both hired by a fast-food chain known for its roast beef sandwiches. We lasted just over a week. Earned enough money for the rent and then quit.

Back at the Canterbury, the good Reverend had allowed some of the tenants to clean up and soundproof the walls in the basement and set up a rehearsal space for bands. The Bags rehearsed there a few times. "It's about time, Gordita!" said Craig Lee, as I walked in late to rehearsal. I'd lost most of my baby fat, but Craig called me Gordita because he thought it would annoy me. He thought right.

"It's good to see you too, Bagel Breath." We walked the fine line between insulting each other and playful teasing. In our book, gorditas and bagels were very distant cousins to terms like *spic* or *kike*; in our vernacular, they were terms of endearment. "Let's get to work!" Patricia yelled, redirecting us to the task at hand; she was usually the one to crack the whip.

The band had been on an extended break since I'd been in New York, and the finishing touches were being put on our Dangerhouse single. I was disinterested in the mixing process, preferring to explore NYC. Now that I'd returned, getting back to work was the order of the day.

Bags rehearsal in the basement of the Canterbury, 1978.

DOWNWARD SPIRAL

The Dilaudid tablets simmered and dissolved into a couple drops of water in the spoon. The flame had to be moved around under it to distribute the heat evenly. Sheila and Shannon watched hungrily, like ravenous vampires waiting to feed. I had never seen the process so I was curious, but I wasn't a fan of needles and wondered why anyone would want to stick something in a syringe and poke themselves when they could just as easily swallow a little tablet. The girls tied off their arms, filled the syringe and, pausing only to wipe the needle with another ball of cotton, shared the mixture.

"Do you want some, Alice?" asked Shannon in her deep Garbo voice. She seemed to be having an orgasm; her head rolled back, eyes semi-closed. She reclined on the toilet seat and let the wall hold her up. Sheila sat on the edge of the bathtub. She smiled like a satisfied cat, her head tilted downward, looking up at me with seductive eyes:

"Try it Alice. It's sooooo gooood."

"No thanks," I said, offering a pained smile. "More for you, right?"

Sheila finished off the contents of the syringe. "*Riiiight*," she purred.

I have to admit that I was afraid of intravenous drugs. It was a time before we knew about HIV/AIDS, but images of Diana Ross as Billie Holiday in *Lady Sings the Blues* came to mind. I remembered the feeling of disgust when I'd seen the part of the movie where she's fixing heroin, and I thought, *So much talent...what a waste.* I guess I imagined that because my choice of drug was legal, it must be less destructive. I took a sip from the can of Dr. Pepper that I had spiked with rum and walked out of the bathroom, leaving my two friends together with their new lover.

Dilaudid and Percodan were the new heartthrobs in town, seducing many of my friends. The stray Quaalude still found its way into the Canterbury from time to time, but, like last month's boyfriend, nobody else was that interested so I sometimes got them. I didn't mind taking an occasional pill or tablet. I never paid for drugs—booze, sometimes; drugs, never. I was in a band, after all, and we were playing again. Fans offered me drugs as gifts, but I was never a big fan of drugs. I had been a sickly kid and had hated swallowing medicine or getting shots at the doctor's office. It was also easier to drink than to go through the whole circus of buying drugs. The clubs gave band members drink tickets or drink tabs, and the Whisky had a punk soft-drink menu designed for the teens who usually made up the bulk of our audiences.

The punk menu included a drink named after me. The bartenders there always comped me the pineapple juice and lime concoction whether I was playing or not, adding a splash of rum to create what they called the Real Alice Bag cocktail. And if my favorite bartenders (who served up the Real Alice Bag) weren't working, I could usually convince someone to buy me a pint of rum at the liquor store across the street.

I was underage, so I still had to talk someone into actually buying the stuff. I had once tried to buy a pint of Bacardi Light at the liquor store nearest the Whisky, a place next door to a club called Filthy McNasty's. When I asked for the bottle, a young man working at the register looked me over before grabbing the bottle and putting it on the counter. He was about to ring me up when an older man walked up behind him. "She's not 21." His eyes bore into me, and as he denounced me I felt myself getting jittery. "What year were you born?"

No mister, please don't make me do math! I thought to myself. I wanted to add two years to my age, so I quickly added two years to my real birth year. "1960," I replied. The man laughed.

"Go back to high school, kid," he said, picking up the bottle and putting it back on the shelf. I stared at him, feeling stupid. "Go take some math classes!" he cackled. I don't think I ever lied about my age again after that, not because I was opposed to being dishonest, it was just too difficult to keep the numbers straight.

My drinking escalated to keep up with my friends' drug use. It wasn't intentional; I wasn't really aware that I was drinking excessively until someone brought it up. A few times, Craig Lee pulled me aside during rehearsals and asked if everything was okay, and I'd said that it was, because that's what I thought. I thought I had it under control.

With my roommates' growing interest in drugs, a seedier group of people entered our social circle. In a sober moment, we all agreed not to allow drug dealers into our apartment. Because the girls were often broke, they couldn't afford to buy drugs all the time. For a while, there was a point of recovery where the girls went back to drinking with me instead of cooking up shots in the bathroom. I think this happened around the same time that our ceiling fell into our bathtub. The tenant upstairs must have left the water running, because one day we noticed water dripping from a crack in the ceiling, and the next day we heard what sounded like a load of garbage being dumped into our bathroom. Shannon and I ran in and saw that large chunks of drywall and plaster had completely filled our tub. Above us, a big dripping pipe continued to rain on the pot of plaster stew that was our bathtub. Instead of being upset, we laughed. It seemed completely absurd to us, so in a way, it totally made sense. The stewpot would stay there until we moved out. We showered at friends' houses once or twice a week, and went around stinky the rest of the time.

Under normal circumstances, a tenant might have asked the landlord to repair the ceiling, but living at the Canterbury was anything but normal. It was an atmosphere of almost complete anarchy. There were no rules to follow other than paying your rent each month. The Reverend didn't seem to be interested in anything other than filling the apartments with whoever could pay the minimal rent. He allowed us to pad the basement walls with old carpets and set up a makeshift rehearsal studio. He never complained when punks climbed in and out of the building through the first-floor windows instead of using the front doors. He turned a deaf ear to the constant partying at all hours. He looked the other way when we set up a projector on the rooftop and projected films onto the side of the building for an evening of movies under the stars. In exchange, we didn't complain when the elevator broke down, we just took the stairs instead. We accepted the risk of living in a place where people had been stabbed and shot. Now that the roof was literally caving in, we just saw it as part of the bargain for our preferred lifestyle. We never even thought to ask anyone to repair it. We lived our lives completely in the moment, with little concern for the future. If an obstacle arose, we just figured out a way to work around it and pressed on with our mission of total freedom.

One afternoon, Shannon, Sheila and I were downstairs when some drug dealers came knocking on our door. We pretended not to be home, because the girls said the guys were there to collect some money that was owed to them, and they didn't have the money to pay. The thugs pounded on the door, but we were silent. We didn't even dare to move for fear they might hear some rustling. The knowledge that they were mad and determined to collect should have made the situation scary, but instead we had to stifle laughter; Shannon made faces at us, pretending to be a big, angry thug yelling at us. Eventually the drug dealers got tired of knocking and left.

Later that evening, we heard Sheila's screams coming from upstairs. They were angry curses, and we figured she was fighting again. Sheila had a very loud voice, and her screams filled the courtyard.

"*FUCK YOU, ASSHOLE!*" she screamed. Shannon and I laughed, thinking, "There she goes again, picking a fight," until one line caught our attention:

"I don't have any money! Why don't you just kill me?" Shannon and I became concerned. "Kill me! KILL ME!" The words seemed to ring out over the whole apartment building. We shot upstairs to the second-floor apartment where the sound was coming from, and now we could hear the pounding on the door as Sheila forced a confrontation. But as we rounded the corner from the stairs, the hall fell silent.

"Sheila!" we yelled.

"It's okay," came a voice from behind the door. "I'll be down." The voice was eerily calm and artificial.

"Let us in!" We banged on the door, but no one opened.

"I'll be down in a few minutes," she repeated.

"You be down in five minutes or we're calling the police," Shannon called through the locked door.

When Sheila finally reappeared, she refused to speak to us. "Leave me alone," she said, throwing herself face down on the bed and holding a pillow tight to her ears.

The next day she told us she'd gone up to yell at the drug dealers so that if they had any ideas about killing her, they would have to think twice. If anything happened to her now, she strategized, she had an apartment building full of witnesses who had heard her screaming at them and they would be the prime suspects. But for all of Sheila's boldness in confronting the thugs, she seemed different after that night, and just a few days later she asked to borrow a dime to make a phone call. When she came back, she told us that Camarillo State Mental Hospital was coming to pick her up. She had committed herself for observation and treatment.

MAKING THE CUT

The Bags started playing on a regular basis again. My performances seemed to be getting more aggressive around this time. Fights would break out in the audience or onstage. Our shows seemed to be a catalyst for fucked-up, angry teens who just needed a little encouragement to vent. Our music at this time was loud, belligerent and frenetic — the perfect soundtrack for the crowds that attended our shows. These audiences were frequently out of control, whipped up into a frenzy by the music and my exhortations to release the inner beast.

Onstage at the Hong Kong Café with a bloody lip. Photo by Louis Jacinto.

At the Canterbury, the total chaos and lack of privacy were starting to get to me. Nickey came by to attempt a reconciliation, but I was not in a conciliatory mood and I began hurling accusations at him. In the heat of an argument, I grabbed a belt and whacked him hard across the face with the metal buckle. An ugly red welt immediately began to bloom. He looked at me as if he'd never seen me before.

"Now we're even," he said, walking away.

I would never be able to look at Nickey again without feeling ashamed of myself. For days afterward, I kept replaying the scene in my mind. He had done nothing but try to apologize for losing his temper, and I had unleashed a furious blow against him. I didn't understand it at the time, but now I can see that I was turning into my father — a monster. The idea that I had any control over my rage was just an illusion; my rage was consuming me. Instead of crying, something inside of me took over and shut me down. I started functioning on autopilot. I felt numb, but numb was better than the feeling I got when I saw what a mess I'd become. I walked around like a zombie, feeling dead inside. I didn't interpret what I was feeling as depression; it felt more like emptiness and a desperate longing for understanding.

Sitting at the kitchen table one afternoon, I had a brief moment of solitude. As I was sitting there, I noticed a razor blade lying next to a freshly sharpened eyebrow pencil. I was inexplicably drawn to it and I picked it up. Seeing the ugly black smudges on the blade, I wiped it clean on my shirt and started to make a tiny incision on my inner arm. The cut was only about an inch long and it barely broke the surface. A fine, red line of blood came stinging to the surface. It was as if my mind and body woke up from a deep slumber and yelled, *Hey, what the hell are you doing?!* I set down the blade and felt myself grow happier as the numbness temporarily lifted. It meant two things:

1. I was not already dead (evidenced by the fact that I could still feel pain)
2. I had no desire to kill myself (I only cut deep enough to cause pain, not serious injury)

Over the next few days, cutting myself with a variety of sharp tools seemed like a medicinal act of bloodletting. I stayed away from razor blades after that first cut for fear of cutting too deep. Whenever the numbness became unbearable, when I felt like I wasn't part of the human race, I'd cut. Before long, it became necessary to wear long sleeves to conceal my new addiction.

One night, Craig Lee caught me standing outside alone. He walked up to me and grabbed my arm. Gently, he pulled up my sweater sleeve and gave me a somber, paternal look.

"Why do you do this, Gordita? Are you trying to kill yourself?"

"No…you don't understand," I said.

"This isn't like you," he muttered, shaking his head from side to side. "Your arm looks like hamburger."

I quickly pulled my sleeve down. I felt embarrassed and ashamed; the abrasions from scraping back and forth with a brooch-backing had left a scab pattern that crisscrossed my forearm. If he thought I was trying to kill myself, he must think this was my cry for help. But it wasn't a cry for help; the thought of suicide stank of cowardice to me, yet I had no way of explaining my behavior.

"I just need to feel *something*, Craig," I said, hoping he would understand. But he didn't.

"You shouldn't drink so much. Why don't you move back home?" His response stunned me. So there it was. He didn't think I was grown up enough to make it on my own. Craig was like an older brother to me. I wanted to prove myself to him, and now he thought I was a wuss who was trying to commit suicide with tiny razor blade incisions and abrasions from safety pins and shards of glass. He thought I should run home to mom and dad.

"Fuck off!" I told him. He gave me a sad, wounded look and walked away.

I continued to cut for months after my conversation with Craig, but now the relief I derived from cutting was tainted with guilt, shame and confusion.

BEYOND GOOD AND EVIL

Around the same time that I was cutting, a strange thing happened to me. It was a quiet, early evening at home, and Shannon and I were just relaxing. Neither of us had been drinking or consuming any drugs. Early evenings were the rare times when there was relative calm at the Canterbury. I was lying on the couch in our apartment, talking to Shannon, who was sitting on a chair facing me. I was listening to her when I suddenly became aware that my body was paralyzed. I willed it to move, but it would not. I tried to speak, but I could not; I instantly became alarmed. I stared at Shannon, hoping she would catch the frightened look in my eyes and realize that something was wrong, but my telepathy wasn't working that evening. She continued talking and gesticulating like always, unaware of my physical prison. I focused on moving just one finger. *If I can move just one finger, I'll get control of my body*, I thought. *Just my pinky, if I can just wiggle my pinky*. Instead, my whole being moved. The only problem was that it left my body behind.

I felt myself rising straight up toward the ceiling, like in a cartoon where the Coyote has been run over by a truck and a transparent coyote spirit is shown rising skyward, except my spirit only made it as far as the ceiling of the apartment. I looked down at my body through my spirit eyes. I was looking at Shannon, and incredibly, Shannon was still talking to the body on the couch, unaware that I was hovering above her. I thought I was dying; terror gripped me and in an instant I willed myself back into my body. I looked at Shannon and tried to sit up and surprisingly, this time I was able to move. "What's the matter?" asked Shannon, looking at me as if for the first time.

"You're not going to believe this," I replied. I told her what had happened, and she laughed at me.

"I bored you to sleep!" she said. But I knew I hadn't been asleep. I had plenty of experience with sleep, and this was different. A few days later, I told Patricia and her boyfriend, Rick, about it. Rick was the only person who seemed to be familiar with the phenomenon I was describing.

"That's happened to me before," he said, reassuringly promising to lend me a book that would explain more about what he called "Astral Projection." Until I could read the book, I was left to ponder the strange out-of-body experience which left me feeling scared and confused. On top of that, there was the ongoing cutting and the feeling of numbness that was with me constantly now. I didn't understand what was happening to me. I was losing myself. Whatever was essential to me, whatever sense I'd had of right and wrong, of good and evil, had ceased to guide my decisions.

The whole time I was growing, up I'd hung onto the belief that although I could not control the situations around me, I was in charge of how I responded to them. Now it seemed that even the comfort of feeling self-possessed, of feeling that my actions were the result of my own will, was questionable. Surely this wasn't who I wanted to be. I looked around me at the hovel I was living in, I looked at my scabby, bleeding arms; I had taken my eyes off the road, and now I was lost. I looked out the window, where only a tiny patch of sky was visible between the building tops, and I felt small, dwarfed by the knowledge of magnificent, boundless galaxies — not just physical galaxies but galaxies of ideas, of life forms, of concepts beyond the scope of my vision. In that moment of understanding my minuscule place in the universe, I also felt a part of it. I heard the universe whisper to me. I had to lose what I thought was me, not just all my baggage, but all of *me* — that was my road map. I was more than an individual, and by thinking of myself as an individual I was narrowing the scope of all that I encompassed. It was a brief moment of lucidity that was quickly swallowed up by fear: fear of losing my self, fear of being nothing. The universe was speaking to me loud and clear, but my hearing was impaired and I only digested what I could.

With my own limited vocabulary, I tried to answer. I made my decision to leave the Canterbury then and there. It was near the end of October, so it was too late to move out right away. When Shannon got home, I told her I'd pay one more month's rent to give her time to look for another roommate, and then I'd be moving out.

KICKIN' IT WITH CLAUDE AND PHILLY

A few days of quiet contemplation were followed by my slipping back into old habits. It was all too easy, because there was always a concert or party happening somewhere, and the punk scene had grown so large that there were lots of options. After a downtown loft party, a few of us were still hanging around, refusing to let the night die without draining it of all the fun it had to offer. Kickboy and I decided more booze was in order.

Even the simple act of going to the market with Claude "Kickboy" Bessy was an adventure. We got into Michael Gira's car, the three of us squeezing into the front seat. While Michael drove 90 miles an hour on a deserted street, trying to make it to the liquor store before it closed, Kickboy and I screamed and laughed, enjoying the sense of fear and excitement like kids on a roller-coaster. It was an unforgettable ride; we screeched around corners, slid coming out of turns and finally reached the liquor store just as the owner was locking the door.

"Wait, wait, wait!" I called, climbing out of the car in a rush. "Can we please just buy a fifth of whiskey?" I begged, using the flirtiest voice I could muster. Kickboy thrust out a handful of crumpled up dollar bills.

"What do you want?" said the man. I let Kickboy choose. "Stay here," the man said, walking back in to get the booze for us and locking the door behind him. He gave us the bottle, we slipped him the dough, got in the car and cruised back, guzzling the whiskey right out of the bottle. Kickboy was his usual self, boisterous and funny, cursing in his thick French accent.

This wasn't the first time Kickboy and I had gone on a frantic, last-minute booze run. We could both drink most of our friends under the table and were usually the last ones standing at a party. Once before, we'd been at a party that had run out of liquor, and Kickboy and I passed the hat, scrounging up just a few dollars from the diehards who were still there. Undeterred, we headed across the street to the supermarket, where we agreed that the meager sum would be best spent on a jug of plain-wrap wine. When we got back to the party, people scoffed at the bottle wrapped in a plain white label with big blue letters spelling out the word "WINE." They assumed Kickboy must have picked wine instead of beer because he was French, when in fact it had been my idea. Kickboy retorted: "If you think it tastes so bad, then why don't you use a syringe? Stick yourself with a needle and shoot it up. That way, you won't have to taste it!" He assured them with a sly smile that he had used this method before with no ill effects.

When Michael, Kickboy and I got back to the loft, Philly was waiting for us. She was Claude's perfect complement. She provided the sanity, stability, sweetness and kindness in the relationship. Claude was the inspired, irreverent editorial genius behind *Slash*, the walking embodiment of the early L.A. punk spirit, which was somehow ironic since he was a French expatriate. Those punks and music critics who only know him from his onscreen appearance with his band Catholic Discipline in *The Decline of Western Civilization* are quick to judge him, but most of us could never be as quick as Claude in his slowest moments. He lived life on his own terms and dared us all to do the same. Philly always seemed to find a way to let Kickboy lean over the edge of a precipice, swiftly pulling him back just before he toppled, and tonight she would also do that favor for me. We drank until dawn, and then Philly and Kickboy, perhaps sensing that I needed a break from the nonstop partying at the Canterbury, took me back to their apartment by the beach and tucked me into bed. Just like our breakneck booze run earlier that morning, I was careening, nearly out of control and about to crash. Philly's concern was sweet and touching, and just what I needed at that time.

AUTUMN

The autumn winds blew in a new legion of punks, some wearing armbands with swastikas. As they walked through the courtyard of the Canterbury, Shannon and I leaned out of our first-floor window and shouted at them: "*Die, Nazi Scum!*"

Not wanting to be ostracized, some of these swastika-wearing fascist-nistas would claim that wearing the symbol of the Third Reich was just a shocking fashion statement. Others denied that they were wearing the symbol for its shock value. Dismissing the Nazi connection, they insisted that the symbol had been around for thousands of years before the rise of Hitler. Their excuses were weak, as the stark, black, bold-type swastikas that were being worn were clearly Nazi ones and not the more organic-looking, multicolored versions of the same bent cross found in religions of old.

A few of us went so far as to make shirts with the words *Die, Nazi Scum!* or similar sentiments scrawled on the front. At the Canterbury, most of the swastika-wearers were not well received, prompting many to give in to peer pressure and stop wearing them. Others, like Rick Wilder who had been in the Berlin Brats, tried to laugh off our criticism and stick to his guns, but eventually he too stopped wearing the offensive symbol, reforming the Berlin Brats into the Mau-Maus with the help of Canterbury tenant Rod Donahue.

Halloween 1978 at the Canterbury: Pat Bag, Terry Graham (in drag), Alice Bag.

The Mau-Maus' first show was at the Roosevelt Hotel on Halloween night, 1978. It was one of the last shows I'd attend while still living at the Canterbury. I went with my bandmates Rob Ritter and Terry Graham, who had to literally drag me into an elevator to save me from a tall, muscle-bound football player I'd been busy picking a fight with. The jock was charging at me like an angry rhino when I'd collapsed to the floor in a drunken, dizzy, laughing spell that inadvertently saved me. Dodging him at the last second, I watched as he slammed his body against the wall, nearly knocking himself out. His friends ran up to him as he clutched his own wrist, which seemed to be injured. Terry and Rob acted quickly; each one grabbed me under an arm and dragged me into an elevator that had been disgorging its passengers. Terry pushed the buttons and the elevator doors shut just in time to escape the dazed jock, who had broken free of his concerned friends.

Terry and Rob thought the whole adventure was comical, but, unlike me, they were aware that I had been in real danger of getting pummeled. I didn't care. Soon, I'd be moving back home with my parents and all this craziness would be behind me, but for now, I was going to savor every last minute of it.

That fall marked the end of my teenage years. I turned 20 on November 7th. I still remember sitting on the stairs of Craig Lee's apartment in Los Feliz, a funky section of L.A. bordering Hollywood proper. He wasn't home, so I waited for him, and as I sat there alone, my tears started to flow. I leaned back against the building and allowed myself the luxury of letting the water run until I ran out of tears. I saw Craig walking up. He was all smiles. "It's my Gordita!" he called out to me as he reached the bottom of the long staircase. I smiled and waved back. "Hey Craig!" I called back. It was uncharacteristic of me not to reply with my own insult, and it made him frown.

"What's going on?" He noticed my red eyes as he got closer. "You're crying, Gordita? What's up?" I hated that he called me Gordita, even when he was trying to be nice to me.

"Don't call me that," I said, irked but unable to huff out a smile. I rubbed my face, trying to erase the evidence. "I'm taking your advice," I said. "I'm moving back home."

"That's great. You'll still be able to go out, and you get along with your parents. So why are you crying?"

"I feel like a failure," I replied. "Wouldn't you if you had to move back home?" He shook his head.

"Don't even compare us; your situation is different. What's really bothering you?"

"I'm old. I'm 20 years old and I haven't done anything with my life." Craig laughed a full-bellied, hearty laugh that I found insulting. "Why are you laughing at me?!" My eyes were welling up again.

"Because you're stupid! You're only 20! You're young!"

"I just feel like I have to act grown-up; I can't act like an idiot anymore. I don't have an excuse anymore."

"When did YOU ever need an excuse to act like an idiot?" he laughed again. This time I punched him in the arm. He hugged me in return.

"Alice...step away from this for a while. You're doing the right thing, moving back with your parents. You need space and time to think." He walked toward the kitchen to put on the tea kettle for us. "Just make sure your arms are healed before your mom sees them."

I'LL BE HOME FOR CHRISTMAS

Moving out of the Canterbury was easy. I didn't want to be there anymore. November had been a month of fires in the stairwells; either a pyromaniac was living there or an arsonist was. Two or three fires mysteriously happened each week, and the perpetrator was never apprehended. Many of us began to fear that the entire building would eventually go up in flames with us inside of it. I started looking forward to home-cooked meals, on-site laundry facilities and, most of all, my own private bedroom. When the end of the month came, I packed up my belongings. I didn't have much stuff, just a suitcase full of clothes, some records, books and makeup. Shannon, Sheila and I loaded up the old Ford Falcon in one trip.

Sheila had returned from her stay at Camarillo State Hospital with tales of her adventures in the asylum. She told us the story of an old woman who walked around carefully guarding her purse wherever she went. Sheila acted out the scene: Tucking a large handbag under her arm, she backed up to the wall and eyed the room suspiciously. She pulled out a chair with one arm, the other arm squeezing tightly down on the bag. She sat in the chair and pushed the bag up to her chest, still surveying the room through squinted eyes. "The woman walked around with that treasured bag for the first week I was there," she said, "until one day, the orderly pissed her off and she started yelling at him. She opened up her bag and threw tissue ball after tissue ball at him!" Sheila cackled and tossed imaginary tissue balls at us. "There was nothing in the bag but used Kleenex!" Sheila laughed. She told us all about the antics of the other inmates but never said a word about herself or what had prompted her to check herself in.

I'd miss her, and Shannon, too. "Sure you didn't forget anything?" Shannon asked.

"If I did, I'll know where to find you," I smiled back at her. We exchanged quick hugs all around, then I got in my Falcon and drove east, back over the river which separated Hollywood from East L.A., the two halves of my life up until that time. My parents were delighted to have me home. My room was just as I'd left it. My mother had a feast simmering on the stove to welcome me. It felt good to be home.

In my absence, my parents had developed a taste for Vegas. A "party bus" took off from the nearby Maravilla Senior Center early in the morning, driving the old geezers out to the desert oasis while they sipped mimosas with their breakfast pastries, if their doctors allowed it. By lunchtime they'd arrive at one of the less popular casinos, off the strip, where they'd eat lunch and then be held hostage for a couple of hours. After that, they'd be driven to downtown Vegas, where some of the hostages might manage to escape their captors and see the town before the dinner bell rang. Then they'd get herded back into the party bus for another out-of-the-way dinner buffet and gambling session designed to shake the last few pension pennies out of their pockets. On the drive home, the party bus became a sleeper car, as most of the seniors enjoyed a long nap after a hard day of partying.

I guess since my dad couldn't make it to Caliente racetrack anymore he had to find another way to satisfy the urge to gamble. But unlike at Caliente, where my mom had largely been a spectator, in Vegas she thought she was a high roller. It was my mom who was really into bright lights and clanging coins and sirens announcing a jackpot payoff. She was a slot-machine queen who kept her nickels in rolls, tucked in casino coin cups, ready to catch the party bus at a moment's notice. It was great to see my parents enjoying each other's company, and it was wonderful to have the whole house to myself, a luxury I'd all but forgotten at the Canterbury.

Blessed, wonderful solitude. I brewed a pot of tea, sat in my dad's recliner, pushed it back until the leg rest rose, leaned back and did nothing.

A NEW DIRECTION

The deal at home was that mom and dad would give me free room and board as long as I was going to school. I could study whatever I wanted and keep any money I made to use as I saw fit. I thought it was a great deal. Tuition at East L.A. College was ridiculously cheap in those days, and I was more than happy to purchase used books to save money, so I picked up a class schedule and selected my classes for the following spring semester. There was only one hitch: I needed money to pay for my classes and books, and I was flat broke. A job was needed.

My friend Sue, who had a cosmetology license, suggested that we go into business together. Her brilliant plan was to hit several local mortuaries and apply for jobs grooming corpses for funeral services. I thought I was good at makeup and Sue wanted to do the hair, so we went out and tried to get hired as corpse beauticians. But people were suspicious of us, perhaps thinking that we might have ulterior motives for being around cadavers, and they didn't even bother to give us applications. One friendly receptionist tipped us off that a nearby floral shop which had just delivered a large casket spray might be looking for help and she suggested we try there. Susan wasn't interested in flowers; for her, it was corpses or nothing, but I found the idea charming. I'd passed the flower shop from time to time when I was at Sacred Heart, and there was something inviting about the self-contained little corner building with its seasonal window displays. It seemed like there was always something to celebrate inside. I pictured myself arranging sweet-smelling flowers in a cheery setting and decided I would give it a try. Susan waited in the car while I went in for an application.

Having learned some lessons from my previous close encounters of the employment kind at Jack LaLanne's, the Roosevelt Hotel and Arby's, I theorized that the key to landing and keeping a job was to look and act the part, and I determined to give it a go. A little bell rang as I walked into the shop, and a pretty, perky brunette with a Dorothy Hamill wedge haircut came out to greet me. "Hi! What can I do for you?" she chirped. She would have been good on a pep squad.

"I'm looking for a job. Do you know if they're hiring?" I asked timidly.

She turned back and called out: "*Lee-ee-o!*" then turned back to me, still smiling, sizing me up. A slim, attractive man in jeans and a plaid shirt appeared from behind a partition. He had a warm smile and a worried look that perhaps explained his thinning hair. "She wants to know if you're hiring," said the perky one. She stared at Leo as though trying to communicate an unspoken secret.

"What do you do? Are you a college student?" he asked, immediately cluing me in to what he was looking for.

"Yes, I'm a college student," I said, doing my best to imitate the smile of the perky one.

"Have you ever worked around plants or flowers?" he asked distractedly.

"No," I replied; my smile faltered a little.

"So, what's your schedule look like? I mean in college," Leo asked.

"I'm thinking of going to school in the afternoon, so I'm looking for a morning and weekend job."

"That's perfect!" the shop girl said. Leo looked up at her, a little irked at her unsolicited comment. He rolled his eyes and turned to look at her now.

"You need the mornings for the post office right?"

"Right, I can come in after that," said the girl, enthusiastically opening her eyes in a wide, hopeful look. Just then a bronze-skinned man in a green smock holding a small knife and a rose came around from behind the partition. He looked me over, then walked behind the counter and shuffled things around without letting go of the rose and knife.

"I can do mornings," I repeated, sensing that Leo just needed a little extra push to hire me.

"Yes, Leo. She can do mornings," said the bronze man, nodding at me and handing me the rose.

"Thank you," I whispered. Leo let out a little laugh.

"Okay, well I guess they've decided. When can you start?"

A few minutes later, I was hired on to a job that would support me all the way through college and provide a desperately needed measure of normality in my tumultuous life. Sometimes, it's the little choices in life that make that the biggest differences. I was so excited that I ran back to the car where Susan was still waiting.

"You took long enough! Where's the application?"

"I got the job! I start Monday!" I said, bouncing up and down on the seat.

"Great," said Susan, in a deadpan voice. "So much for our plan."

DOWN MEXICO WAY

Nineteen seventy-eight expired with a bang as the Bags headlined a New Year's Eve show with a band called Fear at Brendan Mullen's new incarnation of the Masque (cleverly named the New Masque), located just kitty-corner from Nickey Beat's old apartment on Santa Monica Boulevard. By January of 1979, I was living at home but still rehearsing, playing and hanging out in Hollywood. New bands were now entering the scene constantly as the L.A. punk scene had long outgrown the geographical boundaries of Hollywood to encompass the suburbs. Two of my favorites were Middle Class, from Orange County, and Rhino 39, from Long Beach.

Rhino 39 had the distinction of bringing a positive twist to punk music. Their singer, Dave Dacron, was a tall, fresh-faced kid who actually smiled onstage. To the delight of their frenzied audiences, their music was clocking in ahead of most of the established punk bands. Music that was once considered fast by older standards now seemed to plod along. Rhino 39, along with Middle Class, pushed the speed of punk to previously unheard tempos, setting the dance floor on fire. The new crop of bands were too fast to pogo to, and their rise in popularity coincided with an aggressive new style of dancing called *slam dancing*. Outlying venues like the Rock Corporation in Van Nuys had opened their doors to punk in the latter half of 1978, and Chinatown was doing a bustling business in punk rock and new wave at Madame Wong's and the Hong Kong Cafe.

At this point in our development, the Bags were still playing out-of-control gigs. We turned every club we played in into a Wild West saloon, where bar fights, spilled drinks, flying furniture and general pandemonium were commonplace. The newer, speedier bands seemed like a good complement to our style, so we booked a show with Middle Class in San Diego. I don't remember all the details of the show, except for the fact that it was well received. I do remember that after the show, a bunch of us decided to pitch in money to rent a motel room and go to Tijuana the next day. Jeff Atta, Mike Atta, Bruce Atta and Mike Patton (the members of Middle Class), along with Black Randy, Joanie, Rick Jaffee and me, all without a change of clothes, slept in what we'd been wearing all day and then wore our stinky, sweaty clothes on our little sightseeing expedition down Mexico way.

Joanie was a good friend of mine from my front-desk days at the Canterbury. She hung out with me, Shannon and Sheila quite often. She had started

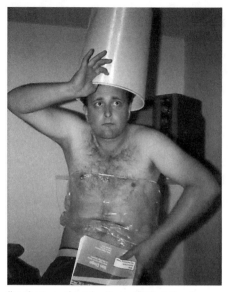

"Look at me, I'm John Denny!" Black Randy cavorts in a San Diego motel room.
Photo by Alice Bag

dating Black Randy, and the two seemed to bring the best out in each other. Joanie had a regular job and a car. As far as I knew, she was drug-free, levelheaded and didn't carry around a lot of emotional baggage. Randy, on the other hand, was legally insane. He rented a little office suite where he sometimes slept, because the rent was less expensive than an actual apartment. He told me and Joanie that he received monthly checks from SSI because he was considered mentally unable to hold down a job. He said that on the day he'd gone in to meet the caseworker who would determine whether to grant him the monthly stipend or not. He'd stopped on his walk to the bus stop and filled his jacket pockets with dog shit he found along the way. "When I walked in she immediately smelled it and started to gag," Randy laughed as he remembered the incident. "I thought she was gonna puke all over her desk!" The caseworker quickly assessed Randy's mental condition, confirming that he was indeed mentally unfit to hold a job. "As I was leaving, I took the dog shit out of my pockets and left it on her desk!" laughed Randy, obviously quite proud of his performance.

Black Randy was an interesting character who'd been around since the early days of the L.A. scene with his band, the Metrosquad. I'd been an occasional backup singer and dancer in various incarnations of the Blackettes/ Randettes, including a featured guest-spot singing my old favorite "Popotitos" (the Spanish version of "Boney Maroney") with Mexican Randy. Randy always insisted on calling me Alice Bag, even in casual conversation: "Alice Bag, would you like another drink?" One time at a party, Randy made the mistake of passing out before me, and I drew all over his face with eyeliner; then I hightailed it out of there before he woke up, as he could be quite vicious in exacting his revenge. But that night in San Diego we were all on our best behavior, drinking rum and Dr Pepper and having fun. With the aid of some clear plastic and a lampshade, Randy treated us all to his impersonation of John Denny from the Weirdos.

The following morning, on our way to Tijuana, we broke off into smaller groups. Sixteen-year-old Middle Class drummer Bruce Atta and I had embarked on a drunken romance the night before; now we were still feeling cuddly, so Joanie asked me and Bruce to join her in her compact car. Bruce and I climbed in the back seat and Joanie and Black Randy rode in front as we crossed the international border ready for a little vacation. That's what I thought, anyway.

The caravan split up to find parking, and we agreed to meet on Avenida Revolución, the main drag in Tijuana. Joanie found a parking spot quickly, and we got out to admire the colorful ceramics, piñatas, sarapes, jewelry and other tourist attractions that lined the street. But the one attraction that most interested Randy was one he called "the Donkey Show." I had been to Tijuana many times but had never heard of the Donkey Show. Standing there on Avenida Revolución, Randy pointed to a crudely rendered mural above the entrance to a bar. It showed a scantily clad woman standing next to a donkey.

"That's where they have the donkey show," Randy pointed at the mural.

"What exactly happens in there?" I asked, not wanting to assume the worst.

"What do you think, Alice Bag? She fucks the donkey!" Randy replied, laughing.

"No way!" I was shocked for the first time in a very long time.

"Let's go see the show, I'll prove it to you."

"No fucking way," I said, disgusted with the picture that my imagination instantly concocted.

"Why don't we meet up with you later?" Bruce suggested. Joanie gave me a pained look. I knew she wanted to be rescued from having to go explore the donkey show, but she was Randy's girl, and she knew that meant hanging out with a certified loony. "She knows what she's getting into," I thought to myself, a little guilty for not saving her. "We'll meet you at the car at five o'clock," I said. I'd leave it to Joanie to speak up if she didn't want to be part of Randy's sick little adventure.

Bruce and I explored the city, and at 5 p.m. we waited at the designated spot. Randy and Joanie were late. When they finally arrived, Joanie looked a little perturbed, but she gave me a forced smile and assured me everything was okay. We got back in the car and joined the long line of cars waiting to go through the customs inspection checkpoint to get back into the US. Randy seemed exhausted from the day's adventures, and a little out of it. He kept falling asleep.

"What's up with Randy?" I asked Joanie.

"He bought some heroin and shot it up in the car just before we met you guys."

"Is that what you guys have been doing?" I asked, feeling bad for my friend, whose idea of fun, I was certain, did not include buying drugs in foreign countries. Then came the clincher.

"He stuffed the rest of it in the glove compartment."

"What?!" I was furious. By now, we were just three or four cars away from the immigration booth and I could see a drug sniffing German Shepherd patrolling in the secondary inspection area, just beyond the checkpoint. The last place on earth I wanted to be was in a car that was smuggling heroin across an international border. I kicked Randy's seat.

"Wake up, you asshole! What the fuck were you thinking?" But Randy couldn't keep his eyes open. Joanie looked worried. Bruce was silent. There was nothing we could do. The cars continued their inexorable advance toward the border and the dozens of cars behind us had us hemmed in. There was no way to get out and dump the heroin; we were too close and would surely be spotted. I was nervous and scared, and, most of all, angry.

"We'll just say he's sleeping," Joanie said, trying to calm me down. We advanced to the booth where the immigration officer asked our nationality. "We're US citizens," Joanie told the officer. Then he looked at me.

"Where are you from?" he asked.

"Los Angeles," I replied. I was sure I could feel sweat starting to bead down my temples. My heart was pounding in my ears.

"What part?" He was still staring at me, suspiciously.

"East L.A." I answered. It started to dawn on me that he was more concerned about illegal immigrants than illegal narcotics.

"What's wrong with your friend?" he turned back to Joanie.

"Too much tequila," Joanie smiled at the officer, who waved us through. He'd been more concerned with what part of L.A. I was from than with the guy passed out on heroin in the front seat. I breathed a sigh of relief and vowed never to go anywhere with Randy again.

IF YOU'RE GOING TO SAN FRANCISCO

Many of my friends had moved on to serious drug abuse, and heroin was now prevalent in the scene, replacing most other pharmaceuticals as the drug of choice. Safe at home in East L.A., I often heard about friends who had overdosed, and though I know it sounds selfish, I have to confess that I was relieved to have put some distance between myself and Hollywood. In retrospect, having a caring and supportive mother and father to provide a safety net spelled the difference between survival and disaster when I felt I was slipping off the tightrope.

I fell into a comfortable routine of working at the flower shop in the mornings, classes at East L.A. College in the afternoon and rehearsals or homework at night. My days were full, and the quotidian rhythm of my life allowed my mind the stillness it needed to keep track of where I was going.

The band played outlying areas more often, as punk spread to the suburbs. We added smaller towns to our regular San Diego–L.A.–San Francisco circuit. Trips to S.F. were still a band favorite and we played San Francisco so often that for a while the whole band considered moving there.

The Temple Beautiful and the Deaf Club became two of my favorite places to play. The Temple Beautiful was a larger venue than most; it had once functioned as a Jewish synagogue and boasted tall, stained-glass windows that let soft light spill in onto the rows and rows of wooden pews built into the balcony. Of course, one could only appreciate the afternoon glow during sound checks, which were typically done while the sun was still up. At night it was just a big auditorium packed with weird-looking people.

The Temple Beautiful was run by a group of Rastafarians, and it was right next door to the People's Temple headquarters, a much smaller building where punks on their way to a concert passed by a shingle reading *The People's Temple, Jim Jones Pastor*. I'm not sure whether the Temple Beautiful just happened to be next door or whether it had ever been used by the large religious cult, but in any case, the eerie memory of the mass suicide orchestrated in Guyana by the Reverend Jim Jones, in which an estimated 900 people died just a few months prior, gave me the willies every time I passed the sign. It always reminded me of the blowout argument I'd had with Darby about leaders and followers, and I took some satisfaction in knowing that I would never drink the grape Flavor Aid.

The loudest and most exciting club in town was the Deaf Club. It had been built as an actual club for the deaf in the 1930s. By the late 1970s, it functioned as a rental hall for special events until punk rock entrepreneur Robert Hanrahan decided to rent the place to book punk shows. He had to complete the rental transaction by passing a notepad back and forth to the club owners. It seemed like a perfect arrangement, because no one would complain about the loud music. I don't think anyone expected it, but what happened is that punk in San Francisco began to gain a large audience of deaf people who frequented the shows at that venue, bringing a wonderful new perspective to what we were doing. I started to notice the unique way in which the deaf reacted to our playing and energy onstage. I remember watching a young woman as we were performing one night. She clung to the PA speakers, absorbing the vibrations with her whole body. Her face never looked away from me as she reacted to the energy onstage with a full-bodied bear hug of the speaker cabinet, and her head swaying to the rhythm of the music; she was at one with the music in a way most people would never experience.

The Bags and Robert Hanrahan became very close; I believe at one point we even considered designating him as our band manager. *Search & Destroy*, a San Francisco–based punk zine, was very supportive, and we made friends with Ruby Ray and Vale, who were two important documenters of the burgeoning scene. I loved our trips to San Francisco and seriously considered the move, but upon discussing it with my parents, my mother told me that my father's health was failing and that I needed to stay close to home. Her appeal weighed heavily on me, but I also reasoned that I had a good job with a kind, flexible boss, and I was enjoying school. I decided to stay put in East L.A. and let my roots take hold.

A SMALL BLADDER IS
A MIXED BLESSING

Despite our four-year age difference, Bruce from Middle Class and I had continued to see each other after returning from our trip to Tijuana with Joanie and Black Randy. Bruce was 16 and still in high school, I was 20 and lived a good 40 miles away, but we managed to see each other on weekends. I found the arrangement perfect for me. I'd briefly dated Terry Graham and Michael Gira after my fling with Zippers, but if the term *player* had existed at the time, I think we all would have fallen into that category. Bruce was different, and our relationship developed along much more romantic and traditional lines… traditional by my standards, at any rate.

Everyone was buzzing about the upcoming concert featuring the Clash, Bo Diddley and the Dils, an unusual lineup, to be sure, but one which somehow fit the early punk attitude of "the more variety, the better." The Clash show took place on February 9, 1979, at the Santa Monica Civic Auditorium, the same place where I had stalked Elton John just a few years earlier. It was an unusually large venue for punk rock, but the Clash had a solid fan base, so we expected it to be crowded. Bruce and I got there early to catch the Dils, who were one of my favorite bands. We claimed a space right up against the stage and were able to hold onto our spot until the curse of my small bladder struck and I had to go to the bathroom. Like most newly smitten couples, we didn't want to be apart for long, so instead of holding our place, Bruce walked with me to the ladies' room. We hung out in the lobby for a while, talking to friends. When we returned, the auditorium was packed and we scooted in as far we could but we had to settle for enjoying the Clash from the sidelines. We still had fun, but I cursed my poorly timed trip to the bathroom.

A month later at the Elks Lodge, my bladder would bring me better luck. The St. Patrick's Day show was supposed to feature X, the Alleycats, the Plugz, the Zeros and the Go-Go's. It was another great bill, indicative of the all-embracing style of the early L.A. scene, so we got there early to see the Go-Go's, who had been progressing very quickly. They were writing catchy pop tunes and practicing all the time, making leaps and bounds with every new performance. I felt something like maternal pride when I saw them play. I'd seen Jane, Margot and Belinda evolve from being fans to self-confident musicians and composers. Charlotte had been able to play since I first met her, but now she, too, was pushing her limits, moving from bass to lead guitar. The girls were driven, and I got a vicarious thrill from watching it happen for them. I guess I also felt like they were family, because our own drummer, Terry, had played their first show with them at the Masque. I remember Craig Lee and I commenting after their first show that the girls had good writing skills and were destined for fame.

The Go-Gos were slated to go on first at the Elks Lodge, which meant we couldn't afford to be fashionably late or we'd miss their set. Once again we made our way toward the front of the stage to watch the show, but as soon as the Go-Gos finished playing I found myself urgently needing to use the ladies room. It was early and the hall was not yet fully packed, so we cruised downstairs, figuring I had plenty of time to go and come back without missing anything. This is where the curse of the small bladder turned out to be a blessing in disguise, because as I walked downstairs and across the foyer toward the ladies room, I caught a glimpse out of the large glass doors in the front of the building. Meandering outside were a few policemen in full riot gear, wearing helmets with plastic eye shields and carrying batons. As I moved closer to the door, I could see all the way up the street. It was a frightening sight: row upon row of policemen in riot gear, standing at attention like storm troopers getting ready to march into the ghettos. Inside the auditorium were hundreds of punk fans peacefully waiting for the next band to take the stage, without a clue that they were about to be attacked. I flashed back to the Chicano Moratorium, where what had started out as a peaceful march had turned ugly in a matter of seconds. All it would take now is for someone, anyone, to strike the match that would ignite the powder keg.

I sprinted back up to where Bruce and some of our friends were seated, on the magnificent, ornate steps of the Elks Lodge Hall, and I told them what was happening outside. "We should get out of here — NOW!" I said decisively. The lead police officers and their commander were just walking through the front doors as we made our way down the steps. The atmosphere in the lobby immediately thickened with tension, and punks started to scatter in fear. Time slowed down, and the air became electrically charged with the threat of imminent danger, like the desert just before a lightning strike. I'd sensed this danger many times before; I'd grown up with it all my life. It was the plight of the defenseless in the face of unrestrained power and force. It happened in East L.A. when the L.A. County Sheriffs had gunned down Chicano activists, when bullies at Stevenson Junior High would kick some little kid's ass just to show them who was in charge, when my dad's anger with my mom had reached the tipping point.

"What's going on?" I asked the commander in a polite tone. The officer turned to look at me, pausing for a second as though thinking of his reply, and then he turned toward the staircase, and, in a loud voice, he said: "You need to disperse!"

There was nothing to do but run for our lives, and we scurried out like cucarachas when the lights go on. The order to march had been given, and we fled through MacArthur Park, grateful that we'd been able to warn those people in the lobby but worried about our friends who were trapped upstairs. Even though we feared the worst, we clung to the hope that the crowd would be dispersed peacefully as we had been.

It turned out that our worst fears were justified.

THE AGE BEFORE CELL PHONES

It was 1979, an age before cell phones and readily available video cameras. If only we'd had cell phones, we'd have been able to text Bruce's brother and his girlfriend, Dorothy, to warn them of the advancing storm troopers. We could have called from the lobby and advised our friends to evacuate. It took only seconds between the time the LAPD commander ordered us to disperse and the advancement of the foot soldiers up the stairs. If only we'd had video cameras, we'd have been able to document the brutal abuse of police power that took place over the next 10 minutes. Instead, it was left to black-and-white photographic images and painful bruises, broken bones and split scalps to tell the story of what really happened on the night when officially sanctioned violence became part of the L.A. punk scene.

I couldn't help looking back as we hurried away, and the images were seared on my brain: LAPD wielding their batons as though they were striking human piñatas rather than young kids made of flesh and blood; concertgoers trying desperately to escape the building had to run past a phalanx of riot police who beat them mercilessly as they fled. More cops arrived to join the ranks of those already making their way into the building. "Get out of here, NOW!" an officer yelled at us as we distanced ourselves from the scene of the growing disaster. We scattered like rats, which is just what we felt like, running away, feeling small and powerless, unable to help our friends. It was a hopeless situation.

When we finally did hear from Bruce's brother, Jeff, and his girlfriend, Dorothy, we discovered that they had been badly beaten by the police. Both of them had been clubbed brutally and their injuries had landed them in the emergency room, where they'd had to have the vicious cuts on their scalps stitched back together.

They weren't the only ones who'd been injured; dozens of innocent bystanders had been clubbed while attempting to leave the building, but perhaps because Jeff was in a well-known band, they attracted more attention than others. They bravely went forth on local television and spoke out against the injustice of what had taken place, forcing the LAPD to respond. They put a human face on what the public saw as just a bunch of weird-looking, troublemaking kids. After receiving a bit of media attention, they met with a lawyer about the possibility of suing the LAPD for use of excessive force, but the lawyer advised them against it. "Sure," he told them. "You could sue, and you might even win, but you better hope you never get pulled over for a traffic ticket." Jeff and Dorothy had plenty of witnesses who had seen what had been done to them, and they had medical documentation of their injuries, but the implication was clear: If you tangled with the LAPD, they'd get you back someday, one way or another. It would be many years before the videotaping of Rodney King's arrest and beating would set the city on fire and bring about some change in the abuse of power by the rotten apples in the Los Angeles Police Department.

It was outrageous that the police could attack so viciously, without the slightest provocation, and get away with it. The only little bit of satisfaction any of us got came from hearing the story of Dorothy's sister Barbara. Dorothy and Barbara had been regulars on the scene for a while. They were known affectionately as the Xerox Twins because they bore a sisterly resemblance to each other. Barbara had earned her tough-girl stripes in a legendary fight with my former roommate Sheila Edwards. Upon hearing of her sister's beating at the hands of the LAPD, the petite but by no means frail Barbara was said to have uprooted a No Parking sign from the park across the street from the Elks Lodge and advanced on the cops, swinging it furiously like a medieval battle-axe. The riot squad advanced on Barbara, but, fueled by a rush of adrenaline, she hoisted the sign up and threw it at them. They looked at each other dumbfounded before swarming her and wrestling her to the ground, where they cuffed her. Barbara somehow broke her restraints and got up swinging. Realizing that cuffing the diminutive she-devil was not enough, the thugs cuffed her again, this time also hog-tying and arresting her.

The LAPD's explanation for Barbara's superhuman strength was that she was on angel dust — PCP. At the time, anyone who tangled with the LAPD with any sort of success was accused of being "dusted," and this gave them license to use what would be considered excessive force under normal circumstances. It was just bullshit. The allegations were untrue. Barbara was squeaky clean, and despite the fact that she had been arrested, the story of her David and Goliath confrontation with the storm troopers at the Elks Lodge Hall became L.A. punk legend.

HARD TO THE CORE

The Bags were kinda hardcore before there was hardcore.
—Nickey Beat

Now that officially sanctioned violence had been introduced to the punk scene courtesy of the LAPD, SoCal punk shows began to take on an increasingly moody, angry tone. At the same time, the rising popularity of hardcore bands led to swelling audiences; quite naturally, many of these bands found opening slots on bills with the Bags.

Although I didn't realize it at the time, the Bags had always had a dark, angry core. It's the reason why Brendan Mullen remarked of our first show at the Masque that he'd "never seen a woman so angry," why Craig Lee had written the songs "Babylonian Gorgon" and "Violence Girl" about me, why Bibbe Hansen later described my stage persona as "woman as Avenging Goddess." There was a point in our musical development where our live shows were all energy and chaos, and I felt like I'd inadvertently unleashed the wrath of Kali upon the world of punk.

Now the seeds of a new movement were falling on fertile ground. The change happened slowly; as in any cultural movement, each artist built upon what came before while at the same time razing some of what they deemed superfluous, supplanting it with their own contribution and reinventing earlier forms. Art does not happen in a vacuum.

During the spring and summer of 1979, the Bags welcomed and supported many of the newer, more aggressive hardcore bands coming out of Orange County and from Southern California's beach cities. Bands were multiplying, springing up everywhere. Most wanted to play Hollywood, where the punk scene was already in full swing; many cultivated venues to play in their own neighborhoods. From backyard parties in East L.A. to abandoned churches in Hermosa Beach, punk was on the rise, picking up the flavors of each region.

Audiences were getting bigger, representing larger and broader sections of the population. But bigger isn't always better. Unlike the band of misfits who had originally shaped the L.A. punk scene, this broader, larger sampling of the general population included its fair share of creators but also some mainstream bandwagon-jumpers, who, instead of expanding creativity, inhibited it.

One night while I was onstage, I noticed that the landscape was changing before my eyes. As I looked out into the audience, I could see that the once quirky men and women artists who prized originality above all else were being replaced by a belligerent, male-dominated mob who became anonymous, camouflaged by their homogeneous appearance. I didn't mind the belligerent part; in fact, playing for a belligerent group of individuals can be quite satisfying. What I didn't like was the sameness. In the past, audiences were full of men and women in wildly colored plumage; now the black leather jacket was emerging as the uniform of the new regime.

As I surveyed these new audiences, I saw a number of young men who were looking around as if they were in a daze, not even listening to the band. They were looking for the next person they could slam their body against, and we just happened to be the band providing the background music. It was disappointing, because what was most important to me as a performer was to be able to connect with people when I was onstage, where I felt like a conduit for energy. The rage that had been bottled up for years came pouring out of me onstage, but I was also a conduit for the energy being put out by the audience. It was a deeply intimate and personal exchange, a give-and-take between audience and performer, not unlike sex.

Good sex is like a good rock show: Both demand constant, active engagement between everyone involved. If someone is not actively engaged, then they're just going through the motions, and that's just missing the point of the whole thing. I wanted my audiences to experience what I felt onstage: complete and utter freedom from convention and rules. I wanted to connect with them on a visceral level, to lead them through a sort of mass catharsis. Rock music has never been an intellectual exercise for me, which explains why I always listen for melody and emotion first, lyrics second. I had always said that I wanted to erase the line between performer and audience, to do away with the barrier of the stage, but now it became apparent to me that hardcore audiences weren't so much there for a live performance as they were looking for a live soundtrack to work out their frustrations. Punk rock had entered a new stage in its evolution, as had I.

TOO MUCH PRESSURE

The band's popularity was still swelling through the spring and summer of 1979. We had consistently good reviews, and a few of the major record companies sent scouts out to our shows, but what the press loved most about us was the energy we created in a live situation, something that could not be duplicated on vinyl. The feedback we were getting from A&R people was that they wanted to know that I could really sing, not just rile people up.

That's when the pressure began to build within the band. Different members started giving me vocal tips, but what stumped them was that I sang well at rehearsal and had done my vocals for the Dangerhouse single in one take, so they knew I was capable of getting it right; I just wasn't doing it live. Patricia, being my oldest friend in the group, was the only one who came right out and told me that it was essentially up to me to start delivering consistent vocal performances if we wanted to get signed. In hindsight, I'm sure that the whole band felt the same way. I started to see Patricia as the bearer of bad news whenever I fucked up. The pressure put some strain on our friendship, but because I knew she was trying to help me I did my best to try to measure up. The pressure I put on myself was much greater than the pressure anyone else put on me.

At a band meeting where my shortcomings were openly discussed, we decided to hire go-go dancers to help keep up the energy onstage while I reined myself in and focused on my singing. I deliberately started holding back onstage, trying to pace myself like an athlete might do when running a long-distance race. In the past, I had tried to sprint through the entire set, which left me breathless halfway through and set me up for a poor vocal performance. The only problem was that my performances were coming from a place that I didn't fully control. Alice Bag was born from chaos.

We said goodbye to the go-go dancers after a few performances.

At the height of our popularity, we decide to turn the band around 180 degrees. We held another band meeting at my parents' house, where we discussed the possibility of adding keyboards for me to play somewhere in the middle of the set. The idea was that the keyboards would force me to remain stationary and give me a break to catch my breath. The band was also eager to prove that we were musically versatile, and the keyboards would add a new dimension to our songs. I thought back to my early piano lessons with Miss Dean and felt certain that I could manage the playing, but I hadn't had a piano since I was 10 years old, so the idea was put on hold until we could afford to purchase one.

My mom and dad were fond of surprises. They showed up one evening at Madame Wong's in Chinatown to hear the band play. "Since you haven't invited us, we just had to show up and surprise you," my dad said. It turned out to be a show that would get female musicians 86'd from Madame Wong's. The Bags and X were on the bill, and our audience had been particularly frisky. My father had to stand atop a chair to watch our set. My mom thought it was hilarious, and I could tell my hell-raiser father was proud of me. "I don't know what you were singing about m'ija, but I loved the way you did it!" Madame Wong didn't think it was so great. The club sustained damage, and Billy Zoom's guitar got stolen. After that night, Madame Wong decided that bands with girls in them meant trouble, and she refused to book them.

Now my parents were ready to spring another surprise on me. I didn't know that my father had been listening in on our conversation during the band meeting, but a few days later, when I got home from school, my mom and dad asked me to take a drive with them. They had something to show me but wouldn't tell me what it was. We drove out to a music store in Montebello, and when we walked in my father led me straight back to where the electric pianos were. "I'm not a rich man, but what I have is yours," my father said. "Your mom and I are buying you a piano to play in your band."

The Hohner piano cost a whopping $1,100 — a small fortune at that time, especially for my parents, who were barely making ends meet. They had raided their savings account for me, and although I felt guilty and tried to refuse, they wouldn't hear of it. I only hoped that if it helped the band I might be able to repay them someday.

FASTEN YOUR SEATBELTS

When Craig informed us that we'd be opening for Iggy Pop in Seattle, we were thrilled. Not only would we be playing with a man whose exploits were legendary, we'd be expanding our touring range north beyond San Francisco. There was a lot of planning that went into the trip. Craig handled most of it by himself. He arranged to borrow a van from the studio where his mother was working, which saved us a bunch of money because we wouldn't have to pay a rental fee.

Craig Lee's mother had started out in Hollywood as an actress, then she'd moved on to writing (for which she won an Emmy award), then TV directing and producing. She was a strong, independent powerhouse of a woman. Like his mom, Craig was also strong, independent and driven, and perhaps that contributed to their frequent feuds. But despite the feuding, Craig and his mother were in constant contact over the years, which led me to believe that they thrived on the mutual tension they created. On more than one occasion, Joanna Lee came to the aid of the Bags, even hiring us to entertain at a garden party she hosted for the cast of the TV show M*A*S*H. We played in a large tent at her palatial residence on one of the numerous Helena Drives in Brentwood. I remember wearing a gold thrift-store evening dress and having actress Loretta Swit compliment me on it. I was so star-struck: There I was, the barrio girl with the self-clipped hair and secondhand clothes eating fancy canapés with Hot Lips Houlihan. We received a warm, if somewhat confused, reception from the party guests, but Joanna was obviously proud of her son. I could see it, even if Craig couldn't.

My share of the preparations for the trip to Seattle was to collect money from my bandmates for anyone wishing to purchase thick foam rubber mats that were being sold at the swap meet near my house. The mats were the perfect size to fit under sleeping bags, and we anticipated sleeping on floors for most of our trip. Oddly, Craig was the only person who did not want to purchase a foam mat. He was the one who had the biggest apartment and was most accustomed to comfort, so it surprised me that he would want to forgo the little bit of extra padding that the mats would afford.

When the day finally came for us to leave for Seattle, Craig picked up the van, then picked up me, Rob, Patricia and Terry, in succession. We hadn't even left Hollywood when it became obvious that we were in for a bumpy trip. The van Craig had borrowed was large and roomy, but it had a stick shift and two small rear windows which were pretty much useless because they were blocked by our equipment, sleeping bags and luggage. "I'll drive first," Craig said, optimistically waiting for someone else to chime in, but no one did. Terry said he couldn't drive because he had outstanding parking tickets that had turned into a warrant for his arrest; Patricia said she'd slept in her contacts and couldn't see properly, and Rob also refused, for some reason I've forgotten.

"I'd help drive," I offered, "but I don't know how to drive a stick shift, and this is a huge van." Craig looked at the loaded van and its less-than-helpful occupants.

"Oh, it's easy, Gordita!" he said, smiling, trying to make me feel confident. But I was worried. Craig drove almost all the way to San Francisco before asking me to take over. Now the whole band was eager to give me driving lessons: "Put one foot on the brake, the other on the clutch." I did as I was told. "Now you're going to put your foot on the gas while slowly letting your foot off the clutch." Craig spoke to me like I was an idiot. Surely it couldn't be that hard. Countless people who were less intelligent than me somehow managed to drive a stick shift; how hard could it be? The van lurched forward violently as I let out the clutch. I stomped on the brake and killed it.

"Slowly, Alice!" "Don't give it that much gas!" "Make it smooth." There was a chorus of suggestions coming from the peanut gallery. "That was good Alice, try it again." After a good 15 to 20 minutes of lessons during which everyone wanted to strangle me, I took over the driving while Craig slept. Terry offered to sit up front with me and be my copilot, in case I ran into trouble. It wasn't bad at all, once I got my speed steady and didn't have to worry about the clutch. I was used to staying up late, but the monotony of a long-distance drive in the dark made me sleepy. Terry was forced to entertain me by playing music and chatting with me whenever I looked like I was falling asleep at the wheel.

We reached Mt. Shasta sometime in the early morning. There was a light snow falling. I had never seen snow before, so it was exciting to see the little puffs floating down. I pulled over and got out of the van, an action which provoked a bit of annoyed mutterings in the back of the van from passengers who had been lulled to sleep by the sound of the road rolling under our tires, but I had been driving for hours and felt entitled to stretch my legs and catch some snowflakes on my palms. Complain, complain, complain… First they didn't want to drive, then they wanted to complain. I felt myself getting annoyed, and so I took my sweet time admiring the snow. I walked out into a wooded area, stretched out my arms and spun around like a helicopter, letting the snow fall on my face. Calls came from the van. "Let's GO!" "C'mon!!!" The increasingly whiny tone in the voices amused me. I pretended to be Butterfly McQueen as Prissy in *Gone with the Wind*, walking back slowly, distractedly, ignoring anxious expectation. It became a game for me. Every time someone called out for me to hurry back, I'd stop in my tracks to look at something just to annoy them. It wasn't until Craig called me back that I finally made haste and climbed back behind the wheel. After two or three attempts, I got the clutch engaged and everyone went back to sleep, but their repose would only last a few more minutes. The murky light of early morning didn't wake them up; the feeling of our van skidding on the ice did.

IT'S GOING TO BE A BUMPY RIDE

We don't get a lot of snow in East L.A. Ice never forms on our cracked and pitted streets. The smooth, shiny glass surface I was driving on had absolutely no traction and the van started to slide. "Don't hit the brakes, whatever you do!" Terry called out to me, but it was too late. I thought I'd eased up on the brakes, but we were still sliding.

"Fuuuuuck!" I yelled. We only slid a few feet, but it was enough to make everyone panic. "What's going on?!" Craig called.

"There's ice on the road," Terry replied. There were still cars behind us, so I had to keep driving.

"Pull over Gordita. I'll drive." I drove to the next exit with every one of my passengers holding their breath. Craig was the driver again, and he knew what he was doing. I got in the back and took out one of the foil-wrapped burrito packages my mom had sent with us and handed a bean-and-cheese burrito to each person. There were six burritos in each package, and she'd sent three packages. We'd unwrapped one package the night before for dinner, and now we were unwrapping breakfast. The burritos were cold, but we had no money for restaurants, so we ate them anyway. After breakfast, I fell asleep, and when I woke up we were in Seattle. I jumped up to the front seat to look around at this new city.

We found the venue by the middle of the afternoon, and we circled several times, looking for a place to park before spotting a car that was leaving. Craig put on his signal and patiently waited for the space until the car left, then he pulled the van up slowly, preparing to back in. A little white sports car came out of nowhere and swooped into our parking spot. Without thinking, I opened the passenger door and, hanging out the open door, called to the driver: "Hey! We're backing into that spot!" But the sporty-looking guy cocked his head down, looked over his sunglasses and waved me away like he thought I was a pesky insect who was going to fly away. "Hey, fuckwad, that's our spot!" I continued to shout. A hand appeared from the back of the van, offering me an open package of burritos. I took a fat, juicy one and flung it onto the hood of the previously pristine white convertible. Mr. Hot Stuff driver turned back, shock registering on his face. I grabbed more Mexican foodstuff projectiles and launched an all out attack on the enemy vehicle. Hot Stuff was running back to his car.

"Bitch!" he screamed at me. I laughed, still flinging burritos and watching them explode, leaving turd-like blobs on the shiny paintjob. As Craig drove away, I climbed all the way in and slammed the door.

"That'll teach him!" Patricia said, and we all burst into uncontrollable laughter.

We decided to unload the equipment and then go find a parking space. We left Rob, Patricia and Terry at the venue, and Craig and I drove around, finally finding a parking spot some distance away. We bumped into our band-mates on the walk back. We were too early for sound check, they said. The sound man wasn't ready for us, and we needed to kill some time. I noticed a big sex shop across the street from where we were standing.

"Let's go in there!" I suggested.

"No, you don't want to go in there," Patricia said, suppressing a laugh.

"Yeah, we've already been in there." Terry added. "They have these little soup cans that look like Campbell's soup…"

"And one said 'Cream of Cum' — YUCK!" Patricia looked completely grossed out.

"I want to see," I enthused, but I was outvoted, and we went for a walk instead. As usual, I wasn't prepared for the cold. We were close to the water, and, even though I was wearing a long-sleeved shirt and a trench coat, the icy wind felt like it blew right through my clothes. Walking around Seattle with winter approaching was not fun. I still vividly recall the sight of a home-less man sitting on the ground. He had lost most of his nose, probably due to frostbite. He quickly covered the hole in the center of his face when he saw me and Patricia staring at him, but we couldn't help it. "Oh my God, poor man," Patricia whispered. The sight made an impression on me, too. *What is wrong with our society when we can let this happen and look the other way?* I asked myself. I had seen beggars and homeless people in Tijuana, and maybe one or two in downtown L.A., but it was rare. There were plenty of shelters in down-town L.A., and government programs were designed to care for people who could not care for themselves.

It was the end of 1979 and things would change dramatically over the next few years. 1980 would be an election year, and already some of the poten-tial nominees were starting to lay the groundwork for their upcoming cam-paigns. I wasn't politically involved at the time. My 18th birthday had come just five days after the 1976 US presidential elections, and I had remained largely uninvolved, but recently I'd read an interesting article on Governor Jerry Brown in *Rolling Stone* and another one in *Playboy* that had made me take notice of the unorthodox, handsome young politician. I loved the fact that he'd refused to move into the governor's mansion. I'd become enamored of him and had even written a song called "Iconoclast" about him.

Residents of Northern California and the Pacific Northwest had always claimed to be more politically and socially aware than their Southern California counterparts. Perhaps it was the gray weather and the presence of the disenfranchised trying to battle the elements alone that made people think about finding a solution to their plight.

THE BAD JUJU VAN

Perhaps I should have seen it coming, because the minute we were all in that van driving up north, I had the feeling that it wasn't going to be smooth sailing. We walked back to do our sound check at the club in Seattle and were quickly cut short without having the opportunity to achieve the sound we wanted. There's a saying that musicians employ whenever they have a discouraging sound check: "Bad sound check, good show." It's rarely true, and that night was no exception; the sound positively sucked. I was doomed from the start, because, lacking perfect pitch, I have no way of judging whether or not I'm on key unless I can hear myself in the monitors. There was feedback coming from the speakers and the noise all but ruined our entire performance. The band played on of course, struggling through our set like desperate soldiers slogging through a muddy retreat. After our set, it was hard to feel good about the show and what had been an inauspicious beginning to our West Coast mini-tour.

Iggy Pop came over to talk to the Bags backstage, but Patricia was still upset about the crappy show and she kept her distance. Iggy was encouraging, telling us not to be too hard on ourselves and that we'd had good energy. He then went on to tell us little bits of trivia about himself, very general stuff that we already knew. Maybe he wasn't aware of his own legendary status or perhaps he felt the need to remind others of his importance in the grand history of rock. Still, we gathered around him, hoping that some gems might drop from his lips, but after several minutes we were left wanting, and I walked back to where Patricia was sitting.

"You're all such groupies — look at you all clustered around him. What was so interesting about him?" she asked pointedly. I looked at her for a long time, searching for an answer.

"He's got really long eyelashes," I replied, and we both burst out laughing. Years later, I learned that Iggy had the Dead Kennedys removed from the bill of our Seattle gig because he had found their name to be in "bad taste and morally reprehensible." Jello Biafra retaliated by saying it was a case of the pot calling the kettle black, and rechristening Iggy as "Piggy Slop."

I quickly fell asleep in the van after the show, crashed on somebody's floor and was awakened early the following morning for a little tour of the city. The Seattle skyline was as gray and bleak as my mood, a light but incessant drizzle had been pestering the city since the previous night. We stopped for coffee at a little corner shop across the street from a big public fish market called Pike's

Place. I don't eat seafood, so the charm of people tossing around fish carcasses was completely lost on me. Instead, I pressed my cup of hot coffee against my lips, hoping the aroma of freshly roasted coffee beans would camouflage the fishy smell in the air. My intense love of coffee notwithstanding, I decided then and there that I didn't care for Seattle. It would take about 20 years for me to go back to the Emerald City and learn to appreciate it, but on that cold morning in 1979 I just wanted to get the hell out of there.

The next night we played in Portland at a club called the Long Goodbye, an oddly prescient omen. We were scheduled to play two sets in one night, an early show for under-21s and a late show for 21 and over. Another difficult sound check ensued, and I was apprehensive about the upcoming sets, but Jello Biafra from the Dead Kennedys showed up early to cheer us on. It was good to see a familiar face in the audience. Over the past few months, Jello had been a sort of goodwill ambassador for the Bags whenever we went to San Francisco. It wasn't unusual for him to jump in the car with us and give us an audio tour on our way to wherever we were going. Jello was never at a loss for words, and he had mastered the art of engaging, provoking and challenging his audiences. Now he stood in front of the stage in Portland, gamely calling out songs and trying to engage our band in our own performance. It was big-hearted of him and temporarily comforting.

The Portland show soon turned tense. I looked at the members of our band, trying to detect some team spirit, but it was everyone for themselves. I had never felt so distant from Patricia, who seemed to scowl at me onstage; I couldn't tell if she was angry at me or at someone else, but when I looked at her she looked tense and upset. Rob Ritter was in his own world; by this time he had become a fully committed recreational drug user, and since he was the only regular user in the band, he practically existed in his own universe. Terry Graham and Craig Lee could barely even stand to look at each other; the animosity between them had grown almost unbearable. The Bags were disintegrating with each successive performance.

We made it through the two shows, and afterward we hung out with some friends we'd made at the club, an all-girl band called the Neo Boys ,with whom I instantly fell in love. Craig and I wanted to party with the Neo Boys all night, and there was talk of going bowling the next day, but not everyone was as smitten with them as Craig and I were. After drinking heavily at a party, we said goodbye to our new friends and drove to the house where we would crash for the night. I must have dozed off in the back of the van while Craig was driving, and when we finally stopped, he came around to open the passenger door and get us all out. He must have bumped Terry awake because before I knew what was happening, Terry had turned around and punched Craig squarely in the jaw. Craig didn't punch him back. Instead he looked at me and said, "He's your friend Alice. You deal with him."

Terry yelled at Craig: "You did that on purpose!" I had no idea what he was talking about or how to fix the situation, and in the end I didn't fix anything. We all went inside, rolled out our cushions and sleeping bags and went to sleep. Craig was the only one who didn't have a cushion and had to sleep on the bare floor. I don't know if it was his simmering anger at Terry or the hard floor that annoyed him most, but he kept trying to talk to me. Desperate to get some sleep, I eventually parted with my sleeping bag, hoping that it would allow him to rest more comfortably and quiet down. I scrunched myself into a ball on my foam pad, pulled my blanket around me and dreamed of being home in my own bed.

The next morning we went thrift-store shopping with the Neo Boys, but the bowling would have to wait until some other day. You know it's a bad tour when the best part about it is meeting another band, and so far, meeting them had been the best thing about this trip. Unfortunately, we had to leave pretty early, as we had a show in San Francisco that night and another the following night. We got in the van again and drove south, the increasing tension now palpable. Nobody was really getting along.

Being in San Francisco was almost like being back home. We had friends there, knew what type of sound to expect at the clubs and how to best compensate for any problems. The first night went well, and we loaded up the van after the show, ready for a good night's rest in real beds at the Sam Wong Hotel on Broadway. It seemed we had finally managed to shake off our bad juju when Craig opened the back door of the van and popped his head in. "That was a good show!" he said cheerfully. Then he dropped a bomb: One of his friends was having a big party that night, and he had invited the Bags to play.

"No," I said flatly. "I don't want to go to a party. I want a nice warm bed."

"But it's a great opportunity for us. There will be lots of people there, people who wouldn't ordinarily hear us." Craig was pleading now.

I felt a fleeting twinge of guilt, but then I insisted, "No, I'm not doing it." I didn't bother to consult anyone else, I didn't look around to take a vote. I was exhausted, not just physically but emotionally by all the negative feelings that were festering in the bad-juju van for the past few days. Craig's face flushed red as he started yelling at me about how I was being so selfish, only thinking of myself. What about everything he'd done for the band? I was so tired that I couldn't focus on what he was saying; instead I saw his cartoon-like red face contorting in front of me as he spit out the ugly accusations. The veins in his neck were suddenly bulging, threatening to burst. He had giant, goggling frog-eyes, and his gesticulating was wildly exaggerated. Suddenly, without meaning to, I began to laugh. Terry immediately followed suit, laughing with me, laughing at Craig. Craig stared at both of us with hurt and anger in his eyes and slammed the door, leaving us in the van.

The last show in San Francisco and the subsequent drive home to Los Angeles were quiet, tense and uncomfortable. Clearly, road trips didn't agree with us.

BAG END

When we got back to L.A., we tried to put the trip behind us. We booked more shows and met with a woman who wanted to film us for a documentary she was making about the L.A. punk scene. We discussed the project with her at Wilshire Fine Arts rehearsal studios during a break, but we didn't commit to do the film immediately; instead, we asked for a chance to discuss it as a group and get back to her. Even though our band was going through a rough patch, we still felt that we had something to protect. Some of the original scene bands were still trying for the brass ring of a major-label record contract; after all, the Dickies had been signed to A&M, hadn't they? Craig offered to have his mother's attorney look at the contract before signing anything.

We played around town, but it wasn't easy, because punk had been banned from many of the established rock clubs by this time. Madame Wong's had banned the Bags for provoking a mini riot, and I had been personally 86'd from Club 88 for punching a crotch-grabbing pervert in the face and slicing open the area under his eye socket. Fortunately, the Hong Kong Cafe saw opportunity where others saw trouble. We started booking double shows there, which meant we could sell the house out twice in one night and make double the money. The shows at the Hong Kong were always fun; the 1940s Chinese-deco building exuded an exotic, retro vibe, and the low ceilings, with their ornate decorative tiles, created a sense of pressure-cooker intensity. Paul Cutler from the Consumers often ran the soundboard there, and he made sure the bands could hear and that no extraneous feedback was coming through the speakers.

We continued to work in songs with keyboards here and there. I started writing again, something I hadn't done in over a year, but my pop influences were showing. I contributed two songs that betrayed my permanent Buzzcocks damage; both songs had an upbeat, poppy sound that didn't gel with our tough, out-of-control image. At the same time, Craig was penning darker, slower songs like "The Balcony" and "Prowlers in the Night," moving toward what would soon be called *post-punk*. At rehearsals our new songs sounded great, but there was still the question of whether I could consistently deliver good pitch in an unpredictable live setting. The answer was no. I could only sing well when I could hear myself and wasn't losing myself in the performance. The jumping, whirling and prowling the stage often left me breathless and unable to sustain notes. The band as a whole was in a state of flux, with each member's tastes pushing and pulling us in different directions.

After the near disastrous trip to the Pacific Northwest, we never fully recovered as a team. Patricia and I were barely speaking to each other, and I didn't even know why. I assumed it was because I was letting the band down, somehow. It all came to a head at a show in San Diego. It was a small show and one that wouldn't ordinarily have been a big deal, but it would be an important turning point for the band. Before the show, Patricia had been drinking, and she was not typically a heavy drinker, so it should have been a red flag. Once onstage, the drinking began to affect her. She started flubbing notes, which was surprisingly unlike her. She had been the most vocal about the need for the band to be more professional, but for once it was her and not me fucking up. Of all people in that group, I knew what it was like to fuck up onstage, but instead of sympathizing with her, I felt angry that she was behaving the way she'd been telling me not to behave. My reaction might have been different if it hadn't been for the fact that over the past few months we'd grown increasingly distant.

I wasn't the only one who was angry. Backstage after the show, Rob was the first to mention Patricia's mistakes, ranting about how she kept playing wrong sections of songs and bumping into his guitar, knocking it out of tune, but he didn't say a word to her when she walked in. He only vented when she wasn't in the room. It was confusing, because he'd been so upset with her just a few minutes earlier. Terry remained diplomatic, silently shaking his head. Craig and I were the bad guys. "What happened to you?" Craig asked, scratching his forearms in frustration until they were red. I joined in, eager to dish back some of the pressure that Patricia had heaped on me over the past few months.

"Yeah, what the hell was that?" I asked. Patricia just looked at us and laughed. She was still drunk and made a woozy bee line to get her things and walk out.

The backbiting was intense. It seemed that every problem any of us had with anyone else in the group was redirected at Patricia. She became the scapegoat. The show had also raised questions about the direction of the band. Speaking privately with Craig, I confessed to him that I was thinking of quitting. I wasn't having as much fun onstage anymore, and I wanted to make big changes that I knew the rest of the band wouldn't agree to. I'd always felt that the most creative artists are those who change often and reinvent themselves, and I felt stuck as Alice Bag. I'd been swallowed by one aspect of my personality and it was overshadowing the rest of me. I don't think either of us understood that I was trapped in the persona I'd created. Craig gave me the usual pep talk and told me to wait. "We can make big changes, you'll see."

The phone lines were still jammed with me, Craig, Terry and Rob talking to each other about the San Diego show, basically blaming Patricia for things she was and wasn't guilty of. We decided it was best for the four of us to sit down and talk. There were many things to discuss, but the main one was Patricia: Should we keep her, or kick her out? We hastily arranged for a meeting at my parents' house in East L.A. We hadn't been there for more than 10 minutes when the phone rang. It was Patricia. She asked if it was true that we were meeting without her. Terry's girlfriend was very good friends with Patricia. We all knew it, but we hadn't thought for a moment that she would tell her about our meeting before we'd had a chance to figure out what we wanted to do. I believe that's what happened.

"Yes," I said. "We want to talk about the San Diego show," I added.

"What about it?" she asked.

"You made a lot of mistakes," I replied. Patricia asked me to hand the phone to Rob, then Terry, then Craig. She spoke to each person briefly before telling Craig that she was quitting. Her actions surprised me, and I thought about all the times that my bandmates had discussed my bad performances, telling me later what I could do to improve. I'd felt bad about it, but I hadn't resigned. Had they ever considered firing me? I don't know. I felt sad almost immediately, but it didn't last. Except for Terry's girlfriend, who sat quietly on the couch, everyone else tried to make light of it: "Well, I guess now we don't have to decide what to do about Patricia."

Years later, Patricia would say that a bass player she knew had told her that he'd been asked to join the band. To my knowledge, nobody else was ever asked to join the band. Rob had volunteered to switch over to bass even before Patricia tendered her resignation. Rob and Craig had made the drive to East L.A. together from Hollywood, and on the ride over they had discussed all the possible options, one of them being Rob switching from lead guitar to bass.

In our minds, Patricia had quit, but rumors circulated, some saying that she quit, others saying that we kicked her out. Patricia had beaten us to the punch. She had made the decision for both herself and us, in the process denying us the satisfaction of ever knowing that we'd done the right thing.

It took 30 years for me and Patricia to be on speaking terms again after that fateful day. When I think back, I can see that the Bags had already torn apart at the seams, both musically and personally, and it was just a matter of time before the band would run its course. Anyone who's ever been in a band will tell you they have their own peculiar dynamics, and it is only by a delicate balance of egos and talents that the ones who stick around manage to survive with all original members intact. The Bags was a band that had taken months and months to form. It was a band that had survived countless false starts, a couple of different names, the loss of a finger, the hiring and firing of a dozen different members, the trashing of the Troubadour and innumerable triumphs and travesties. But the main reason the Bags existed in the first place was because two good friends dared to dream of having their own all-girl band.

It only took 10 minutes on a fall afternoon in 1979 to kill that dream forever.

READY FOR MY CLOSE-UP

At the end of 1979, the remaining members of the band filmed *The Decline of Western Civilization*, as planned. Director Penelope Spheeris gave us one specific request: "Please don't wear dark colors. Everyone we've shot so far is wearing black or dark colors." I went to my favorite thrift store and bought a hot pink mod dress. I also had the brilliant idea that I was going to get my hair finger-waved. I visualized combining a '60s dress with a '20s hairdo, and the mental image looked good, but, as it usually turned out, the idea was much better in my imagination. My too-frequently dyed and too-rarely conditioned hair sizzled with the perm solution, and I don't mean it sizzled because it was so fashionably hot; no, it was *chicharron*-hot, crispy noodle hot. When I washed out the solution, my hair felt like seaweed, limp and slimy. I flashed back to my junior high school girls' bathroom days where, with a pair of school scissors I'd clipped a bald spot on the side of my head. What the fuck do I do now?

"Miss Spheeris, I'm ready for my close-up!"

The filming of the performance was an ordeal. It was supposed to be a live show, but because several bands were being filmed and there were five bands on the bill, it became a marathon. Fights broke out backstage as people tried to change the order of performance. In a small area overflowing with testosterone, I was the only woman, and nobody was fucking with me. For some stupid reason, I took it upon myself to think of a peaceful solution to the problem of the evening's lineup. "Let's draw straws," I offered. Oddly, everyone agreed to abide by whatever straw we drew. I went first and immediately picked the shortest one, which meant we were screwed.

We were nearly out of steam even before we went on. The show had gone on far too long. The film crew was packing up equipment, members of the audience looked spent and it was hard to get excited about playing, but we went out and tried to revive the night. I knew it wasn't our best show, but it wasn't our worst, either. I was just glad to be done with it, figuring it was probably going to be another student film that the director would screen for a class full of film students. I imagined it would never be heard of again.

Within weeks, Patricia contacted the director and claimed copyright of the name "the Bags." Penelope in turn contacted us, convinced that she risked being sued if she used the band name without permission from the copyright holder. The band met to discuss this new development. It was the first indication we'd had that Patricia was feeling vindictive. Any bit of sympathy or remorse that might have lingered from our messy breakup with her flew out the window. After assassinating her character, maligning her playing and any other aspect of her we could think of, we moved on to the task of thinking up a new name for the band. Maybe it's a good thing, I thought to myself. Maybe it will be a chance to reinvent ourselves. For the next month or so, at least half an hour of every rehearsal was set aside for brainstorming ridiculous band names. By the time 1980 rolled around, we had settled on two finalists. The first name on the short list was Plan 9, after the film *Plan 9 from Outer Space*, a sort of homage to Craig's mom, Joanna Lee, who had played an extraterrestrial in the Ed Wood cult classic. The second name on the list was Buffy's Ghost, a reference to one of our favorite 1960s TV shows, *Family Affair*. Buffy was the name of a little girl character on the show. The actress who played Buffy had died a couple of years earlier of a drug overdose. The image of sweet little Buffy and her constant companion, the bespectacled doll Mrs. Beasley, appearing as a ghost seemed perversely comical.

While we'd been spinning our wheels thinking of stupid names for the band, Penelope Spheeris had taken matters into her own hands. "You guys never gave me a name," she told us at a band meeting.

"I'm sorry, we hadn't thought of one, but we have one now." I was looking forward to announcing that we'd finally decided to go with Plan 9, but she cut me off.

"No, I'm sorry. I had to move ahead. I listed you as 'the Alice Bag Band.'" We looked at each other in disbelief.

"But that's not our name!" I protested immediately, aware that the name would make me appear like a megalomaniac.

"Can't we change it?" Craig asked.

"I wasn't aware we had a deadline," Terry joined in, but Ms. Spheeris stuck to her guns. She was like no one I'd ever met. She wasn't going to let anything stand in the way of completing this film on her terms and on her schedule. There was something about the way she spoke that instantly made it clear she was not there to negotiate.

"I just wanted to let you know," she informed us. "Look — the name works because it tells your fans who's in the band. That way you can still get Bags' fans without risk of copyright infringement." Craig nodded, seeming to agree with her. "This film WILL be released, and it will generate interest in your band. You might think about starting to play under that name," Penelope said as we ended the meeting.

I felt sick. It's not that I was modest — heavens no, modesty has no place on a list of an entertainer's virtues. The truth is, I was aware of the perception that choosing a name like that would create. If it had truly been my solo project, my songs, my vision, it might have been a different story, but it wasn't that at all. The band was very much a democracy. Craig still wrote most of the songs and booked most of the shows; Terry and Rob wrote their own parts and had a say in every aspect of the band.

I don't think anyone was happy with the name, but in the end we decided to use it. Terry, Craig and Rob all seemed to agree with Penelope that the Bags name recognition factor was important. I was the lone protesting voice. My hopes for a new name and new direction for the band were fading fast.

OLD FRIENDS, NEW GAMES

"They waited too long!" Shannon's voice trembled with a mixture of anger and sadness on the other end of the phone line. "They could have saved her, but they were too stupid and scared!"

Shannon was telling me about some of her new friends, people I had met only in passing but with whom she'd formed a bond based on drug use. It seemed that one of them — a young girl — had accidentally died from an overdose of heroin. The girl had been shooting up with these friends when her eyes rolled back in her head and she'd slumped to the floor. When she couldn't be revived, they realized that they'd have to call for help. They'd panicked, frightened of being arrested when the police arrived. Several critical minutes passed while they argued over the best course of action, finally deciding to place an anonymous phone call and then flee the scene. It was too little, too late. Shannon's friend died in the ambulance on the way to the hospital.

Even though I was saddened by this young girl's death, my instinct for self-preservation told me to insulate myself from her and from the goings-on in Hollywood. The harsh reality of my friends becoming junkies had just started to hit me during my last days at the Canterbury. The increasingly frequent close calls of my neighbors overdosing on their drugs of choice was one of the reasons I'd wanted to move back to my parents' house, but at the same time I didn't want to just abandon my old friends. We'd been through too much together; we'd become each other's extended family.

"Wanna come over and cheer me up, Alice?" I hadn't seen Shannon as often as I would have liked since I'd moved home. Sheila, Shannon and I had been pretty tight when we were roommates at the Canterbury, now I only saw the girls at concerts or at parties. "Come over, we'll go have Thai food at that place you like on Hollywood Boulevard." Shannon insisted.

We went to Lee's Thai, where the spicy food made our eyes water and the sweet, creamy iced tea soothed our burning tongues. I listened to Shannon rant about the unfortunate overdose of her young friend until she ran out of things to say. Shannon was not a person who could dwell on sorrow for very long; her irrepressible sense of humor usually wouldn't allow it. And so, with a few bad jokes, I managed to pull her out of her grief. I treated her to lunch, because I had a regular job and Shannon was the one who needed cheering up. At first, Shannon refused to let me pay, since she was the one who'd insisted we meet for lunch. She gave in reluctantly, smiling the sneaky smile I'd missed so much.

"Okay, you get lunch, but you've got to let me get dessert, okay?"

"Deal," I replied.

"I've got a treat for us at home," she smiled. By home, she meant her mother's house. Shannon had left the Canterbury shortly after I had, briefly moving into a different apartment before ending up back with her mom. No one was home at her house when we got back from lunch. Shannon's mood had lifted considerably, and she no longer seemed to be thinking about her dead friend or even the fact that I was there to cheer her up. Instead, she rummaged through a bag that she took out of the closet. "Come with me," she said, walking from the living room into the hall.

"You want me to go to the bathroom with you?" I asked, kidding with her.

"Yes," she replied in her deep, velvety voice. "I'm too distraught to wipe my own ass, I need your help." We laughed and she locked the door behind me. It dawned on me that our dessert wasn't going to be the cookie or brownie I'd imagined. She held a small paper package in her hand.

"I don't want any of that," I said, figuring out what my present was.

"How do you know you don't want any? You've never even tried it," she said in a half-seductive, half-mocking tone. "You're not going to turn down my present, are you? You said you'd let me do something for you." I watched Shannon as she unfolded the package, shook out some of its contents and started dissolving what looked like light brown sugar on an old spoon. "Are you afraid?" she asked, suddenly serious.

"I guess so," I replied but there was a part of me that felt safe around Shannon. As if reading my mind, she filled the syringe and stopped to look at me.

"I won't hurt you. I know what I'm doing." Her bedside manner was flawless. Shannon expertly lassoed my virgin arm with a tourniquet, gently penetrated my vein with the needle and gave me my first taste of heroin.

The initial pinch and sting of the needle was quickly replaced by the total absence of any kind of pain. It took only seconds for the drug to get from my forearm to my brain. My head fell back and I felt myself swoon. A dreamy sense of calmness and well-being washed over me; it was like I was floating in a warm bath or amniotic fluid. I watched as Shannon tied herself off and shot the remainder of the drug into her own vein. We were smiling at each other happily when we heard the front door of the house open and Shannon's mother call up the stairs. "Shannon! Are you here?" She was walking up the stairs.

"We're in the bathroom, mom. Putting on our makeup!" Shannon called out through the locked door. The doorknob turned back and forth in a futile attempt to open it.

"Why do you have to lock the door to put on makeup?" Her mom sounded annoyed.

"We'll be right out, mom!" Shannon said, quickly shaking off the pleasant stupor and getting rid of any incriminating evidence.

Shannon had given me a smaller, beginner's dose but I started feeling nauseous and the good feeling turned into a groggy, queasy high. Before long I was back in Shannon's bathroom, vomiting up Lee's Thai, shooting brown rice and hot chiles out through my nose and burning my mucous membranes. Now I knew why junkies were so thin. I quietly cursed myself for having allowed Shannon to shoot me up, but once the unpleasantness of being sick had passed, I was left with the best high ever, only slightly diminished by an annoyingly itchy, runny nose.

Later that night, as I drove myself back home to East L.A., I wondered if my parents would somehow know that I'd used heroin. Did I look different? I knew I had crossed some imaginary line, one that my trusting and loving parents would never have wanted me to cross. I felt terribly guilty, and I promised myself now that my curiosity had been satisfied, and I would never do it again.

BEAUTY SCHOOL DROPOUT

After our name change, the Alice Bag Band hobbled along for two or three more shows. We went back into the studio to record some demos which never saw the light of day before we eventually dissolved. There were no fights, no drama; I think we all realized that the band had simply run its course. I told the guys that I wanted to focus on school (which was true), and everyone was fine with it. If I did nothing else right, I was determined to at least graduate from college and fulfill my promise to my parents and myself.

By this time, I'd taken every philosophy class offered at East L.A. College. My old friend Sue prompted me to make the move to Cal State L.A., where we could both major in philosophy, and, maybe later, go on to law school. I'd had poor grades in high school, but luckily I scored well on the ACT and was admitted to Cal State on probation. Sue and I got back into a habit of hanging out at Googie's in Atlantic Square between classes. I couldn't help but notice that Sue always seemed to have plenty of pocket money, and I asked her about it. She told me that she'd started working at her mom's beauty shop after our corpse-beautician plan had fallen through. She made more money in tips alone than I made working for minimum wage, which at that time was about three dollars an hour.

In the spirit of Lucy and Ethel, Sue and I hatched another ingenious get-rich plan. I switched my hours at the flower shop so that I could work more evenings and weekends, and I applied for a vocational training program to earn a cosmetology license before starting at Cal State L.A. in the fall. The beauty school was so eager to have me that they filled out all the paperwork so that I would be able attend without having to pay tuition, and because they had continuous enrollment, I was able to start as soon as I gathered my supplies. I purchased a little case with hair rollers, different combs, bottles of mysterious solutions, a blow-dryer, manicure supplies and scissors. I also had to purchase a training manual and a Gloria Head, which is basically a decapitated manne-quin's head for practicing beauticians but could also be a cool punk rock name. I felt like a kid with a new box of Tinker Toys! The Gloria Head particularly fascinated me. I took my black nail polish and gave it Soo Catwoman eyes before my classes even started.

Learning new skills had always been exciting for me, and this was no dif-ferent. We had lectures in the mornings, then usually attempted some styling assignments on our Gloria Heads. Once you had a few hours under your belt, you were allowed to experiment on real people. People would actually pay to let clueless students cut their hair! The prices for being a hairstyle guinea pig were seductively low, and people on fixed budgets found comfort in the belief that an instructor would surely step in before a student made a serious error. But the instructors had several students to oversee at once, so it was luck of the draw for the customers. Some students were very good, while others — like me — were not really bad, we just had a different idea of what was fashionable.

Well, maybe I was just bad. My fellow students laughed at my punk rock Gloria Head, and I retaliated by laughing at their meager reading skills. It shocked me to hear some of the students struggle with the unfamiliar words in the beautician's guide. Some hadn't learned how words were put together, so they had no idea how to sound out an unfamiliar word. I have to confess that for the first week or two, knowing that I could read better than most of the people in my cosmetology class foolishly gave me a feeling of superiority. Things changed after I started getting to know the girls; I realized that they had gone to some of the same public schools I'd attended.

I told my friend Sue about my classmates, and she didn't seem surprised. "Hairdressers have a bad reputation. People make jokes about stupid hairdressers just like they do about dumb blondes."

"Sue, some of the girls can't even read. They're not dumb, they pick up the lessons quickly if someone is demonstrating, but if they're assigned to read the chapter then you might as well forget about it." It bothered me that I'd been so quick to judge them and that their shortcomings had made me feel superior, but it was still hard to be nice to them when they laughed at my hairdressing skills. By now I had chopped off most of the hair from my Gloria Head, and all it was good for was spiky punk rock cuts. I had painted a dark purple nail color over the mannequin's lips that looked shiny and, in my opinion, very fashion-forward.

My beauty school days lasted just a few months before I figured out that I wasn't right for the job, but my time there hadn't been wasted. My experience made me realize that there was something very wrong with an educational system that allowed students to graduate without knowing how to read, and I told myself that some day I'd try to do something about it. My brief stay at beauty school also spawned a musical project that never quite got off the ground. The Dumb Hairdressers was a concept band which was supposed to challenge people's ideas about hair, music and fashion with comedy and by poking fun at stereotypes. I recruited my friends Sue and Phranc, but the band fizzled. Phranc wrote a song for the project called "Ballad of a Dumb Hairdresser," and when the project didn't take off, she performed the song solo as part of her lesbian "pholk" singer act. I would also take some ideas from this project and squirrel them away for a later date, when I would join another concept band called Cholita.

THE CASTRATION SQUAD, PART 1

Petit Trianon in East L.A. — I think that was the look I was going for in my bedroom at my parents' house. All those stories of the kings and queens of France that Miss Sarkesian had told us to make our French lessons more interesting really worked on me. They'd captured my imagination. I'd convinced my dad to buy me peel 'n' stick mirrored tiles with gold veins running through them, then I'd covered one whole wall behind my bed with them. The other three walls were painted a buttercup gold, and the windows were trimmed with ornately tacky, hand-me-down heavy drapery swept back with gold ropes and tassels. Incongruously juxtaposed against this poor girl's cheap imitation of opulence were punk rock concert posters, accessorizing the walls where gilt-framed paintings might have been more cohesive. The pièce de résistance was a bright yellow happy-face lamp that had hung in my bedroom for many years, to which I gave a magic-marker makeover, turning the face into a disconcerting hybrid between Cleopatra and a chola.

I was studying in my little punk rock Versailles when the phone rang. It was Shannon. "Aliiiice, I need your help!" Her sultry, baritone voice was sounding a little whiny today.

"You need professional help," I quipped, but my joke fell flat as Shannon ignored it. "What is it?" I asked, starting to worry about the possibilities.

"My band has a show, and we don't have a bass player!" She sounded desperate.

"What band?"

"Castration Squad!" Back when I was still living at the Canterbury, I had come home one evening to find Patricia and Shannon sitting on the sofa, working on a song called "The Ex-Girlfriend." It was about a vicious ex-lover who tries to win back her boyfriend by telling lies and causing trouble for him and his new girlfriend. I wasn't there when the subject came up, but I could see that they were all fired up and that their songwriting was serving some therapeutic purpose.

"That's a great song," I'd said, laughing at the *Why don't you just die! Why don't you just die! Why don't you just die!* chorus. "Is she anyone I know?"

"No!" they shouted back in unison. Now they were cracking up, too.

"What is up with you guys?"

"We're starting a new band," said Shannon.

"That's right. It going to be called the Castration Squad." Patricia was beaming like she'd just given birth to a new baby.

"Great, sign me up for the fan club." I decided not to keep asking about the inspiration for the song, because I figured if they wanted me to know, they'd tell me. That was the first and last I'd heard of Castration Squad. It was a project that had either gone dormant or had served its purpose and died a quiet death, at least until my phone rang and Shannon began petitioning me to be her bassist.

"I didn't even know you had a real band. What about Patricia? I thought she was supposed to be in the band with you."

"She can't do it."

"Why not?"

"She's busy," she pushed on. "That's why I want YOU to play."

"Shannon, I can't play bass."

"Why not?"

"Because I don't know how!" I laughed to myself at the ludicrous request, but I had made the critical error of forgetting one of the punk commandments: Thou Shalt Not Need To Know How To Play Before Starting a Band.

Shannon insisted: "But I remember Hector Zero was giving you bass lessons." I hesitated, not wanting to be trapped.

"Well, yeah, he taught me a few things on bass, but I don't think I'm good enough to play in a band."

"That's okay, I'm sure you're good enough." After a several minutes of relentless arm-twisting, I finally agreed to fill in for just one show.

The Castration Squad rehearsal would take place at Mary Sim's house, where Mary lived with her mom and aunt. The two older women were supportive of Mary's interest in music and agreed to let us rehearse in their garage. The house was on the Westside, about a 30-minute drive from East L.A. on the freeway. Despite the fact that I got there about a half hour late, I was the first one there. Mary answered the door. I had met her before when I was living at the Canterbury. At the time, she'd been going out with Don Bolles, the drummer for the Germs. Back then, she was a young, shy blonde who hadn't yet blossomed into the ghostly apparition that now greeted me at the door. Standing in front of me was an otherworldly beauty with snow-white hair and ivory skin, dressed in a short skirt and billowy scarves. She invited me in and told me the other girls would arrive soon.

After a few minutes, Shannon Wilhelm and her posse of strikingly beautiful bandmates showed up. Shannon was quick to apologize. I allowed her to beg forgiveness without telling her that I'd been late too. Shannon graciously made the introductions.

"You've met Mary. Let me introduce you to the rest of the band," Shannon said.

Tiffany Kennedy was first, a tall, model-thin young lady with impeccable manners that immediately communicated a good upbringing. She stretched out her hand to me as she uttered a soft-spoken hello. Her movements were effortlessly elegant and graceful, she

Castration Squad: Tracy Lea, Alice Bag, Tiffany Kennedy, Mary Bat Thing, Shannon Wilhelm (kneeling) and Elissa Bello.

had regal carriage, and, as I got to know her, I would discover that she was intelligent, articulate and very, very much in love with the late President John F. Kennedy. Tiffany would be playing keyboards for the band.

The spunky, magnetic guitarist Tracy Lea was introduced next. She seemed much younger than any of us, and she gave me a big smile, putting her hand up and spreading her fingers as if to wave. "Hi Alice!" she said in a cheery tone, then went back to chewing her gum. She seemed energetic and fun-loving, and her long shorts and tennis shoes gave her a tomboyish quality. Tracy's dark brown hair was buzz-cut, leaving only a few long strands in front that fell over her big brown eyes, making her look like a punk Veronica Lake. She had an hourglass figure and a snappy sense of humor.

I was impressed by how well put-together my future bandmates were. By punk standards they were all very fashionable, but they were also pretty by anyone's standards. They smiled sweetly, thanking me for filling in, and I felt glad that Shannon had talked me into doing the show, because I liked these girls right away.

The final arrival that day would be drummer Elissa Bello. I'd met Elissa before when she'd first joined the Go-Go's, but her Go-Go's days were behind her, and now she'd been drafted into the Castration Squad and was reluctant to commit. As a consequence, she was spotty about making rehearsals, the other girls told me. Since I also was reluctant to commit, I immediately hit it off with Elissa. The curly-topped Italian spitfire was always wisecracking. She simply could not stop smiling and laughing at rehearsals, which often provoked my own smiling, which in turn made Tracy smile, leaving Tiffany unable to resist giggling, which caused Mary to lose her focus and crack up, which meant Shannon would stop the rehearsal and yell at us…but all that was still to come.

THE CASTRATION SQUAD, PART 2

I was still a little nervous about my limited playing skills, but as soon as we shut the garage door and started practicing, I realized that everyone was a little unsure of their skills. It made me feel better right away, and it wasn't long before I found myself really enjoying playing with Castration Squad.

Subsequent rehearsals would put a damper on my initial good experience. I soon found out that at least two-thirds of the band was enjoying an intravenous happy hour before each rehearsal. Often, this meant that procurement of the drug interfered with our rehearsal schedule. "Nothing comes between me and my heroin," Shannon would later joke, twisting the famous Brooke Shields tagline for Calvin Klein jeans. Sadly, it was true. One of the main reasons I had moved away from Hollywood was to distance myself from the destructive self-indulgence that was so easy to give in to. Drinking all the time, doing drugs, staying out all night…it had been fun for a while, but I'd seen too many people overindulge and overdose. For completely selfish reasons, I didn't want to get close to people who were habitual drug users. It didn't seem glamorous or bohemian to me anymore. Each time I played with Castration Squad, I felt seduced by the friendship and camaraderie that I enjoyed with the girls, while at the same time I was repelled by the ever present use of drugs.

As much as I tried to distance myself from the increasingly drug-infested punk scene, my instincts for self-preservation failed me at times, and one night I found myself back in Shannon's mother's bathroom, fixing heroin. This time Shannon had gone first but she'd saved a bit of junk for me. "Just wipe the top with the cotton ball," she told me. I did as she instructed, but I couldn't bear to stick the needle in my own arm.

"You do it, I can't," I said, cringing. Shannon obliged me, and once again I enjoyed the warm feeling of euphoria as it swelled inside me, followed a few minutes later by the nausea. This time, I hadn't gorged on Thai food, so when the urge to vomit came, it was a minor inconvenience. Shannon and I cleaned up the evidence in the bathroom and went back into the living room.

After a few minutes I started to feel uncomfortable. "Can we open the windows? It's hot in here," I complained.

Shannon shot me a funny look. "You're hot?"

"Aren't you? It's burning up in here." She felt my forehead with a look of concern on her face.

"How do you feel?" she asked. Actually, I wasn't feeling too good. When

Shannon opened the windows I started to shiver and shake uncontrollably. "Oh shit — you have cotton fever," she said quietly.

Tracy and I sneak a smile behind a scowling Shannon.

She placed a pillow on the couch and told me to lie down. "It's not that bad," she said, trying to be cheerful. "It just means you got a little cotton fiber in your veins. Here, I'll get you some cool water. You rest." I spent the next few hours miserably sweating and shivering, reassured by Shannon that it would all be over soon enough. When Shannon's mom got home, Shannon told her that I might have the flu and she needed to take care of me because my parents weren't home. I don't know if her mom believed it, but I think the will to believe is a liar's best friend. When my fever finally broke, much later that night, I felt that I had somehow escaped serious danger with a mere warning. I would never be tempted by heroin again.

Despite my reluctance to commit, I played with Castration Squad for the next year, always "just for this one show." Over time, I fell in love with the girls. Phranc played with us a few times, too. The former Nervous Gender and Catholic Discipline singer had started playing acoustic shows which really allowed people to hear her clever lyrics and catchy songs. Shannon would ask Phranc to pinch-hit whenever one of us couldn't make it, and Phranc always managed not only to save the day but to add her own personal signature style to CS performances. We even did our own CS version of a song Phranc had written about Charlotte Caffey called "I like Charlotte." It was a sweet declaration of lesbian love. Phranc's barbershop flattop and lack of makeup made her a handsome girl, except for the voluptuous tatas which blew this sister's mister-look, in a good way.

The band always seemed to get along well, but inevitably it would split along the lines of habitual drug users and those of us who were not governed by the need to score. It became frustrating during rehearsal breaks, when most of the band would disappear into the bathroom for a fix. One time, we were rehearsing at a studio, and some of the girls left to take care of their business. After waiting for a while, I needed to use the bathroom. There was only one toilet, so I walked in and made my way behind the crowd at the sink to get into the stall.

"Hey!!!"

"Wait, Alice!"

"DON'T... MOVE..." Shannon commanded. She had grabbed my foot and was now holding it up in the air. I'd stepped on a newspaper that had some of the precious powder on it. Shannon scraped the dust off my Converse back onto the newspaper and the girls quickly moved in and scooped it up onto the spoon, melted it down and stuck it in their arms. From the bottom of my dirty sneaker into their veins; I was blown away.

Fortunately, most of my memories of Castration Squad are not about drugs but about all the silly things we did, like buying a bag full of stuffed bats from a discount store on Vine St. called Pic 'n' Save. These Halloween decoration bats weren't at all scary looking; they were fat bats with goofy faces and floppy wings onto which we'd sewn little red armbands with the letters CS for Castration Squad, just like the armbands the band members wore. We had started playing an impromptu version of "Wild Thing" at rehearsal one day when Mary picked up the microphone and decided to change the lyrics and title of the song to "Bat Thing." Shannon recognized genius and insisted that we add it to our set, along the way rechristening Mary Sims as Mary Bat Thing. Mary would go on to change her name again when she formed the band 45 Grave and became known as Dinah Cancer. To celebrate our new song, we decided to buy the little stuffed bats and throw them out at the audience during our set. That night, Shannon and Mary Bat Thing sent the bats flying at the unsuspecting audience members, who were pelted by the ridiculously cute little creatures.

Despite the undeniable humorous elements of Castration Squad, Shannon insisted that the band appear deadly serious whenever we were onstage or in public. She drafted a Castration Squad manifesto based on Valerie Solanas's *SCUM Manifesto*. She instructed us to wear armbands and tried to cultivate a paramilitary look for us, then she laid down the No Smiling law. She complained that we giggled too much and broke character while we were performing, so she insisted that we practice not smiling at rehearsals too. How this was supposed to work while she and Mary were attacking audience members with stuffed toys is beyond me, but the more she tried to enforce the rule, the worse the rest of us behaved.

As if to underscore the satiric nature of the band, Castration Squad did a cover of the song, "Cruella de Vil," from *One Hundred and One Dalmations*. While Shannon sang about Cruella, she'd narrow her eyes like she was telling a ghost story to a group of scouts: "At first you think Cruella is the devil…" Behind her back, those of us who could would let go of our instruments and hold up our index fingers on either side of our heads to make little devil horns. If Shannon didn't see us, we'd continue, but if she saw one of us, that person would get yelled at. It was like being in junior high school and getting caught goofing off by the teacher.

Despite the band's faults and weaknesses, in many ways Castration Squad was a visionary glimpse of a group of girls trying to give feminism and femininity a much-needed punk rock makeover. The band was described by Peter Ivers on New Wave Theatre as "the end of stuff-your-pants rock and roll." Castration Squad anticipated the styles of death punk, goth and riot grrrl, and would continue to perform sporadically even after I had played my "one last time" with them and moved on to other projects and endeavors.

DEATH LENDS A NEW PERSPECTIVE

You're watching yourself
But you're too unfair
You got your head all tangled up
But if I could only make you care
Oh, no love, you're not alone
No matter what or who you've been
No matter when or where you've seen
All the knives seem to lacerate your brain
I've had my share, I'll help you with the pain
You're not alone.
    —David Bowie, "Rock 'n' Roll Suicide"

We were sitting in Tracy Lea's bedroom, going over some song ideas for Castration Squad, when her phone rang.

"No…no…no…." she repeated into the phone. I could tell immediately that something was very wrong, but I tried not to listen to her conversation. "How did it happen?" she continued. She was pacing now, which made it extra hard for me to ignore her, since I was sitting on the floor. She stopped in front of me. "Darby's dead," she said, covering the mouthpiece. Her eyes were tearing up and she was visibly upset. I stopped plucking my bass and looked off into my vanishing surroundings. Images of my old friend Bobby Pyn were projected on my mental screen, and a terrible sadness crept up from the pit of my stomach to my throat and spread out to my limbs like a blooming plant. Then the images began to change. It was me and Darby arguing; Darby, trying to burn my wrist with his cigarette; me punching Darby on the stairs of the Canterbury; Darby outside the Hong Kong Cafe with his new British accent after returning from a brief European vacation; Darby falling down drunk and drugged. My sadness was replaced by anger.

Tracy hung up the phone. "It was a suicide," she informed me. Darby and one of his girlfriends had made a suicide pact and had ingested massive doses of heroin. The girl had survived, Darby had not. Tracy was crying and I put my arms around her, trying to comfort her. My own feelings were a jumble of competing emotions, pushing each other out of the way as each tried to monopolize my mood. There was the sadness of losing a once-close friend and confidante, the anger that it had been a suicide, a feeling of guilt and helplessness about whether I or anyone else could have prevented it, and general confusion about what would make Darby want to take his own life. After trying to provide the strong shoulder to cry on, I finally spoke up.

"I'm sorry Tracy, I need to go home."

"That's okay, I understand," she said, probably thinking that I wanted to cry in private, but it wasn't that at all.

On the drive home, I thought about how badly things had ended between Darby and me, how we'd stopped speaking to each other. I'd always held onto the hope that one day we'd come back and talk things through; that we'd laugh at our youthful mistakes as we got older and wiser. Now our unfinished conversations would remain unfinished forever. An unspoken apology would wither on my lips, we'd never have the opportunity to revisit our beliefs, to see how time and experience would color and change our views. We'd never again talk for hours on the phone, laugh at stupid jokes, discuss philosophy or share a bottle of booze. It was all over. Darby was really gone for good. Instead of making me cry, my grief and lack of answers made my temper flare. I was angry not only at Darby but at myself, and at those around him who had allowed it to happen.

I'm the kind of person who squeezes the last bit of toothpaste from the tube, who uses the last teaspoon of mustard in the jar and won't throw out the jar before it's all gone, even if it takes room in the fridge, but that's me. I'm that way about life, too. I'd seen too much poverty, misery and wasted opportunity as a kid, and I want to extract as much knowledge, adventure, excitement and love from this life as I can, for as long as I can. I wondered if Darby's life didn't still have a few surprises in store for him. I think it did. I have to remind myself that it was his choice to make, not mine. But I can't seem to stop myself from second-guessing him, just like he second-guessed me when he thought I was wrong. That's part of what friends do, isn't it? They tell you when you're wrong. I wondered if other people were thinking the same things I was thinking. I wondered if others wished they'd been around to argue the wisdom of suicide with him.

I suppose I just don't understand suicide. I understand euthanasia, I understand wanting to end suffering if you're ill. I understand dying for a cause, fighting to defend your loved ones, defending a principle or fasting for peace or freedom. I just didn't feel that I understood the cause behind Darby's death. Why did he die? What did he die for? I knew that he believed that dying young was the key to becoming a legend, but the idea that he would kill himself because he thought it would bring him fame made me sick to my stomach. I knew he wasn't shallow, and I couldn't imagine he'd want fame without wanting to accomplish something with it, or at least be around to enjoy its rewards. I pushed the idea away; another question that wouldn't be answered. I almost preferred to believe that he was depressed and that we had all failed in helping him overcome his depression. Once again, I had to stand back and tell myself that only he knew for sure. I would never know the answers to these questions.

The guilt, the anger, the sadness grabbed me by the throat and threatened to pull me down. I fought back, just like I had been fighting back all my life. I would always fight and rage against the dying of the light. I dug my fingernails into the soft rubber of the steering wheel. My throat tightened, my eyes watered and the road in front of me blurred as I muttered, "You fucking asshole!"

MASTER OF NONE

As 1980 gave way to 1981, hardcore emerged as the dominant style, while several of the original scene bands fell apart and morphed into new styles and genres: death rock, art rock, rockabilly, roots rock, noise, performance art. The mood of the nation was also changing: Ronald Reagan defeated Jimmy Carter in the November presidential elections, ushering in an era of social conservatism and militarism that would reward the rich and punish the poor and disenfranchised at home and around the world. It was fertile ground for rebellion, and punk swelled in popularity, expanding well beyond the major cities and reaching deep into the heartland.

I couldn't believe that such an obviously senile corporate shill as Ronald Reagan could be chosen to be the "leader of the free world" — it completely fucked up my confidence in the democratic process. As if to put an authoritative, final period on the optimism of the early punk scene, *Slash*'s literary firebrand, Claude "Kickboy" Bessy, and his muse, Philly, checked their US credentials at the door and fled the States forever on the day Reagan was sworn in. In protest, I wore a dress fashioned from a white sheet, emblazoned with the words "Kill Reagan" onstage at the Vex when I performed with Castration Squad, only to be harassed and threatened with arrest by the police. It was a foreshadowing of much worse things to come over the next eight years.

My relationship with Bruce during this time helped to keep me grounded. The fact that he lived in Orange County and didn't drive made for a long-distance relationship which allowed us to satisfy our need for romance while giving us the breathing room to accomplish our individual goals. As pedestrian as it sounds, our relationship was comfortable and relatively drama-free. I was able to do for him what Nickey had done for me: I introduced him to new things like the joys of dim sum in Chinatown or cult films at the art-house movie theater. He also enjoyed reading and discussing philosophy, important aspects of which would play a major role in a relationship that would last for seven years.

With a boss who was willing to accommodate my changing schedules, part-time band projects and a long-distance boyfriend, I felt fortunate to be in a very comfortable situation. Being a free agent suited me perfectly. I think I played most of the shows Castration Squad asked me to play without ever feeling like I was compelled to do something I didn't want to do. Around the same time, I started getting offers to participate in bands with some of my other friends.

I'd met Mikey Ochoa and Gerardo Velasquez through Phranc and their work together in the band Nervous Gender. Since they both lived in East L.A., it was really easy for me to get together with them. I still had my keyboard and was eager to continue to get some use out of my parents' costly gift. The three of us formed a band called the Imports, using their synthesizers and my electric piano. It was kind of like Kraftwerk, only with a punk rock, Mexican twist. We only rehearsed a few times, and I don't think we ever played live, but it was fun, and somehow we ended up with a track credited as "Alice's Song" on the Nervous Gender/Beelzebub Youth record. I wrote a crazy-making piano ditty, and Gerardo quickly penned some lyrics that went with the mood of the music. It was a repetitious, demented-sounding piece, and I believe Mikey Ochoa came up with the chorus, which was just incessant chanting: "Neurotic, neurotic, neurotic…" It still makes me laugh when I think that the same basic rehearsal track we recorded was later remixed and turned into a record.

Another band I played with from time to time was the Boneheads. This band included Trudie Arguelles, Chase Holiday, Robert Lopez, Craig Lee and Elissa Bello. It was a truly wacky band, with eclectic taste that married Polynesian flavors with pop, punk and just plain silliness. The band was one big party, because everyone was really open to any idea. Rehearsals felt more like art therapy than the serious drill and practice that some bands (like the Bags) followed. Each member's unique quirks helped me appreciate different approaches to music and encouraged me to explore musical extremes and incongruities in my own playing.

I have to admit that whether playing bass or keyboards, I had very limited skills, but that was never an issue. There was no pressure to perform on a more professional level with any of these bands. I, in turn, felt liberated, free to be inventive. I turned down invitations to sing because I didn't want to go back to doing what I'd been doing. I also didn't want to go back to being the focal point. I loved being just another member of the band without anyone pinning their hopes on me.

I never would master either the bass or the keyboards, but I played as well as I needed to play, and for me, at that time, it was all about the pleasure of playing and being creative. The world is full of proficient musicians who play like technicians; mastery of an instrument is wonderful, but it's not necessary to be a master to be able to express yourself. Punk taught me never to be afraid to try something I really wanted, not to let a lack of experience stand in my way.

It's funny how we're told in school that we have to choose a career path and stick to it. That is wrong. There are so many different things a person can be and so many ways to go about it. The longer you live, the more dreams you should have to keep you occupied. In those days, I had convinced myself that I had to choose between school and playing music, and when I first left the Bags, I shied away from playing at all, because I thought I would have to give up the distraction of music if I was going to take school seriously; but music always seemed to find me. My friends would call and invite me to play with them, or I'd meet new friends and collaborators. I figured out that participating in bands part-time gave me the opportunity to continue playing and didn't really interfere with getting an education. In fact, playing gave me a respite from my school work and, in the end, helped me to accomplish my educational goals. In turn, focusing on my school work and living at home sheltered me from some of the destructive elements that were now beginning to take their toll on the Hollywood scene.

THE MAGIC OF RELIGION

The first thing I did when I got to Cal State L.A. was declare my major as philosophy. I'd finished some of my general ed courses at East L.A. College, so here I could focus on taking the classes that most interested me. Not surprisingly, my grades improved. It wasn't just the fact that the subject matter appealed to me; now that I was working hard and shelling out my own money for an education, I wanted to get my money's worth.

I took courses in logic, religion, feminism, ancient, medieval and modern philosophy, even ritual magic, all offered through the philosophy department. I immersed myself in school, making friends with the professors, meeting some of them for coffee or going to dinner at their homes. It was a small department, and, with only a few students majoring in philosophy, we got to know each other and each person's views pretty quickly.

I took a class offered by the Religious Studies department called Women in Religion, which taught me a little about the many ways in which patriarchal societies infuse sexism into some of their religious practices, effectively making the religion support the values of the patriarchy. I thought about the ritual magic class I'd had and remembered how sympathetic magic works: like affects like, microcosm affects macrocosm and vice versa. I wondered how my own little world was influenced by my religious upbringing.

Growing up Mexican, the fine line between magic and religion was blurred from the moment the concepts were introduced to me. In my world, magic and religion were used to explain the unexplainable and/or accomplish the improbable or impossible, because neither had to adhere to the laws of logic — they were governed by laws of their own. At home, my mother would burn candles in propitiation to saints or *la virgen de guadalupe*; she sometimes cleansed herself of the evil eye by bathing in special, blessed oils, or rubbed her temples with the magical water that my brother had brought from Lourdes. Clearly, in my mother's world, God and his host of helpers were external, supernatural beings who were open to making deals with common mortals.

Listening to the professor speak, I was struck by the realization that the oppression of women could be carried out at a much deeper level, beyond the level of logic and thus could not be countermanded by logic alone. Sexism wasn't just in society, out in the open for all to see; it was programmed deep into our psyches, hidden and out of sight, embedded in the darkest recesses of our beings when we were just impressionable little boys and girls trying to figure out our places in the world.

At my parish when I was growing up, I'd seen the hierarchy of the Catholic Church at work. The male priests were called "Fathers," and were served by lesser nuns. The priests also had female housekeepers to clean and cook for them. I wondered if the nuns had housekeepers, but somehow I doubted it. It bothered me that there were no female priests, cardinals, bishops or popes. I thought about how I'd learned to trust that this order was somehow approved by God himself and therefore correct. I had stopped being a Catholic long ago, but just because I wasn't going to mass didn't mean I was free of the indoctrination I'd received. I felt like my mind was sometimes at odds with the image that automatically popped up into my head when I thought or spoke of the divine.

For years, I'd been struggling with the shedding of old religious beliefs, and with defining and refining a set of personal beliefs to replace the ones I'd tossed out. I thought about the image of God I'd grown up with, a Caucasian-looking portrait of Jesus, and all I could think of was sympathetic magic: as in heaven so below, like affects like, Jesus as the God of one big Caucasian patriarchy. I thought of Mary Daly's book, *Beyond God the Father*, which I'd read in my Philosophy of Feminism class. In it, Daly argues that the image of God as male hinders the spiritual growth and full participation of women in Judeo-Christian religions. Her arguments had firmly cemented my belief that describing God in anthropomorphic terms was not only simplistic but was in fact promoting a truncated, inaccurate portrayal of what I believed was an omnipresent deity.

The realization made me angry. I felt like I'd been duped. If God was omnipresent, then God was present in me — why had I been robbed of this knowledge? I wasn't the only one being cheated. I'd been raised to believe that God was omnipresent, omniscient and omnipotent. If God was omnipresent, then God was in everyone and everything, and if God was in everything, then God must BE everything, for what ingredient could be named that is devoid of God? It was an epiphany. I hadn't taken my search far enough. I felt a physical certainty that extended my belief in God beyond the limits of the rational mind. I felt like I was knowing for the first time — not just with my brain, but knowing with my whole being.

After my emotional realization, I wanted time to analyze what had happened and digest what I'd experienced, because giving myself time to think was a habit I'd fallen into. I spoke to my philosophy mentor, Professor Vick, who had once tried to teach me to meditate. He told me that logic was not the only way to gain knowledge. He spoke to me about allowing the world to reveal itself. It was an enormous task for me; I kept getting in my own way. Eventually, I learned not to be so afraid of losing myself. My concept of self, like my concept of God, was so limited that had I not been willing to let it go, I would never have been able to understand what the universe was showing me. I took a leap of faith and was finally rewarded with a steadfast belief that I am part of the omnipresent, omniscient, omnipotent deity.

Here at last was a God I could believe in, a God that was not transcendent, not a separate, otherworldly being. In the past, I had reasoned that my concept of God was incomplete, but reason hadn't been enough, I hadn't been able to shake the emotional connection I had to "God the father." It wasn't until my understanding went beyond a rational understanding that I was able to let it go.

I thought about Bobby/Darby and how he'd seen the universe around him and determined that it was devoid of God. I'd seen the same universe and determined that it was all a manifestation of God. The reason I'd hit Darby that day on the steps of the Canterbury was that I'd felt threatened, vulnerable because my faith was limited to a logical argument. I wished he was around now, not to argue the existence of God but to agree on something. I realized that we both believed that God was not an external being who could be found by looking in a church window; we both believed there would be no judge or jury; we both believed in ourselves.

A TURN FOR THE WORSE

My father's health continued to deteriorate. Because of his diabetes, he developed sores on his feet which seemed to never fully heal, and eventually the skin tissue around the sores began to decay and darken. Gangrene set in. A daily ritual of bathing his feet in a tub of Betadine solution was prescribed to help stave off the inevitable deterioration. The putrid smell of rotting flesh and disinfectant filled our living room. Despite the battle that my father put up against it, gangrene got the better of him, and the doctor informed him that some of his toes were beyond repair and would have to be amputated.

My dad took it really hard. His regular dialysis treatment took up a good part of his day three times a week, but he had been able to enjoy a measure of independence. Even though he was weakened by the treatment, he was still able to get around on his own. Now the amputation of several toes on one foot and his big toe on the other brought that small bit of independence under attack. He was *un machote*, a man's man who prided himself on being tough, strong and self-reliant. Now, he wouldn't even be able to walk without assistance, and the prospect terrified him.

"I won't be able to work," he complained. He had already curtailed his daily physical activities to overseeing my mother on her small construction projects. "I may even need to be in a wheelchair." I had never seen my father look so vulnerable, so defeated. He sounded like a little boy.

"It'll be okay, dad," I told him. "You don't have a choice. The gangrene could spread, and then it might be even worse." I didn't know if that was true; I was making it up as I went along. The truth is that I didn't know what to say to him. Comforting my father was something completely new to me. He'd always been the one to comfort me. This man who had always seemed so strong, who had always loomed so large and powerful in my life — what could I say to ease his mind? I felt totally inadequate and unprepared to comfort him. I searched my mind for the right words but I came up empty, so I just held his hand, unable to think of anything else to say or do.

The room was quiet as my father and I clutched each other's hands. He looked in my eyes, then he placed his free hand over our intertwined fingers.

"*Quien te quiere mucho?*" (Who loves you very much?) It was the same question he'd been asking me for years and years, ever since I was a little girl.

"*Tu,*" I responded. Throughout my sad and violent childhood, my father and I would repeat this question-and-answer as a sort of mantra, a magic spell that was supposed to lessen the pain of the atrocities I'd seen him commit against my mother. And it was a good spell. Even though it left me deeply conflicted about loving the man who beat my mom, it always held me up when I needed to be held up. It was an amulet, invisibly carried in my heart forever.

After the amputations, my father spent long periods of time in bed. I don't know if it was due to pain from the surgery or from the injury to his pride. The rest periods he'd take after dialysis treatments seemed to lengthen. Now when I came home from work or from school, I'd frequently find my father in bed. One day he called me over.

"Alicia, help me put my socks on. I can't do it." I looked at his horribly disfigured feet, fresh wounds emitting the familiar, fetid smell. I couldn't do it. I didn't want to touch his feet, to look at them or smell the gangrene on them.

"Why don't I get you the socks and you put them on?" I offered, trying to smile.

"You can't do this for me? You can't help me?! Forget it!" His brow furrowed; the temper I'd once known still simmered under his narrowed eyelids. "I don't need you, get out of here!"

I realized too late that I'd wounded him. "I'm sorry, Dad. I'll help you." I took his injured leg in my hand and clumsily tried to force the sock onto his misshapen foot, but he angrily kicked at my hands with his other foot.

"I said, get OUT of here!" He glared at me.

I left the room, sobbing, feeling sorry that I hadn't been able to do such a little thing for my father. I wished to God that I could take the moment back and do this one small favor for my dad, who'd done so much for me; but of course it was too late. He'd seen the disgust on my face. I'd made the man who called me *La Reina del mundo y de otras partes* (The Queen of the World and Other Places) the whole time I was growing up feel bad about something he had no control over. The

My dad in failing health.

man who had told me I could be president of the United States, or a brain surgeon, or anything I wanted; I'd been unable to even help him put his socks on. He had given me so much and I had given nothing. I felt like the lowest creature on the planet.

From then on, I made a real effort to go in and talk to him whenever he was in bed. I tried to talk to him and he tried to talk to me, but it felt forced. There seemed to be an invisible barrier that kept us from really communicating. One day, in an effort to break through the barrier, I decided that I had to talk to my father about the violence he'd wreaked on our household while I was growing up. I went into the bedroom where he and my mother had slept in separate beds since we moved into the house on Bonnie Beach Place. I pulled up a little stool and sat opposite his bed, watching him for a while in silence as he held up his hands over his body, turning them slowly in midair. He seemed to be staring at the shadows they were casting on the wall. My stomach was in knots, anticipating what I was about to say.

"Dad, I wanted to talk to you about some stuff," I said, not knowing where or how to begin.

"What is it?" He immediately stopped staring at the shadows on the wall and turned to look at me.

I was like an actor frozen with stage fright, forgetting her lines. His eyes were like spotlights, bearing down on me. I took a deep breath.

"It's about when you used to hit Mom." There it was, I'd said it. The words hung in the air for what seemed like an eternity.

"When I used to hit Mom?" He looked at me blankly. "What are you talking about?"

A locked door inside of me suddenly opened and a torrent of memories and words spilled out, one after the other.

"When you hit her, you tried to strangle her, you punched her and dragged her, and spit on her, and kicked her. I'm talking about when you busted her nose and the blood flew on her dress and on your shirt and on the wall! I'm talking about when you beat her with the belt buckle and tore open her scalp, and the blood dripped down her face, when she kneeled in front of you before you kicked her in the face and then kicked her some more when she couldn't get up! That's what I'm talking about! That's what I'm talking about! *That's what I'm talking about, Papi!*"

I was carried away in a flood of emotion, tears, snot, nausea. I stopped only because I couldn't talk anymore. My vocal cords cramped tight like a muscle clenching shut, flood gates trying to stop the words that needed to be

screamed and launched like angry missiles, words that had lived in me, infect-
ing my body and soul like the gangrene in my father's feet. My father stared at
me like I was a stranger. I wished he would hold me and tell me he was sorry,
but instead he sat up on his bed and said just three words.

"That never happened."

FORGIVE

I rushed out of the bedroom and right into the arms of my mother who had been listening in the next room. She held me by the shoulders as she turned her head to yell into the other room: "Yes, it did happen!"

"You're both crazy!" my father yelled in return, and then he lay back in his bed, covering his entire body and face with a blanket.

"*Que bueno, mija, que bueno que le dijiste.*" My mother was glad that I'd finally confronted my father. She walked outside with me, her arm around my shoulder. My mom was not a physically affectionate person, she very rarely hugged me or any of my siblings. Whenever we tried to hug her at Christmas or on her birthday she'd turn her head, stiffen and look uncomfortable. She made up for it by being warm in many other ways. We sat outside on the porch and she confided in me. "Your father doesn't want to think about that. He wants to pretend it never happened. He doesn't want you to think of him that way."

"But he should admit it and apologize..." I was calmer now but still upset.

"You know how your dad treated me when you were little? He doesn't treat me that way anymore."

"I know that." It had been years since my father had been strong enough to physically abuse my mother; his diabetes had seen to that.

"Mija, he never once said he was sorry for anything he ever did to me. He would just come around the next day smiling, being nice, trying to act like nothing happened, until things went back to normal after a day or two." My mom was gazing off into the distance now, sifting through her many painful memories.

"One day a young policeman tried to help your father stay out of trouble. He gave him a choice, he said, 'You can apologize to your wife and family, or you can spend the night in jail.' Your father chose the night in jail."

"That's why you used to tell me not to smile at him, not to talk to him after those times."

Sighing, my mother continued. "Yes, but you were just a *niña*, you wanted things to go back to normal, too, so you'd smile and hug and kiss him and he never had to answer for anything he did."

"Did you ever confront him, Ma?"

"No, I never did, because as he got older and weaker, I knew he couldn't hurt me anymore."

"But did you forgive him?" My mom didn't answer at first, then she turned to face me.

"No, I don't forgive him, it just doesn't matter to me anymore. It makes me mad at him when I think that it still hurts you, but he can't hurt me anymore. Alicia, you need to let it go, for yourself, not for your dad. I don't think your dad will ever be able to face up to what he did. He's going to die soon, he's very sick."

"I know, that's why I wanted to make peace with him." My eyes began to fill with tears as I realized that this would be one more conflict I might not be able to resolve. My heart began to ache with competing emotions: love, hate, sadness, regret, anger… I felt like I would burst at any moment.

"Make peace with yourself, Alicia. Let God deal with your dad." My mother touched me once more, lightly on the shoulder, then she got up and went back into the house, leaving me alone on the porch with my confused emotions.

I decided to take a walk to clear my head. Ever since we'd moved into the house on Bonnie Beach, I'd been fond of walking to one of the cemeteries that was near our house. A block away, just beyond the freeway overpass, was a small Jewish cemetery that was always quiet and deserted, with very little space between the graves. It had been there since the days when East L.A. had been a Jewish neighborhood. Today I walked past it, heading instead a few blocks farther up Downey Road, toward Calvary Cemetery. Calvary is a large Catholic cemetery with acres of rolling green lawns, dotted with sculptures of crosses, angels and shrouded figures in mourning. I needed the space, I needed a chance to walk and think.

Maybe my mother was right. Maybe forgiveness was not for the recipient but for the giver. I replayed the scene that had just happened with my father over and over again in my mind, watering the graves with my tears as I walked aimlessly. I sensed the poison that was still inside of me and I could physically feel it starting to make me sick.

I thought about my conversation with my mother and I suddenly knew with complete certainty that my father would never admit nor apologize for the violence and pain he had brought into our home, and I tried to accept it. When I'd circled the entire perimeter of the cemetery, I walked back to our house. My father was still in bed.

"Dad?"

He pulled down the blanket and looked at me.

"I forgive you."

He covered his face with the blanket and turned his body toward the wall.

We would never discuss the subject again.

THE CALLING

For the next couple of years, I followed my routine of working part-time, going to school and practicing with bands or playing at night. Castration Squad gave birth to a splinter group called the Cambridge Apostles, which featured several of the Squad's smiling members. The group would undergo several mutations, and at times would include Barbara James, Elizabeth Anthony, Tiffany Kennedy, Dinah Cancer, Bruce and Mike Atta, Tracy Lea and even my old friend Marlene. I also formed a group called Funhouse, with Flipside's X-8, Craig Lee and my boyfriend, Bruce Atta. That group was into funky grooves.

At the end of the summer quarter in 1984, I received my bachelor's degree in philosophy. I didn't attend the ceremony, but my parents were thrilled when I got my certificate in the mail. My father was jubilant that I'd held up my side of our bargain.

My plan during the whole time I'd been in college was to go on to law school, but, as with most of my plans, I hadn't really done the research. I quit my job at the flower shop and treated myself to a trip to Mexico City to visit my aunt and cousins. When I returned, I was still no closer to deciding what my next step should be. I'd spent all my savings on my trip, so I looked around for a part-time job while I figured out my next move. I didn't want to go back to the flower shop; I knew they would have been happy to have me, but I wanted to try something new. My mother had worked as a teacher's aide for a while during my teen years, and she suggested I try that. She showed me a help-wanted ad in a local newspaper soliciting TA applications for the Alhambra School District. "What do I have to lose?" I thought to myself. I went in and was hired on the spot. Within the first few weeks, my dreams of going on to law school hopped a tricycle on the playground and pedaled away. I realized I'd found my calling. I loved working with the kids and immediately started investigating the ins and outs of becoming a teacher.

I saw another ad, this one in the *L.A. Times*. USC was holding an informational presentation about their Accelerated Teaching Program. When I got there, the auditorium was already nearly full. I sat at the back and listened to a conservatively attired panel expound on the perks and the requirements of the program, and I, along with hundreds of other hopefuls, decided to take home an application. It was quite a coup to be admitted; I believe only seven of us made the cut. I spent two semesters at USC, and at the end of six weeks of student teaching I was granted an emergency bilingual credential and hired at the school where I'd done my practicum.

At Hoover Street Elementary School in gang-infested Koreatown, I started working with the children of immigrants, children who were limited English speakers, just as I'd been when I entered school. It was enormously satisfying to be able to help them acquire English skills with the kindness, patience and understanding that I wished some of my own teachers had shown me. I wanted my students to value and maintain their own culture and language and to build upon that firm foundation of self-esteem. I loved my work. I'd found a brand new audience, one that was eager to engage with me on a daily basis. The children taught me patience, a virtue I'd never had. I encouraged my students to question everything and everybody, especially me and any other authority figure. I felt useful, needed, valued, even loved — and I loved them back. I told my students, "If you work hard you can be president of the United States, you can be brain surgeons; you can be anything you want…" and my students grew and blossomed and made me swell with pride.

Many of the students at Hoover Street Elementary were the children of families from Central America. By the mid-1980s, several countries, including Honduras, El Salvador and Nicaragua, were caught in brutal, horrific civil wars between communist revolutionaries and US-backed governmental forces. The Reagan administration had authorized covert CIA operations to train and fund the "counter-revolutionary forces" without seeking the approval of congress to wage what was essentially a war by proxy. Few details of these secret wars were made public at the time, but the swelling population of Central American refugees in Los Angeles was evidence of a growing humanitarian crisis. Growing up in East L.A., I had seen my share of hardship, but it was nothing compared to what some of these little kids and their families had been through.

Early in my teaching career, I was sitting with a small group of kindergartners. The children were talking about their backgrounds. One little girl raised her hand and said, "*Maestra, yo soy mojada.*" Another voice joined in.

"*Yo tambien, maestra.*" Their trust compelled me to share my own story.

"It's okay. My father was illegal, too." I told them about how my father used to cross over for work. As I shared my family's story, their faces brightened, as my own revelations somehow assuaged their shame. I realized that I was in a unique position to help these children; that they could relate to me in a way they couldn't with most of their other teachers.

A shy boy who rarely spoke in class raised his hand and began telling us his story, haltingly at first. He told us about his family raising money to send him and his older brother to the United States. As he spoke and recalled more details, his speech came more rapidly, the words tumbling out one after the other. He told us about the frightening experience of crossing the river by foot with a group of other people he didn't know, led by a coyote, and then being squeezed into a single truck, having to be quiet and still, afraid of being caught. When he arrived in San Diego, he was supposed to be met by relatives who would pay the coyote the balance of the transport fee, but the relatives hadn't been able to come up with the full amount for both brothers. Only the older, teenage boy was released; my student had to stay behind until his relatives could raise the money. He had to remain behind, trapped in a dark, filthy, cockroach-infested motel with people he didn't know for over a week, not knowing if he'd ever see his family again, wishing that his mother would rescue him. His classmates sat and listened sympathetically, and the girl who had initially spoken reached over and put her arm around him, giving him a reassuring squeeze.

Looking into the faces of those students, I was more determined than ever to help them. Unlike Daedelus, I hoped to give my students wings that might someday allow them to rise above their present limitations. My life had come full circle.

LITERACY FOR ALL!

I did some of my graduate work at USC and, due to the high tuition there, I also did some graduate studies back at Cal State. In one of my Cal State classes, I was assigned a book called *Pedagogy of the Oppressed*, by Brazilian author Paulo Freire. This little book packed a big punch. It opened my eyes to the ways in which traditional education was failing students. In the book, Freire describes the common methods used to fill students with information and turn them into receptacles of facts, rather than empowering the students to become active participants in the process of inquiry. Freire envisioned an educational process where the students become a combination of teacher and student. The role of the traditional teacher was to facilitate the circumstances for this self-teaching to take place. His ideas were exciting to me; I believed my own teaching methods were very much in sync with his ideology, but I hoped I could do more.

I was talking to a fellow teacher about Paulo Freire when she informed me that she'd heard Freire had been consulted by the postrevolutionary Sandinista government in Nicaragua to help them come up with a literacy campaign designed to educate the illiterate poor who'd had no access to education prior to the revolution. I chased down the lead and soon found myself trying to convince my philosophy professor to allow me to take an independent study on the philosophy of education.

I found out about a program in Nicaragua called Escuela NICA, which billed itself as a school for internationalists. It combined Spanish-language instruction with a brief history of the country, visits to co-ops in the Nicaraguan countryside and participation in community development programs, along with opportunities for volunteering. In addition, the school would provide room and board with a local family in Estelí, Nicaragua. I spoke with them about my plan to do an independent study of their national literacy campaign, to see if it could be adapted for use in inner-city schools in the United States, and they were eager to assist me.

When I told my parents that I was planning to go to Nicaragua, they were immediately concerned. The revolutionary Sandinista forces had successfully deposed the corrupt, US-backed dictatorship of Anastasio Somoza in 1979 and had installed a socialist democracy in its place. Television news showed tanks rolling through the capital city of Managua, and the US support of the Contras (counter-revolutionaries) was hotly debated in the American news media. My parents feared that I'd be caught in a war-torn country during an insurgency. I did my best to calm them, reassuring them that I'd be living in a small town far from Managua, and that I'd be busy researching and assisting with their literacy program as well as doing volunteer work. "Don't worry," I told them. "I'm not there to join the revolution." Little did I know that much of the fighting was taking place in the northern part of the country, where I'd be living, and that the very act of teaching someone to read could be revolutionary.

I booked my flight and, in the weeks leading up to my departure, I began collecting school supplies to take with me, raising funds in anyway I could. When the day of my departure finally arrived, I felt like a beast of burden, trudging through the airport with a huge suitcase packed so tightly with pencils, erasers, notebooks, crayons and more that it threatened to burst. A small duffel bag held my clothes, insect repellant and a mosquito net. Being short on money, I caught a red-eye flight to Houston, where I'd have a five-hour layover before catching a connecting flight to Managua. Despite the late hour, I was wide awake when I boarded the flight to Houston. The people next to me turned off their reading lights and quickly fell asleep, but I couldn't. I was too excited. I was thumbing through the in-flight magazine when I found myself distracted by a conversation between the two men in the seats behind me.

"So where are you headed?" one of them asked.

"I'm catching a connecting flight down to Central America from Houston," the other voice replied. I smiled, thinking I might turn around and make friends with the guy right then and there, but something stopped me. I held my tongue and pushed my head further back so I could hear them better.

"What takes you to Central America?"

"I'm on assignment. We're doing some training down there in Honduras and Nicaragua. Just helping out."

"You mean you're with the Contras."

"Yeah," the guy laughed. "We're just helping these people take back their country from the communists."

I felt sick to my stomach. I wondered if I'd be seeing this guy face to face on the bad side of a gun; just being on the same plane with him made me uneasy. Now I really wasn't going to get any sleep. I tried to listen to as much as I could, and was relieved to discover that this particular "civilian consultant" would be flying into Honduras, so I wouldn't be on the same plane with him after Houston.

When I got up to use the bathroom, I took a good look at him. He was young, his curly hair was neatly groomed, and he didn't look like a killer at all. I hoped I'd never see him again.

In Houston, I waited the five hours for my plane while trying to catch a bit of sleep on a bench in the ladies lounge, but I was all too aware that I had to watch my luggage and not fall so deeply asleep that I miss my flight. Sleep was elusive, and by the time I finally squeezed into the tiny coach-section seat, I thought for sure I'd doze off; but my sleep was intermittent and fitful. The woman next to me ordered a glass of orange juice and promptly spilled it over both of us, leaving us and our plane seats sticky for the rest of the long flight. Sometime the next day, I got off the plane and rubbed my bleary eyes, blinking in the hazy sunlight of Managua.

OUT OF MY COMFORT ZONE

From the moment I stepped off the plane, I knew that I wasn't in Kansas anymore. The airport was full of men in military uniforms carrying automatic rifles as they monitored who was entering and leaving the city. The airport itself was small, but it buzzed with noise and activity. I was questioned briefly, my paperwork was scrutinized, and then I was allowed to walk out into the waiting room. I expected to see someone holding a sign that said "Escuela Nica," or maybe a paper with my name on it, but there was no one there. I'd already collected my luggage, and I walked around for about a half hour with my heavy load, wondering if the school had forgotten about me — or worse, if it was a scam, and I was about to be left stranded in a foreign country.

Someone eventually showed up about half an hour late — a young American man with short, curly, sandy brown hair. He didn't have a sign, he just walked around calling out, "Escuela Nica!" A few of us scattered about in the waiting room, got up and followed him out the door. The school representative made no apology for being late; instead he seemed distracted, looking for someone who hadn't arrived. We boarded a dust-covered old bus and waited for him to return. He'd have to come back later, I overheard him tell the bus driver. The missing student's flight had been delayed.

The drive through the city was a revelation. I'd expected Managua to be similar to Mexico City. I thought there would be a downtown area with businesses and poorer neighborhoods around the periphery, but I waited and waited and we never got to the nice part of town. Every part of Managua bore witness to the war. The bombed-out buildings and poverty were not politely contained in a less desirable part of town; the whole city lay wounded before us, exposed for all to see. Buildings showed the battle scars of war. Some had whole sections that had been blown away by bombs, and yet they continued to operate; in other areas stood mounds of broken concrete, wood, glass and twisted metal where an office building or a factory had once been. Ancient trucks and buses exhaled thick plumes of black smoke, pedestrians clogged the streets, hitchhikers waited to be picked up by large flatbed military or construction vehicles which allowed the hitchers to ride on the back, thereby easing the burden on an overtaxed public transit system. The city's buses were jammed to overflowing with people hanging out of the doors, sitting cross-legged on the roof or holding on to a rear ladder designed to load luggage. Despite the fact that a good portion of Managua lay in ruins, the city still crackled with life and energy. Women walked through the streets with baskets on their heads, others wore heels and office attire; men and women rode bicycles on their way to work while foreign volunteers like me, who had come to this country eager to lend a helping hand, gaped in amazement and took it all in.

We ended up at a place called Hospedaje Norma. It was a student hostel where we would spend the night and wait for the other students to arrive on different flights from all over the world. I'd had some experience with hostels in Europe; I knew they were usually very simple, no-frills places, but this one was like no hostel I'd ever stayed in. This was a collection of ramshackle, temporary barracks held together by a maze of two-by-fours and a hodgepodge of sheets of wood, corrugated metal and whatever other castoff building material was at hand. The "walls" dividing the rooms were just makeshift planks of plywood which neither reached the ceiling nor went all the way down to the ground. Some of the surfaces had been painted in a turquoise blue color in an effort to dress the place up.

Outside, in the common area, stood a row of dirty, seatless toilets which hadn't been flushed and contained disgusting, coffee-colored water. The stench was enough to keep all but the most desperate away. The toilet stalls faced a Sparkletts water bottle set up on a metal holder with a single tin cup on top. I watched others who had been there longer pour themselves a drink. Tiny bits of debris floated up inside the bottle as air displaced the water, rousing the settled particles. After drinking, each person replaced the cup on top of the bottle with not so much as a courtesy rinse. Being somewhat germophobic, my mind reeled as I thought of the bacteria and residual saliva from countless other mouths that lived on the surface of that cup.

Anti U.S. imperialism mural in Leon, Nicaragua. The figure is a silhouette of Augusto Sandino , who is often villified in U.S. history books but was a national hero to the Nicaraguan working class, stomping Uncle Sam with his boot. Photo by Alice Bag.

"Water is scarce," the school rep informed us, as if reading my mind. "It is rationed, so each city has two or three days a week without water. You will not be able to shower, flush the toilet or wash on those days, so be frugal with it." He continued. "Each family keeps a container of water for drinking and cooking. The families you'll be staying with will tell you more about that." The school rep allowed us some time to put our things away before taking us to get some food. I fell asleep on a cot and didn't wake up until the next morning.

We drove two hours north through the beautiful Nicaraguan countryside to the little town of Estelí. There, we unloaded our luggage and prepared to meet our host families. After a few words of welcome from the head of the school, the names of the students and families that had been paired up were called out. Each NICA student was introduced to their host family as their new son or daughter. Cheers rose from the crowd as the families joined in the spirit of the event.

"*M'ijo, I'm so happy to see you*," said one old woman taking a tall African-American student into a big bear hug. The diminutive woman smiled through her few remaining teeth as the student played along.

"Mama!" he cried, lifting her off the ground. The group laughed. I watched as whole families came over and put their arms around their newly adopted son or daughter. I scanned the small crowd, looking around for my family. I noticed a young girl with short, curly hair, longer on top than it was on the sides. She was wearing Bermuda shorts, and her dark skin stood out against her trim, white cotton blouse. She couldn't have been more than 10 years old. She smiled a toothpaste-ad smile at me.

"*Bienvenida, hermana*," she welcomed me in Spanish. I began speaking to her in Spanish, asking her name and thanking her for coming. I could see that my Spanish fluency came as a relief to her.

"My name is Lizette. My mother couldn't come. She had to work, so she sent me. I hope you don't mind."

"I don't mind," I replied.

"*Ustedes llegaron tarde*," she said. ("You got here late.")

"Yes," I told her. "One of the flights was late."

"So soon and you're already on *Nica-time*," she joked as she helped me carry my luggage back to what would be my new home. *Nica-time*, I would come to find out, meant that things always occurred considerably later than the stated time.

I cursed the useless wheels on my suitcase that were not designed to roll over the cobblestone streets. Weighed down with school supplies, the walk seemed interminable. It felt like the house was miles and miles away. We got there just as people were making their way home from their jobs for the mid-afternoon lunch break. I met my new family, which was made up of five young girls with a strong matriarch at the helm. I felt at home immediately.

The family I lived with, in front of the house I stayed in, Esteli, Nicaragua. Photo by Alice Bag.

BEYOND THE CLASSROOM

I soon realized that nothing in my relatively comfortable upbringing had prepared me for the reality of living in a country at war. The pops of automatic rifle fire in the distance were almost as common as the clucking of the hens and roosters that woke me at sunrise. Nevertheless, I quickly fell into the rhythm of the household with the warm support and encouragement of my new family. The three regular meals each day were invariably beans, tortillas and a thick, muddy coffee. You could count on eating the same thing pretty much every day, but on special days, we'd have a dish called *Gallo Pinto*, which was just red beans and rice; sometimes a bit of *queso fresco* would find its way onto the table.

En Nicaragua, Jesus carga un fusil.
("In Nicaragua, Jesus carries a rifle.")
Photo taken in Nicaragua by Alice Bag.

After a few days, I decided to rescue the family from our culinary monotony by going to the market to buy some groceries I could contribute to the household. After all, I'd been in town for three days and hadn't spent any money at all, which was an unfamiliar feeling. When I got to the store, I noticed that many of the shelves were empty. There were some bottles of hot sauce, dry beans, dry rice, a small selection of ugly-looking vegetables, a few household items and not much else. Everything was inexpensive. I asked the woman behind the counter about the scarce selection. She informed me that when something was in stock, it was priced cheaply enough that anyone could buy it and so it would sell out quickly. The very idea of setting the price of groceries based on the law of supply and demand was counterrevolutionary to her. I understood her ideology, but I still didn't fully understand the empty shelves.

"The US has declared an embargo against us, but they will not break us. We'll eat beans forever if we have to." There was disapproval in the woman's voice. "You are a guest in this country. You do not buy the groceries." It suddenly struck me that what I was doing was rude. Who did I think I was, coming to their country, thinking I could buy better food because I had more money? I immediately felt foolish and decided against the groceries, hoping to buy some toilet paper instead. I had brought a roll of toilet paper with me because I knew that it was scarce, but what I didn't know was that it was not only scarce, it was nonexistent. I'd put the single roll in the bathroom and it was quickly gone, to be replaced by little squares of cut-up newspaper. I hoped to score a four-pack of toilet paper, but here, again, I was thwarted.

"*Papel hygienico?*" I asked.

She looked amused. "*No hay.* There isn't any. You need to go back to your family and live like a Nicaraguan," she said, still smiling in a tolerant way. I walked out of the market, my sole purchase a baggie filled with a frozen fruit punch concoction known to the locals as *posicle* (which I thought sounded like Popsicle). I bit off the corner of the baggie, sucked on the sweet frozen treat and tried to cheer myself up after being exposed in all my ethnocentric ignorance.

I got right to work after that. I made arrangements to visit and deliver supplies to some of the local teachers. School buildings were used for morning, afternoon and evening classes: waste not, want not. The literacy program was open to everyone. Men, women, boys and girls would gather around a few large, mismatched tables. Some people stood for the entire class while others walked in carrying chairs they'd brought from their respective homes. There were men in dirty work uniforms, *campesinos* with calloused hands who had worked the farms all day and still found time and energy to attend classes, women with toddlers on their laps. They all wanted one thing—to learn to read. Unlike the schoolbooks I'd grown up with, here there was no Tom and Jane to read about. These texts were meaningful, with stories of Augusto Sandino, Carlos Fonseca and the FSLN. The simple stories were first read for meaning, then broken down into simple sentences; the sentences were then broken down into syllables and finally into individual letter sounds. It was the exact opposite of how it's done here in the US. When I learned to read, I was taken from abstract letters and sounds to concrete meaning; why not start with meaning and then break it down?

Going from concrete to abstract was a strategy that made sense to me, especially for second-language learners, but it also occurred to me that the historical texts that were used in the literacy campaign were a form of political indoctrination. They all espoused the revolutionary ideals of the ruling socialist party. The literacy classes inevitably included some open discussion of the material, but it would be difficult for dissenting voices to gain an audience.

Given the circumstances of a social revolution, it would have been hard to disagree with the material or the socialist economic philosophies being taught. I thought about the ways we Americans were indoctrinated by the mass media in our own country, and I wondered how much of my own core beliefs and values had been hard-wired by my education.

My oldest "sister," Carelia, told me: "All of Nicaragua is a classroom — there are people learning new things everywhere." She liked to tell me stories of her days on the literacy youth brigades. "We were, and still are, fighting a war against ignorance," she explained. "Teens are expected to help without necessarily picking up a rifle. Many of us chose to fight the war against illiteracy. After a training session, we were sent out to the countryside to teach farmers and their families to read. It was hard for me at first, really hard, probably like it is for you coming here. Some places I went to didn't even have an outhouse or running water. We had to squat behind a tree and use leaves to wipe ourselves." She reminded me of how I'd felt the first time I'd seen the little squares of newsprint in the bathroom and asked if we were out of toilet paper. "I imagine it seemed as strange to you to have to use old newspaper as it was for me to have to use leaves." She paused and we laughed, picturing each other's moment of realization, trying to figure out how we were going to wipe our asses.

It wasn't too long before I realized that what this town needed even more than literacy coaches were strong legs, arms and backs to do the heavy lifting of rebuilding neighborhoods that had been destroyed by the war. I signed on to volunteer on a building project. Since I had no construction skills, I was given the simple task of transporting bricks from the brick pile to a construction site on top of a hill. My out-of-shape body was struggling to steer and push the full wheelbarrow over the uneven earth when I accidently rolled over a rock, causing the cart to tip over, dumping and breaking most of the precious bricks down the side of the hill.

The building of houses on rural farmland was a cooperative project similar to a barn raising. People came from all over to help, and the future tenants were expected to feed the workers as a sign of gratitude in exchange for the free labor. I felt guilty taking the bowl of beans and handful of corn tortillas, not only because I hadn't accomplished much and had probably actually set them back, but because it didn't feel right taking anything from a family so poor that the children wore tattered clothes and no shoes. I hadn't done much to deserve it but everyone's spirits were so high that I gratefully accepted the food and the smiles. With every bite, my vision got sharper and I saw how fortunate I was to have grown up in East L.A., where we have indoor plumbing and schools and gas stoves, and if you walked around barefoot, usually it was because you wanted to. Sure, in comparison to the families who lived on the west side of L.A. we were poor, but compared to this family, we lived like kings. I felt a new appreciation for what life had given me, and a greater sense of perspective filled me.

Back at the school, the director had been told of my exploits by the frustrated foreman who had shuffled me from a failed farmwork assignment to the construction assignment until he figured out that I was pretty much unfit for manual labor. The director looked at me, not insensitive to my shame, and asked gently, "What can you do?"

Thinking back to my muralist days at Garfield High, I responded that I could paint. He thought for a few moments, then smiled and assigned me the task of painting seeds with the likeness of Augusto Sandino. These were fashioned into different types of jewelry which could then be sold.

The fact that I was bilingual in English and Spanish was also valuable, since they needed to translate documents. I was happy to have found a skill I could use, not realizing that the documents in need of translation were repair manuals for truck engines, sewing machines and power generators. Of course, I didn't know the Spanish words for such technical terms as "flywheel" or "spark plug," so that was a bit of a challenge. I did a fair job of translating the *charlas* (discussions) between the community members and the foreign students who had a limited Spanish vocabulary. These weekly meetings helped keep the school at the service of the community. I'd listen and simultaneously translate Spanish to English and then back again. It's harder than it sounds — it gave me a real appreciation for the role of translators.

I spent a month in Estelí, helping out in some of the classrooms, interviewing people who had learned to read through the literacy campaign and then had gone out to remote villages to teach others, forming youth brigades which fought against ignorance and battled illiteracy as an extension of a social revolution. It was then I realized that teaching someone to read was itself a revolutionary act. I observed and learned as much as I could, but mostly I learned about myself and about my government, which had imposed an embargo against this tiny country and was helping to train and fund the *contra-revolucionarios* — Contras, as they were known in the States, or "Freedom Fighters," as Ronald Reagan had attempted to name them (but even in the US, the name wouldn't stick).

Aside from constant volunteer work, I spent my spare time hitching rides through the Nicaraguan countryside, seeing some of the outlying towns and visiting with the people who lived there. But this was no tourist vacation. Once, while walking down a dusty street and talking to a villager, I found myself face down in the dirt when loud bursts of automatic rifle fire popped just a block away. Being so close to the border with Honduras, where the Contras were staging their counter-revolutionary attacks, meant that I had to be constantly aware of my surroundings and prepared to duck and cover at the first sign of a gun battle. Every place I went — from the largest city to the tiniest hamlet — had its own personality, but they all shared a common vision: to rebuild their war-torn country from the inside out.

As poor as these people were, and despite the difficulty of their circumstances, I found in their spirit a warmth and generosity that I'd rarely experienced before. I learned by watching their daily examples that what was most important in life was neither wealth nor material possessions, but rather purpose, community and resourcefulness. Being in Nicaragua at that time also allowed me to witness firsthand some of the effects of war in a way that was not sanitized for my consumption.

After more than a month of living, teaching and working in Nicaragua, I boarded a flight for the return trip to the States and to my job as a schoolteacher with a renewed sense of purpose and dedication. The most lasting impression I have of Nicaragua is of the indomitable spirit of its people. Their hunger for knowledge and self-determination would teach me to never be complacent about what I have and what I have to lose.

Children of Esteli. Photo by Alice Bag.

CHILDREN ARE THE BALM

Upon returning to Los Angeles and Hoover Street Elementary, I settled into my job as a kindergarten teacher. The months passed, and my parents were no longer able to come visit me at school. Complications from my father's diabetes progressed to the point where he needed to rest most of the time, and he began making more frequent trips to the hospital; but he was still stubborn and strong, and always came back home after a day or two. During one of these trips to the hospital, my father lay in bed, plugged into various monitors that ticked off his vital signs. An IV tube fed a steady drip of saline solution to one of the bulging, overworked veins in his arms. His skin had taken on the appearance of ancient parchment, like a wrinkled papyrus scroll covered with markings that told the story of his rough life. I stood by his side while he talked to me about seeing my classroom for the first time.

"I'm so proud of you. You kept your promise and you're doing a great job," he said affectionately.

"Thank you, Papi," I replied, happy to be able to hold up a carton of juice to his lips so he could take sips through a straw. I stroked his hair gently. "You're going to get better. Just don't fight with the nurses so much." My father had a bad reputation for being abusive with the nurses who sometimes bossed him around.

"Who do they think they are? They're really rough sometimes, so I had to set them straight." He put on his mean face, but this time it wasn't working and there was a kind, bittersweet smile eager to replace it.

"*Mi'ja*… I don't think I'm going home this time," he said in a gentle tone.

"Dad, they've been telling you you're going to die for years. Are you going to let them be right this time?" I tried to make light of this conversation which was not going anywhere I wanted to go. "You're a fighter, Dad. You can beat this."

His smile turned into a grimace.

"It hurts a lot; you don't understand. I'm done fighting with my body. I'm ready to go."

I couldn't believe my ears. The room seemed to spin as my whole body tensed, trying to resist the impact of the blow. My eyes betrayed me and started to overflow with tears.

"Why? You've fought it for years. It always hurt. What's changed?"

"Damn it, Alicia, you don't feel what I feel! I'm tired of living with the pain, I'm tired of fighting. I held on because I wanted to make sure you'd be okay and you are, so now you have to let me go!"

"No!" I said stubbornly, raising my voice. "I don't want to let you go. I love you! I still need you!" One of the nurses must have heard me and hustled into the room.

"You'll have to keep your voice down. There are other patients trying to sleep."

"Go to hell!" my father yelled at the nurse. I quickly stepped in to try and soften my dad's wrath.

"Please leave us alone for a few more minutes. I'll keep it down." I composed myself, then turned to my father once more and said, "Please Dad, let's talk about this tomorrow. I don't want them to kick me out." He looked at me but didn't reply. I bent down to kiss him. "I'm sorry you're in so much pain, Dad. I'll talk to the doctor about ways to manage it."

My father was still looking at me, and time seemed to slow as he gazed silently at my face. I could see the pain hiding in his eyes, although he had done his best to smother it with love. My father, my superhero, my villain; he was all things rolled into one, and he had finally stepped into the ring with the one opponent he couldn't beat.

Another nurse came in. She was polite but very firm as she turned toward me. "You're going to have to leave now. It's time for your father's medication, and he needs to rest."

"Okay," I replied. "I'll see you tomorrow morning. Please listen to the doctors and nurses, promise?"

"I don't promise you anything."

"I love you, Dad. Don't forget that." I gathered my belongings and moved toward the door.

"I love you, too, and I'm very proud of you. You don't forget that."

That night I was awakened by a phone call. It was my mother.

"Alicia, your father got really sick in the middle of the night."

"What happened?" I squeezed the receiver anxiously.

"He died."

I dissolved into the carpet, my bones completely liquefied. "*No...*" I moaned, unable to do anything more than lie on the ground, choking on my tears.

By the following day, I realized that I couldn't allow myself to wallow in my grief. As much to distract myself as to help out, I threw my full attention into making all the necessary arrangements for the funeral. I kept busy by picking out the plot, a casket and a tombstone, and attending to every minute detail of my father's burial. I knew that if I stopped long enough to think, I would realize that a cannonball had just been fired through my chest.

My mother insisted on a Catholic rosary service, even though my father, an atheist to the end, had specifically asked that nobody pray for him. He said it would be hypocritical. Despite my father's wishes, I agreed to the religious service, telling myself that funerals were for the living, because the dead were already gone

The rosary was beyond sad. We should have hired mourners, because so few people showed up. I can't imagine that seeing the tiny mortuary viewing room so sparsely attended brought my mother any solace.

I sat at the back of the room, and, after the first dozen Hail Marys, I snuck out the back door. I took a solitary walk on the busy street in front of the funeral home, feeling grateful for the fact that I no longer believed in a heaven or a hell. My father was immortal for me. He had made an indelible imprint on me, and his presence would be felt by anyone who met me.

My mother found solace in prayer and in her children. My siblings and I hovered around her as much as possible, and my sister Yolanda began an unsuccessful campaign to get me to move in with my mother on the grounds that I was still unmarried and would be a good companion for her. But my mother was a strong woman who needed little in the way of emotional support. She simply picked herself up and carried on with her life the way she always had.

I struggled to find my footing. I slipped in and out of denial, thinking that this was all a bad dream from which I would suddenly awake. Grief tortured me to the point where I thought I couldn't take anymore. Then it would loosen its grip on me just long enough to let me think that life had gone back to normal, before pulling me back down into an even deeper level of despair. There was no remedy for it but to endure. I remembered my father, who rarely spoke in platitudes, once telling me that time was the only thing that could heal a broken heart. I had nowhere to turn but back to everyday life.

When my three days of bereavement leave were up, I went back to work at my school in the inner city of Los Angeles. I wasn't sure how I'd hold up, but seeing the faces of my students again was comforting. They had been told of my loss by another teacher, and now they took turns hugging me, trying to comfort me. Oddly, their affection did not make me want to cry. It made me want to be strong for them. After the brief break from routine, my students found their way back to their favorite places on the rug where they sat cross-legged, waiting patiently for me to teach them the next lesson.

In Jeffrey Eugenides's Pulitzer Prize–winning novel *Middlesex*, there is a line that reads, "Children were the only balm against death." I couldn't agree more. That afternoon, I watched the children as they played during recess: laughing, yelling, tossing a rubber ball back and forth, skipping ropes and riding tricycles. The trees in the kindergarten yard looked the same as before my father died. Only the leaves would change, some would die and fall off, but they'd always be replaced by new ones. Everything had changed in my world, and yet the world looked exactly the same.

WEIGHTLESS

Within a few weeks I'm back in the swing of things, still reeling from the loss of my father but carrying on with my life. I begin another school year and am assigned a new teaching assistant, a young man with blue hair who performs in women's clothes under the name Fertile LaToya Jackson with a six-foot-five drag queen named Vaginal Davis. We become fast friends and before long start collaborating on a new concept band called Cholita.

Vaginal Davis, a seasoned performance artist, has a clear vision for this new band. She insists that every member dress the part and adopt the persona of a teenage Latina, the more colorful and over the top, the better. Vaginal becomes 13-year-old Graciela, Fertile morphs into Guadalupe, and I turn into La Sad Girl, who, at 16, is the oldest member of the group and thus always on the verge of being kicked out. Just like with the Latino boy-band Menudo, 16 was over the hill by Cholita's standards.

To the casual observer, being backstage at a Cholita performance is a bit like seeing a bomb explode in a drag queen's closet. Costumes include a chopped and tailored '50s prom gown customized with pink feathers and sequins, and a bra constructed of a pair of children's Power Ranger masks. The band's sound has been described as "the Germs and Gloria Trevi getting down in a back alley." Our performances are chaotic, but there is a message of social and sexual equality behind the mascara. Cholita's members are from diverse ethnic backgrounds, and we enjoy poking fun at stereotypes. Vaginal Davis is our lead singer and I play rhythm guitar, which is just fine with me. I welcome the opportunity to let someone else have the pressure that comes with the spotlight and the lead vocals after being the front-person for the Bags.

This particular night, Cholita is performing at a club in Hollywood, and we are busy getting into our costumes and makeup just before show time. I lean over the bathroom sink backstage at the club and carefully apply a single teardrop of eyeliner on my cheek, mimicking the look of a chola-style tattoo, symbolizing the death of a close loved one. I stop and stare at my own reflection in the mirror. I can hear the muffled sound of the audience clapping in time and stomping their feet, impatient for the band to go on. I take a swig of booze to calm my nerves and walk out to join the rest of the band.

The group gathered in a last pre-show huddle before taking the stage. Placing our right hands into the middle of a circle we began chanting, in ever increasing volume, "Pussy Power, Pussy Power, PUSSY POWER!" As we finish screaming our chant, we throw our right hands up into the air in a triumphant display of unity. The other musicians backstage watch us with a look of concern on their faces.

One, two, uno, dos, tres, quatro! My band rips into the first song. The music bounces and swells and the audience starts to dance. I feel a heaviness lifting from me, and I realize that I am grinning from ear to ear as I play and sing along.

I am flying, weightless and free, *en mi mero mole*.

EPILOGUE

The characters and events in Violence Girl are real; however, my memories of them are not meant to be impartial historical documentation. I have shared these snapshots of my life from the only perspective I can share — my own. I hope that if you've taken this ride with me, you have felt not only my quest for knowledge and self-preservation but my fears, confusion, uncertainty, anger and desperation as well, because it was the hurdles I've had to surmount in life that made me who I am today. What a waste my life would be without all the beautiful mistakes I've made.

The lifestyle I've written about in *Violence Girl* was not without risks, and I owe a good deal of my survival to my mother and father, who provided me with the sacred amulet of their unconditional love. I hope that I may provide the same protection to my own daughters. Sadly, many of the friends and characters who appear in Violence Girl are no longer living. The early L.A. punk scene encouraged a fast lifestyle that exacted a heavy toll among the gifted and creative individuals who were part of it.

When I was younger, I felt like I was just stumbling around in the dark, looking for a light switch, and I walked into my share of walls in the process. I learned a lot during that first quarter. I learned to walk, talk, feed myself, deal with my anger, define my God and understand my place in the universe. Music always seemed to be there, lighting a path for me, helping me get beyond the limitations of my left-brain thinking. It was a source of power for me and a way to express the ineffable, even before I knew I had anything to say. Like magic and religion, it gave me access to an alternate fountain of information, one which I have continued to drink from over the years.

During the next chapter in my life, I was part of several exciting musical projects including the Afro Sisters, Cholita!, El Vez, the Cambridge Apostles, Las Tres, Stay at Home Bomb and Swing Set. I got married, then divorced, then remarried; I became a stepparent; I dealt with the deaths of my mother and sister. I watched Craig Lee and Shannon battle and then succumb to AIDS. I saw my smiling Castration Squad angels come back from the depths of hell, stronger and more beautiful for having struggled with and triumphed against their personal demons. I had a life-changing, long-distance love affair with a man in prison, fought against the intrusion of educational fascists in my inner-city classroom, had a baby, learned to become an advocate for children with special needs. I danced in my underwear in the land of the midnight sun;

I turned down dinner with Oprah. I took big, hungry bites out of life, and I'm still not full.